Essential
Atlas
of the
WORLD

Helicon

Contents

Key Map and Legend

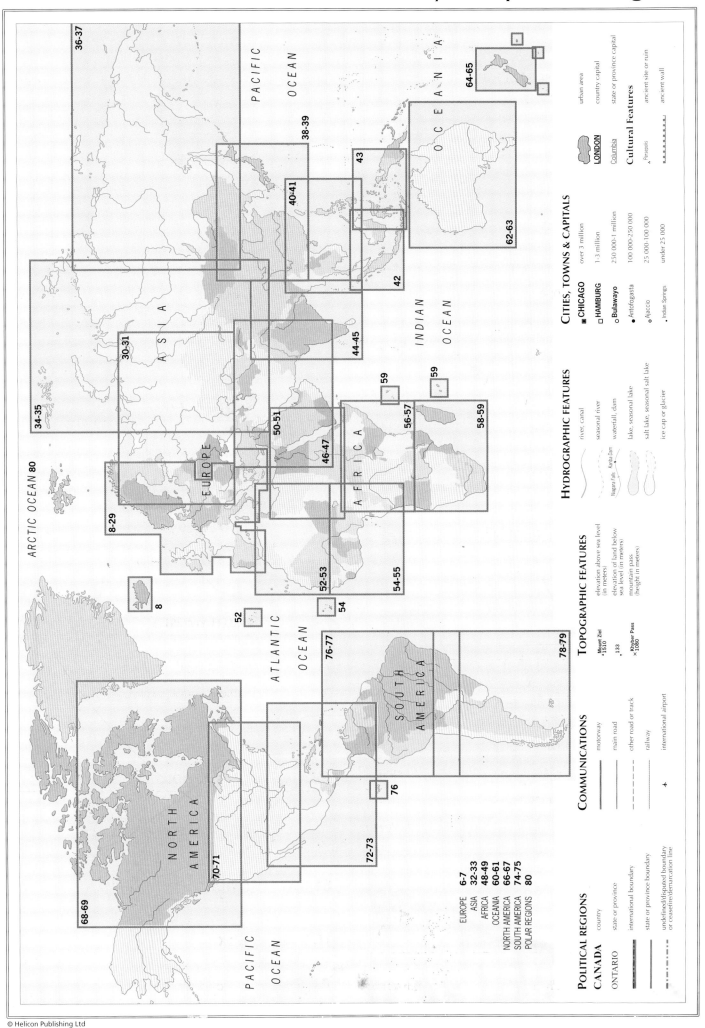

POLITICAL REGIONS

EUROPE	6-7
ASIA	32-33
AFRICA	48-49
OCEANIA	60-61
NORTH AMERICA	66-67
SOUTH AMERICA	74-75
POLAR REGIONS	80

POLITICAL REGIONS

CANADA — country
ONTARIO — state or province

——— international boundary
——— state or province boundary
- - - - undefined/disputed boundary
or ceasefire/demarcation line

COMMUNICATIONS

——— motorway
——— main road
- - - - other road or track
——— railway
✈ international airport

TOPOGRAPHIC FEATURES

Mount Ziel ▴1510 — elevation above sea level (in meters)
▪133 — elevation of land below sea level (in meters)
╳ Khyber Pass 1080 — mountain pass (height in meters)

HYDROGRAPHIC FEATURES

river, canal
seasonal river
Niagara Falls / Kariba Dam — waterfall, dam
lake, seasonal lake
salt lake, seasonal salt lake
ice cap or glacier

CITIES, TOWNS & CAPITALS

▪ CHICAGO — over 3 million
◻ HAMBURG — 1–3 million
○ Bulawayo — 250 000–1 million
● Antofagasta — 100 000–250 000
○ Ajaccio — 25 000–100 000
· Indian Springs — under 25 000

urban area
LONDON — country capital
Columbia — state or province capital

Cultural Features

▴ Persepolis — ancient site or ruin
· · · · ancient wall

© Helicon Publishing Ltd

3

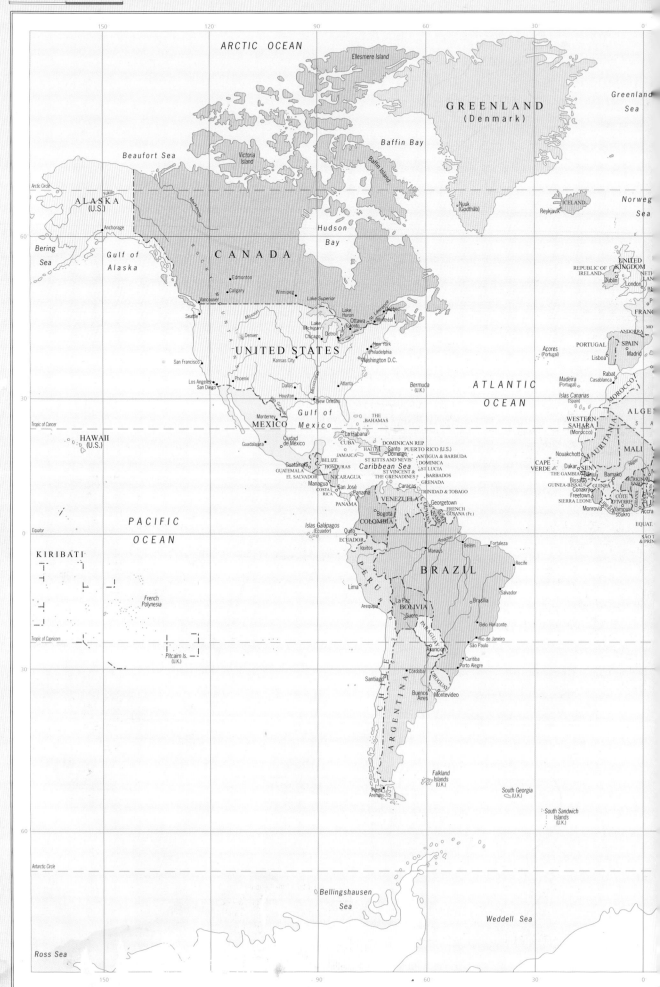

Equatorial Scale 1 : 112 000 000

0   1000   2000   3000   4000 km
0   1000   2000 miles

ARCTIC OCEAN

Ellesmere Island

GREENLAND
(Denmark)

Greenland
Sea

Baffin Bay

Baffin Island

Beaufort Sea

Victoria
Island

Arctic Circle

Yukon

ALASKA
(U.S.)

Nuuk
(Godthåb)

ICELAND

Norweg

Reykjavík

Sea

Anchorage

Hudson
Bay

Bering
Sea

Gulf of
Alaska

CANADA

REPUBLIC OF
IRELAND

UNITED
KINGDOM

NETH
LAN

Edmonton

Dublin

London

Calgary

Winnipeg

Lake Superior

Québec

FRANC

Vancouver

Lake
Huron

Montréal

MO

Seattle

Missouri

Lake
Michigan

Ottawa
Toronto

Chicago

Detroit

ANDORRA

PORTUGAL

SPAIN

Denver

UNITED STATES

New York

Açores
(Portugal)

Philadelphia

Washington D.C.

Lisboa

Madrid

San Francisco

Kansas City

Madeira
(Portugal)

Rabat
Casablanca

Los Angeles
San Diego

Phoenix

Dallas

Atlanta

Bermuda
(U.K.)

Islas Canarias
(Spain)

ATLANTIC

WESTERN
SAHARA
(Morocco)

ALGE

Houston

New Orleans

OCEAN

MOROCCO

Tropic of Cancer

HAWAII
(U.S.)

Monterrey

Gulf of

Mexico

MEXICO Mexico

THE
BAHAMAS

Nouakchott

MAURITANIA

MALI

Ciudad
de México

CUBA

La Habana

DOMINICAN REP

CAPE
VERDE

Dakar

SEN

Guadalajara

HAITI

Santo
Domingo

PUERTO RICO (U.S.)

ANTIGUA & BARBUDA

THE GAMBIA

Banjul

Bamako

Guatemala

BELIZE

JAMAICA

ST KITTS AND NEVIS

DOMINICA

Bissau

BURKINA
FASO

GUATEMALA
EL SALVADOR

HONDURAS

Caribbean Sea

DOMINICA

GUINEA-BISSAU

GUINEA

Managua

NICARAGUA

ST VINCENT &
THE GRENADINES

ST LUCIA

BARBADOS

Conakry

Freetown

San José

Caracas

GRENADA

SIERRA LEONE

CÔTE
D'IVOIRE

Yamou
soukro

Accra

COSTA
RICA

Panamá

TRINIDAD & TOBAGO

Monrovia

PANAMA

VENEZUELA

Georgetown

FRENCH
GUIANA (Fr.)

EQUAT.

Bogotá

PACIFIC

Islas Galápagos
(Ecuador)

COLOMBIA

Quito

SÃO T
& PRIN

OCEAN

Equator

ECUADOR

Iquitos

Amazon

Belém

Fortaleza

Manaus

KIRIBATI

BRAZIL

Recife

PERU

Lima

French
Polynesia

La Paz

BOLIVIA

Brasília

Salvador

Arequipa

Sucre

Belo Horizonte

Tropic of Capricorn

Rio de Janeiro

PARAGUAY

São Paulo

Asunción

Curitiba

Pitcairn Is.
(U.K.)

Porto Alegre

Córdoba

URUGUAY

Santiago

CHILE

Buenos
Aires

Montevideo

ARGENTINA

Falkland
Islands
(U.K.)

South Georgia
(U.K.)

Punta
Arenas

South Sandwich
Islands
(U.K.)

Antarctic Circle

Bellingshausen

Sea

Weddell Sea

Ross Sea

Country Abbreviations

ALB.	ALBANIA	LITH.	LITHUANIA
AZER.	AZERBAIJAN	LUX.	LUXEMBOURG
BANG.	BANGLADESH	MAC.	MACEDONIA
BEL.	BELGIUM	MAL.	MALAWI
BHT.	BHUTAN	RUS.	RUSSIA
BOS.	BOSNIA-HERZEGOVINA	RW.	RWANDA
BUR.	BURUNDI	SEN.	SENEGAL
CAMB.	CAMBODIA	SL.	SLOVENIA
CRO.	CROATIA	SLOVAK.	SLOVAK REPUBLIC
EST.	ESTONIA	SWITZ.	SWITZERLAND
HUNG.	HUNGARY	U.A.E.	UNITED ARAB EMIRATES
LAT.	LATVIA	YUG.	YUGOSLAVIA
LEB.	LEBANON	ZIMB.	ZIMBABWE

• London   Selected capital cities

• Brisbane   Other cities

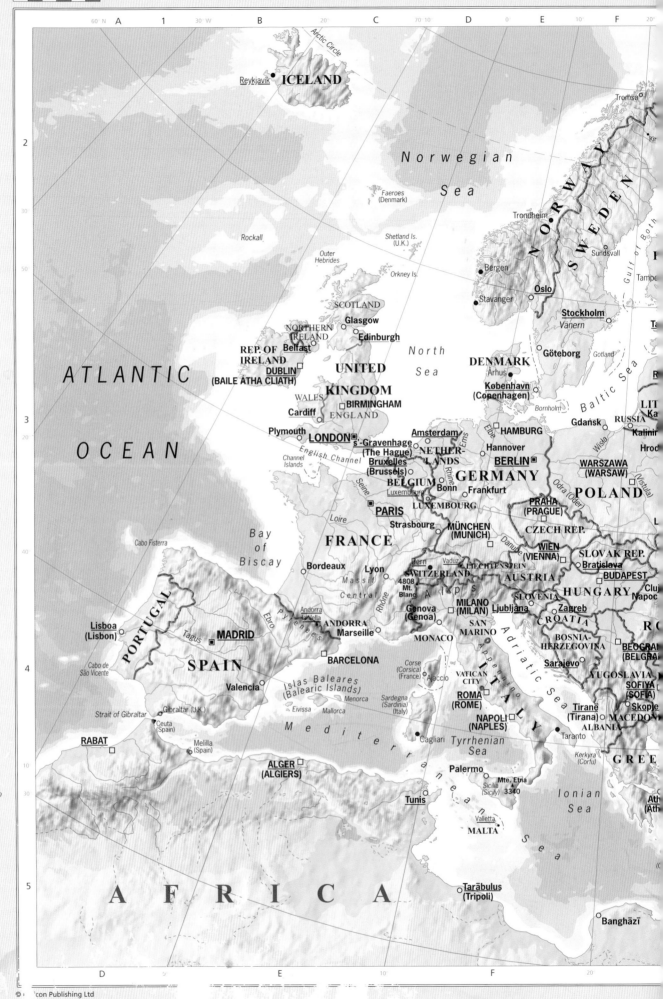

Scale 1 : 20 200 000

| | 0 | 250 | 500 | 750 km |
| 0 | 100 | 200 | 300 miles |

ICELAND
Reykjavik •

Arctic Circle

ATLANTIC

OCEAN

Norwegian

Sea

Faeroes (Denmark)

Rockall

Shetland Is. (U.K.)

Outer Hebrides

Orkney Is.

SCOTLAND
Glasgow
Edinburgh

NORTHERN
IRELAND
REP. OF Belfast
IRELAND
DUBLIN
(BAILE ÁTHA CLIATH)

North
Sea

UNITED
KINGDOM

WALES
Cardiff ENGLAND
BIRMINGHAM

Plymouth
LONDON
s-Gravenhage
(The Hague)
Bruxelles
(Brussels)
English Channel
Channel Islands

Amsterdam
NETHER-
LANDS
BELGIUM
Luxembourg

DENMARK
Århus •
København
(Copenhagen)
Bornholm

NORWAY
Trondheim
Bergen •
Oslo
Stavanger •

SWEDEN
Göteborg
Gotland
Stockholm
Vänern

Gulf of Both
Sundsvall
Tampe
Ta

Baltic Sea

R

LIT
Ka
RUSSIA
Gdańsk Kalinir
Hrod

HAMBURG
Hannover
BERLIN
WARSZAWA
(WARSAW)

POLAND

Bay
of
Biscay

Cabo Fisterra

FRANCE
PARIS
Seine
Loire
Strasbourg
Bordeaux Lyon
Massif
Central
Rhône

Bonn
Frankfurt
GERMANY
Elbe
Ems
Rhine
LUXEMBOURG

PRAHA
(PRAGUE)
CZECH REP.
Danube
WIEN
(VIENNA)
AUSTRIA
Vaduz
LIECHTENSTEIN
SWITZERLAND
Bern
4808
Mt.
Blanc
Alps

Odra (Oder)
Wista

SLOVAK REP.
Bratislava
BUDAPEST
HUNGARY
SLOVENIA
Ljubljana
Zagreb
CROATIA

Cluj
Napoc

R

BEOGR
(BELGRA

YUGOSLAVIA
SOFIYA
(SOFIA)

PORTUGAL
Lisboa
(Lisbon)
Tagus
MADRID
Cabo de
São Vicente

SPAIN

Valencia
BARCELONA
Ebro
Pyrenees
Andorra
la Vella
ANDORRA
Marseille
MONACO

MILANO
(MILAN)
Genova
(Genoa)
SAN
MARINO
VATICAN
CITY
ROMA
(ROME)

Appennino

Adriatic Sea

BOSNIA-
HERZEGOVINA
Sarajevo

Tiranë
(Tirana)
ALBANIA
MACEDON
Skopje

GREE
Ath
(Ath

Corse (Corsica) (France)
Ajaccio

Islas Baleares (Balearic Islands)
Menorca
Mallorca
Eivissa

Gibraltar (U.K.)
Ceuta (Spain)
Strait of Gibraltar
Melilla (Spain)

RABAT

Sardegna (Sardinia) (Italy)

ITALY
NAPOLI
(NAPLES)
Taranto

Cagliari
Tyrrhenian Sea
Palermo
Sicilia (Sicily)
Mte. Etna
3340

Ionian Sea

Kerkyra
(Corfu)

Mediterranean

ALGER
(ALGIERS)

Tunis

Valletta
MALTA

Sea

AFRICA

Tarābulus
(Tripoli)

Banghāzī

metres	feet
4000	13120
2000	6560
1000	3280
500	1640
200	656
0	0
200	656
1000	3280
2000	6560
4000	13120
6000	19690
8000	26250
metres	feet

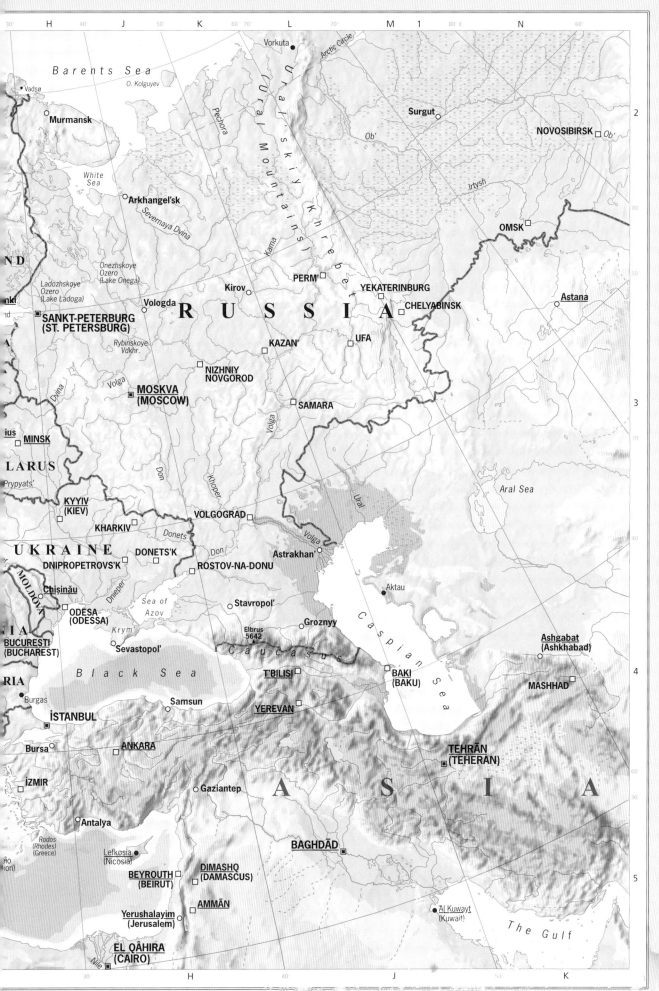

Barents Sea

Vadsø

Murmansk

O. Kolguyev

Vorkuta

Arctic Circle

(Ural'skiy

White Sea

Pechora

Ural Mountains) Khrebet

Surgut

Ob'

NOVOSIBIRSK Ob'

Irtysh

OMSK

Arkhangel'sk

Severnaya Dvina

Kama

Onezhskoye Ozero (Lake Onega)

Ladozhskoye Ozero (Lake Ladoga)

nki

ND

Vologda

Kirov

PERM'

YEKATERINBURG

CHELYABINSK

Astana

R U S S I A

SANKT-PETERBURG (ST. PETERSBURG)

Rybinskoye Vdkhr.

KAZAN'

UFA

Volga

NIZHNIY NOVGOROD

Dvina

MOSKVA (MOSCOW)

SAMARA

ius

MINSK

Volga

LARUS

Prypyats'

Don

Khoper

Ural

KYYIV (KIEV)

Aral Sea

KHARKIV

Donets

VOLGOGRAD

UKRAINE

Don

Volga

DNIPROPETROVS'K

DONETS'K

Astrakhan'

ROSTOV-NA-DONU

MOLDOVA

Chişinău

Sea of Azov

Stavropol'

Aktau

ODESA (ODESSA)

Krym'

Groznyy

Caspian Sea

IA

Sevastopol'

Elbrus 5642

Ashgabat (Ashkhabad)

BUCUREŞTI (BUCHAREST)

C a u c a s u s

T'BILISI

BAKI (BAKU)

RIA

Black Sea

MASHHAD

Burgas

Samsun

YEREVAN

İSTANBUL

Bursa

ANKARA

TEHRĀN (TEHERAN)

İZMIR

A S I A

Gaziantep

Antalya

Rodos (Rhodes) (Greece)

elo

Lefkosia (Nicosia)

BAGHDĀD

ion)

BEYROUTH (BEIRUT)

DIMASHQ (DAMASCUS)

AMMĀN

Al Kuwayt (Kuwait)

Yerushalayim (Jerusalem)

The Gulf

EL QĀHIRA (CAIRO)

Nile

Scale 1 : 5 800 000

Scale 1 : 3 450 000

© Helicon Publishing Ltd

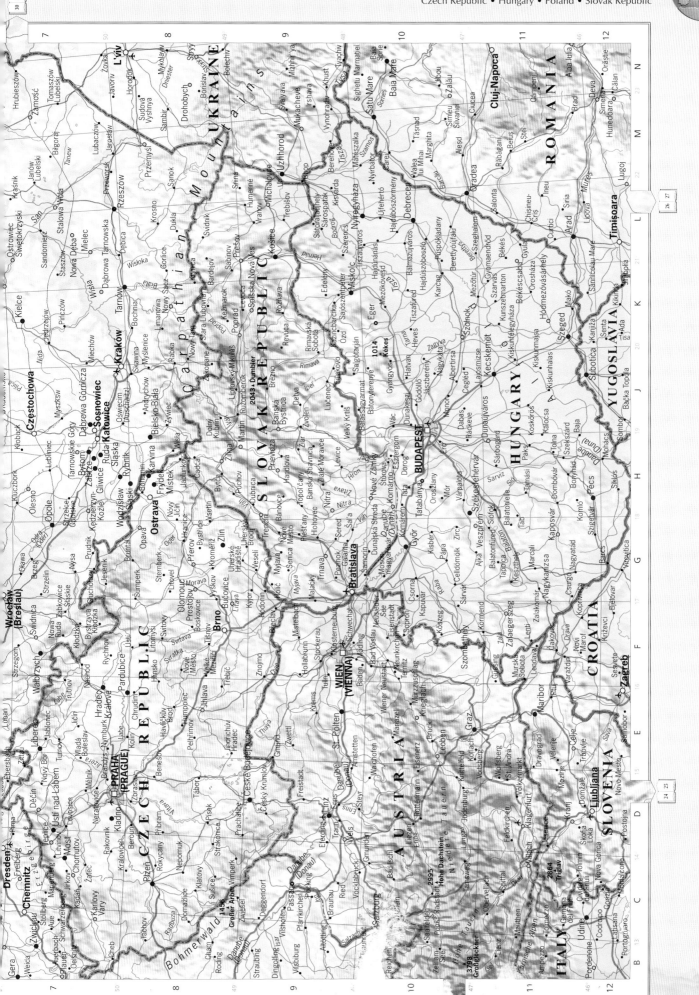

Scale 1 : 2 600 000

© Helicon Publishing Ltd

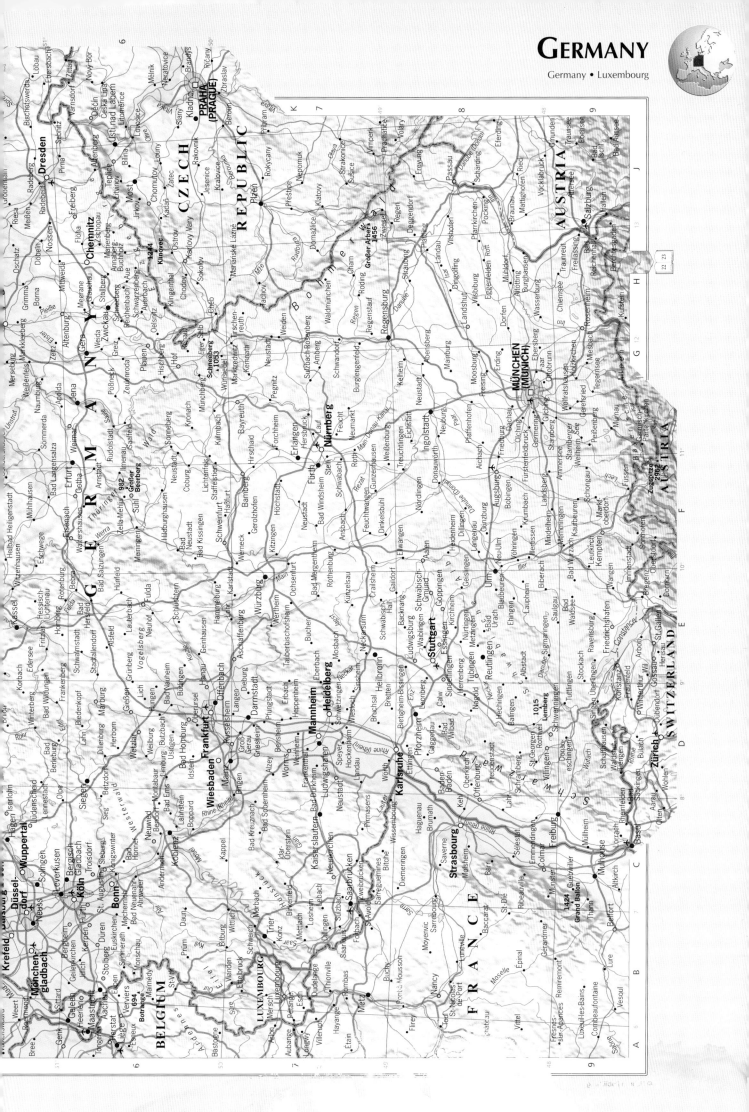

GERMANY

Germany • Luxembourg

Scale 1 : 2 300 000

UNITED KINGDOM

NORTH SEA

ENGLAND

LONDON

English Channel

The Weald

South Downs

Strait of Dover

Isle of Wight

Baie de la Seine

PARIS

© Helicon Publishing Ltd

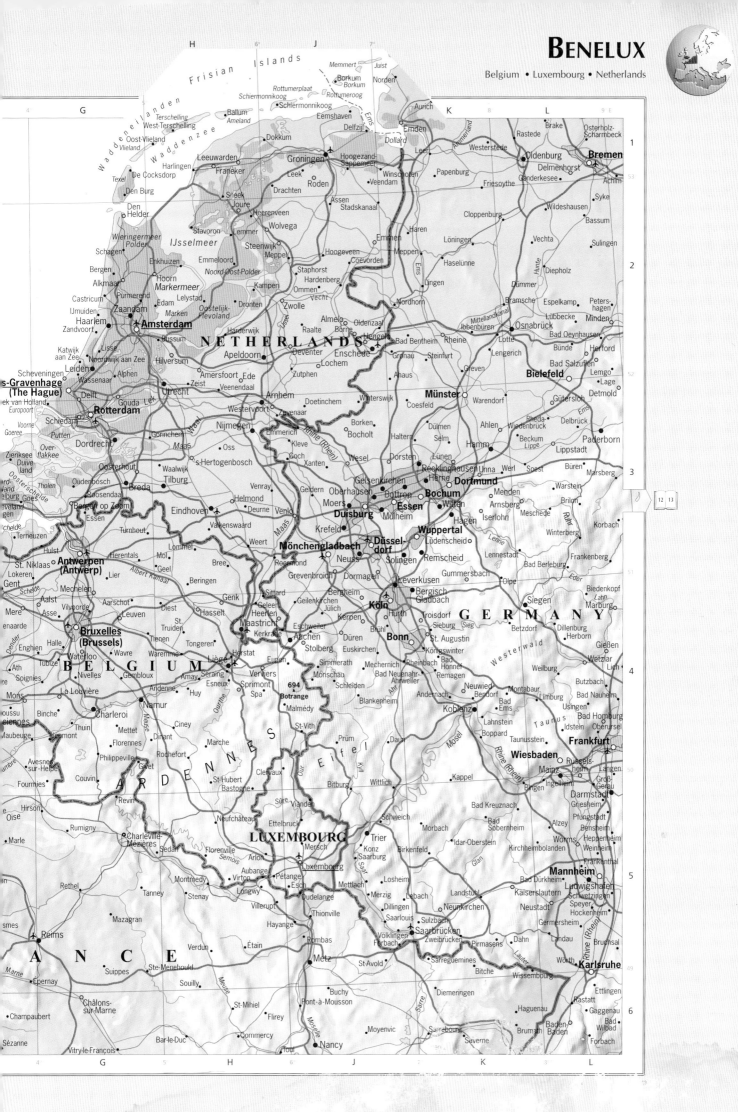

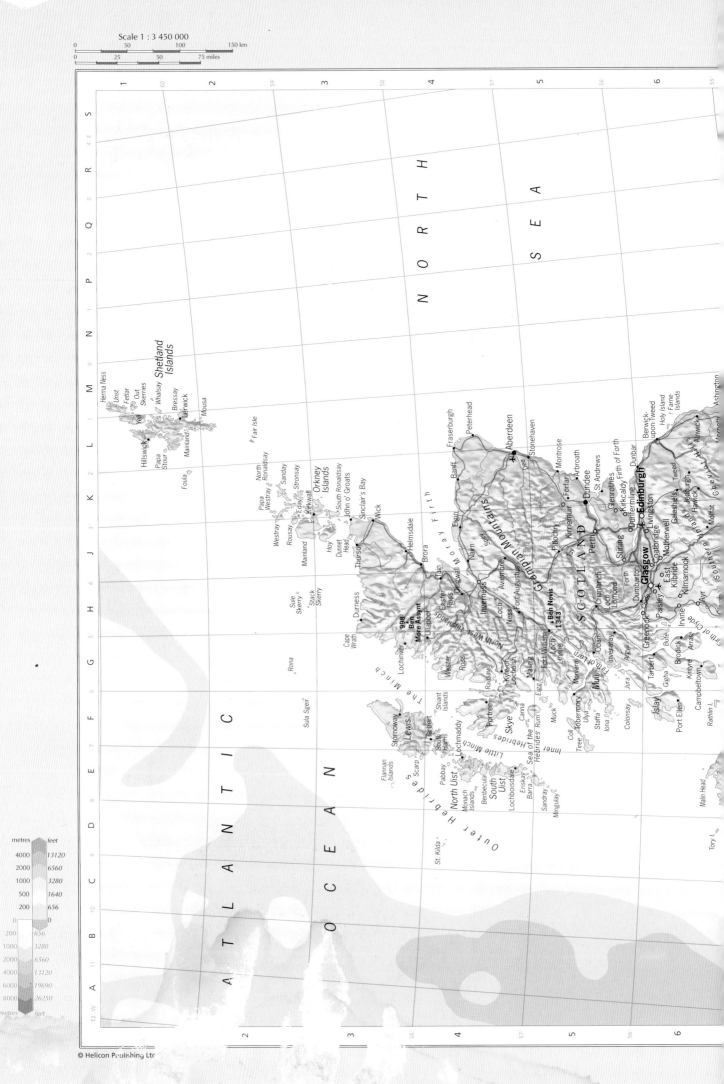

Scale 1 : 3 450 000

© Helicon Publishing Ltd

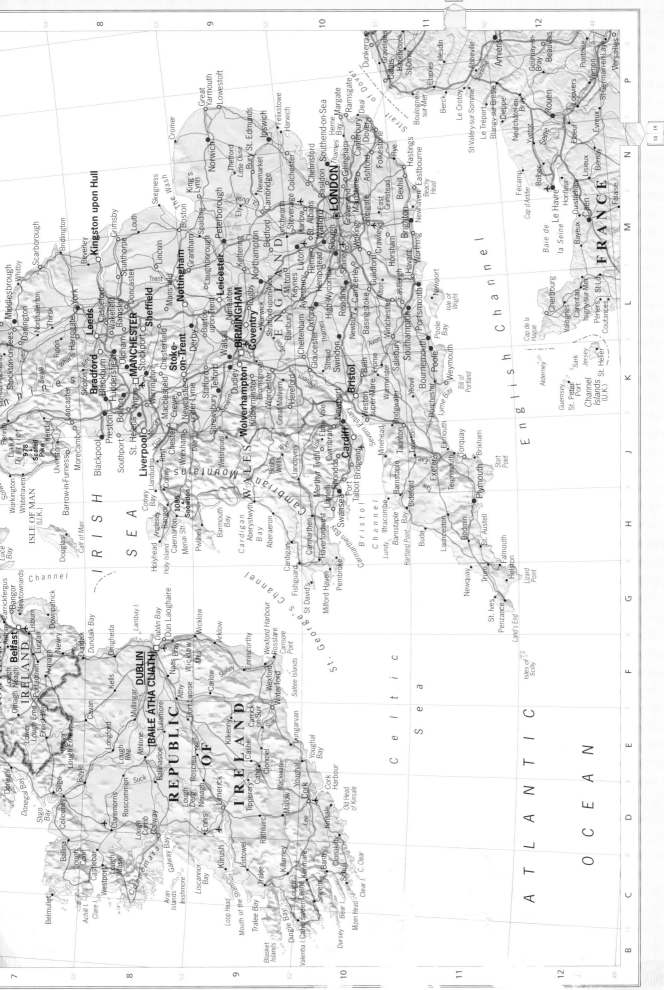

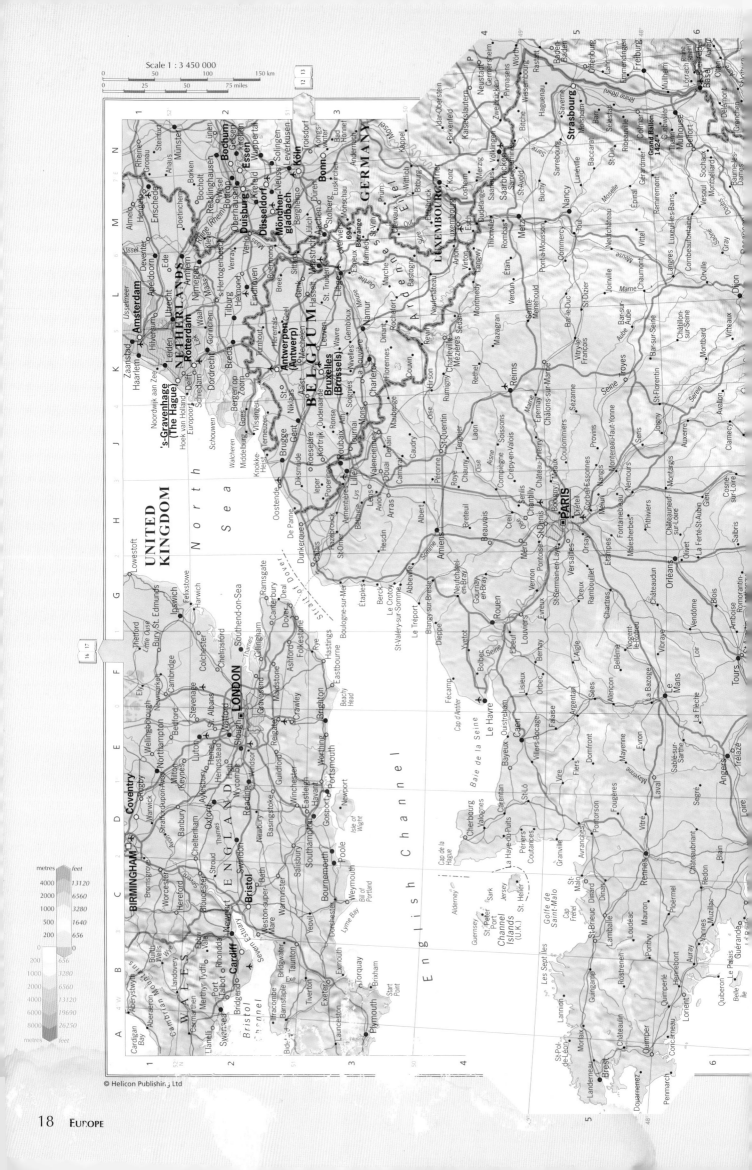

© Helicon Publishing Ltd

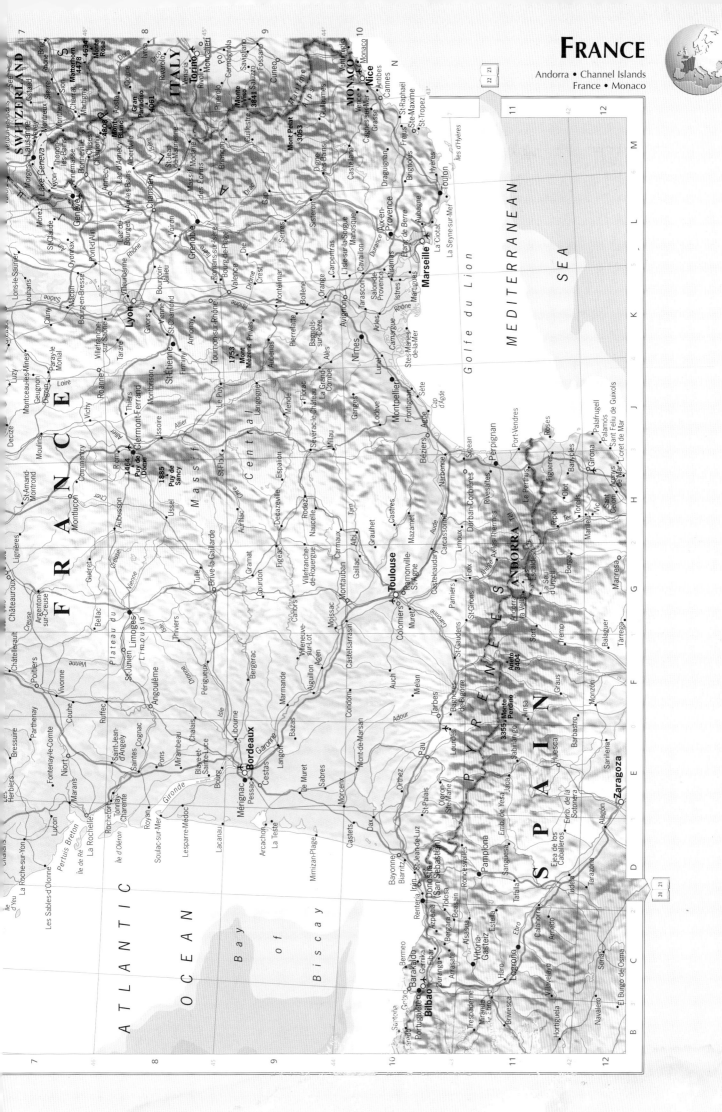

FRANCE

Andorra • Channel Islands
France • Monaco

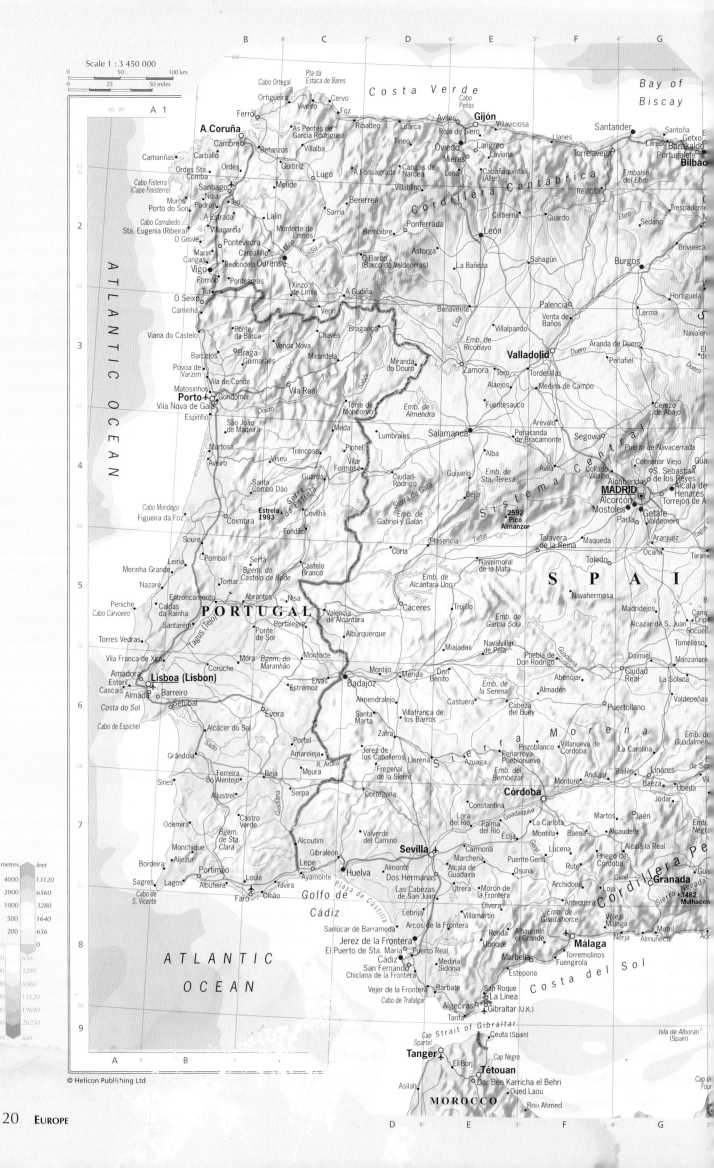

© Helicon Publishing Ltd

18 19

FRANCE

Bayonne
Biarritz
Orthez
Muret
Béziers
Agde
Sète
Cap d'Agde

Irún
St-Jean-de-Luz
St-Palais
Castelnaudary
Aude
Carcassonne
Narbonne

Donostia
(San Sebastián)
Oloron-Ste-Marie
Pau
Tarbes
Garonne
Limoux
Sigean
Golfe du Lion

Beasain
Roncesvalles
Lourdes
Bagnères-de-Bigorre
St-Gaudens
Pamiers
Foix
Rivesaltes
Perpignan

Alsasua
Pamplona
Jaca
PYRENEES
Ax-les-Thermes
Le Perthus
Port-Vendres

Estella
Emb. de Yesa
3355 Monte Perdino
Aneto 3404
ANDORRA
Andorra la Vella
Les Escaldes
Roses

Tafalla
Sangüesa
Sabiñánigo
Ainsa
Sort
La Seu d'Urgell
Ripoll
Figueres
Costa Brava

Ejea de los Caballeros
Huesca
Graus
Tremp
Berga
Torelló
Manlleu
Banyoles
Olot

Tudela
Emb. de la Sotonera
Bárbastro
Balaguer
Vic
Girona
Palafrugell
Palamós

Tarazona
Monzón
Manresa
Sant Celoni
Sant Feliu de Guixols

Alagón
Sariñena
Lleida
Tárrega
Terrassa
Granollers
Arenys de Mar
Lloret de Mar

Torrelapaja
El Burgo de Ebro
Cinca
Fraga
Igualada
Sabadell
Mataró

Zaragoza
Calatayud
Azaila
Caspe
Montblanc
Vilafranca del Penedès
Sant Boi
BARCELONA
Badalona

Daroca
Alcañiz
Gandesa
Valls
Vilanova y la Geltrú
El Prat de Llobregat

Molina de Aragón
Calamocha
Montalbán
Tortosa
Cambrils
Tarragona
Sitges
Gavà

Monreal del Campo
Morella
Amposta
Cabo Tortosa
Costa Dorada

Teruel
Sierra de Gúdar
Sant Carlos de la Ràpita
Vinaròs
Benicarló

Cuenca
Torreblanca
Islas Baleares
(Balearic Islands)
Ciutadella
Menorca

Emb. de Contreras
Barracas
Onda
Castelló de la Plana
Pollença
Cap de Formentor
Mahón

Utiel
Vila-real
Borriana
Islas Columbretes
Sóller
Sa Pobla
Inca
Artà

Motilla del Palancar
Requena
La Vall d'Uixó
Sagunt
Golfo de Valencia
Palma de Mallorca
Manacor

Paterna
Burjassot
Valencia
Sa Dragonera
Llucmajor
Mallorca

Torrent
Cofrents
Carlet
Algemesí
Santanyí
Cap de ses Salines

Albacete
Júcar
Cullera
Eivissa (Ibiza)
Cabrera

Chinchilla de Monte-Aragón
Xàtiva
Gandia
San Juan Bautista

Almansa
Alzira
Oliva
Dénia
San Antonio Abad
Eivissa (Ibiza)

Yecla
Ontinyent
Xàbia
Cabo de la Nao
Formentera

Hellín
Villena
Alcoi
Costa Blanca

Jumilla
Elda
Benidorm
La Vila Joiosa

Cieza
Novelda
Aspe
Alicante
Santa Pola

Caravaca de la Cruz
Crevillent
Elch

Molina de Segura
Orihuela

Alcantarilla
Murcia
Torrevieja

Zarzadilla de Totana
Alhama de Murcia
Torre-Pacheco

Lorca
La Unión
Cabo de Palos

Huércal-Overa
Águilas
Golfo de Mazarrón
Cartagena

Albox
Vera

Níjar
Carboneras
Mediterranean Sea

Almería
Cabo de Gata

Dellys
Tizi Ouzou

ALGER (ALGIERS)
Aïn Taya
Thenia

Bou Ismail
Rouïba
Lakhdaria
Boghni

Cherchell
Hadjout
Boufarik
Bouira

Ténès
Gouraya
Blida
Aïn Bessem

Bouzghaïa
Miliana
Médéa
Beni Slimane
Sour el Ghozlane
Berrouaghia

Khemis Miliana
Atlas Mountains

Ech Chélif
Bordj Bou
ALGERIA
Ksar el Boukhari
Aïn el Hadjel

Aïn-Tédélès
Chélif
Bou Kadir
Bougzoul

Mostaganem
Arzew
Relizane

Mers el Kébir
Gdyel
Mohammadia

Oran
Oued Tlélat
Sig

Cap Figalo
El Amria
Mascara

Beni Saf
Hammam Bou Hadjar

Aïn Témouchent

52 53

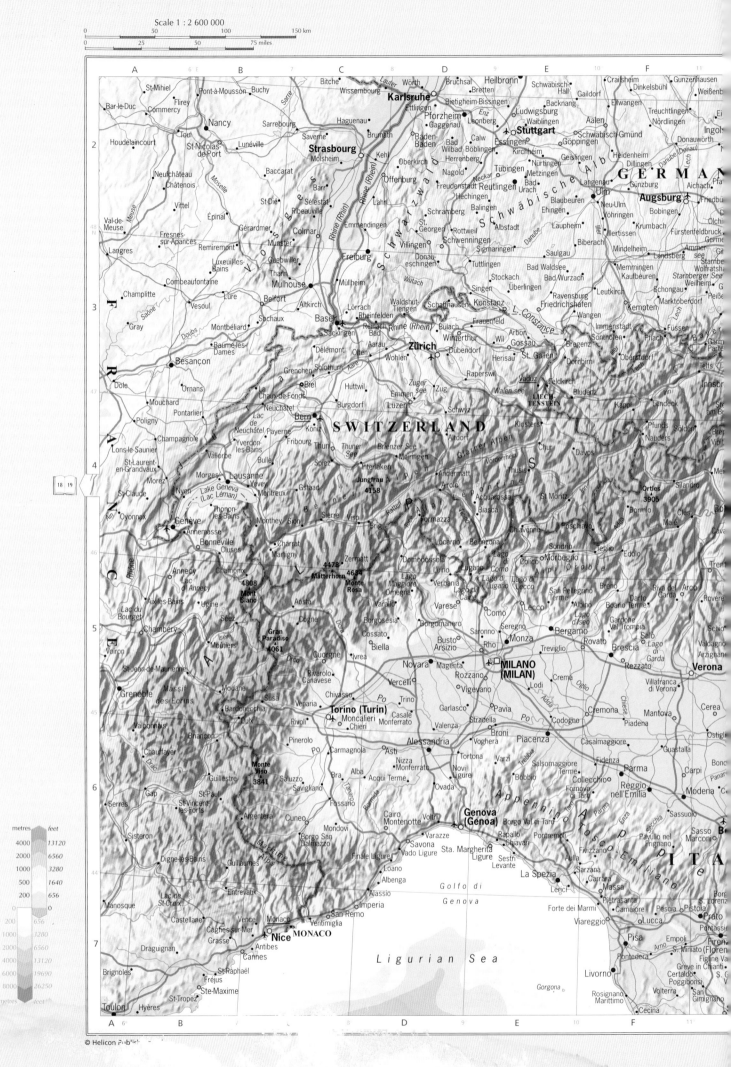

Scale 1 : 2 600 000

© Helicon Publishing

THE ALPINE STATES

Austria • Liechtenstein • Slovenia • Switzerland

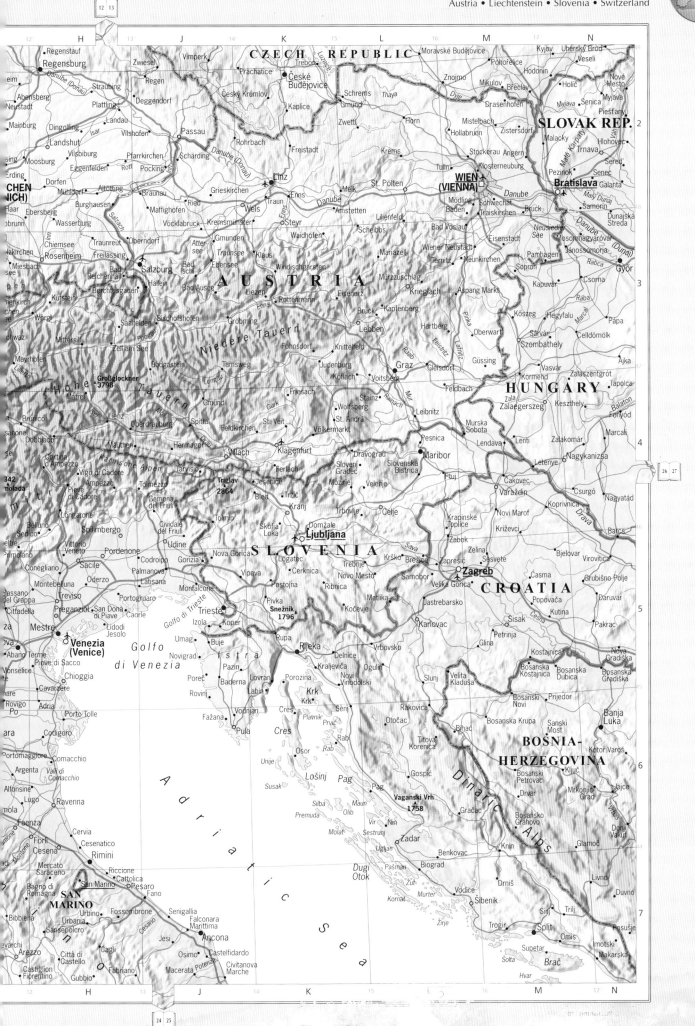

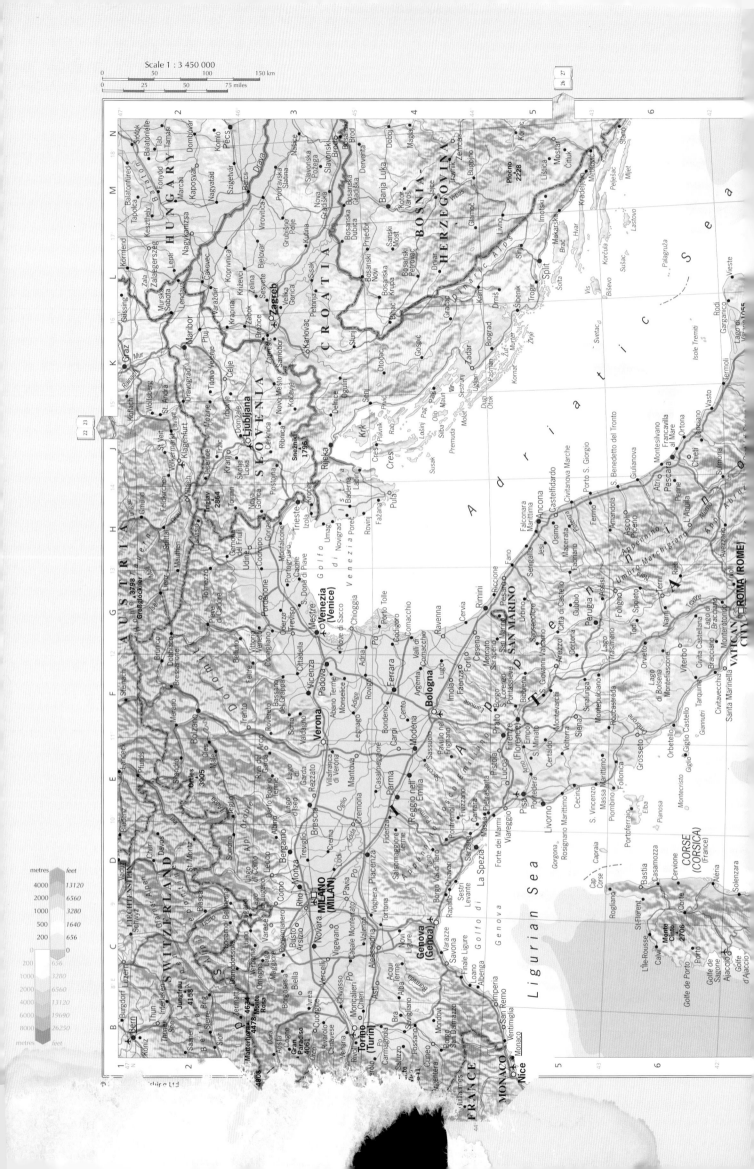

Otranto
Squinzano
Lecce
Copertino
Maglie
Trapani
Casarano
Capo S. Maria di Leuca
Brindisi
Ostuni
Mesagne
Francavilla Fontana
Mola di Bari
Bari
Bisceglie
Molfetta
Andria
Ruvo di Puglia
Noci
Fasano
Martina Franca
Gioia del Colle
Gravina in Puglia
Altamura
Matera
Cerignola
Lacedonia
Melfi
Rionero in Vulture
Potenza
Pisticci
Bernalda
Castellaneta
Taranto
Golfo di Taranto

Punta Alice
Cirò Marina
Crotone
Isola di Capo Rizzuto
Ciro
S. Giovanni in Fiore
Petilia Policastro
Cutro
Capo Colonna
Corigliano Calabro
Rossano
Cariati
Acri
Luzzi
Catanzaro
Golfo di Squillace
2248 Spulico
Monte Pollino
Castrovillari
Cosenza
Nicastro
Soverato
Siderno
Locri
Capo Spartivento
Cetraro
Montalto Uffugo
Paola
Vibo Valentia
Amantea
Rosarno
Gioia Tauro
Palmi
Polistena
Scalea
Golfo di Policastro
Golfo di Sant'Eufemia
Capo Vaticano

Ionian Sea

Tyrrhenian Sea

Sapri
Lauria
Sala Consilina
Eboli
Battipaglia
Salerno
Golfo di Salerno
Agropoli
Ascea
Capo Palinuro

Stromboli
Basiluzzo
Panarea
Salina
Isole Lipari
Lipari
Vulcano
Filicudi
Alicudi

Messina
Reggio di Calabria
Milazzo
S. Giovanni
Villa
Taormina
Giarre
Acireale
Catania
Golfo di Catania
Lentini
Siracusa
Capo Murro di Porco
Augusta
Golfo di Augusta
Patti
Sant'Agata di Militello
Randazzo
Monte Etna 3323
Adrano
Paternò
Palagonia
Caltagirone
Vizzini
Palazzolo Acreide
Modica
Avola
Noto
Pachino
Capo Passero
I. delle Correnti
Ispica
Scicli
Ragusa
Vittoria
Comiso
Gela
Golfo di Gela
Licata

Cefalù
Castelbuono
Gangi
Troina
Leonforte
Nicosia
Enna
Piazza Armerina
Caltanissetta
Mazzarino
Niscemi
Riesi

Capo Gallo
Palermo
Monreale
Termini Imerese
Bagheria
Corleone
Partinico
Alcamo
Castelvetrano
Sciacca
Ribera
Agrigento
Palma di Montechiaro
Canicattì
S. Cataldo
Caltanissetta

SICILIA (SICILY)

Capo S. Vito
Castellammare del Golfo
Trapani
Calatafimi
Marsala
Mazara del Vallo
Capo Granitola
Capo Feto
Menfi

Levanzo
Favignana
Marettimo
Isole Egadi
Égadi

MALTA
Gwardex (Gozo)
Kemmuna (Comino)
Victoria
Rabat
Valletta

Malta Channel

MEDITERRANEAN SEA

Sicilian Channel

Isola di Pantelleria (Italy)

Linosa (Italy)

Napoli (NAPLES)
Vesuvio 1281
Pozzuoli
Ercolano
Afragola
Nola
Avellino
Benevento
Caserta
Capua
Mondragone
Aurunca
Sessa
Fondi
Terracina
Formia
Gaeta
Golfo di Gaeta
Sorrento
Capri
Ischia
Isole Ponziane
Ventotene
Zannone
Ponza
Palmarola

SARDEGNA (SARDINIA) (Italy)

Strait of Bonifacio
La Maddalena
Palau
Costa Smeralda
Golfo di Olbia
Olbia
Budoni
Siniscola
Tempio Pausania
Monte Limbara 1359
Ozieri
Bitti
Nuoro
Orosei
Golfo di Oroso
Bono
Bonorva
Macomer
Sassari
Porto Torres
Alghero
Bosa
Punta La Marmora 1834
Lago del Flumendosa
Tortolì
Villaputzu
Sorso
Sennori
Lago del Coghinas
Oristano
Golfo di Oristano
Laconi
Capo di Monte Santu
Sestu
Quartu Sant'Elena
Cagliari
Assemini
Iglesias
Carbonia
Villacidro
Guspini
San Pietro
Sant'Antioco
Golfo di Palmas
Capo Spartivento
Capo Carbonara
Asinara
Golfo dell'Asinara

TUNISIA
Tunis
Bizerte
Cap Blanc
Cap Serrat
Menzel Temime
Korba
Nabeul
Hammamet
Golfe de Hammamet
La Goulette
La Marsa
Soliman
Grombalia
Menzel Bouzelfa
Kelibia
Ras Mostefa
Cap Bon
Ile Zembra
Golfe de Tunis
Béja
Mateur
Menzel Bourguiba
Jedeida
Medjez el Bab
El Fahs
Enfida
Siliana
Tébourba
Téboursouk
Jendouba
El Kef
Nefza
Tabarka
La Galite
Cap Serrat

ALGERIA
El Tarf
Souk Ahras
El Kala
Cap Rosa

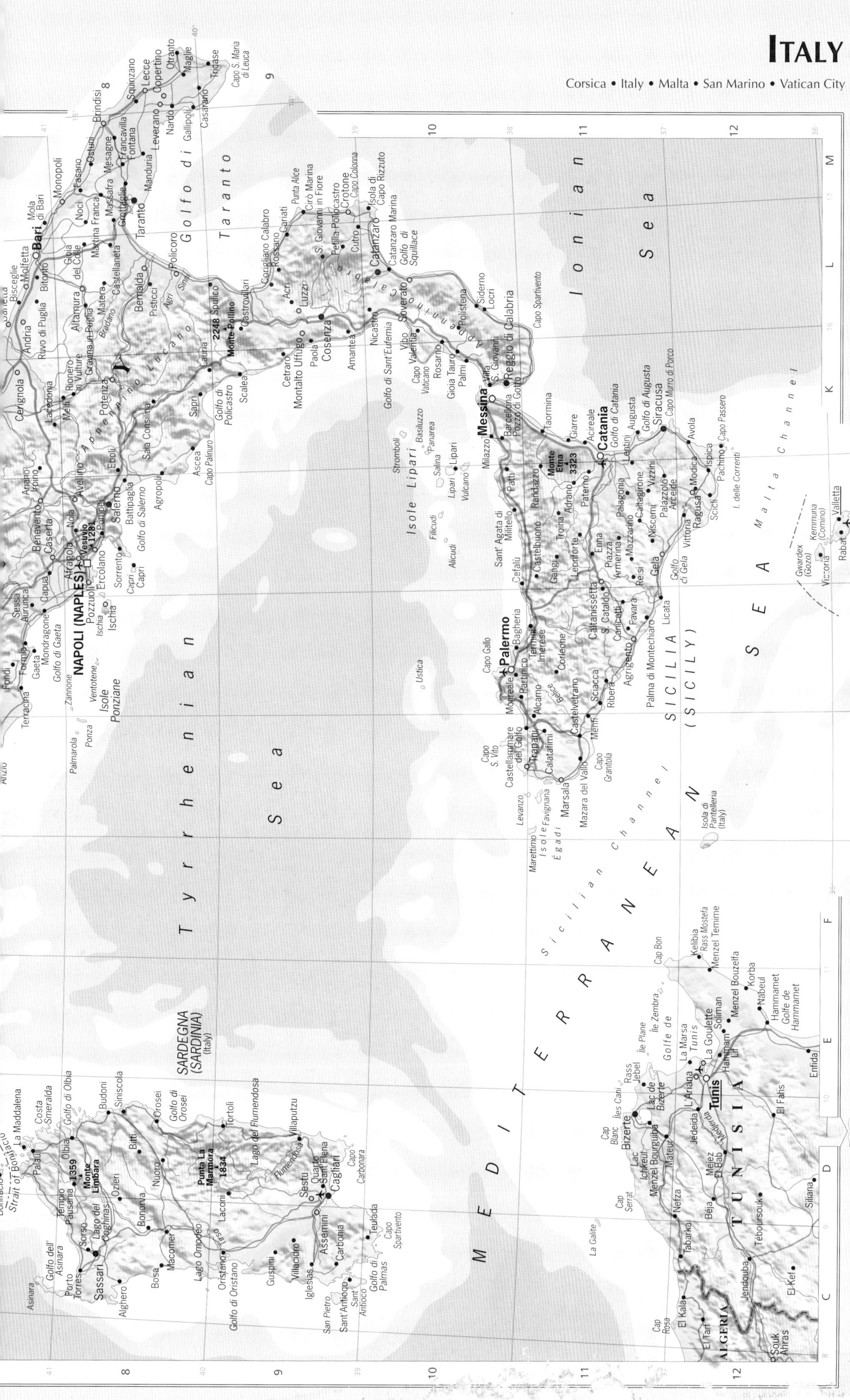

Scale 1 : 3 450 000

THE BALKANS

Bosnia-Herzegovina • Bulgaria
Croatia • Moldova • Romania • Yugoslavia

UKRAINE

MOLDOVA

Chişinău

ROMANIA

Cluj-Napoca

Târgu Mureş

BUCUREŞTI
(BUCHAREST)

Constanţa

BULGARIA

SOFIJA
(SOFIA)

Plovdiv

Varna

B L A C K   S E A

TURKEY

İSTANBUL
Kartal

GREECE

ODESA
(ODESSA)

Mouths of
the Danube

Marmara Denizi
(Sea of Marmara)

Scale 1 : 3 450 000

© Helicon Publish...

BLACK SEA

Varna
Provadija
Devnja
Staro
Orjahovo
Bjala
Ajtos
Nos Emine
Nesebár
Karnobat
Pomorie
Burgas
Burgaski Zaliv
Sozopol
Grudovo
Mičurin
Málko
Tárnovo
Resovo
Iğneada
Yıldız Dağları
Kirklareli
Kıyıköy
Pınarhisar
Vize
Babaeski
Saray
Karacaköy
Lüleburgaz
Çerkezköy
İstanbul Boğazı (Bosporus)
Hayrabolu
Çorlu
Silivri
İSTANBUL
Sarıyer
Beykoz
Şile
Ağva
Muratlı
Büyükçekmace
Yeşilköy
Kartal
Pendik
Gebze
İzmit
Hendek
Düzce
İnecik
Tekirdağ
Büyükada
Sapanca
Sakarya
Bolu
Şarköy
Kumbağ
Marmara Denizi (Sea of Marmara)
Yalova
Karamürsel
Mudurnu
Köroğlu Tepesi 2400
Marmara Adası
Kapıdağı Yarımadası
İmralı Adası
Geyve
Nallıhan
Beypazarı
Türkeli Adası
Paşalimanı Adası
Erdek
Bandırma
Mudanya
Gemlik Körfezi
Gemlik
İznik Gölü
İznik
Bilecik
Sakarya
Çubuk
Biga
Karacabey
Bursa
Can
Gönen
Mustafakemalpaşa
Ulubat Gölü
İnegöl
ANKARA
Elmadağ
Kırıkkale
Susurluk
Bozüyük
Eskişehir
Balıkesir
Burhaniye
Dursunbey
Tavşanlı
Kütahya
Kaymaz
Sivrihisar
Polatlı
Balâ
Savaştepe
Bigadiç
Simav
TURKEY
Bergama
Soma
Demirci
Gediz
ANATOLIA
Dikili
Kınık
Kırkağaç
Emirdağ
Yunak
Tuz Gölü
Akhisar
Gediz
Uşak
Banaz
Afyon
Cihanbeyli
Aliağa
Saruhanlı
Gölmarmara
Manisa
Salihli
Kula
Çay
Bolvadin
Menemen
Gediz
Akşehir
İZMİR
Turgutlu
Alaşehir
Sandıklı
Sarayönü
Kemalpaşa
Egridir Gölü
İlgin
Kadınhanı
Bayındır
Ödemiş
Dinar
Seferihisar
Torbalı
Tire
Sarıkaraağaç
Selçuk
Sarayköy
Keçiborlu
Konya
Kuşadası
Germencik
Aydın
Nazilli
Açı Göl
Isparta
Egirdir
Beyşehir Gölü
Beyşehir
Ortaklar
İncirliova
Kocarlı
Çumra
Söke
Çine
Denizli
2528 Esler Dağ
Burdur
Burdur Gölü
Bucak
Camıçıgölu
Kale
Yenihisar
Yatağan
Boz Dağ 2419
Kızılkaya
Cevizli
Bozkır
Karaman
Milas
Muğla
Korkuteli
Seydişehir
Akseki
Bodrum
Ören
Köyceğiz
Serik
Geyik Dağ 2877
Kara Ada
Gökova Körfezi
Marmaris
Dalaman
Gölhisar
Antalya
Manavgat
Ermenek
Mut
Datça
Fethiye
Elmalı
Kemer
Alanya
3073
Kumluca
Karacal T. 2339
Gazipaşa
Anamur
Kalkan
Finike
Antalya Körfezi
Silifke
Megisti (Greece)
Yardımcı Burnu
Ovacık
Aydıncık
MEDITERRANEAN SEA

Zonguldak
Kozlu
Çaycuma
Ereğli
Karabük
Akçakoca
Karasu
Kandıra
Gerede
Çerkes Dağları
Cankırı
Köroğlu Dağları
Kızılcahamam
Beypazarı
Çerikli
Kursünlü
Kızılırmak
Cide
Azdavay
İnebolu
Kerempe Burnu
Bartın
Taşköprü
Kastamonu
Safranbolu
Tosya
Yerkoy
Kaman
Kırşehir
Mucur
Gülşehir
Nevşehir
Şereflikoçhisar
Sultanhanı
Aksaray
Niğde
Bor
Ereğli
Karapınar
İçel (Mersin)
Erdemli
Kızıllalan

CYPRUS
Keryneia
Lefkosia (Nicosia)
Morfou
Ammochostos (Famagusta)
Polis
C. Arnaoutis
Troodos
Olympus 1952
Larnaka
Cape Greko
Aigialousa

Rodos (Rhodes)
Lindos
Kattavia
Saria
Karpathos
Nisyros
Symi
Tilos
Chalki
Kos
Samos
Dodekanisos (Dodecanese)

Scale 1 : 10 400 000

© Helicon Publishing Ltd

O. Kolguyev

Bugrino
Tobseda
Nosevaya
Indiga
Malozemel'skaya Tundra
Pechora
Shapkina
Khoreyver
Severnyy
Khoseda Khard
Vorkuta
Yar Sale
Aksarka
Nyda
Novyy
Urengoy
Urengoy
Krasnosel'kup
shskaya
Guba
Oksino
Nar'yan
Mar
Chum
1499
Salekhard
Nadym
Tarko Sale
Tol'ka
Tol'ka
Volonga
Sula
Yermitsa
Adz'vavom
Abez'
Petrun
Shuryshkary
Taniovo
Kharampur
afonovo
Sula
Krestovka
Ust'-Usa
Inta
Khashgort
Gorki
Noyabr'sk
Izhas
Trusovo
Ust'-Tsil'ma
Mutnyy
Materik
Synya
Kos'yu
Ustrem
Vanzevat
Numto
Raduzhny
ma
Koynas
Izhma
Kadzherom
Saranpul
Berezovo
Beloyarskiy
Nizhnevartovsk
Strezhevoy
hukonskoye
Shegmas
1883
Lyapin
Sos'vinskaya
Peregrebnoye
Sherkaly
Bol. Atlym
Surgut
Lokosovo
Vozhgora
Bol. Pyssa
KOMI
Kartayel'
Kyrta
Sartyn'ya
Igrim
Nyagan'
Nov. Karymkary
Sytomino
Nefteyugansk
Aleksandrovskoye
Vazhgort
Ukhta
Vuktyl
Zapadno-Sibirskaya Ravnina
ukhcha
1185
Troitsko-
Pechorsk
Ilych
Ust' Tapsuy
Khanty-Mansiysk
Salym
Koslan
Mikun'
Yaksha
Pechora
Ust'
Ur'ya
Pionerskiy
(West Siberian Plain)
Charymovo
Loptyuga
Aykino
Storozhevsk
Ust' Nem
Ivdel'
Pelym
Uray
Dem'yanskoye
Nefedovo
ya
Yarensk
Irta
Vychegda
Karepino
Los'va
Kondinskoye
Konda
Irtysh
Denyanka
asnoborsk
Kotlas
Syktyvkar
Vizinga
Koygorodok
Krasnovishersk
Severoural'sk
Yagodnyy
Kuma
Tobol'sk
Sumkino
Irtysh
Ust'-Ishim
Tevriz
Znamenskoye
Tara
Tara
Luza
Ust'-Alekseyevo
Ob'yachevo
Cherdyn'
Krasnotur'insk
Sos'va
Turtas
Kolosovka
hug
Oparino
Luza
Gayny
Kosa
Solikamsk
1562
Serov
Tavda
Yarkovo
Vagay
Ozero
Saltaim
Bol'sherech'ye
Ust'-Tarka
inskoye
Nagorsk
Vyatka
Kirs
Yurla
Berezniki
Kizel
Nov. Lyalya
Turinsk
Tavda
Ishim
Omi
chug
Murashi
Kudymkar
Chermoz
Gubakha
Verh.
Tura
Nitsa
Tyumen'
Golyshmanovo
Nazyvayevsk
Kalachinsk
Yaransk
Kirov
Kirovo-Chepetsk
Glazov
Dobryanka
Chusovoy
Lys'va
Nizhniy Tagil
Irbit
Talitsa
Vinzili
Yalutorovsk
Ishim
OMSK
Kotel'nich
Kumeny
Igra
Okhansk
PERM'
Kungur
Pervoural'sk
Asbest
Isetskoye
Belozerskoye
Petukhovo
Petropavlovsk
Sovetsk
Nolinsk
Urzhum
Kil'mez
Votkinsk
Achit
Revda
YEKATERINBURG
Kamensk-Ural'skiy
Yoshkar Ola
UDMURTIYA
Izhevsk
Krasnoufimsk
Kasli
Tugoz
Kurgan
MARIY EL
Malmyzh
Agryz
Mozhga
Chernushka
CHELYABINSK
Kopeysk
Shumikha
Presnogorkovka
Kokshetau
oksary
KAZAN'
Mamadysh
Nizhnekamskoye
Vodokhranilishche
Sarapul
Kambarka
Neftekamsk
Zlatoust
Miass
Korkino
Krasnoarmeysk
Oz.
Seletyteniz
Nizhnekamsk
TATARIYA
Al'met'yevsk
Birsk
Asha
Min'yar
Yuzhnoural'sk
Sergeyevka
Ishim
Makinsk
Aksu
Naberezhnyye
Chelny
UFA
Plast
Troitsk
Fedorovka
Borovskoy
Uritskiy
Volodarskoye
Alekseyevka
latyr
Buinsk
Tuymazy
1638
Verkhneural'sk
Kostanay
Lomonosovka
Zholymbet
Ul'yanovsk
Oktyabr'skiy
Beloretsk
Magnitogorsk
Rudnyy
Koluton
Zhaltyr
Astana
Dimitrovgrad
Severnoye
BASHKIRIYA
Kartaly
Ozero
Kushmurun
Zhaksy
Atbasar
Tol'yatti
Sterlitamak
Meleuz
Sibay
Kizil'skoye
Tobol
Kushmurun
Yesil'
Ladyzhenka
Syzran'
SAMARA
Buguruslan
Buzuluk
Bredy
Dzhetygara
Semiozernoye
Kurgal'dzhinskiy
uznetsk
Novokuybyshevsk
Sorochinsk
Novo-
sergiyevka
Saraktash
Zhailma
Ozero
Tengiz
ov
Balakovo
Volga
Ilek
Ural
Orenburg
Mednogorsk
Energetik
Arkalyk
Yershov
Ozinki
Burlin
Ilek
Novotroitsk
Orsk
Svetlyy
Turgayskaya
Amengel'dy
Zhaksykon
Krasnyy Kut
Ural'sk
Una
Ilek
Yasnyy
Stolovaya
Goly Ulytau
Novouzensk
Dzhambeyty
Novoalekseyevka
Aktyubinsk
Karabutak
Strana
Turgay
Ulytau
Kzyl-Dzhar
Karazhal
Chapayev
Karatobe
Oktyabr'sk
Mugodzhary
Turgay
Ozero
Zhamanakkol'
Dzhezkazgan
Zhezkazgan
Furmanovo
Mergenevo
Ural
Kalmykovo
Uil
264
Irgiz
Karsakpay
Baykonur
Sarysu
Nov.
Kasanka
Masteksay
Kushum
Uil
Shubarkuduk
Emba
Ulytau
Ozero
Aralsor
KAZAKHSTAN
Peski Priaral'skiye
Karakumy
Betpak-Dala
Kharabali
Ryn-
Peski
Kulagino
Sagiz
Sagiz
Chelkar
Prikaspiyskaya Nizmennost'
Makat
Zharkamys
408
249
Aral'sk
Novokazalinsk
Dzhusaly
Kyzylorda
Suzak
khan
Ozero
Zhaltyr
Atyrau
-24
Zal.
Paskevicha
Syrdarya
Tasbuget
Chiili
-13
Balykshi
Caspian
Sea
Karaton
Opornyy
Aral Sea
Kamyzyak
Lagan'

Scale 1 : 11 600 000

0   200   400   600 km

0   100   200   300 miles

95° E

A | **B** | 100 | **C** | 105 | **D**

BHUTAN

Tashigang Hápoli Dibrugarh Pangin Zayû Dêgên Gongshan Zhongdian Xichang **Zunyi** Huaihua Jish

Barpeta Itanagar Brahmaputra Tinsukia Tazungdam Putao Weixi Bijie Liupanshui **GUIYANG**

Goalpara Nagaon Golaghat Tabóng Maingkwan Lijiang Dukou Weining Anshun Duyun Kaili

Guwahati Dimapur Kohima Myitkyina Lushui Yongren Yuanmou Guanling Xingyi Heshan **Guilin**

I N D I A Shillong Mogaung Hopin Baoshan Dali **KUNMING** Qujing Yanshan Hechi Yangsf

Sylhet Silchar Imphal Bhamo Mong Yu Wandingzhen Lincang Jinggu **Chuxiong** Kaiyuan Funing Pingguo Binyang **Liuz**

Bhairab Bazar Aizawl Karnafuli Reservoir Kalemyo Mabein Hsweni Gengma Cangyuan Simao Gejiu Yuanjiang Lai Chau Cao Bang Wuxu **Nanning** Qinzhou

CHITTAGONG Haka Chindwin Mogok Lashio Lancang Jinghong Mong Yai Yun Xian Song Hong (Red River) Tuyên Quang Thai Nguyên **Pingxiang** Beihai **Zhanjia**

BANGLADESH Cox's Bazar Paletwa 3053 Pakokku Monywa Myingyan Amarapura Kyauske Mongkung Kunhing **MANDALAY** Kengtung Muang Sing Louang Namtha Muang Khoua **HA NÔI (HANOI)** Tien Yen **Zhanjia**

Teknaf Mt. Victoria Chauk Meiktila Taunggyi Wan Hsa-la Muang Xai Xam Nua Son La Viêt Tri Hon Gai Hepu

Sittwe **MYANMAR (BURMA)** Magwe Minbu Taungdwingyi Salween Chiang Rai Louangphrabang Ban Ban Môc Châu **HAI PHONG** Nam Dinh **Haikot**

Kyaukpyu Sinbaungwe Loikaw Mekong Phôngsaly Xianghoang Ninh Binh Thanh Hoa Dan Xian Wen

Ramree Island Taungup Pyinmana Nan **LAOS** **Qion**

Cheduba Island Pyè Toungoo Pasawng Papun Chiang Mai Siri Kit Dam Muang Pakxan Vinh Dongfang Tongshi **Hainan**

Bay of Sandoway Zigon Letpadan Mae Sariang Lampang **Viangchan (Vientiane)** Chiang Khan Khamkkeut Sanyá

Bengal Kyeintali Henzada Uttaradit Nong Khai Loei Muang Khammouan Dông Hôi

Bassein Pegu Thaton Tak Nam Ping Phitsanulok Udon Thani Muang Phin Quang Tri **Huê**

Myaungmya Insein Moulmein Phichit Sakhon Nakhon Savannakhet **Da Năng**

Cape Negrais Bogale **YANGON (RANGOON)** Kawkareik Chaiyaphum Khon Kaen Mukdahan Hôi An

Labutta Ye Sangkhla Buri Chainat Nakhon Lam Chi Roi Et Khemmarat Ban M. Khôngxédôn Pakxé Quang Ngai

Mouths of the Irrawaddy Gulf of Martaban **Nakhon Sawan** **Nakhon Ratchasima** Suwannaphum Mae Nam Mun Ubon Ratchathani Attapu **VIETNAM**

Preparis North Channel Sara Buri Surin Det Udom Kon Tum Qui Nhor

Preparis Island **THAILAND** Phumi Sâmraông M. Không Virôchey Play Cu

Preparis South Channel Ayutthaya **KRUNG THEP (BANGKOK)** Sisôphôn Siêmréab Stœng Trêng **Buôn Mê Thuôt** Tuy Hoa

Coco Island Rat Buri Aranyaprathet Bâtdâmbâng Ninh Hoa

Coco Channel Phet Buri Samut Songkhram **CAMBODIA** Kâmpông Cham Da Lat **Nha Tra**

North Andaman Bight of Bangkok Pattaya Rayong Kâmpông Chhnang Krông Kaôh Kông Chon Thanh Bao Lôc Cam Ran

Andaman Islands (India) Ban Hua Hin Chanthaburi Ko Chang Tay Ninh Biên Hoa Phan Rang

Ritchie's Archipelago Mergui Prachuap Khiri Khan Tônlé Sab Ta Khmau **HÔ CHI MINH (SAIGON)** Phan Thiêt

South Andaman Bang Saphan Yai Kâmpôt **Phnum Penh**

Port Blair Mergui Archipelago Gulf Sihanoukville Long Xuyên Bien Hoa Vung Tau

Duncan Passage Chumphon of Dao Phu Quoc My Tho

Little Andaman Thailand Rach Gia **Cân Tho**

Ten Degree Channel Kawthaung Ranong Ca Mau Bac Liêu Mouths of the Mekong

A n d a m a n Ko Samui Nam Can Côn Son

S e a Takua Pa Surat Thani

Car Nicobar Phuket Krabi Nakhon Si Thammarat

Katchall Nicobar Islands (India) Thung Song Phatthalung

Little Nicobar Trang Thale Luang Songkhla

Great Nicobar Hat Yai

Satun Pattani

Sabang Langkawi Kangar Yala Narathiwat

Banda Aceh Alor Setar Ban Betong Kota Bharu

Sungei Petani Kuala Kerai **M A L A**

Bireun George Town Gerik Kuala Terengganu

Lhokseumawe Pinang Taiping G. Korbu 2182 Dungun

I N D I A N Takengon Langsa Kemasik Laut

Ipoh Kuala Lipis

SUMATERA (SUMATRA) 3145 Meulaboh Gunung Leuser Bagun Datuk Kuantan Natuna Besar Panarik

O C E A N **MEDAN** Tebingtinggi Temerloh Kepulauan Natuna

Sibigo Simeulue Sinabang Danau Toba Bentong Malay Peninsula Subi Besar

Pematangsiantar Prapat **KUALA LUMPUR** Seremban Jemaja Kepulauan Anambas (Indonesia) Tanjung Datu

Balige Segamat Mersing Kud

Barus Baganssiapiapi Strait of Malacca Melaka Muar Batu Rahat

Sibolga Kotapinang Dumai Keluang **SINGAPORE** Sambas Siluas

Gunungsitoli Nias Duri Johor Bahru **SINGAPORE** Pemangkat

INDONESIA 100 105

metres / feet: 4000/13120, 2000/6560, 1000/3280, 500/1640, 200/656, 0/0, 200/656, 1000/3280, 2000/6560, 4000/13120, 6000/19690, 8000/26250

44 45

40 ASIA

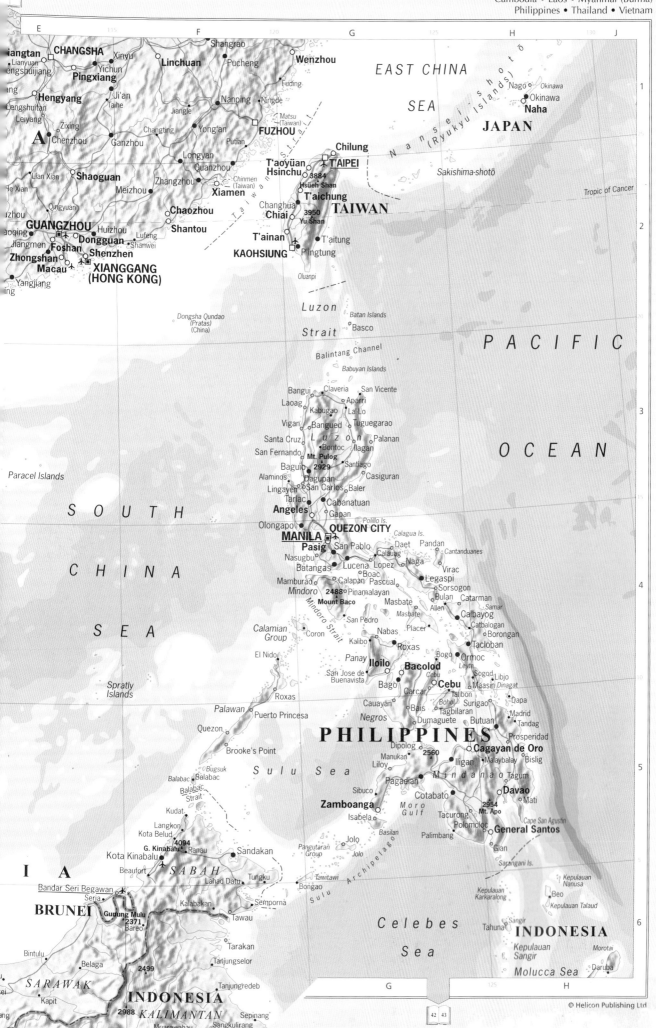

© Helicon Publishing Ltd

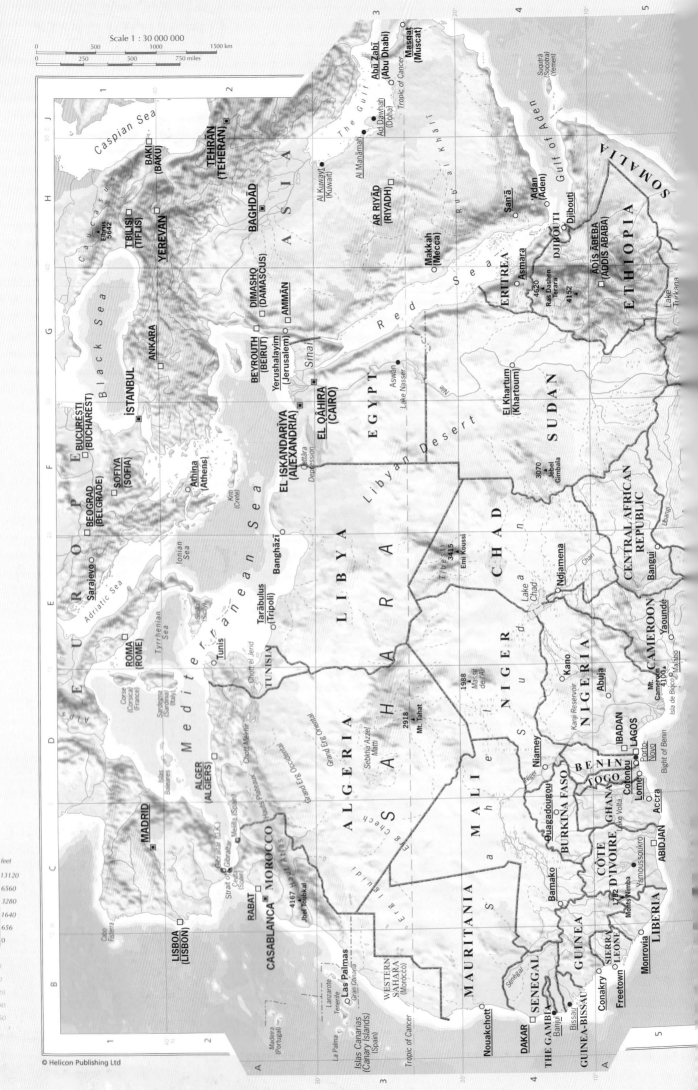

Scale 1 : 30 000 000

© Helicon Publishing Ltd

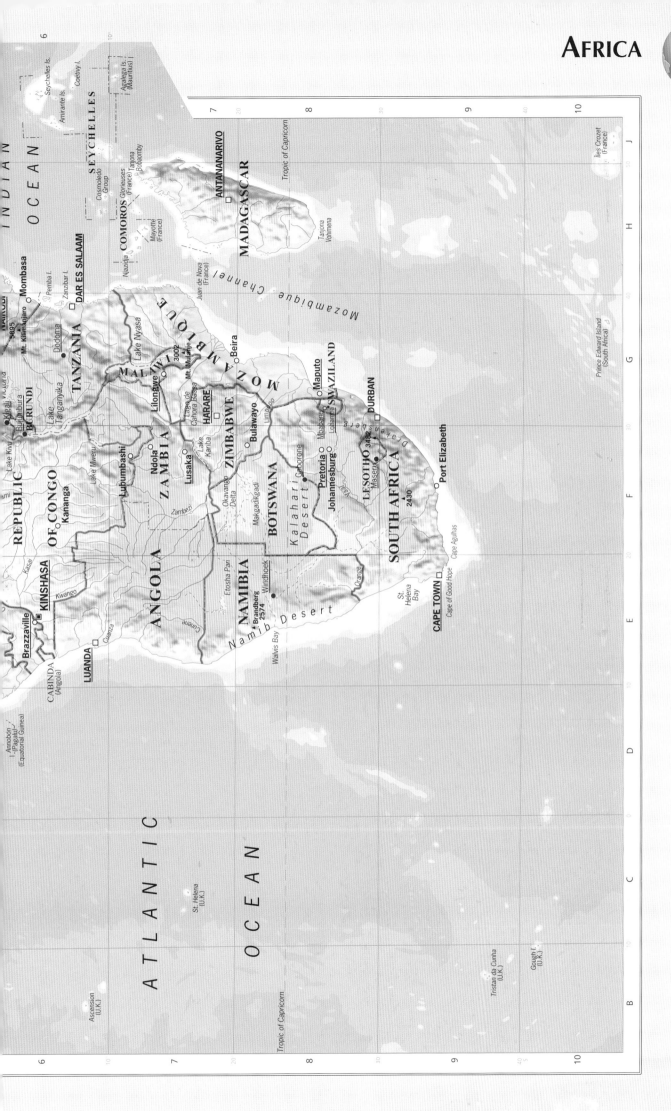

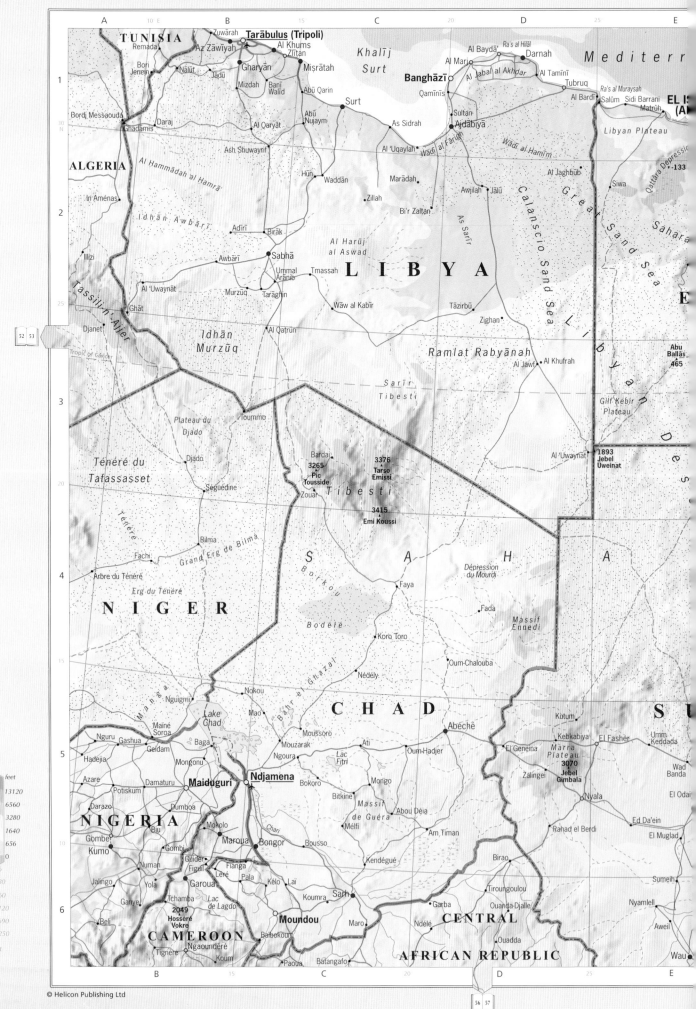

Scale 1 : 11 600 000

© Helicon Publishing Ltd

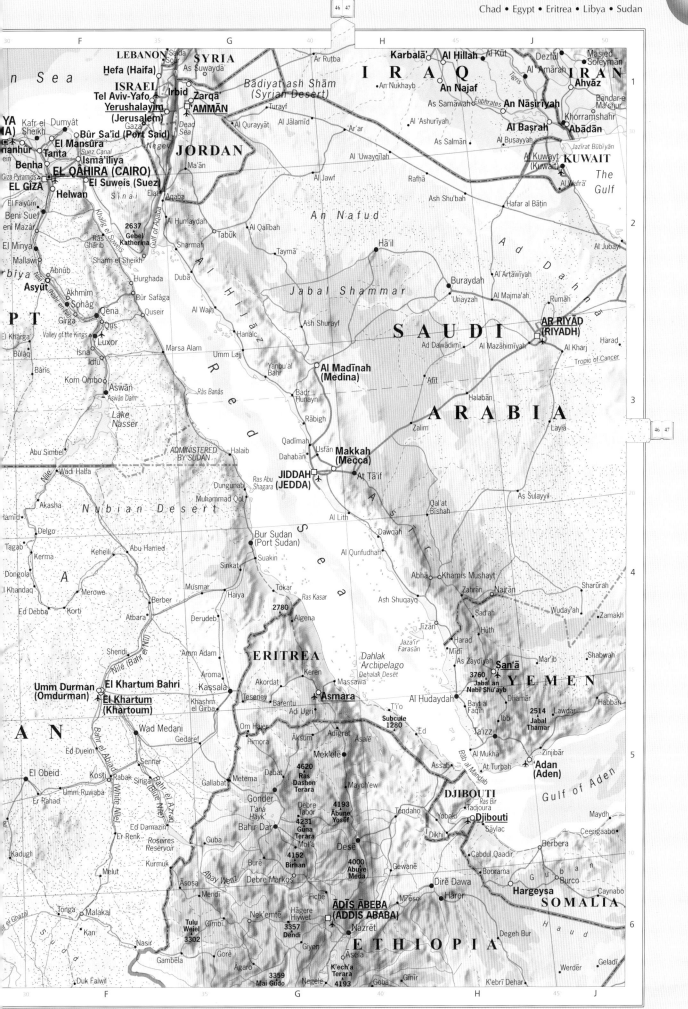

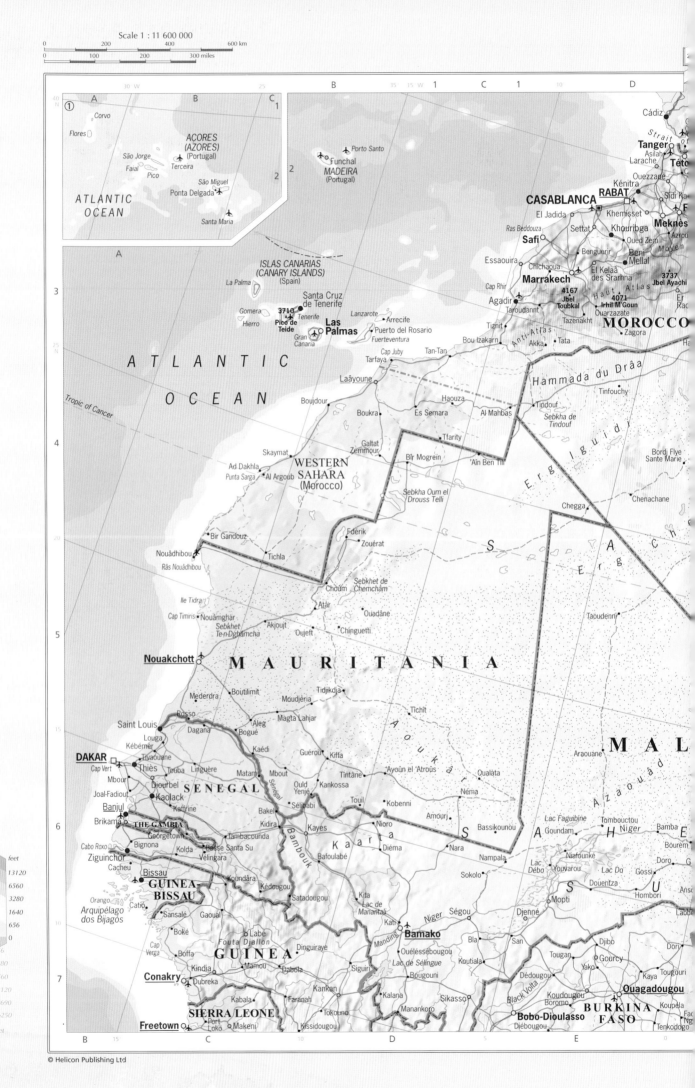

Scale 1 : 11 600 000

0   200   400   600 km
0   100   200   300 miles

① A   B   C 1
40 N

Corvo
Flores

AÇORES
(AZORES)
(Portugal)

São Jorge
Faial   Terceira
Pico

São Miguel
Ponta Delgada

ATLANTIC
OCEAN

Santa Maria

2

Porto Santo
Funchal
MADEIRA
(Portugal)

ISLAS CANARIAS
(CANARY ISLANDS)
(Spain)

La Palma

Gomera   Santa Cruz
Tenerife   de Tenerife
Hierro   3710
Pico de
Teide   Las
Palmas
Gran
Canaria

Lanzarote
Arrecife
Puerto del Rosario
Fuerteventura

ATLANTIC

OCEAN

Tropic of Cancer

WESTERN
SAHARA
(Morocco)

Cádiz

Strait
Tanger
Asilah   Této
Larache
Ouezzane
Kénitra
CASABLANCA   RABAT
El Jadida   Khemisset   Meknès
Settat   Azrou
Ras Beddouza   Khouribga   Oued Zem   Moyen
Safi   Benguerir   Beni
Mellal
Essaouira   Chichaoua   El Kelaâ   3737
Cap Rhir   des Srarhna   Jbel Ayachi
Marrakech   4167   4071
Agadir   Jbel   Irhil M'Goun
Taroudannt   Toubkal
Tazenakht   Ouarzazate
Tiznit   MOROCCO
Zagora
Anti-Atlas

Cap Juby   Tan-Tan   Bou Izakarn   Akka   Tata
Tarfaya   Hammada du Drâa
Laâyoune   Tinfouchy
Haouza
Boujdour   Es Semara   Al Mahbas   Tindouf
Boukra   Sebkha de
Galtat   Tfarity   Tindouf
Skaymat   Zemmour   Bîr Mogrein   'Aïn Ben Tili   Erg   Iguidi
Ad Dakhla   Bordj Flye
Punta Sarga   Al Argoub   Sante Marie
Sebkha Oum el   Chenachane
Drouss Telli   Chegga
Bir Gandouz   Fdérik
Nouâdhibou   Zouérat   Taoudenni
Râs Nouâdhibou   Tichla
Choûm   Sebkhet de
Ile Tidra   Chemchâm
Cap Timiris   Ouadâne
Nouâmghâr   Atâr   Ouadâne
Sebkhet   Akjoujt   Chînguetti
Ten-Dgâmcha   Oujeft
Nouakchott

MAURITANIA

Boutilimit   Tidjikdja
Mederdra   Tichît
Moudjéria
Boutilimit   Magta Lahjar   Aouker
Rosso   Aleg   Araouane   M A L
Saint Louis   Dagana   Bogué   Tombouctou
Louga   Kaédi   Kiffa   Oualâta   Lac Faguibine   Niger   Bamba
Kébémer   Guérou   Tintâne   'Ayoûn el 'Atroûs   Goundam   Bourem
DAKAR   Tivaouane   Néma   Gourma
Cap Vert   Thiès   Touba   Linguère   Matam   Kankossa   Amoûrj   Niafounké   Doro
Mbour   Diourbel   Mbout   Touil   Kobenni   Bassikounou   Lac   Gossi
Joal-Fadiout   Kaolack   SENEGAL   Ould   Nioro   Faguibine
Banjul   Kaffrine   Bakel   Yenjé   Kayes   Nara   Youvarou   Lac Do   Douentza
Brikama   Kidira   Diéma   Nampala   Lac   Hombori
THE GAMBIA   Tambacounda   Kaarta   Sokolo   Débo   Mopti
Georgetown   Basse Santa Su   Bafoulabé   Ségou
Cabo Roxo   Bignona   Kolda   Vélingara   Niafounké
Ziguinchor   Kédougou   Lac de   Djenné
Cacheu   Koundâra   Manantali   Bamako   Ségou   Bla   San   Djibo   Gourcy
Bissau   Satadougou   Kati   Tougan   Yako   Tougouri
GUINEA-   Orango   Kita   Niger   Ouéléssébougou   Koutiala   Dédougou   Kaya
BISSAU   Sansalé   Gaoual   Lac de Sélingue   Siguiri   OUAGADOUGOU
Arquipélago   Catió   Boké   Labé   Dinguiraye   Bougouni   Sikasso   Koudougou   Koupéla
dos Bijagós   Cap   Boffa   Fouta Djallon   Boromo   BURKINA
Verga   Mamou   Dabola   Kalana   Black Volta   Bobo-Dioulasso   FASO   Tenkodogo
GUINEA   Kindia   Siguiri   Manankoro   Dori
Conakry   Dubreka   Faranah   Kankan   Diébougou   Fag
Kabala   Kissidougou   Tokounou   Koudougou
SIERRA LEONE   Port   Makeni
Freetown   Loko

B   15   C   10   D   5   E

© Helicon Publishing Ltd

metres   feet
4000   13120
2000   6560
1000   3280
500   1640
200   656
0   0
200   656
1000   3280
2000   6560
4000   13120
6000   19690
8000   26250
metres   feet

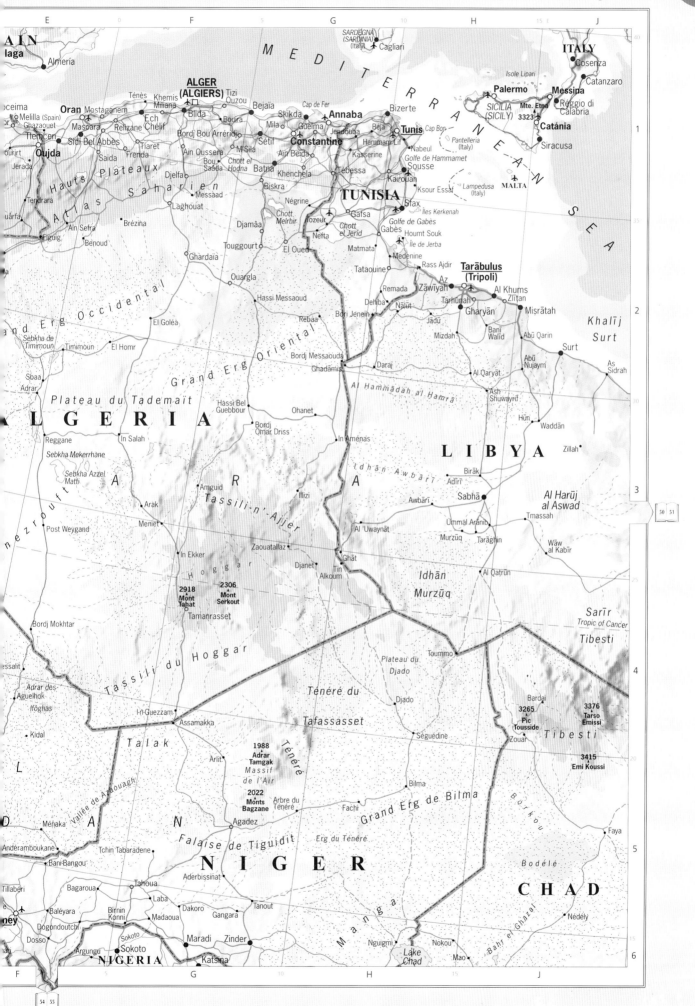

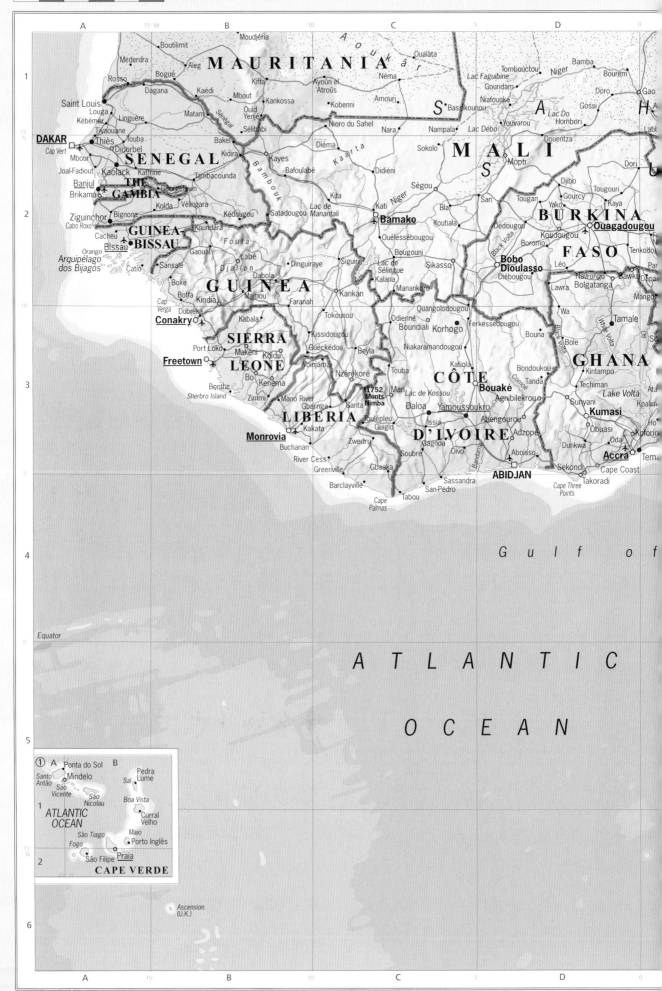

Scale 1 : 11 600 000

0   200   400   600 km
0   100   200   300 miles

A   15°W   **B**   10   **C**   5   **D**   0

Moudjéria
Boutilimit
Méderdra
Aleg
Bogué
Rosso
Dagana
Kaédi
Kiffa
Kankossa
Kobenni
Amourj
Oualâta
Néma
Basikounou
Tombouctou
Goundam
Bamba
Bourem
Niger
Gao
Gossi
Doro

M A U R I T A N I A
Aoukâr
S A H
Lac Faguibine

Saint Louis
Louga
Kébémer
Linguère
Tivaouane
Matam
Ould Yenjé
Nioro du Sahel
Nara
Nampala
Youvarou
Lac Débo
Lac Do
Hombori
Douentza

15°N

DAKAR
Cap Vert
Thiès
Diourbel
Mbour
Joal-Fadiout
Kaolack
Kaffrine
Touba
Bakel
Kidira
Kayes
Didiéni
Diéma
Ségou
San
Tougan
Djibo
Gourcy
Yako
Kaya
Dori
Mopti

S E N E G A L
Bambouk
M A L I
S

Banjul
Brikama
Georgetown
Bignona
THE GAMBIA
Bafoulabé
Kita
Bla
Koutiala
Dédougou
Koudougou
Boromo
Ouagadougou

Ziguinchor
Cabo Roxo
Kolda
Vélingara
Kédougou
Satadougou
Lac de Manantali
Kati
Bamako
Bougouni
Sikasso
BURKINA

GUINEA-BISSAU
Bissau
Cacheu
Catió
Koundâra
Gaoual
Labé
Dinguiraye
Siguiri
Lac de Sélingué
Kalana
Manankoro
Diébougou
Léo
Bobo Dioulasso
Lawra
FASO

Arquipélago dos Bijagos
Orango
Sansalé
Boké
Boffa
Dabola
Mamou
Faranah
Tokounou
Kankan
Quangolodougou
Wa
Navrongo
Bolgatanga
Bawku

Cap Verga
Dubreka
Kindia
Kabala
Kissidougou
Odienné
Boundiali
Korhogo
Ferkessédougou
Bouna
Bole
Tamale

GUINEA
Djallon
Fouta
Kabala

Conakry
SIERRA LEONE
Port Loko
Makeni
Koidu
Guéckédou
Beyla
Touba
Katiola
Bondoukou
Tanda
Techiman
Sunyani
GHANA

Freetown
Bo
Kenema
Voinjama
Nzérékoré
Man
Lac de Kossou
CÔTE
Bouaké
Agnibilekrou
Kumasi
Kintampo

Bonthe
Sherbro Island
Zimmi
Manó River
Gbarnga
Santa
1752 Monts Nimba
Daloa
Yamoussoukro
Abengourou
Obuasi
Oda
Koforidua

LIBERIA
Kakata
Toulépleu
Guiglo
Issia
D'IVOIRE
Adzopé
Dunkwa
Accra

Monrovia
Buchanan
River Cess
Zwedru
Gagnoa
Divo
Aboisso
Sekondi
Cape Coast

Greenville
Gbaaka
Soubré
Sassandra
San-Pédro
ABIDJAN
Cape Three Points
Takoradi

Barclayville
Tabou
Cape Palmas

G u l f   o f

Equator

A T L A N T I C

0

O C E A N

①   **A**   Ponta do Sol   **B**
Santo Antão
Mindelo
São Vicente
São Nicolau
Sal
Pedra Lume
Boa Vista

ATLANTIC OCEAN
Curral Velho

1

São Tiago
Maio
Porto Inglês

Fogo
São Filipe
Praia

15°N

2

CAPE VERDE

Ascension (U.K.)

6

metres / feet
4000 / 13120
2000 / 6560
1000 / 3280
500 / 1640
200 / 656
0 / 0
200 / 656
1000 / 3280
2000 / 6560
4000 / 13120
6000 / 19690
8000 / 26250
metres / feet

WEST AFRICA

Benin • Burkina Faso • Cameroon • Cape Verde • Congo • Côte d'Ivoire • Equatorial Guinea • Gabon • The Gambia
Ghana • Guinea • Guinea-Bissau • Liberia • Nigeria • São Tomé & Príncipe • Senegal • Sierra Leone • Togo

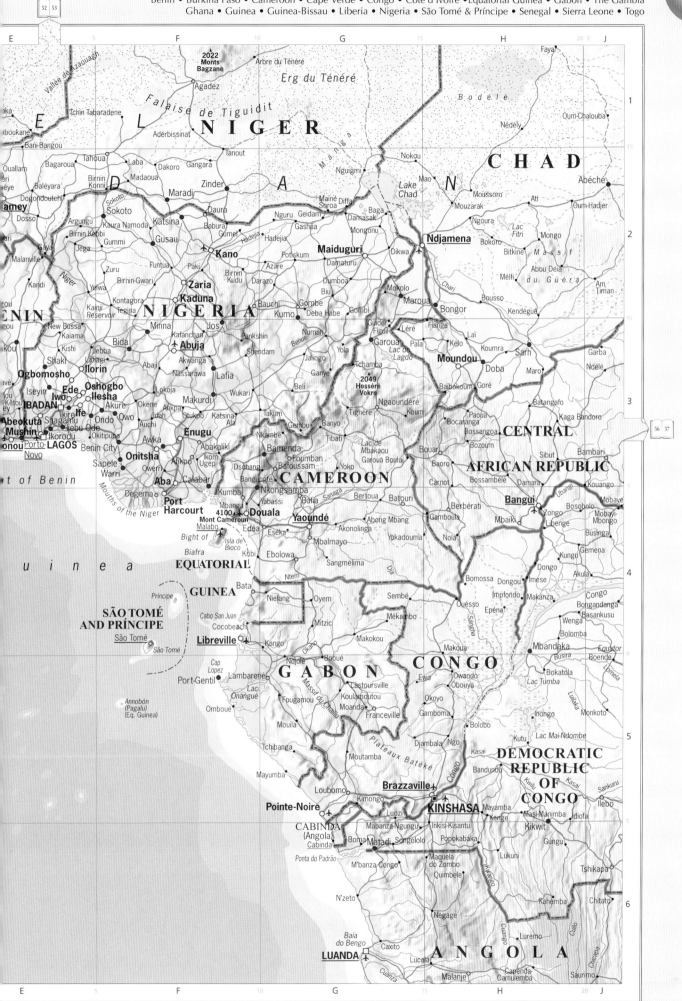

56 | 57

Scale 1 : 11 600 000

© Helicon Publishing Ltd

CENTRAL AFRICA

Angola • Burundi • Central African Republic • Democratic Republic of Congo
Djibouti • Ethiopia • Kenya • Rwanda • Somalia • Tanzania • Uganda

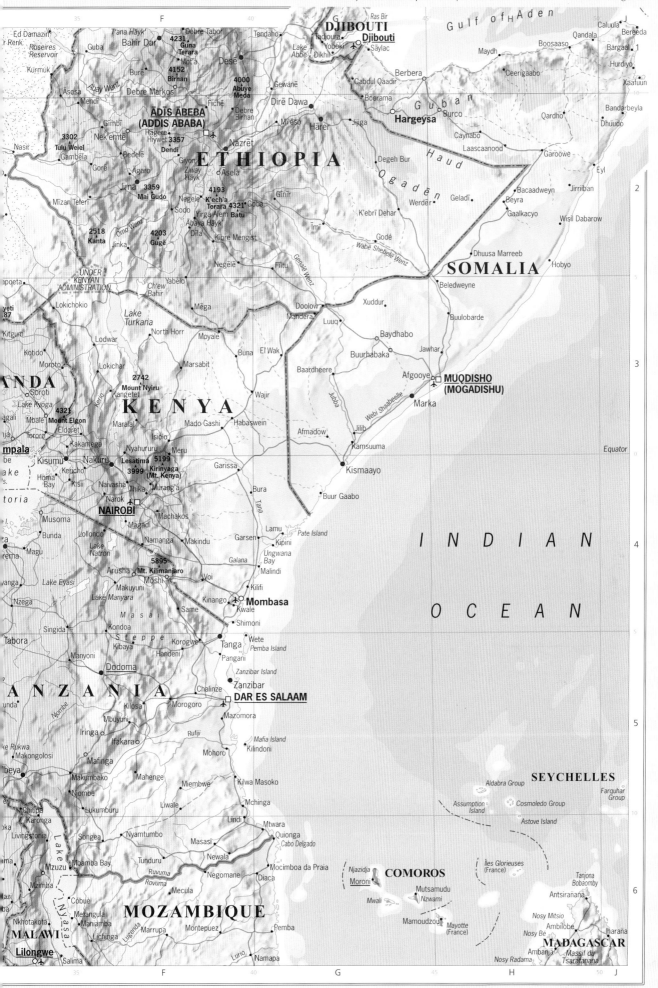

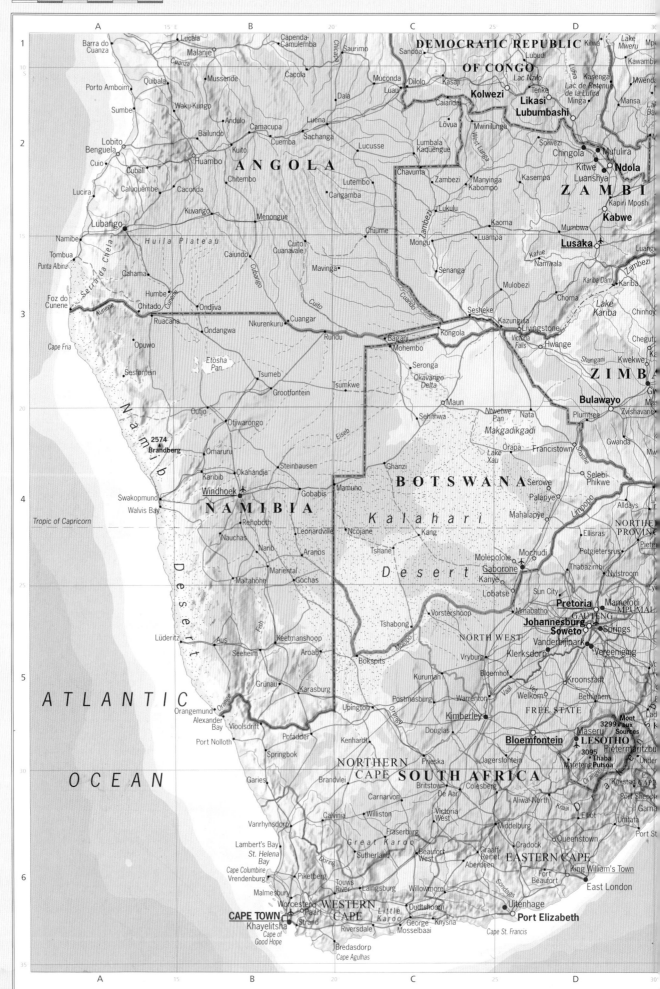

© Helicon Publishing Ltd

SOUTHERN AFRICA

Botswana • Comoros • Lesotho • Madagascar • Malawi • Mauritius
Mozambique • Namibia • Seychelles • South Africa • Swaziland • Zambia • Zimbabwe

TANZANIA

Nakonde
Nyombe
Lukumburu
Liwale
Lindi
Mtwara
Quionga
Cabo Delgado

SEYCHELLES
Aldabra Group
Assumption Island
Cosmoledo Group
Astove Island
Farquhar Group

Chitipa
Karonga
Isoka
Songea
Nyamtumbo
Masasi
Newala
Mocímboa da Praia

COMOROS
Mitsamiouli
Mutsamudu
Îles Glorieuses (France)
Tanjona Bobaomby

Chama
Mzuzu
Mbamba Bay
Tunduru
Masuguru
Rovuma
Negomane
Diaca
Moroni
Njazidja
Foumboni
Mwali
Nzwami
Nosy Mitsio
Antsiranana

Chikwa
Mzimba
Cobuè
Mecula
Mecufi
Mamoudzou
Mayotte (France)
Nosy Bé
Ambilobe
Iharaña

Lundazi
Nkhotakota
Metangula
Maniamba
Lichinga
Marrupa
Montepuez
Pemba
Ambanja
Massif du

Mfuwe
MALAWI
Salima
Mandimba
Namapa
Memba
Nosy Radama
Bealanana
2876
Sambava
Andapa

Chipata
Lilongwe
Dedza
Cuamba
Lake Chilwa
Nacaroa
Nacala
Analalava
Tsaratanana
Antalaha
Maroansetra

Songo
Zomba
2419
Nampula
Moçambique
Mahajanga
Mitsinjo
Mandritsara
Farihy Alaotra

Bene
Ulongue
Blantyre
Monte Namuli
Alto Molócuè
Soalala
Ambato Boeny
Soanierana-Ivongo
Andilamena
Nosy Boraha

Lago de Cahora Bassa
3002
Lugela
Angoche
Besalampy
Maevatanana
Ambatondrazaka
Helodrano Antongila

Tete
Chiromo
Mount Mulanje
Mocuba
Moma
Tanjona Masoala

MOZAMBIQUE
Changara
Caia
Pebane
Morafenobe
Maintirano
Beravina
MADAGASCAR
Toamasina

ARE
gwiza
Catandica
Mopeia
Namidobe
Quelimane
Nosy Barren
Antsalova
Tsiroanomandidy
ANTANANARIVO
Moramanga

Mutare
Chimoio
Inhaminga
Chinde
Miandrivazo
2643 Tsiafajavona
Antsirabe
Vatomandry
Mahanoro

Cashel
Beira
Belo Tsiribihina
Mania
Marolambo

Save
Espungabera
Morondava
Malaimbandy
Fandriana
Nosy-Varika

angle
Save
Nova Mambone
Mandabe
Matsiatra
Ambositra
Ambohimahasoa
Manjary

Chicualacuala
Chigubo
Ilha do Bazaruto
Manja
Mangoky
Fianarantsoa
Ifanadiana

Mapinhane
Bassas da India (France)
Morombe
Tanjona Ankaboa
Ankazoabo
Zazafotsy
Ihosy
Manakara
Vohipeno

Mabalane
Chicualacuala
Massinga
Île Europa (France)
Mahaboboka
Sakaraha
Ivohibe
Vangaindrano

Mabalane
Inhambane
Toliara
Betroka
Tropic of Capricorn

Chókwe
Macia
Chibuto
Ponta Zavora
Betioky
Onilahy
Bekily
Manantenina

Xai-Xai
Ampanihy
Beloha
Ambovombe
Tôlañara

Maputo
Ponta Khehuene
Bela Vista
Tanjona Vohimena

ILAND

Mkuze
Lake St. Lucia

I N D I A N

nozi
Empangeni
O C E A N

BAN

SEYCHELLES

Praslin I.
Silhouette I.
Mahé
Victoria

Amirante Is.

Coëtivy I.

INDIAN OCEAN

① A
Port Louis
Phoenix
St-Denis
MAURITIUS
St-Pierre
Réunion (France)
INDIAN OCEAN

② **A**
Aldabra Islands
St. Pierre I.
Providence I.
Assumption Island
Cosmoledo Group
Astove Island
Farquhar Group
Agalega Islands (Mauritius)

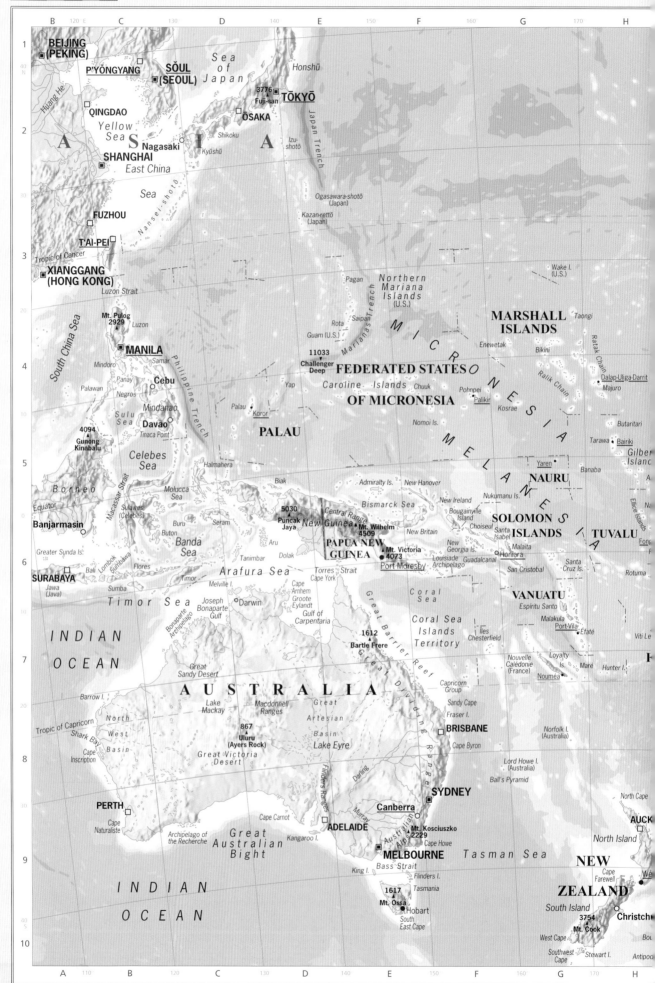

J 170 K 160 L 150 M 140 N 130 P 120 W Q

NORTH AMERICA

LOS ANGELES ■
SAN DIEGO □

P A C I F I C

Guadalupe
(Mexico)

Hawaiian Islands

Lysan I.

Necker I.

HAWAII
(U.S.)

Tropic of Cancer

Kauai
Oahu
Honolulu ○ Maui

Hawaii

Johnston I.
(U.S.)

Is. Revillagigedo
(Mexico)

O C E A N

N. W. Christmas Island Ridge

Palmyra I.
(U.S.)

Tabuaeran

Line Islands

Kiritimati

owland (U.S.)
Baker (U.S.)

Jarvis
(U.S.)

enix Islands

Birnie
Rawaki
KIRIBATI
ona
Manra
Malden I.

Equator

Starbuck I.

O L Y N E S I A

Atafu
Nukunonu
Tokelau
(New Zealand)
Tongareva
Vostok I.
Caroline I.
Nuku Hiva

Marquesas Islands

Swains I.
Danger Is.
Nassau
Manihiki
Hiva Oa

SAMOA
American
Samoa
Savaii
e) Apia Tutuila
Upolu
Tatahi
Rose I.
Suvorov I.
Motu One
Îles Palliser
Îles de
Désappointement

Archipel des Tuamotu

Pukapuka

Islands

Cook Islands
Raroia

TONGA
Niue
Palmerston I.
(New Zealand)
Aitutaki
Arch.
de la Société
Tahiti
Hao

ofa
Rarotonga
French
Polynesia
Îles Duc de
Gloucester

Ata
Mangaia
Îles
Maria
Rurutu
Groupe Actéon

orizon Depth
10882
Tubuai Islands
Tubuai
Mururoa
Morane
Gambier
Is.

Raevavae
Mangareva

Oeno
Tropic of Capricorn

Rapa
Henderson I.

Pitcairn Is. Ducie I.
(U.K.)

Marotiri

Easter I.
(Chile)

South West

Pacific

Basin

ec Islands
Zealand)

Tonga Trench

Trench

J 170 K 160 L 150 M 140 N 130 P 120 Q 110 R

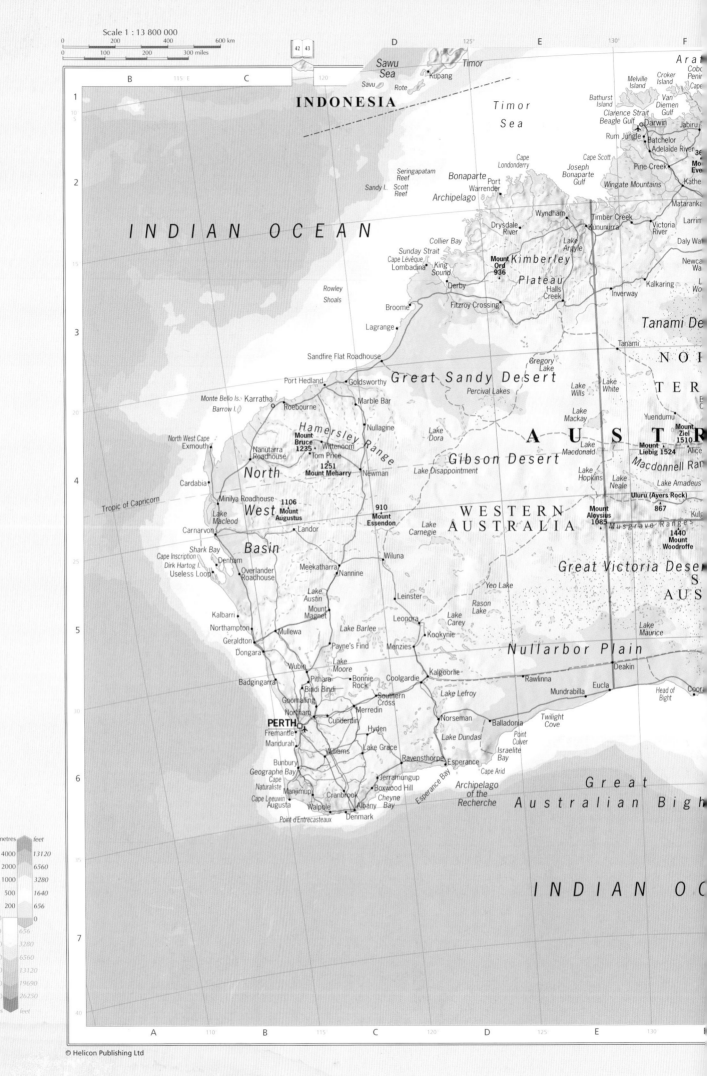

Scale 1 : 13 800 000

© Helicon Publishing Ltd

G 140° H 145° J 150° K 155° L

Cape Wessel
Wessel Islands

Nangalala Nhulunbuy
Cape Arnhem

hem Bickerton Island
nd Groote
Eylandt
Numbulwar

er Bar

Borroloola
Sir Edward
Pellew Group

Cape
Crawford

rkly Tableland

t Creek

RN Lake Nash
ORY Mount Isa

Simpson
Desert

L I A

Lake Eyre
Basin

oodnadatta

I A
ber Pedy
Lake Eyre
South

Lake
Gairdner

ler Ranges
y Bay
Eyre
Pen.

colmo
not

Mulgrave I. Moa (Banks Island)
Torres Strait
Prince of Wales Cape York
Island Somerset
Bamaga

Duifken Point
Weipa
Albatross Bay
Aurukun

Cape
Grenville

Cape
Direction

Cape
York
Peninsula

Port
Moresby

PAPUA
NEW GUINEA

D'Entrecasteaux
Islands
Alotau

Louisiade
Archipelago

Coral Sea Islands
CORAL SEA

Territory
(Australia)

PACIFIC

OCEAN

Kowanyama

Dunbar

Coen

Princess Charlotte Bay

Silver
Plains

Cape
Flattery
Laura Cooktown
Cape Melville

Osprey Reef

Shark Reef

Bougainville Reef

Holmes Reefs Diane Bank

Willis Group

Magdelaine Cays

Diamond Islets

Herald
Cays

Flinders
Reefs

Malay Reef

Turtle I.

Tregosse Islets

Swain
Reefs

Burketown
Karumba

Normanton

Croydon

Georgetown
Forsayth
Greenvale

Mareeba
1612 Mount Bartle Frere

Mount Garnet
Innisfail

Ingham
Halifax Bay

Mutarnee
Townsville

Port Douglas Cairns

GREAT

DIVIDING

RANGE

BARRIER

REEF

Lorraine

Camooweal

Cloncurry

Richmond

McKinlay

QUEENSLAND

Hughenden

Charters
Towers

Ayr Bowen The
Whitsundays
Proserpine
Repulse Bay
Mackay

Dalrymple
Lake

Nebo Sarina

Broad Sound
Clairview

Townshend I.

Tobermorey

Great

Boulia

Winton

Muttaburra

Clermont

Barcaldine
Longreach Jericho Emerald
Blackwater

Springsure

Yeppoon
Rockhampton
Curtis I.

Capricorn
Group

Cato I.

Tropic of Capricorn

Artesian

Birdsville
Betoota

Windorah

Jundah

Yaraka

Blackall

Tambo

Banana

Gladstone

Bundaberg
Sandy Cape

Sturt Stony
Desert Basin

Lake
Yamma
Yamma

Augathella

Charleville

Taroom

Biloela

Tirari
Desert

Lake Eyre
North

Quilpie

Muckadilla

Miles

Roma

Gayndah

Eidsvold

Hervey Bay
Fraser I.
Maryborough

Gympie

Caloundra

Marree

Lake
Blanche

Thargomindah

Glenmorgan

Kingaroy

Moonie Dalby Toowoomba

BRISBANE

Moreton I.

Leigh Creek

Lake
Callabonna

Tibbooburra
Wanaaring

Hungerford

Cunnamulla

Dirranbandi

St
George

Bungunya

Goondiwindi
Boggabilla

Beenleigh
Surfers Paradise
Gold
Coast

North Stradbroke I.

Mount
Roberts
1387

Glendambo
Lake
Torrens
Pimba

Lake
Frome

Tibooburra

White
Cliffs

Brewarrina

Moree

Casino

Cape Byron
Ballina

Tenterfield

Marree

Flinders Ranges

Lake

Bourke

Walgett

Narrabri

Armidale

Glen Innes

Grafton

Round
Mountain
1608

Coffs Harbour

Port Augusta

Whyalla
Kyancutta
Cowell

Port Pirie

Orroroo

Burra

Hawker

Broken
Hill

Menindee

Wilcannia

Louth

Coolabah

Cobar

NEW

SOUTH

WALES

Gunnedah

Coonabarabran

Nyngan

Gilgandra

Tamworth

Quirindi

Black
Sugarloaf
1494

Port Macquarie

Morgan

ADELAIDE

Gawler

Murray Bridge
Tailem Bend

Renmark

Wentworth

Darling

Ivanhoe

Roto

Condobolin

Dubbo

Orange 1274

Bathurst

1204

Singleton
Taree

Cessnock
Newcastle

Innamincka
Victor
Harbor
Investigator Strait
Cape Borda

Kingscote

Kangaroo I.

Murray River
Basin

Morgan

Murray

Balranald

Hay

Swan
Hill

Narrandera

Wagga Wagga

Gigowan
Marsden

Cowra
1204
Cootamundra

Lithgow Katoomba
SYDNEY
Wollongong

Nowra

Border Town

VICTORIA

Hopetoun

Ouyen

Deniliquin

Finley

Albury

Tumut

A.C.T.
Canberra

Batemans Bay

Lacepede Bay
Cape Jaffa
Robe

Big Desert

Little
Desert

Horsham

Shepparton

Seymour

Yea

Omeo

2229
Mount
Kosciuszko

Cooma

GREAT

DIVIDING

Hamilton

Ballarat

Mount Bogong
1986

Mount Gambier

Portland
Cape Nelson

Geelong

Morwell

MELBOURNE

Bombala

Eden

Cape Howe

Bairnsdale

Sale

N

Warrnambool

Apollo
Bay

Korumburra

Port Albert
Wilson's Promontory
South East Point

Walkerville

King Island

Currie

Bass Strait

Furneaux
Group
Cape Grim Stanley Whitemark
Burnie George
Devonport Town Launceston
Queenstown 1617
Mount
Ossa

TASMANIA

Lake Gordon

South West
Cape

Hobart
Dover

Swansea

Cape Forestier

Port Arthur
Storm Bay

South
East Cape

Flinders I.

Banks Strait

Cape Barren I.

TASMAN SEA

A.C.T. = Australian Capital Territory

Lord Howe I.

Ball's Pyramid

64 65

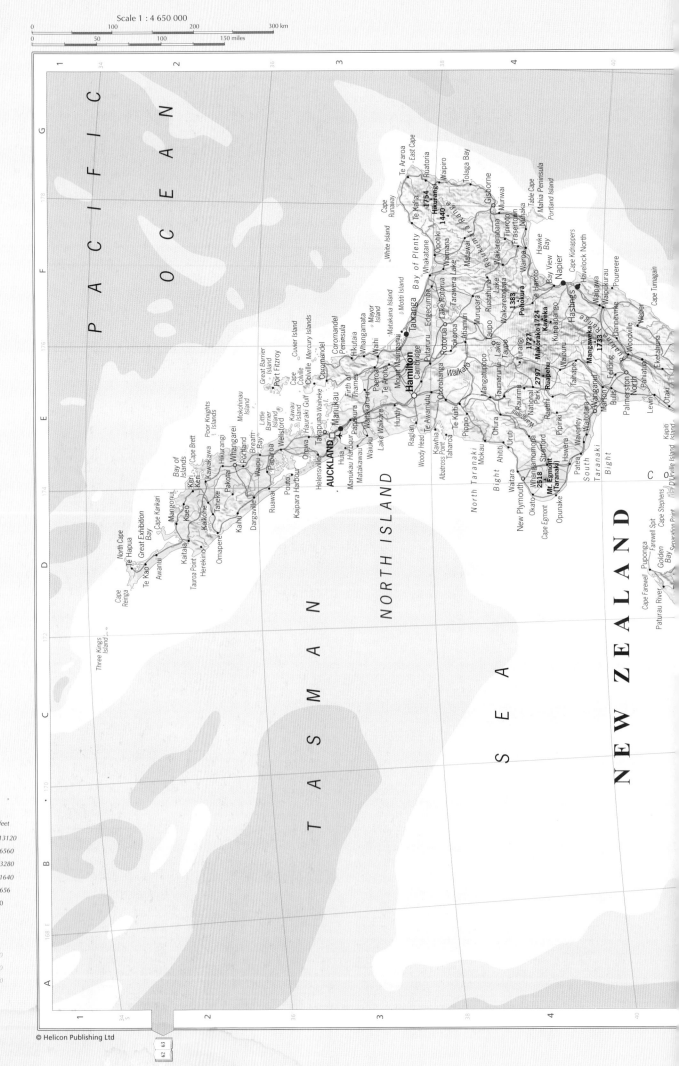

Scale 1 : 4 650 000

© Helicon Publishing Ltd

NEW ZEALAND

Antipodes Islands • Auckland Island
Campbell Island • Chatham Islands

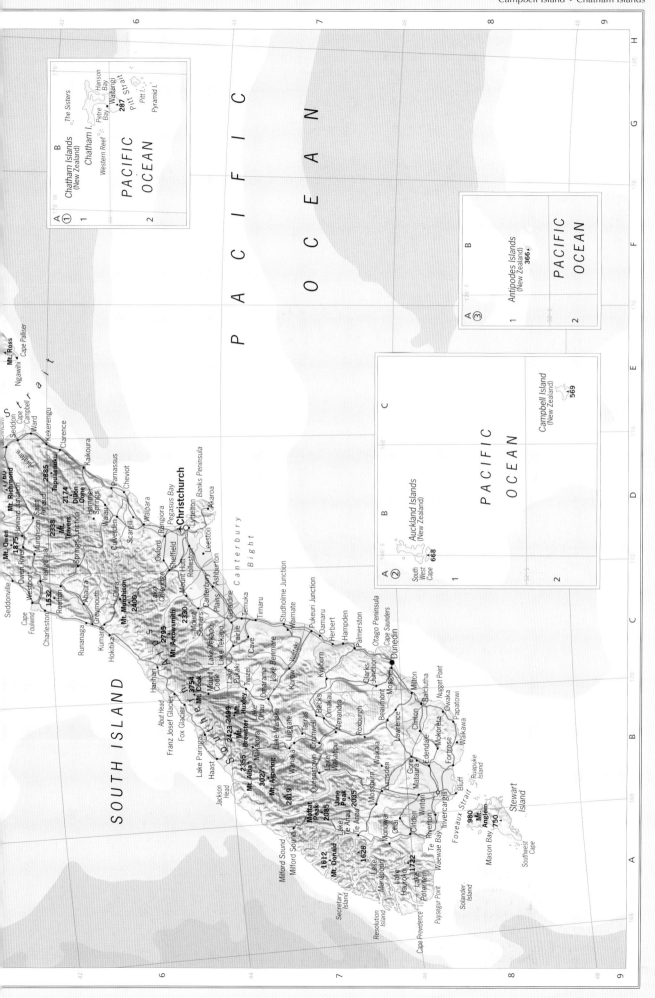

SOUTH ISLAND

PACIFIC OCEAN

Christchurch

Dunedin

Stewart Island

Chatham Islands
(New Zealand)

Chatham I.

The Sisters

Hanson Bay
Waitangi 287
Pitt Strait
Pitt I.
Pyramid I.

Western Reef

Petre Bay

PACIFIC OCEAN

Antipodes Islands
(New Zealand)

366

PACIFIC OCEAN

Auckland Islands
(New Zealand)

668

South West Cape

Campbell Island
(New Zealand)

569

PACIFIC OCEAN

0 500 1000 1500 km
0 250 500 750 miles

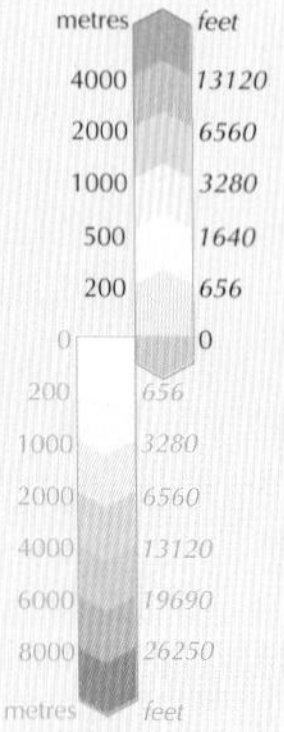

A B C 10 20 D 4 30 E 40 50 F 5 50 40

NORWAY

Shetland Is. (U.K.)

Faeroes (Denmark)

ICELAND • Reykjavik

Arctic Circle

Greenland Sea

Jan Mayen (Norway)

Denmark Strait

ATLANTIC

OCEAN

Cape Farewell

St. John's
Cape Race
St. Anthony
Newfoundland
St-Pierre-et-Miquelon (France)
Cape Breton I.
Nova Scotia
Halifax

Svalbard (Spitzbergen) (Norway)

Wandel Sea

GREENLAND (Denmark)

Nuuk (Godthåb)

Davis Strait

Cape Dyer

Resolution I.
Iqaluit
Cumberland Sd

Labrador Sea

Cape Harrison

Smallwood Reservoir

Cape Chidley

Réservoir Manicouagan

Baffin Bay

Baffin Island

Peninsule d'Ungava
Ungava Bay

Île d'Anticosti
Gulf of St. Lawrence

Baie Comeau
Chicoutimi
Québec
MONTRÉAL

St. Lawrence

ARCTIC

North Pole

OCEAN

Ellesmere Island
Queen Elizabeth Islands
Parry Islands
Devon Island

Nares Strait

Bylot I.
Arctic Bay
Brodeur Pen.
Prince Charles Island
Foxe Pen.
Melville Pen.

Foxe Basin

Southampton Island
Coats I.
Marsel I.

Hudson Bay

Belcher Islands

James Bay

Winisk

Akimiski I.
Fort George
Val-d'Or
Kapuskasing

Ottawa

Lake Nipigon

Thunder Bay

Melville Island
Prince Patrick Island
Viscount Melville Sound
Somerset Island
Prince of Wales Island
Boothia Pen.
Gulf of Boothia
King William Island

Banks Island
Amundsen Gulf

Victoria Island

Bathurst Inlet
Garry Lake
Baker Lake
Nueltin Lake
Cape Churchill
Churchill

Reindeer Lake
Nelson
Sandy Lake

Winnipeg
Lake Winnipeg
Manitoba
Lake Winnipegosis

Beaufort Sea

Mackenzie Bay

Inuvik

Great Bear Lake

Great Slave Lake
Yellowknife
Slave
Peace
Dawson Creek

Lake Athabasca
Churchill
Thompson

Lake Saskatchewan

Regina
Saskatoon
Lethbridge

CANADA

Point Barrow

Point Hope
Kotzebue Sound

Brooks Range

ALASKA (U.S.)

Fairbanks
Yukon
Whitehorse
Yukon

Mackenzie Mts

Mt. Roosevelt 2972

Mackenzie

R O C K Y

Edmonton
Calgary

Kelowna
Kamloops

Fraser

Seattle
Spokane

Mt. Waddington 4042

Mt. McKinley 6194
Anchorage

Alaska Range

Coast Mountains

Mt. Logan 6050

Juneau

Alexander Archipelago
Prince of Wales I.
Graham I.
Queen Charlotte Islands
Queen Charlotte Sound
Prince Rupert

Vancouver I.
Victoria
Vancouver
Portland

Blue Mts

ASIA

RUSSIA

East Siberian Sea

Ostrov Vrangelya

International Date Line

Arctic Circle

Anadyrskiy Zaliv

St. Lawrence I.

Bering Strait

Norton Sound

Nunivak I.

Bristol Bay

St. Matthew I.
Pribilof Is.

Bering

Sea

Kodiak I.
Gulf of Alaska

Aleutian Islands

Fox Islands
Aleutian Trench

metres | feet
4000 | 13120
2000 | 6560
1000 | 3280
500 | 1640
200 | 656
0 | 0
200 | 656
1000 | 3280
2000 | 6560
4000 | 13120
6000 | 19690
8000 | 26250
metres | feet

W V U T S R
170 E 180 170 W 160 150 40
60 N

© Helicon Publishing Ltd

NORTH AMERICA

ATLANTIC OCEAN

SOUTH AMERICA

Bermuda (U.K.)

PHILADELPHIA
Baltimore
Washington D.C.
Virginia Beach
Cape Hatteras
Raleigh
Charlotte
Cleveland
Cincinnati
Columbus
Indianapolis
CHICAGO
Milwaukee
St. Louis
Nashville
Knoxville
Memphis
Little Rock
Kansas City
Denver
Oklahoma City
Abilene
DALLAS
Fort Worth
Austin
SAN ANTONIO
HOUSTON
Corpus Christi
El Paso
Ciudad Juárez
Albuquerque
Tucson
PHOENIX
Las Vegas
Salt Lake City
Sacramento
San Francisco
San Jose
Fresno
LOS ANGELES
SAN DIEGO
Mexicali
Ensenada

UNITED STATES

Great Salt Lake
4123
Grand Canyon
3951
Colorado
Death Valley
Mojave Desert
Great Basin
Sierra Nevada
Channel Is.
Guadalupe (Mexico)

Tropic of Cancer

Atlanta
Savannah
Jacksonville
Tampa
Miami
Cape Canaveral
Florida Keys
Straits of Florida

THE BAHAMAS
Grand Bahama
Great Abaco
Nassau
Andros
Great Inagua
Turks and Caicos Is. (U.K.)

Puerto Rico Trench
Virgin Is. (U.S.)
San Juan
Puerto Rico (U.S.)
Virgin Is. (U.K.)

DOMINICAN REPUBLIC
HAITI
Pico Duarte
3175
SANTO DOMINGO
PORT-AU-PRINCE
Santiago de Cuba
CUBA
LA HABANA (HAVANA)
Isla de la Juventud
Cabo Beata

Lesser Antilles
Netherlands Antilles
Aruba (Neth.)
CARACAS
Punta Gallinas

JAMAICA
Kingston
Cayman Is. (U.K.)

Caribbean Sea

Swan Is. (Honduras)
Cabo Gracias á Dios

Gulf of Mexico
MEXICO
Yucatán Channel
I. de Cozumel
Cozumel
Mérida
Bahía de Campeche
Yucatán
Ciudad Madero
Veracruz
Vol. Citlaltépetl
5610
CIUDAD DE MEXICO
León
MONTERREY
Matamoros
Reynosa
Rio Grande
Sierra Madre Occidental
Sierra Madre del Sur
GUADALAJARA
Acapulco
Islas Marías
Islas Revillagigedo (Mexico)
I. Clarión
Cedros
La Paz
Cabo San Lucas
Golfo de California
Baja California
Hermosillo
Ciudad Obregón

Belmopan
BELIZE
GUATEMALA
4210
GUATEMALA
San Salvador
EL SALVADOR
HONDURAS
Tegucigalpa
NICARAGUA
Lago de Nicaragua
Managua
COSTA RICA
San José
PANAMA
Panamá
Canal de Panamá (Panama Canal)
Golfo del Darién
Golfo de Panamá
Punta Mariato
Isla Coiba
I. de Coco (Costa Rica)
Isla de Malpelo (Colombia)

Middle America Trench

BARRANQUILLA
Cristóbal Colón
5775
MEDELLÍN
CALI
5750
Cordillera Occidental
Cordillera Central
BOGOTÁ
Orinoco
Meta

SOUTH AMERICA

QUITO
6310
GUAYAQUIL
Golfo de Guayaquil
Chiclayo
Iquitos
Amazonas

Islas Galápagos (Galápagos Is.) (Ecuador)
Isla Isabela

Clipperton Island (France)

PACIFIC OCEAN

Equator

Tropic of Cancer

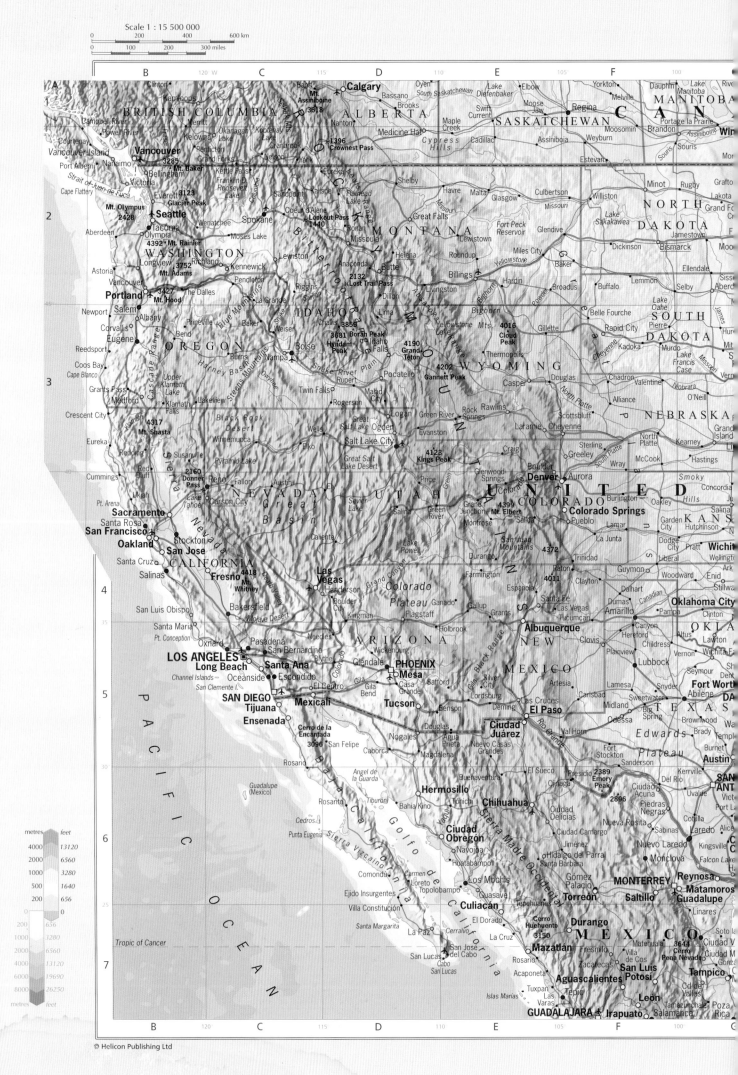

Scale 1 : 15 500 000

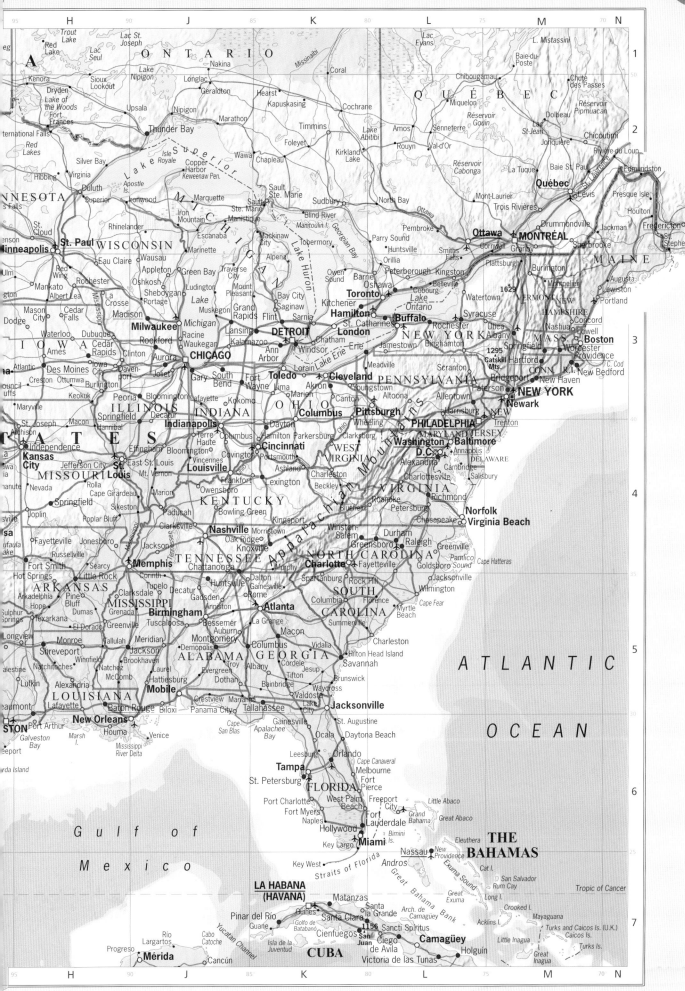

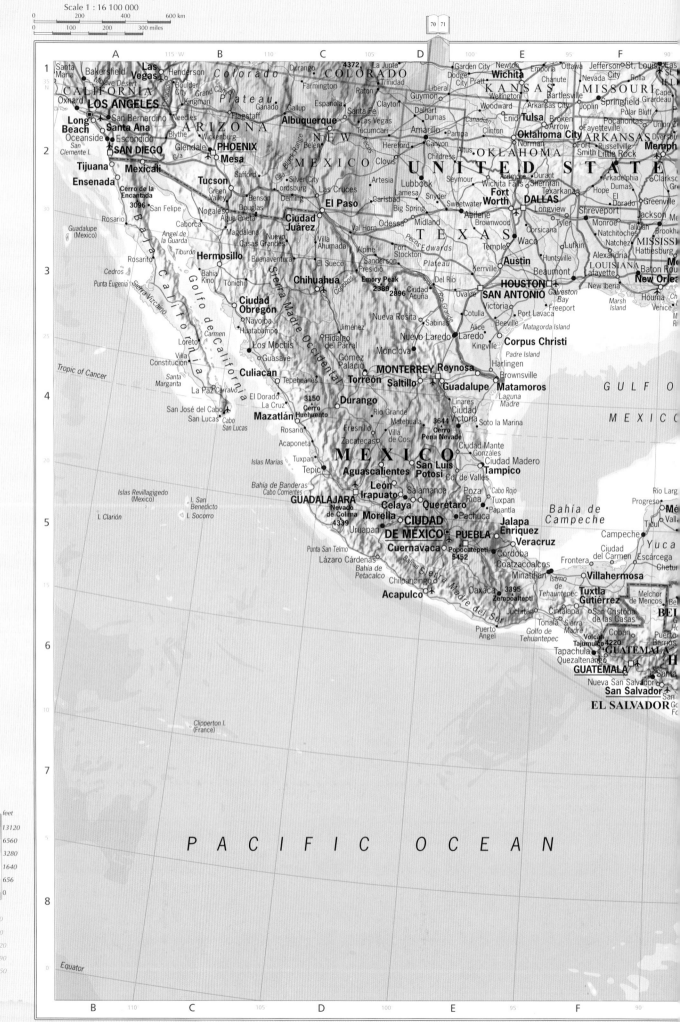

Scale 1 : 16 100 000

© Helicon Publishing Ltd

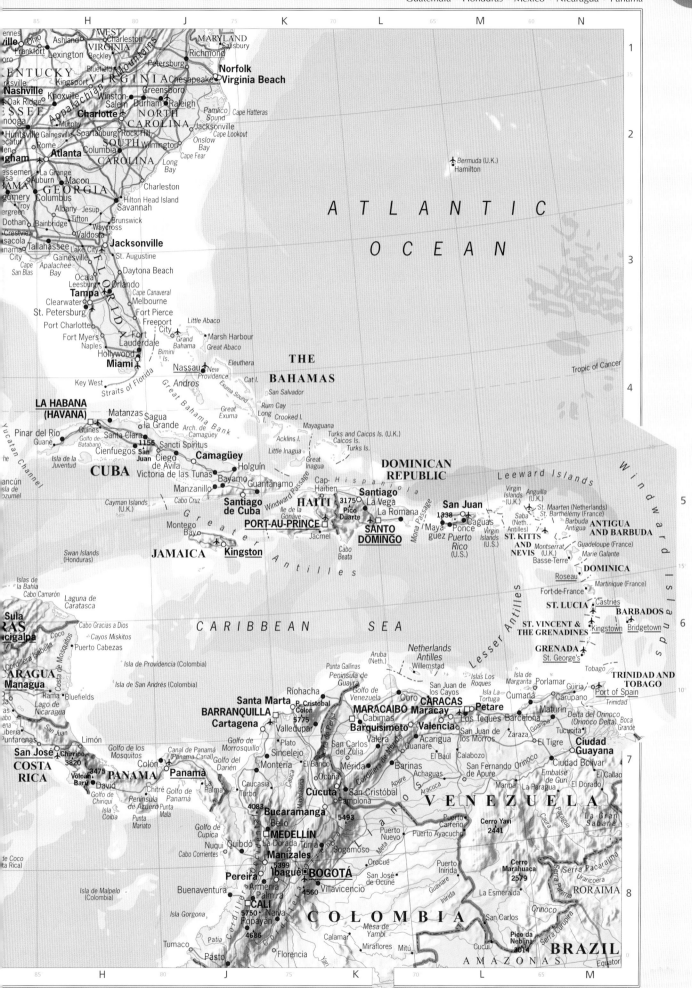

ATLANTIC OCEAN

CARIBBEAN SEA

THE BAHAMAS

CUBA

JAMAICA

HAITI

DOMINICAN REPUBLIC

VENEZUELA

COLOMBIA

BRAZIL

Scale 1 : 28 000 000

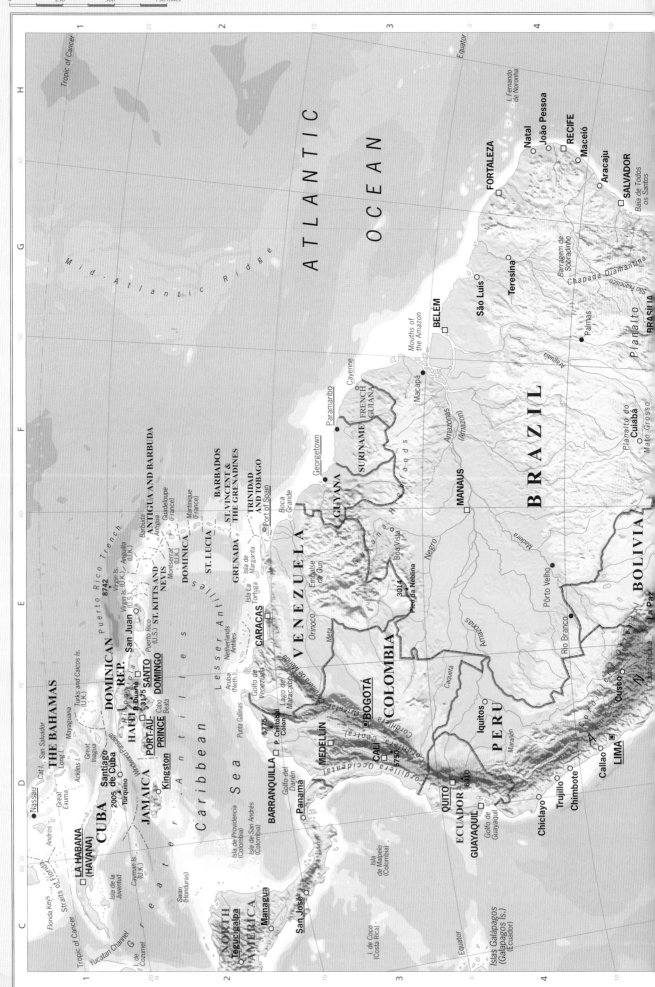

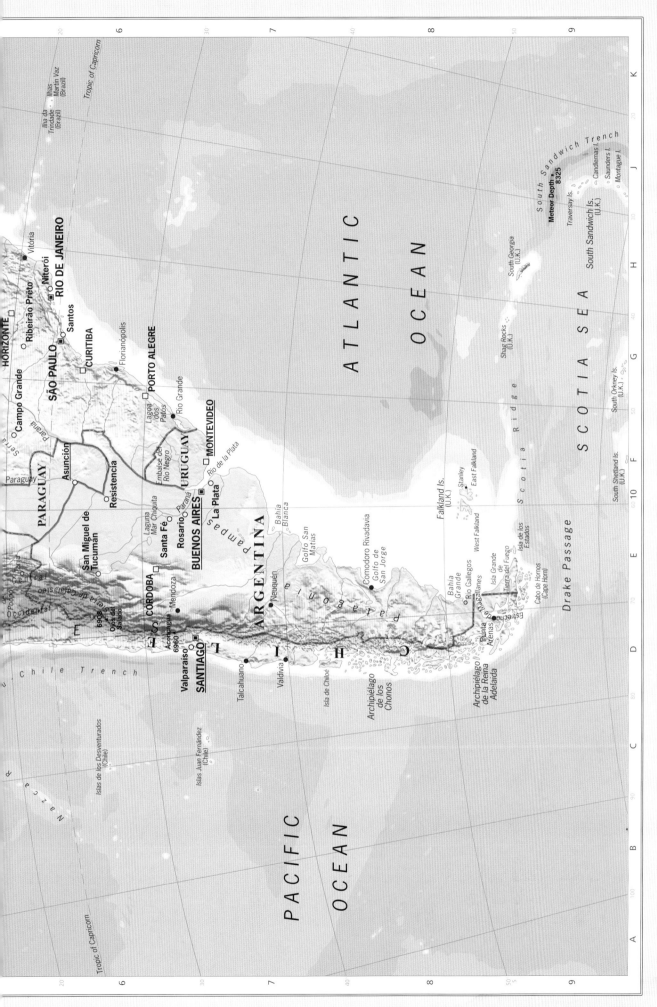

Scale 1 : 16 100 000

| 72 | 73 |

© Helicon Publishing Ltd

ATLANTIC
OCEAN

Georgetown
New Amsterdam
Corriverton
Nieuw Amsterdam
Nickerie
Apoera
Brokopondo
Embalse
Toekomstig
W. J. van
Blommestein-
meer
FRENCH
GUIANA
Cayenne
Kourou
St. Laurent
Iracoubo
Albina
SURINAME
1230
Juliana Top
Cabo Orange
Oiapoque
Vila Velha
Calcoene
Amapá
Camopi
Regina
AMAPÁ
Merirumá
Azauri
Pôrto
Grande
Pôrto Santana
Macapá
Mazagão
Afuá
Cabo Norte
Mouths of
the Amazon
Equator

Georgetown
New Amsterdam
Corriverton
Nieuw
Nickerie
Apoera
SURINAME
ghlands

I. Fernando
de Noronha
Atol das
Rocas

Chaves
Baía de
Marajó
Salinópolis
Ilha Grande
de Gurupá
Ilha de
Marajó
BELÉM
Vigia
Castanhal
Bragança
Viseu
Camiranga
Óbidos
Monte
Alegre
Prainha
Almeirim
Breves
Pará
Acará
Baião
Cametá
Badajós
São Luís
Ilha de
São Luís
Parnaíba
Camocim
Itapipoca
Sobral
Acaraú
Caucaia
FORTALEZA
Amazonas
(Amazon)
Santarém
Portel
Pindaré
Mirim
Rosário
Rapicuru
Mirim
Luzilândia
Canindé
Aracati
Altamira
Belo
Monte
Tucuruí
Jacundá
Represa
Tucuruí
Bacabal
Codó
Piripiri
Campo
Maior
CEARÁ
Mossoró
Areia Branca
Macau
Cabo de São Roque
Itaituba
Paga Conta
PARÁ
Marabá
Araguatins
Imperatriz
Pedreiras
Caxias
Teresina
Amarante
Tauá
Iguatu
Juàzeiro
do Norte
Rio Grande
do Norte
Currais Novos
Natal
Jacareacanga
Araras
São Félix
Conceição do
Araguaia
Carolina
Pôrto Franco
Grajaú
Barra do Corda
Pastos
Bons
Floriano
Oeiras
PIAUÍ
Picos
Crato
Ouricuri
PARAÍBA
Souza
Guarabira
João Pessoa
Campina Grande
Jaboatão
Olinda
RECIFE
Manuelzinho
Santa Maria
das Barreiras
Balsas
Urucuí
Canto do Buriti
São Raimundo
Nonato
PERNAMBUCO
Caruaru
Garanhuns
Palmares
Cachimbo
Pedro
Afonso
São Félix
Alto
Parnaíba
Gilbués
Barragem
de Sobradinho
Petrolina
Juàzeiro
Paulo Afonso
ALAGOAS
Maceió
Arapiraca
TOCANTINS
Macaúba
Palmas
Pôrto
Nacional
Dianópolis
Barra
Irecê
Xique Xique
Jacobina
Tucano
Senhor do
Bonfim
SERGIPE
Aracaju
Estância
Campo de
Diauarum
São Félix
Peixe
Paraná
Barreiras
Ibotirama
Mundo
Novo
Serrinha
Esplanada
Alagoinhas
MATO GROSSO
Lucas
Diamantino
Nova Xavantina
Porangatu
Bom Jesus
da Lapa
BAHIA
Santo Antônio
de Jesus
SALVADOR
Baía de Todos
os Santos
Camaçari
Nova Xavantina
Rosário
Oeste
Cuiabá
Barra do
Garças
Uruaçu
Niquelândia
Guanambi
Brumado
Ipiaú
Ubaitaba
Jequié
Gandu
Ilhéus
Cáceres
Rondonópolis
GOIÁS
Ceres
Goiás
Formosa
Planalto
Manga
Vitória da
Conquista
Itabuna
Itapetinga
BRASÍLIA
DISTRITO
FEDERAL
Januária
Monte
Azul
Pardo
Itapebi
Belmonte
Ipora
Alto Garças
Anápolis
Cristalina
Central
Salinas
Pedra Azul
Pôrto Seguro
Goiânia
Piers do Rio
Montes Claros
Bocaiúva
Minas Novas
Prado
MATO GROSSO
DO SUL
Jataí
Rio Verde
Itumbiara
Ipameri
Paracatu
MINAS
GERAIS
Minas Novas
Teófilo Otoni
Caravelas
Itambacuri
Itiquira
Campo
Grande
Rio Verde de Mato Grosso
Araguari
Patos
de Minas
Corinto
Diamantina
2033
Pico de
Itambé
Governador Valadares
ESPÍRITO SANTO
Linhares
Pantanal
Taquari
Jardim
Aquidauana
Ribas do
Rio Pardo
Paranaíba
Ituiutaba
Uberlândia
Uberaba
Araxá
Sete Lagoas
Itabira
Ipatinga
Caratinga
São José do
Rio Prêto
Barretos
Curvelo
Para de Minas
BELO HORIZONTE
Vitória
Dourados
Andradina
Franca
Passos
Divinópolis
Formiga
Manhuaçu
2890
Pico da
Bandeira
Cachoeiro de
Itapemirim
Ponta Porã
Presidente
Prudente
Marília
SÃO
PAULO
Ribeirão Prêto
Lavras
Muriaé
Campos
Assis
Bauru
Lins
Piracicaba
Limeira
São Carlos
Três Corações
Agulhas Negras
2797
Volta
Redonda
Juiz de Fora
RIO DE JANEIRO
RIO DE JANEIRO
Nova Iguaçu
Niterói

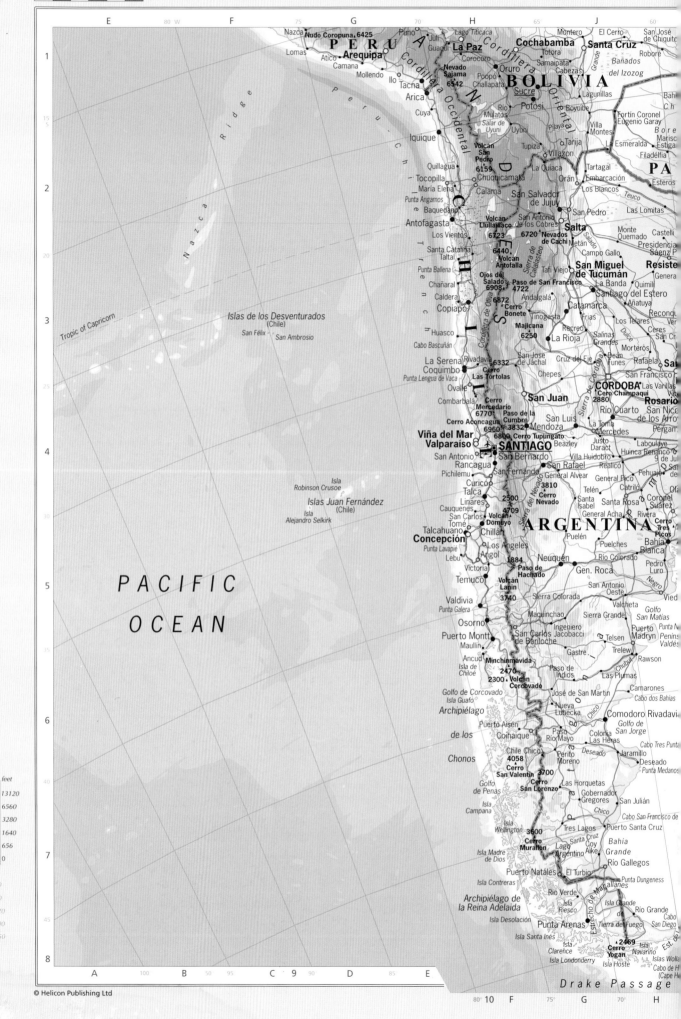

© Helicon Publishing Ltd

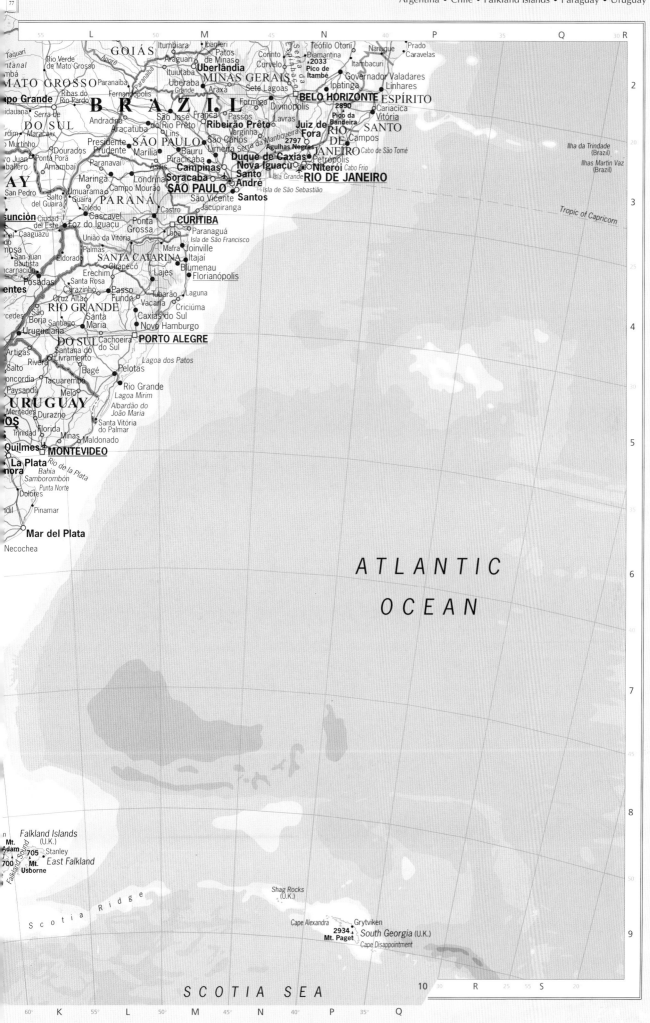

77

L · 50 · M · 45 · N · 40 · P · 35 · Q · 30 · R

Taquari
GOIÁS
Itumbiara
Ipanieri
Teófilo Otoni
Nariqué
Prado
Rio Verde
de Mato Grosso
Araguari
Patos
de Minas
Corinto
Diamantina
Caravelas
antbá
Ituiutaba
Uberlândia
Curvelo
2033
Pico de
Itambé
Itambacuri
MATO GROSSO
Paranaíba
Uberaba
MINAS GERAIS
Sete Lagoas
Governador Valadares
2
po Grande
Ribas do
Rio Pardo
Araxá
Formiga
Ipatinga
Linhares
iduauna
Serra de
BRAZIL
Franca
Divinópolis
BELO HORIZONTE ESPÍRITO
DO SUL
Andradina
São José
do Rio Prêto
Passos
Lavras
2890
Cariacica
SANTO
Aracatuba
Ribeirão Prêto
Vitória
Murtinho
Presidente
Prudente
SÃO PAULO
São Carlos
Vanginha
Juiz de
Fora
Pico da
Bandeira
dim
Dourados
Marília
Bauru
2797
RIO
Campos
Ponta Porã
Piracicaba
Agulhas Negras
DE
Juan
Amambai
Paranavaí
Assis
Campinas
Nova Iguaçu
Petrópolis
JANEIRO
Cabo de São Tomé
3
Ilha da Trindade
(Brazil)
Ilhas Martin Vaz
(Brazil)
Tropic of Capricorn

ATLANTIC

OCEAN

Falkland Islands
(U.K.)
Mt.
Adam
705
Stanley
700
Mt.
Usborne
East Falkland

Shag Rocks
(U.K.)

Scotia Ridge

Cape Alexandra
Grytviken
2934
Mt. Paget
South Georgia (U.K.)
Cape Disappointment

SCOTIA SEA

POLAR REGIONS

Scale 1 : 50 700 000

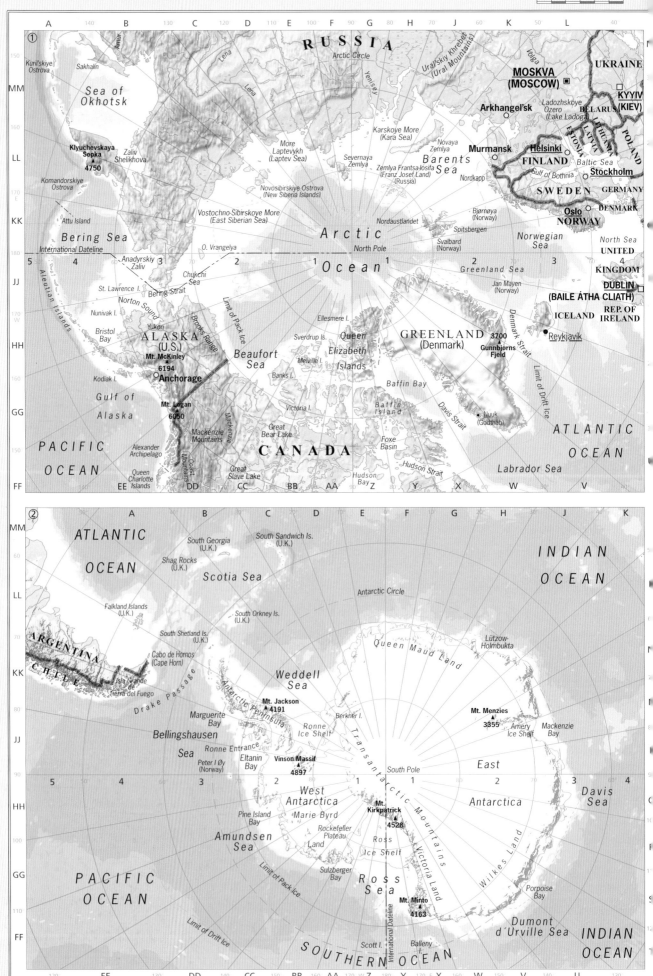

Nations of the World

AFGHANISTAN

Map page 46

National name: Dowlat-e Eslāmi-ye Afghānestān/Islamic State of Afghanistan
Area: 652,225 sq km/ 251,825 sq mi
Capital: Kābul
Major towns/cities: Kandahār, Herāt, Mazār-e Sharīf, Jalālābād, Konduz, Qal'eh-ye Now
Physical features: mountainous in center and northeast (Hindu Kush mountain range; Khyber and Salang passes, Wakhan salient, and Panjshir Valley), plains in north and southwest, Amu Darya (Oxus) River, Helmand River, Lake Saberi
Currency: afgháni
GNP per capita (PPP): (US$) 800 (1999 est)
Resources: natural gas, coal, iron ore, barytes, lapis lazuli, salt, talc, copper, chrome, gold, silver, asbestos, small petroleum reserves
Population: 22,720,000 (2000 est)
Population density: (per sq km) 34 (1999 est)
Language: Pashto, Dari (both official), Uzbek, Turkmen, Balochi, Pashai
Religion: Muslim (84% Sunni, 15% Shiite), other 1%
Time difference: GMT+4.5

ALBANIA

Map page 28

National name: Republika e Shqipërisë/Republic of Albania
Area: 28,748 sq km/11,099 sq mi
Capital: Tirana
Major towns/cities: Durrës, Shkodër, Elbasan, Vlorë, Korçë
Major ports: Durrës
Physical features: mainly mountainous, with rivers flowing east-west, and a narrow coastal plain
Currency: lek
GNP per capita (PPP): (US$) 2,892 (1999)
Resources: chromite (one of world's largest producers), copper, coal, nickel, petroleum and natural gas
Population: 3,113,000 (2000 est)
Population density: (per sq km) 108 (1999 est)
Language: Albanian (official), Greek
Religion: Muslim, Albanian Orthodox, Roman Catholic
Time difference: GMT +1

ALGERIA

Map page 52

National name: Al-Jumhuriyyat al-Jaza'iriyya ad-Dimuqratiyya ash-Sha'biyya/Democratic People's Republic of Algeria
Area: 2,381,741 sq km/ 919,590 sq mi
Capital: Algiers (Arabic al-Jaza'ir)
Major towns/cities: Oran, Annaba, Blida, Sétif, Constantine
Major ports: Oran (Ouahran), Annaba (Bône)
Physical features: coastal plains backed by mountains in north, Sahara desert in south; Atlas mountains, Barbary Coast, Chott Melrhir depression, Hoggar mountains
Currency: Algerian dinar
GNP per capita (PPP): (US$) 4,753 (1999)
Resources: natural gas and petroleum, iron ore, phosphates, lead, zinc, mercury, silver, salt, antimony, copper
Population: 31,471,000 (2000 est)
Population density: (per sq km) 13 (1999 est)
Language: Arabic (official), Berber, French
Religion: Sunni Muslim (state religion) 99%, Christian and Jewish 1%
Time difference: GMT +/-0

ANDORRA

Map page 20

National name: Principat d'Andorra/ Principality of Andorra
Area: 468 sq km/181 sq mi
Capital: Andorra la Vella
Major towns/cities: Les Escaldes
Physical features: mountainous, with narrow valleys; the eastern Pyrenees, Valira River
Currency: French franc and Spanish peseta
GNP per capita (PPP): (US$) 18,000 (1996 est)
Resources: iron, lead, aluminum, hydroelectric power
Population: 78,000 (2000 est)
Population density: (per sq km) 146 (1999 est)
Language: Catalan (official), Spanish, French
Religion: Roman Catholic (92%)
Time difference: GMT +1

ANGOLA

Map page 48

National name: República de Angolo/Republic of Angola
Area: 1,246,700 sq km/ 481,350 sq mi
Capital: Luanda (and chief port)
Major towns/cities: Lobito, Benguela, Huambo, Lubango, Malanje, Namibe, Kuito
Major ports: Huambo, Lubango, Malanje
Physical features: narrow coastal plain rises to vast interior plateau with rain forest in northwest; desert in south; Cuanza, Cuito, Cubango, and Cunene rivers
Currency: kwanza
GNP per capita (PPP): (US$) 632 (1999)
Resources: petroleum, diamonds, granite, iron ore, marble, salt, phosphates, manganese, copper
Population: 12,878,000 (2000 est)
Population density: (per sq km) 10 (1999 est)
Language: Portuguese (official), Bantu, other native dialects
Religion: Roman Catholic 38%, Protestant 15%, animist 47%
Time difference: GMT +1

ANTIGUA AND BARBUDA

Map page 72

Area: 440 sq km/169 sq mi (Antigua 280 sq km/108 sq mi, Barbuda 161 sq km/62 sq mi, plus Redonda 1 sq km/0.4 sq mi)
Capital: St. John's (on Antigua) (and chief port)
Major towns/cities: Codrington (on Barbuda)
Physical features: low-lying tropical islands of limestone and coral with some higher volcanic outcrops; no rivers and low rainfall result in frequent droughts and deforestation. Antigua is the largest of the Leeward Islands; Redonda is an uninhabited island of volcanic rock rising to 305 m/1,000 ft
Currency: East Caribbean dollar
GNP per capita (PPP): (US$) 8,959 (1999 est)
Population: 68,000 (2000 est)
Population density: (per sq km) 246 (1999 est)
Language: English (official), local dialects
Religion: Christian (mostly Anglican)
Time difference: GMT -4

ARGENTINA

Map page 78

National name: República Argentina/Argentine Republic
Area: 2,780,400 sq km/1,073,518 sq mi

Capital: Buenos Aires
Major towns/cities: Rosario, Córdoba, San Miguel de Tucumán, Mendoza, Santa Fé, La Plata
Major ports: La Plata and Bahía Blanca
Physical features: mountains in west, forest and savannah in north, pampas (treeless plains) in east-central area, Patagonian plateau in south; rivers Colorado, Salado, Paraná, Uruguay, Río de La Plata estuary; Andes mountains, with Aconcagua the highest peak in western hemisphere; Iguaçu Falls
Territories: disputed claim to the Falkland Islands (Islas Malvinas), and part of Antarctica
Currency: peso (= 10,000 australs, which it replaced in 1992)
GNP per capita (PPP): (US$) 11,324 (1999)
Resources: coal, crude oil, natural gas, iron ore, lead ore, zinc ore, tin, gold, silver, uranium ore, marble, borates, granite
Population: 37,032,000 (2000 est)
Population density: (per sq km) 13 (1999 est)
Language: Spanish (official) (95%), Italian (3%), English, German, French
Religion: predominantly Roman Catholic (state-supported), 2% protestant, 2% Jewish
Time difference: GMT -3

ARMENIA

Map page 46

National name: Hayastani Hanrapetoutioun/Republic of Armenia
Area: 29,800 sq km/ 11,505 sq mi
Capital: Yerevan
Major towns/cities: Gyumri (formerly Leninakan), Vanadzor (formerly Kirovakan), Hrazdan, Aboyvan
Physical features: mainly mountainous (including Mount Ararat), wooded
Currency: dram (replaced Russian ruble in 1993)
GNP per capita (PPP): (US$) 2,210 (1999)
Resources: copper, zinc, molybdenum, iron, silver, marble, granite
Population: 3,520,000 (2000 est)
Population density: (per sq km) 118 (1999 est)
Language: Armenian (official)
Religion: Armenian Orthodox
Time difference: GMT +4

AUSTRALIA

Map page 62

National name: Commonwealth of Australia
Area: 7,682,850 sq km/ 2,966,136 sq mi
Capital: Canberra
Major towns/cities: Adelaide, Alice Springs, Brisbane, Darwin, Melbourne, Perth, Sydney, Hobart, Newcastle, Wollongong
Physical features: Ayers Rock; Arnhem Land; Gulf of Carpentaria; Cape York Peninsula; Great Australian Bight; Great Sandy Desert; Gibson Desert; Great Victoria Desert; Simpson Desert; the Great Barrier Reef; Great Dividing Range and Australian Alps in the east (Mount Kosciusko, 2,229 m/7,136 ft, Australia's highest peak). The fertile southeast region is watered by the Darling, Lachlan, Murrumbridgee, and Murray rivers. Lake Eyre basin and Nullarbor Plain in the south
Territories: Norfolk Island, Christmas Island, Cocos (Keeling) Islands, Ashmore and Cartier Islands, Coral Sea Islands, Heard Island and McDonald Islands, Australian Antarctic Territory
Currency: Australian dollar
GNP per capita (PPP): (US$) 22,448 (1999)
Resources: coal, iron ore (world's third-largest producer),

bauxite, copper, zinc (world's second-largest producer), nickel (world's fifth-largest producer), uranium, gold, diamonds
Population: 18,886,000 (2000 est)
Population density: (per sq km) 2 (1999 est)
Language: English (official), Aboriginal languages
Religion: Anglican 26%, Roman Catholic 26%, other Christian 24%
Time difference: GMT +8/10

AUSTRIA
Map page 22

National name: Republik Österreich/Republic of Austria
Area: 83,859 sq km/32,367 sq mi
Capital: Vienna
Major towns/cities: Graz, Linz, Salzburg, Innsbruck, Klagenfurt
Physical features: landlocked mountainous state, with Alps in west and south (Austrian Alps, including Grossglockner and Brenner and Semmering passes, Lechtaler and Allgauer Alps north of River Inn, Carnic Alps on Italian border) and low relief in east where most of the population is concentrated; River Danube
Currency: schilling
GNP per capita (PPP): (US$) 23,808 (1999)
Resources: lignite, iron, kaolin, gypsum, talcum, magnesite, lead, zinc, forests
Population: 8,211,000 (2000 est)
Population density: (per sq km) 98 (1999 est)
Language: German (official)
Religion: Roman Catholic 78%, Protestant 5%
Time difference: GMT +1

AZERBAIJAN
Map page 46

National name: Azärbaycan Respublikasi/Republic of Azerbaijan
Area: 86,600 sq km/ 33,436 sq mi
Capital: Baku
Major towns/cities: Gäncä, Sumqayit, Naxçivan, Xankändi, Mingäçevir
Physical features: Caspian Sea with rich oil reserves; the country ranges from semidesert to the Caucasus Mountains
Currency: manat (replaced Russian ruble in 1993)
GNP per capita (PPP): (US$) 2,322 (1999)
Resources: petroleum, natural gas, iron ore, aluminum, copper, barytes, cobalt, precious metals, limestone, salt
Population: 7,734,000 (2000 est)
Population density: (per sq km) 89 (1999 est)
Language: Azeri (official), Russian
Religion: Shiite Muslim 68%, Sunni Muslim 27%, Russian Orthodox 3%, Armenian Orthodox 2%
Time difference: GMT +4

THE BAHAMAS
Map page 72

National name: Commonwealth of the Bahamas
Area: 13,880 sq km/ 5,383 sq mi
Capital: Nassau (on New Providence island)
Major towns/cities: Freeport (on Grand Bahama)
Physical features: comprises 700 tropical coral islands and about 1,000 cays; the Exumas are a narrow spine of 365 islands; only 30 of the desert islands are inhabited; Blue Holes of Andros, the world's longest and deepest submarine caves
Currency: Bahamian dollar
GNP per capita (PPP): (US$) 13,955 (1999 est)
Resources: aragonite (extracted from seabed), chalk, salt
Population: 307,000 (2000 est)
Population density: (per sq km) 22 (1999 est)
Language: English (official), Creole
Religion: Christian 94% (Baptist 32%, Roman Catholic 19%,

Anglican 20%, other Protestant 23%)
Time difference: GMT -5

BAHRAIN
Map page 46

National name: Dawlat al-Bahrayn/State of Bahrain
Area: 688 sq km/266 sq mi
Capital: Al Manāmah (on Bahrain island)
Major towns/cities: Sitra, Al Muharraq, Jidd Ḥafş, Madinat 'Īsá
Physical features: archipelago of 35 islands in Arabian Gulf, composed largely of sand-covered limestone; generally poor and infertile soil; flat and hot; causeway linking Bahrain to mainland Saudi Arabia
Currency: Bahraini dinar
GNP per capita (PPP): (US$) 11,527 (1999 est)
Resources: petroleum and natural gas
Population: 617,000 (2000 est)
Population density: (per sq km) 882 (1999 est)
Language: Arabic (official), Farsi, English, Urdu
Religion: 85% Muslim (Shiite 60%, Sunni 40%), Christian; Islam is the state religion
Time difference: GMT +3

BANGLADESH
Map page 44

National name: Gana Prajatantri Bangladesh/People's Republic of Bangladesh
Area: 144,000 sq km/ 55,598 sq mi
Capital: Dhaka
Major towns/cities: Rajshahi, Khulna, Chittagong, Sylhet, Rangpur, Narayanganj
Major ports: Chittagong, Khulna
Physical features: flat delta of rivers Ganges (Padma) and Brahmaputra (Jamuna), the largest estuarine delta in the world; annual rainfall of 2,540 mm/100 in; some 75% of the land is less than 3 m/10 ft above sea level; hilly in extreme southeast and northeast
Currency: taka
GNP per capita (PPP): (US$) 1,475 (1999)
Resources: natural gas, coal, limestone, china clay, glass sand
Population: 129,155,000 (2000 est)
Population density: (per sq km) 881 (1999 est)
Language: Bengali (official), English
Religion: Muslim 88%, Hindu 11%; Islam is the state religion
Time difference: GMT +6

BARBADOS
Map page 72

Area: 430 sq km/166 sq mi
Capital: Bridgetown
Major towns/cities: Speightstown, Holetown, Oistins
Physical features: most easterly island of the West Indies; surrounded by coral reefs; subject to hurricanes June-November; highest point Mount Hillaby 340 m/1,115 ft
Currency: Barbados dollar
GNP per capita (PPP): (US$) 12,260 (1998)
Resources: petroleum and natural gas
Population: 270,000 (2000 est)
Population density: (per sq km) 625 (1999 est)
Language: English (official), Bajan (a Barbadian English dialect)
Religion: 40% Anglican, 8% Pentecostal, 6% Methodist, 4% Roman Catholic
Time difference: GMT -4

BELARUS
Map page 30

National name: Respublika Belarus/Republic of Belarus
Area: 207,600 sq km/80,154 sq mi
Capital: Minsk (Belorussian Mensk)
Major towns/cities: Homyel', Vitsyebsk, Mahilyow, Babruysk, Hrodna, Brest
Physical features: more than 25% forested; rivers Dvina, Dnieper and its tributaries, including the Pripet and Beresina; the Pripet Marshes in the east; mild and damp climate
Currency: Belarus ruble, or zaichik
GNP per capita (PPP): (US$) 6,518 (1999)
Resources: petroleum, natural gas, peat, salt, coal, lignite
Population: 10,236,000 (2000 est)
Population density: (per sq km) 50 (1999 est)
Language: Belorussian (official), Russian, Polish
Religion: 80% Eastern Orthodox; Baptist, Roman Catholic Muslim, and Jewish minorities
Time difference: GMT +2

BELGIUM
Map page 14

National name: Royaume de Belgique (French), Koninkrijk België (Flemish)/Kingdom of Belgium
Area: 30,510 sq km/ 11,779 sq mi
Capital: Brussels
Major towns/cities: Antwerp, Ghent, Liège, Charleroi, Brugge, Mons, Namur, Louvain
Major ports: Antwerp, Oostende, Zeebrugge
Physical features: fertile coastal plain in northwest, central rolling hills rise eastward, hills and forest in southeast; Ardennes Forest; rivers Schelde and Meuse
Currency: Belgian franc
GNP per capita (PPP): (US$) 24,200 (1999)
Resources: coal, coke, natural gas, iron
Population: 10,161,000 (2000 est)
Population density: (per sq km) 333 (1999 est)
Language: Flemish (a Dutch dialect, known as Vlaams; official) (spoken by 56%, mainly in Flanders, in the north), French (especially the dialect Walloon; official) (spoken by 32%, mainly in Wallonia, in the south), German (0.6%; mainly near the eastern border)
Religion: Roman Catholic 75%, various Protestant denominations
Time difference: GMT +1

BELIZE
Map page 72

Area: 22,963 sq km/8,866 sq mi
Capital: Belmopan
Major towns/cities: Belize, Dangriga, Orange Walk, Corozal, San Ignacio
Major ports: Belize, Dangriga, Punta Gorda
Physical features: tropical swampy coastal plain, Maya Mountains in south; over 90% forested
Currency: Belize dollar
GNP per capita (PPP): (US$) 4,492 (1999)
Population: 241,000 (2000 est)
Population density: (per sq km) 10 (1999 est)
Language: English (official), Spanish (widely spoken), Creole dialects
Religion: Roman Catholic 62%, Protestant 30%
Time difference: GMT -6

BENIN
Map page 54

National name: République du Bénin/Republic of Benin
Area: 112,622 sq km/43,483 sq mi

Capital: Porto-Novo (official), Cotonou (de facto)
Major towns/cities: Abomey, Natitingou, Parakou, Kandi, Ouidah, Djougou, Bohicon, Cotonou
Major ports: Cotonou
Physical features: flat to undulating terrain; hot and humid in south; semiarid in north; coastal lagoons with fishing villages on stilts; Niger River in northeast
Currency: franc CFA
GNP per capita (PPP): (US$) 886 (1999)
Resources: petroleum, limestone, marble
Population: 6,097,000 (2000 est)
Population density: (per sq km) 53 (1999 est)
Language: French (official), Fon (47%), Yoruba (9%) (both in the south), six major tribal languages in the north
Religion: animist 70%, Muslim 15%, Christian 15%
Time difference: GMT +1

BHUTAN
Map page 44

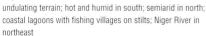

National name: Druk-yul/Kingdom of Bhutan
Area: 47,500 sq km/18,147 sq mi
Capital: Thimphu
Major towns/cities: Paro, Punakha, Mongar, Phuntsholing, Tashigang
Physical features: occupies southern slopes of the Himalayas; Gangkar Punsum (7,529 m/24,700 ft) is one of the world's highest unclimbed peaks; cut by valleys formed by tributaries of the Brahmaputra; thick forests in south
Currency: ngultrum, although the Indian rupee is also accepted
GNP per capita (PPP): (US$) 1,496 (1999 est)
Resources: limestone, gypsum, coal, slate, dolomite, lead, talc, copper
Population: 2,124,000 (2000 est)
Population density: (per sq km) 44 (1999 est)
Language: Dzongkha (a Tibetan dialect; official), Tibetan, Sharchop, Bumthap, Nepali, English
Religion: 70% Mahayana Buddhist (state religion), 25% Hindu
Time difference: GMT +6

BOLIVIA
Map page 76

National name: República de Bolivia/Republic of Bolivia
Area: 1,098,581 sq km/424,162 sq mi
Capital: La Paz (seat of government), Sucre (legal capital and seat of the judiciary)
Major towns/cities: Santa Cruz, Cochabamba, Oruro, El Alto, Potosí, Tarija
Physical features: high plateau (Altiplano) between mountain ridges (cordilleras); forest and lowlands (llano) in east; Andes; lakes Titicaca (the world's highest navigable lake, 3,800 m/12,500 ft) and Poopó
Currency: boliviano
GNP per capita (PPP): (US$) 2,193 (1999)
Resources: petroleum, natural gas, tin (world's fifth-largest producer), zinc, silver, gold, lead, antimony, tungsten, copper
Population: 8,329,000 (2000 est)
Population density: (per sq km) 7 (1999 est)
Language: Spanish (official) (4%), Aymara, Quechua
Religion: Roman Catholic 90% (state-recognized)
Time difference: GMT -4

BOSNIA-HERZEGOVINA
Map page 26

National name: Bosna i Hercegovina/Bosnia-Herzegovina
Area: 51,129 sq km/19,740 sq mi
Capital: Sarajevo

Major towns/cities: Banja Luka, Mostar, Prijedor, Tuzla, Zenica, Bihac, Gorazde
Physical features: barren, mountainous country, part of the Dinaric Alps; limestone gorges; 20 km/12 mi of coastline with no harbor
Currency: dinar
GNP per capita (PPP): (US$) 450 (1996 est)
Resources: copper, lead, zinc, iron ore, coal, bauxite, manganese
Population: 3,972,000 (2000 est)
Population density: (per sq km) 75 (1999 est)
Language: Serbian, Croat, Bosnian
Religion: 40% Muslim, 31% Serbian Orthodox, 15% Roman Catholic
Time difference: GMT +1

BOTSWANA
Map page 58

National name: Republic of Botswana
Area: 582,000 sq km/224,710 sq mi
Capital: Gaborone
Major towns/cities: Mahalapye, Serowe, Francistown, Selebi-Phikwe, Molepolole, Maun
Physical features: Kalahari Desert in southwest (70-80% of national territory is desert), plains (Makgadikgadi salt pans) in east, fertile lands and Okavango Delta in north
Currency: franc CFA
GNP per capita (PPP): (US$) 6,032 (1999)
Resources: diamonds (world's third-largest producer), copper-nickel ore, coal, soda ash, gold, cobalt, salt, plutonium, asbestos, chromite, iron, silver, manganese, talc, uranium
Population: 1,622,000 (2000 est)
Population density: (per sq km) 3 (1999 est)
Language: English (official), Setswana (national)
Religion: Christian 50%, animist 50%
Time difference: GMT +2

BRAZIL
Map page 74

National name: República Federativa do Brasil/Federative Republic of Brazil
Area: 8,511,965 sq km/3,286,469 sq mi
Capital: Brasília
Major towns/cities: São Paulo, Belo Horizonte, Nova Iguaçu, Rio de Janeiro, Belém, Recife, Porto Alegre, Salvador, Curitiba, Manaus, Fortaleza
Major ports: Rio de Janeiro, Belém, Recife, Porto Alegre, Salvador
Physical features: the densely forested Amazon basin covers the northern half of the country with a network of rivers; south is fertile; enormous energy resources, both hydroelectric (Itaipú Reservoir on the Paraná, and Tucuruí on the Tocantins) and nuclear (uranium ores); mostly tropical climate
Currency: real
GNP per capita (PPP): (US$) 6,317 (1999)
Resources: iron ore (world's second-largest producer), tin (world's fourth-largest producer), aluminum (world's fourth-largest producer), gold, phosphates, platinum, bauxite, uranium, manganese, coal, copper, petroleum, natural gas, hydroelectric power, forests
Population: 170,115,000 (2000 est)
Population density: (per sq km) 20 (1999 est)
Language: Portuguese (official), Spanish, English, French, 120 Indian languages
Religion: Roman Catholic 70%; Indian faiths
Time difference: GMT -2/5

BRUNEI
Map page 42

National name: Negara Brunei Darussalam/State of Brunei
Area: 5,765 sq km/2,225 sq mi
Capital: Bandar Seri Begawan (and chief port)
Major towns/cities: Seria, Kuala Belait
Physical features: flat coastal plain with hilly lowland in west and mountains in east (Mount Pagon 1,850 m/6,070 ft); 75% of the area is forested; the Limbang valley splits Brunei in two, and its cession to Sarawak in 1890 is disputed by Brunei; tropical climate; Temburong, Tutong, and Belait rivers
Currency: Bruneian dollar, although the Singapore dollar is also accepted
GNP per capita (PPP): (US$) 24,824 (1999 est)
Resources: petroleum, natural gas
Population: 328,000 (2000 est)
Population density: (per sq km) 56 (1999 est)
Language: Malay (official), Chinese (Hokkien), English
Religion: Muslim 66%, Buddhist 14%, Christian 10%
Time difference: GMT +8

BULGARIA
Map page 26

National name: Republika Bulgaria/Republic of Bulgaria
Area: 110,912 sq km/42,823 sq mi
Capital: Sofia
Major towns/cities: Plovdiv, Varna, Ruse, Burgas, Stara Zagora, Pleven
Major ports: Burgas, Varna
Physical features: lowland plains in north and southeast separated by mountains (Balkan and Rhodope) that cover three-quarters of the country; River Danube in north
Currency: lev
GNP per capita (PPP): (US$) 4,914 (1999)
Resources: coal, iron ore, manganese, lead, zinc, petroleum
Population: 8,225,000 (2000 est)
Population density: (per sq km) 75 (1999 est)
Language: Bulgarian (official), Turkish
Religion: Eastern Orthodox Christian, Muslim, Jewish, Roman Catholic, Protestant
Time difference: GMT +2

BURKINA FASO
Map page 54

Area: 274,122 sq km/105,838 sq mi
Capital: Ouagadougou
Major towns/cities: Bobo-Dioulasso, Koudougou, Banfora, Ouahigouya, Tenkodogo
Physical features: landlocked plateau with hills in west and southeast; headwaters of the River Volta; semiarid in north, forest and farmland in south; linked by rail to Abidjan in Côte d'Ivoire, Burkina Faso's only outlet to the sea
Currency: franc CFA
GNP per capita (PPP): (US$) 898 (1999 est)
Resources: manganese, zinc, limestone, phosphates, diamonds, gold, antimony, marble, silver, lead
Population: 11,937,000 (2000 est)
Population density: (per sq km) 42 (1999 est)
Language: French (official), 50 Sudanic languages (90%)
Religion: animist 40%, Sunni Muslim 50%, Christian (mainly Roman Catholic) 10%
Time difference: GMT+/-0

BURUNDI
Map page 56

National name: Republika y'Uburundi/République du Burundi/Republic of Burundi

Area: 27,834 sq km/10,746 sq mi
Capital: Bujumbura
Major towns/cities: Bururi,
Ngozi, Ruyigi, Kayanaza
Physical features: landlocked
grassy highland straddling
watershed of Nile and Congo;
Lake Tanganyika, Great Rift Valley
Currency: Burundi franc
GNP per capita (PPP): (US$) 553 (1999 est)
Resources: nickel, gold, tungsten, phosphates, vanadium,
uranium, peat, petroleum deposits have been detected
Population: 6,695,000 (2000 est)
Population density: (per sq km) 236 (1999 est)
Language: Kirundi, French (both official), Kiswahili
Religion: Roman Catholic 62%, Pentecostalist 5%, Anglican 1%,
Muslim 1%, animist
Time difference: GMT +2

CAMBODIA
Map page 40

National name: Preah
Réaché'anachâkr
Kâmpuchéa/Kingdom of Cambodia
Area: 181,035 sq km/
69,897 sq mi
Capital: Phnum Penh
Major towns/cities:
Bătdâmbâng, Kâmpŏng Cham,
Siĕmréab, Prey Vêng
Major ports: Kâmpŏng Cham
Physical features: mostly flat, forested plains with mountains in
southwest and north; Mekong River runs north-south; Lake Tonle
Sap
Currency: Cambodian riel
GNP per capita (PPP): (US$) 1,286 (1999 est)
Resources: phosphates, iron ore, gemstones, bauxite, silicon,
manganese
Population: 11,168,000 (2000 est)
Population density: (per sq km) 66 (1999 est)
Language: Khmer (official), French
Religion: Theravada Buddhist 95%, Muslim, Roman Catholic
Time difference: GMT +7

CAMEROON
Map page 54

National name: République du
Cameroun/Republic of Cameroon
Area: 475,440 sq km/
183,567 sq mi
Capital: Yaoundé
Major towns/cities: Garoua,
Douala, Nkongsamba, Maroua,
Bamenda, Bafoussam,
Ngaoundéré
Major ports: Douala
Physical features: desert in far north in the Lake Chad basin,
mountains in west, dry savannah plateau in the intermediate area,
and dense tropical rain forest in south; Mount Cameroon 4,070
m/13,358 ft, an active volcano on the coast, west of the Adamawa
Mountains
Currency: franc CFA
GNP per capita (PPP): (US$) 1,444 (1999)
Resources: petroleum, natural gas, tin ore, limestone, bauxite,
iron ore, uranium, gold
Population: 15,085,000 (2000 est)
Population density: (per sq km) 31 (1999 est)
Language: French, English (both official; often spoken in
pidgin), Sudanic languages (in the north), Bantu languages
(elsewhere); there has been some discontent with the emphasis
on French - there are 163 indigenous peoples with their own
African languages
Religion: animist 50%, Christian 33%, Muslim 16%
Time difference: GMT +1

CANADA
Map page 68

Area: 9,970,610 sq km/
3,849,652 sq mi
Capital: Ottawa
Major towns/cities: Toronto,
Montréal, Vancouver,
Edmonton, Calgary, Winnipeg,
Québec, Hamilton, Saskatoon,
Halifax, London, Kitchener, Mississauga, Laval, Surrey
Physical features: mountains in west, with low-lying plains in
interior and rolling hills in east; St. Lawrence Seaway, Mackenzie
River; Great Lakes; Arctic Archipelago; Rocky Mountains; Great
Plains or Prairies; Canadian Shield; Niagara Falls; climate varies
from temperate in south to arctic in north; 45% of country
forested
Currency: Canadian dollar
GNP per capita (PPP): (US$) 23,725 (1999)
Resources: petroleum, natural gas, coal, copper (world's third-
largest producer), nickel (world's second-largest producer), lead
(world's fifth-largest producer), zinc (world's largest producer),
iron, gold, uranium, timber
Population: 31,147,000 (2000 est)
Population density: (per sq km) 3 (1999 est)
Language: English (60%), French (24%) (both official),
American Indian languages, Inuktitut (Inuit)
Religion: Roman Catholic 45%, various Protestant
denominations
Time difference: GMT -3.5/9

CAPE VERDE
Map page 54

National name: República de
Cabo Verde/Republic of Cape
Verde
Area: 4,033 sq km/1,557 sq mi
Capital: Praia
Major towns/cities: Mindelo,
Santa Maria
Major ports: Mindelo
Physical features: archipelago of ten volcanic islands 565
km/350 mi west of Senegal; the windward (Barlavento) group
includes Santo Antão, São Vicente, Santa Luzia, São Nicolau, Sal,
and Boa Vista; the leeward (Sotovento) group comprises Maio,
São Tiago, Fogo, and Brava; all but Santa Luzia are inhabited
Currency: Cape Verde escudo
GNP per capita (PPP): (US$) 3,497 (1999 est)
Resources: salt, pozzolana (volcanic rock), limestone, basalt,
kaolin
Population: 428,000 (2000 est)
Population density: (per sq km) 104 (1999 est)
Language: Portuguese (official), Creole
Religion: Roman Catholic 93%, Protestant (Nazarene Church)
Time difference: GMT -1

CENTRAL AFRICAN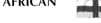
REPUBLIC
Map page 56

National name: République
Centrafricaine/Central African
Republic
Area: 622,436 sq km/
240,322 sq mi
Capital: Bangui
Major towns/cities: Berbérati,
Bouar, Bambari, Bossangoa,
Carnot, Kaga Bandoro
Physical features: landlocked flat plateau, with rivers flowing
north and south, and hills in northeast and southwest; dry in
north, rain forest in southwest; mostly wooded; Kotto and Mbali
river falls; the Oubangui River rises 6 m/20 ft at Bangui during the
wet season (June–November)
Currency: franc CFA
GNP per capita (PPP): (US$) 1,131 (1999 est)
Resources: gem diamonds and industrial diamonds, gold,
uranium, iron ore, manganese, copper
Population: 3,615,000 (2000 est)
Population density: (per sq km) 6 (1999 est)
Language: French (official), Sangho (national), Arabic, Hunsa,

Swahili
Religion: Protestant 25%, Roman Catholic 25%, animist 24%,
Muslim 15%
Time difference: GMT +1

CHAD
Map page 50

National name: République du
Tchad/Republic of Chad
Area: 1,284,000 sq km/
495,752 sq mi
Capital: Ndjamena (formerly Fort
Lamy)
Major towns/cities: Sarh,
Moundou, Abéché, Bongor, Doba,
Kélo, Koumra
Physical features: landlocked state with mountains (Tibetsi)
and part of Sahara Desert in north; moist savannah in south;
rivers in south flow northwest to Lake Chad
Currency: franc CFA
GNP per capita (PPP): (US$) 816 (1999 est)
Resources: petroleum, tungsten, tin ore, bauxite, iron ore, gold,
uranium, limestone, kaolin, titanium
Population: 7,651,000 (2000 est)
Population density: (per sq km) 6 (1999 est)
Language: French, Arabic (both official), over 100 African
languages
Religion: Muslim 50%, Christian 25%, animist 25%
Time difference: GMT +1

CHILE
Map page 78

National name: República de
Chile/Republic of Chile
Area: 756,950 sq km/
292,258 sq mi
Capital: Santiago
Major towns/cities:
Concepción, Viña del Mar,
Valparaíso, Talcahuano, Puente
Alto, Temuco, Antofagasta
Major ports: Valparaíso,
Antofagasta, Arica, Iquique, Punta Arenas
Physical features: Andes mountains along eastern border,
Atacama Desert in north, fertile central valley, grazing land and
forest in south
Territories: Easter Island, Juan Fernández Islands, part of Tierra
del Fuego, claim to part of Antarctica
Currency: Chilean peso
GNP per capita (PPP): (US$) 8,370 (1999)
Resources: copper (world's largest producer), gold, silver, iron
ore, molybdenum, cobalt, iodine, saltpeter, coal, natural gas,
petroleum, hydroelectric power
Population: 15,211,000 (2000 est)
Population density: (per sq km) 20 (1999 est)
Language: Spanish (official)
Religion: Roman Catholic 80%, Protestant 13%, atheist and
nonreligious 6%
Time difference: GMT -4

CHINA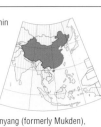
Map page 32

National name: Zhonghua Renmin
Gongheguo (Zhongguo)/People's
Republic of China
Area: 9,572,900 sq km/
3,696,000 sq mi
Capital: Beijing (or Peking)
Major towns/cities: Shanghai,
Hong Kong, Chongqing, Tianjin,
Guangzhou (English Canton), Shenyang (formerly Mukden),
Wuhan, Nanjing, Harbin, Chengdu, Xi'an
Major ports: Tianjin, Shanghai, Hong Kong, Qingdao, Guangzhou
Physical features: two-thirds of China is mountains or desert
(north and west); the low-lying east is irrigated by rivers Huang
He (Yellow River), Chang Jiang (Yangtze-Kiang), Xi Jiang (Si
Kiang)

Territories: Paracel Islands
Currency: yuan
GNP per capita (PPP): (US$) 3,291 (1999)
Resources: coal, graphite, tungsten, molybdenum, antimony, tin (world's largest producer), lead (world's fifth-largest producer), mercury, bauxite, phosphate rock, iron ore (world's largest producer), diamonds, gold, manganese, zinc (world's third-largest producer), petroleum, natural gas, fish
Population: 1,277,558,000 (2000 est)
Population density: (per sq km) 133 (1999 est)
Language: Chinese (dialects include Mandarin (official), Yue (Cantonese), Wu (Shanghaiese), Minbai, Minnah, Xiang, Gan, and Hakka)
Religion: Taoist, Confucianist, and Buddhist; Muslim 2-3%; Christian about 1% (divided between the 'patriotic' church established in 1958 and the 'loyal' church subject to Rome); Protestant 3 million
Time difference: GMT +8

COLOMBIA

Map page 76

National name: República de Colombia/Republic of Colombia
Area: 1,141,748 sq km/440,828 sq mi
Capital: Bogotá
Major towns/cities: Medellín, Cali, Barranquilla, Cartagena, Bucaramanga, Cúcuta, Ibagué
Major ports: Barranquilla, Cartagena, Buenaventura
Physical features: the Andes mountains run north-south; flat coastland in west and plains (llanos) in east; Magdalena River runs north to Caribbean Sea; includes islands of Providencia, San Andrés, and Mapelo; almost half the country is forested
Currency: Colombian peso
GNP per capita (PPP): (US$) 5,709 (1999 est)
Resources: petroleum, natural gas, coal, nickel, emeralds (accounts for about half of world production), gold, manganese, copper, lead, mercury, platinum, limestone, phosphates
Population: 42,321,000 (2000 est)
Population density: (per sq km) 36 (1999 est)
Language: Spanish (official) (95%)
Religion: Roman Catholic
Time difference: GMT -5

COMOROS

Map page 58

National name: Jumhuriyyat al-Qumur al-Itthadiyah al-Islamiyah (Arabic), République fédérale islamique des Comores (French)/Federal Islamic Republic of the Comoros
Area: 1,862 sq km/718 sq mi
Capital: Moroni
Major towns/cities: Mutsamudu, Domoni, Fomboni, Mitsamiouli
Physical features: comprises the volcanic islands of Njazídja, Nzwani, and Mwali (formerly Grande Comore, Anjouan, Moheli); at northern end of Mozambique Channel in Indian Ocean between Madagascar and coast of Africa
Currency: Comorian franc
GNP per capita (PPP): (US$) 1,360 (1999 est)
Population: 694,000 (2000 est)
Population density: (per sq km) 363 (1999 est)
Language: Arabic, French (both official), Comorian (a Swahili and Arabic dialect), Makua
Religion: Muslim; Islam is the state religion
Time difference: GMT +3

CONGO, DEMOCRATIC REPUBLIC OF

Map page 56

National name: République Démocratique du Congo/Democratic Republic of Congo
Area: 2,344,900 sq km/905,366 sq mi

Capital: Kinshasa
Major towns/cities: Lubumbashi, Kananga, Mbuji-Mayi, Kisangani, Kolwezi, Likasi, Boma
Major ports: Matadi, Kalemie
Physical features: Congo River basin has tropical rain forest (second-largest remaining in world) and savannah; mountains in east and west; lakes Tanganyika, Albert, Edward; Ruwenzori Range
Currency: congolese franc
GNP per capita (PPP): (US$) 731 (1999 est)
Resources: petroleum, copper, cobalt (65% of world's reserves), manganese, zinc, tin, uranium, silver, gold, diamonds (one of the world's largest producers of industrial diamonds)
Population: 51,654,000 (2000 est)
Population density: (per sq km) 21 (1999 est)
Language: French (official), Swahili, Lingala, Kikongo, Tshiluba (all national languages), over 200 other languages
Religion: Roman Catholic 41%, Protestant 32%, Kimbanguist 13%, animist 10%, Muslim 1-5%
Time difference: GMT +1/2

CONGO, REPUBLIC OF

Map page 54

National name: République du Congo/Republic of Congo
Area: 342,000 sq km/132,046 sq mi
Capital: Brazzaville
Major towns/cities: Pointe-Noire, Nkayi, Loubomo, Bouenza, Mossendjo, Ouésso, Owando
Major ports: Pointe-Noire
Physical features: narrow coastal plain rises to central plateau, then falls into northern basin; Congo River on the border with the Democratic Republic of Congo; half the country is rain forest
Currency: franc CFA
GNP per capita (PPP): (US$) 897 (1999)
Resources: petroleum, natural gas, lead, zinc, gold, copper, phosphate, iron ore, potash, bauxite
Population: 2,943,000 (2000 est)
Population density: (per sq km) 8 (1999 est)
Language: French (official), Kongo, Monokutuba and Lingala (both patois), and other dialects
Religion: Christian 50%, animist 48%, Muslim 2%
Time difference: GMT +1

COSTA RICA

Map page 72

National name: República de Costa Rica/Republic of Costa Rica
Area: 51,100 sq km/19,729 sq mi
Capital: San José
Major towns/cities: Alajuela, Cartago, Limón, Puntarenas, San Isidro, Desamparados
Major ports: Limón, Puntarenas
Physical features: high central plateau and tropical coasts; Costa Rica was once entirely forested, containing an estimated 5% of the earth's flora and fauna
Currency: colón
GNP per capita (PPP): (US$) 5,770 (1999 est)
Resources: gold, salt, hydro power
Population: 4,023,000 (2000 est)
Population density: (per sq km) 77 (1999 est)
Language: Spanish (official)
Religion: Roman Catholic 95% (state religion)
Time difference: GMT -6

CÔTE D'IVOIRE

Map page 54

National name: République de la Côte d'Ivoire/Republic of the Ivory Coast
Area: 322,463 sq km/124,502 sq mi

Capital: Yamoussoukro
Major towns/cities: Abidjan, Bouaké, Daloa, Man, Korhogo, Gagnoa
Major ports: Abidjan, San Pedro
Physical features: tropical rain forest (diminishing as exploited) in south; savannah and low mountains in north; coastal plain; Vridi canal, Kossou dam, Monts du Toura
Currency: franc CFA
GNP per capita (PPP): (US$) 1,546 (1999)
Resources: petroleum, natural gas, diamonds, gold, nickel, reserves of manganese, iron ore, bauxite
Population: 14,786,000 (2000 est)
Population density: (per sq km) 45 (1999 est)
Language: French (official), over 60 ethnic languages
Religion: animist 17%, Muslim 39% (mainly in north), Christian 26% (mainly Roman Catholic in south)
Time difference: GMT +/-0

CROATIA

Map page 26

National name: Republika Hrvatska/Republic of Croatia
Area: 56,538 sq km/21,829 sq mi
Capital: Zagreb
Major towns/cities: Osijek, Split, Dubrovnik, Rijeka, Zadar, Pula
Major ports: chief port: Rijeka (Fiume); other ports: Zadar, Šibenik, Split, Dubrovnik
Physical features: Adriatic coastline with large islands; very mountainous, with part of the Karst region and the Julian and Styrian Alps; some marshland
Currency: kuna
GNP per capita (PPP): (US$) 6,915 (1999)
Resources: petroleum, natural gas, coal, lignite, bauxite, iron ore, salt
Population: 4,473,000 (2000 est)
Population density: (per sq km) 79 (1999 est)
Language: Croat (official), Serbian
Religion: Roman Catholic (Croats) 76.5%; Orthodox Christian (Serbs) 11%, Protestant 1.4%, Muslim 1.2%
Time difference: GMT +1

CUBA
Map page 72

National name: República de Cuba/Republic of Cuba
Area: 110,860 sq km/42,803 sq mi
Capital: Havana
Major towns/cities: Santiago de Cuba, Camagüey, Holguín, Guantánamo, Santa Clara, Bayamo, Cienfuegos
Physical features: comprises Cuba and smaller islands including Isle of Youth; low hills; Sierra Maestra mountains in southeast; Cuba has 3,380 km/2,100 mi of coastline, with deep bays, sandy beaches, coral islands and reefs
Currency: Cuban peso
GNP per capita (PPP): (US$) N/A
Resources: iron ore, copper, chromite, gold, manganese, nickel, cobalt, silver, salt
Population: 11,201,000 (2000 est)
Population density: (per sq km) 101 (1999 est)
Language: Spanish (official)
Religion: Roman Catholic; also Episcopalians and Methodists
Time difference: GMT -5

CYPRUS

Map page 28

National name: Kipriakí Dimokratía/Greek Republic of Cyprus (south); Kibris Cumhuriyeti/Turkish Republic of Northern Cyprus (north)
Area: 9,251 sq km/3,571 sq mi (3,335 sq km/1,287 sq mi is Turkish-occupied)

Capital: Nicosia (divided between Greek and Turkish Cypriots)
Major towns/cities: Limassol, Larnaka, Pafos, Lefkosia, Famagusta
Major ports: Limassol, Larnaka, and Pafos (Greek); Keryneia and Famagusta (Turkish)
Physical features: central plain between two east-west mountain ranges
Currency: Cyprus pound and Turkish lira
GNP per capita (PPP): (US$) 18,395 (1999 est)
Resources: copper precipitates, beutonite, umber and other ochres
Population: 786,000 (2000 est)
Population density: (per sq km) 84 (1999 est)
Language: Greek, Turkish (both official), English
Religion: Greek Orthodox 78%, Sunni Muslim 18%, Maronite, Armenian Apostolic
Time difference: GMT +2

CZECH REPUBLIC
Map page 10

National name: Ceská Republika/Czech Republic
Area: 78,864 sq km/30,449 sq mi
Capital: Prague
Major towns/cities: Brno, Ostrava, Olomouc, Liberec, Plzen, Hradec Králové, Ceské Budějovice
Physical features: mountainous; rivers: Morava, Labe (Elbe), Vltava (Moldau)
Currency: koruna (based on the Czechoslovak koruna)
GNP per capita (PPP): (US$) 12,289 (1999)
Resources: coal, lignite
Population: 10,244,000 (2000 est)
Population density: (per sq km) 130 (1999 est)
Language: Czech (official), Slovak
Religion: Roman Catholic 39%, atheist 30%, Protestant 5%, Orthodox 3%
Time difference: GMT +1

DENMARK
Map page 8

National name: Kongeriget Danmark/Kingdom of Denmark
Area: 43,075 sq km/16,631 sq mi
Capital: Copenhagen
Major towns/cities: Århus, Odense, Ålborg, Esbjerg, Randers, Kolding, Horsens
Major ports: Århus, Odense, Ålborg, Esbjerg
Physical features: comprises the Jutland peninsula and about 500 islands (100 inhabited) including Bornholm in the Baltic Sea; the land is flat and cultivated; sand dunes and lagoons on the west coast and long inlets on the east; the main island is Sjæland (Zealand), where most of Copenhagen is located (the rest is on the island of Amager)
Territories: the dependencies of Faroe Islands and Greenland
Currency: Danish krone
GNP per capita (PPP): (US$) 24,280 (1999)
Resources: crude petroleum, natural gas, salt, limestone
Population: 5,293,000 (2000 est)
Population density: (per sq km) 123 (1999 est)
Language: Danish (official), German
Religion: Evangelical Lutheran 87% (national church), other Protestant and Roman Catholic 3%
Time difference: GMT +1

DJIBOUTI
Map page 50

National name: Jumhouriyya Djibouti/Republic of Djibouti
Area: 23,200 sq km/8,957 sq mi
Capital: Djibouti (and chief port)
Major towns/cities: Tadjoura, Obock, Dikhil, Ali-Sabieh

Physical features: mountains divide an inland plateau from a coastal plain; hot and arid
Currency: Djibouti franc
GNP per capita (PPP): (US$) 1,200 (1999 est)
Population: 638,000 (2000 est)
Population density: (per sq km) 27 (1999 est)
Language: French (official), Issa (Somali), Afar, Arabic
Religion: Sunni Muslim
Time difference: GMT +3

DOMINICA
Map page 72

National name: Commonwealth of Dominica
Area: 751 sq km/290 sq mi
Capital: Roseau
Major towns/cities: Portsmouth, Marigot, Mahaut, Atkinson, Grand Bay
Major ports: Roseau, Portsmouth, Berekua, Marigot
Physical features: second-largest of the Windward Islands, mountainous central ridge with tropical rain forest
Currency: East Caribbean dollar, although the pound sterling and French franc are also accepted
GNP per capita (PPP): (US$) 4,825 (1999)
Resources: pumice, limestone, clay
Population: 71,000 (2000 est)
Population density: (per sq km) 100 (1999 est)
Language: English (official), a Dominican patois (which reflects earlier periods of French rule)
Religion: Roman Catholic 80%
Time difference: GMT -4

DOMINICAN REPUBLIC
Map page 72

National name: República Dominicana/Dominican Republic
Area: 48,442 sq km/18,703 sq mi
Capital: Santo Domingo
Major towns/cities: Santiago, La Romana, San Pedro de Macoris, La Vega, San Juan, San Cristóbal
Physical features: comprises eastern two-thirds of island of Hispaniola; central mountain range with fertile valleys; Pico Duarte 3,174 m/10,417 ft, highest point in Caribbean islands
Currency: Dominican Republic peso
GNP per capita (PPP): (US$) 4,653 (1999 est)
Resources: ferro-nickel, gold, silver
Population: 8,495,000 (2000 est)
Population density: (per sq km) 173 (1999 est)
Language: Spanish (official)
Religion: Roman Catholic
Time difference: GMT -4

ECUADOR
Map page 76

National name: República del Ecuador/Republic of Ecuador
Area: 270,670 sq km/104,505 sq mi
Capital: Quito
Major towns/cities: Guayaquil, Cuenca, Machala, Portoviejo, Manta, Ambato, Santo Domingo
Major ports: Guayaquil
Physical features: coastal plain rises sharply to Andes Mountains, which are divided into a series of cultivated valleys; flat, low-lying rain forest in the east; Galapagos Islands; Cotopaxi, the world's highest active volcano. Ecuador is crossed by the Equator, from which it derives its name
Currency: sucre
GNP per capita (PPP): (US$) 2,605 (1999)
Resources: petroleum, natural gas, gold, silver, copper, zinc,

antimony, iron, uranium, lead, coal
Population: 12,646,000 (2000 est)
Population density: (per sq km) 46 (1999 est)
Language: Spanish (official), Quechua, Jivaro, other indigenous languages
Religion: Roman Catholic
Time difference: GMT -5

EGYPT
Map page 50

National name: Jumhuriyyat Misr al-'Arabiyya/Arab Republic of Egypt
Area: 1,001,450 sq km/386,659 sq mi
Capital: Cairo
Major towns/cities: El Giza, Shubrâ el Kheima, Alexandria, Port Said, El-Mahalla el-Koubra, El Mansûra, Suez
Major ports: Alexandria, Port Said, Suez, Dumyât, Shubra Al Khayma
Physical features: mostly desert; hills in east; fertile land along Nile valley and delta; cultivated and settled area is about 35,500 sq km/13,700 sq mi; Aswan High Dam and Lake Nasser; Sinai
Currency: Egyptian pound
GNP per capita (PPP): (US$) 3,303 (1999)
Resources: petroleum, natural gas, phosphates, manganese, uranium, coal, iron ore, gold
Population: 68,470,000 (2000 est)
Population density: (per sq km) 67 (1999 est)
Language: Arabic (official), Coptic (derived from ancient Egyptian), English, French
Religion: Sunni Muslim 90%, Coptic Christian and other Christian 6%
Time difference: GMT +2

EL SALVADOR
Map page 72

National name: República de El Salvador/Republic of El Salvador
Area: 21,393 sq km/8,259 sq mi
Capital: San Salvador
Major towns/cities: Santa Ana, San Miguel, Nueva San Salvador, Apopa, Delgado
Physical features: narrow coastal plain, rising to mountains in north with central plateau
Currency: US dollar (replaced Salvadorean colón in 2001)
GNP per capita (PPP): (US$) 4,048 (1999 est)
Resources: salt, limestone, gypsum
Population: 6,276,000 (2000 est)
Population density: (per sq km) 288 (1999 est)
Language: Spanish (official), Nahuatl
Religion: about 75% Roman Catholic, Protestant
Time difference: GMT -6

EQUATORIAL GUINEA
Map page 54

National name: República de Guinea Ecuatorial/Republic of Equatorial Guinea
Area: 28,051 sq km/10,830 sq mi
Capital: Malabo
Major towns/cities: Bata, Mongomo, Ela Nguema, Mbini, Campo Yaunde, Los Angeles
Physical features: comprises mainland Río Muni, plus the small islands of Corisco, Elobey Grande and Elobey Chico, and Bioko (formerly Fernando Po) together with Annobón (formerly Pagalu); nearly half the land is forested; volcanic mountains on Bioko
Currency: franc CFA
GNP per capita (PPP): (US$) 3,545 (1999 est)
Resources: petroleum, natural gas, gold, uranium, iron ore, tantalum, manganese
Population: 453,000 (2000 est)
Population density: (per sq km) 16 (1999 est)
Language: Spanish (official), pidgin English, a Portuguese

patois (on Annobón, whose people were formerly slaves of the Portuguese), Fang and other African patois (on Río Muni)
Religion: Roman Catholic, Protestant, animist
Time difference: GMT +1

ERITREA

Map page 50

National name: Hagere Eretra al-Dawla al-Iritra/State of Eritrea
Area: 125,000 sq km/ 48,262 sq mi
Capital: Asmara
Major towns/cities: Assab, Keren, Massawa, Adi Ugri, Ed
Major ports: Assab, Massawa
Physical features: coastline along the Red Sea 1,000 km/620 mi; narrow coastal plain that rises to an inland plateau; Dahlak Islands
Currency: Ethiopian nakfa
GNP per capita (PPP): (US$) 1,012 (1999 est)
Resources: gold, silver, copper, zinc, sulfur, nickel, chrome, potash, basalt, limestone, marble, sand, silicates
Population: 3,850,000 (2000 est)
Population density: (per sq km) 30 (1999 est)
Language: Tigre, Tigrinya, Arabic, English, Afar, Amharic, Kunama, Italian
Religion: mainly Sunni Muslim and Coptic Christian, some Roman Catholic, Protestant, and animist
Time difference: GMT +3

ESTONIA

Map page 8

National name: Eesti Vabariik/Republic of Estonia
Area: 45,000 sq km/ 17,374 sq mi
Capital: Tallinn
Major towns/cities: Tartu, Narva, Kohtla-Järve, Pärnu
Physical features: lakes and marshes in a partly forested plain; 774 km/481 mi of coastline; mild climate; Lake Peipus and Narva River forming boundary with Russian Federation; Baltic islands, the largest of which is Saaremaa
Currency: kroon
GNP per capita (PPP): (US$) 7,826 (1999)
Resources: oilshale, peat, phosphorite ore, superphosphates
Population: 1,396,000 (2000 est)
Population density: (per sq km) 31 (1999 est)
Language: Estonian (official), Russian
Religion: Eastern Orthodox, Evangelical Lutheran, Russian Orthodox, Muslim, Judaism
Time difference: GMT +2

ETHIOPIA

Map page 48

National name: Ya'Ityopya Federalawi Dimokrasiyawi Repeblik/Federal Democratic Republic of Ethiopia
Area: 1,096,900 sq km/ 423,513 sq mi
Capital: Addis Ababa
Major towns/cities: Dirë Dawa, Harar, Nazrët, Desë, Gonder, Mek'ele, Bahir Dar
Physical features: a high plateau with central mountain range divided by Rift Valley; plains in east; source of Blue Nile River; Danakil and Ogaden deserts
Currency: Ethiopian birr
GNP per capita (PPP): (US$) 599 (1999)
Resources: gold, salt, platinum, copper, potash. Reserves of petroleum have not been exploited
Population: 62,565,000 (2000 est)
Population density: (per sq km) 56 (1999 est)
Language: Amharic (official), Arabic, Tigrinya, Orominga, about 100 other local languages
Religion: Muslim 45%, Ethiopian Orthodox Church (which has

FIJI

Map page 60

National name: Matanitu Ko Viti/Republic of the Fiji Islands
Area: 18,333 sq km/ 7,078 sq mi
Capital: Suva
Major towns/cities: Lautoka, Nadi, Ba, Labasa, Nausori
Major ports: Lautoka, Levuka
Physical features: comprises about 844 Melanesian and Polynesian islands and islets (about 100 inhabited), the largest being Viti Levu (10,429 sq km/4,028 sq mi) and Vanua Levu (5,556 sq km/2,146 sq mi); mountainous, volcanic, with tropical rain forest and grasslands; almost all islands surrounded by coral reefs; high volcanic peaks
Currency: Fiji dollar
GNP per capita (PPP): (US$) 4,536 (1999)
Resources: gold, silver, copper
Population: 817,000 (2000 est)
Population density: (per sq km) 44 (1999 est)
Language: English (official), Fijian, Hindi
Religion: Methodist 37%, Hindu 38%, Muslim 8%, Roman Catholic 8%, Sikh
Time difference: GMT +12

FINLAND

Map page 8

National name: Suomen Tasavalta (Finnish)/Republiken Finland (Swedish)/Republic of Finland
Area: 338,145 sq km/ 130,557 sq mi
Capital: Helsinki (Swedish Helsingfors)
Major towns/cities: Tampere, Turku, Espoo, Vantaa, Oulu
Major ports: Turku, Oulu
Physical features: most of the country is forest, with low hills and about 60,000 lakes; one-third is within the Arctic Circle; archipelago in south includes Åland Islands; Helsinki is the most northerly national capital on the European continent. At the 70th parallel there is constant daylight for 73 days in summer and 51 days of uninterrupted night in winter.
Currency: markka
GNP per capita (PPP): (US$) 21,209 (1999)
Resources: copper ore, lead ore, gold, zinc ore, silver, peat, hydro power, forests
Population: 5,176,000 (2000 est)
Population density: (per sq km) 15 (1999 est)
Language: Finnish (93%), Swedish (6%) (both official), Saami (Lapp), Russian
Religion: Evangelical Lutheran 87%, Greek Orthodox 1%
Time difference: GMT +2

FRANCE

Map page 18

National name: République Française/French Republic
Area: (including Corsica) 543,965 sq km/210,024 sq mi
Capital: Paris
Major towns/cities: Lyon, Lille, Bordeaux, Toulouse, Nantes, Marseille, Nice, Strasbourg, Montpellier, Rennes, Le Havre
Major ports: Marseille, Nice, Le Havre
Physical features: rivers Seine, Loire, Garonne, Rhône; mountain ranges Alps, Massif Central, Pyrenees, Jura, Vosges, Cévennes; Auvergne mountain region; Mont Blanc (4,810 m/15,781 ft); Ardennes forest; Riviera; caves of Dordogne with relics of early humans; the island of Corsica
Territories: Guadeloupe, French Guiana, Martinique, Réunion,

St. Pierre and Miquelon, Southern and Antarctic Territories, New Caledonia, French Polynesia, Wallis and Futuna, Mayotte, Bassas da India, Clipperton Island, Europa Island, Glorioso Islands, Juan de Nova Island, Tromelin Island
Currency: franc
GNP per capita (PPP): (US$) 21,897 (1999)
Resources: coal, petroleum, natural gas, iron ore, copper, zinc, bauxite
Population: 59,080,000 (2000 est)
Population density: (per sq km) 108 (1999 est)
Language: French (official; regional languages include Basque, Breton, Catalan, Corsican, and Provençal)
Religion: Roman Catholic, about 90%; also Muslim, Protestant, and Jewish minorities
Time difference: GMT +1

GABON

Map page 54

National name: République Gabonaise/Gabonese Republic
Area: 267,667 sq km/ 103,346 sq mi
Capital: Libreville
Major towns/cities: Port-Gentil, Franceville (or Masuku), Lambaréné, Oyem, Mouila
Major ports: Port-Gentil and Owendo
Physical features: virtually the whole country is tropical rain forest; narrow coastal plain rising to hilly interior with savannah in east and south; Ogooué River flows north-west
Currency: franc CFA
GNP per capita (PPP): (US$) 5,325 (1999)
Resources: petroleum, natural gas, manganese (one of world's foremost producers and exporters), iron ore, uranium, gold, niobium, talc, phosphates
Population: 1,226,000 (2000 est)
Population density: (per sq km) 4 (1999 est)
Language: French (official), Fang (in the north), Bantu languages, and other local dialects
Religion: Christian 60% (mostly Roman Catholic), animist about 4%, Muslim 1%
Time difference: GMT +1

THE GAMBIA

Map page 54

National name: Republic of the Gambia
Area: 10,402 sq km/4,016 sq mi
Capital: Banjul
Major towns/cities: Brikama, Bakau, Farafenni, Gunjur, Basse
Physical features: consists of narrow strip of land along the River Gambia; river flanked by low hills
Currency: dalasi
GNP per capita (PPP): (US$) 1,492 (1999)
Resources: ilmenite, zircon, rutile, petroleum (well discovered, but not exploited)
Population: 1,305,000 (2000 est)
Population density: (per sq km) 122 (1999 est)
Language: English (official), Mandinka, Fula, Wolof, other indigenous dialects
Religion: Muslim 85%, with animist and Christian minorities
Time difference: GMT +/-0

GEORGIA

Map page 46

National name: Sak'art'velo/Georgia
Area: 69,700 sq km/ 26,911 sq mi
Capital: T'bilisi
Major towns/cities: K'ut'aisi, Rust'avi, Bat'umi, Zugdidi, Gori
Physical features: largely mountainous with a variety of landscape from the subtropical Black Sea shores to the ice and snow of the crest line of the Caucasus; chief rivers are Kura and

Rioni
Currency: lari
GNP per capita (PPP): (US$) 3,606 (1999)
Resources: coal, manganese, barytes, clay, petroleum and natural gas deposits, iron and other ores, gold, agate, marble, alabaster, arsenic, tungsten, mercury
Population: 4,968,000 (2000 est)
Population density: (per sq km) 72 (1999 est)
Language: Georgian (official), Russian, Abkazian, Armenian, Azeri
Religion: Georgian Orthodox, also Muslim
Time difference: GMT +3

GERMANY

Map page 12

National name: Bundesrepublik Deutschland/Federal Republic of Germany
Area: 357,041 sq km/ 137,853 sq mi
Capital: Berlin
Major towns/cities: Koln, Hamburg, Munich, Essen, Frankfurt am Main, Dortmund, Stuttgart, Düsseldorf, Leipzig, Dresden, Hannover
Major ports: Hamburg, Kiel, Bremerhaven, Rostock
Physical features: flat in north, mountainous in south with Alps; rivers Rhine, Weser, Elbe flow north, Danube flows southeast, Oder and Neisse flow north along Polish frontier; many lakes, including Müritz; Black Forest, Harz Mountains, Erzgebirge (Ore Mountains), Bavarian Alps, Fichtelgebirge, Thüringer Forest
Currency: Deutschmark
GNP per capita (PPP): (US$) 22,404 (1999)
Resources: lignite, hard coal, potash salts, crude oil, natural gas, iron ore, copper, timber, nickel, uranium
Population: 82,220,000 (2000 est)
Population density: (per sq km) 230 (1999 est)
Language: German (official)
Religion: Protestant (mainly Lutheran) 38%, Roman Catholic 34%
Time difference: GMT +1

GHANA

Map page 54

National name: Republic of Ghana
Area: 238,540 sq km/ 92,100 sq mi
Capital: Accra
Major towns/cities: Kumasi, Tamale, Tema, Sekondi, Takoradi, Cape Coast, Koforidua, Bolgatanga, Obuasi
Major ports: Sekondi, Tema
Physical features: mostly tropical lowland plains; bisected by River Volta
Currency: cedi
GNP per capita (PPP): (US$) 1,793 (1999 est)
Resources: diamonds, gold, manganese, bauxite
Population: 20,212,000 (2000 est)
Population density: (per sq km) 83 (1999 est)
Language: English (official), Ga, other African languages
Religion: Christian 40%, animist 32%, Muslim 16%
Time difference: GMT +/-0

GREECE

Map page 28

National name: Elliniki Dimokratia/Hellenic Republic
Area: 131,957 sq km/ 50,948 sq mi
Capital: Athens
Major towns/cities: Thessaloniki, Peiraias, Patra, Iraklion, Larisa, Peristerio, Kallithéa
Major ports: Peiraias, Thessaloniki, Patra, Iraklion

Physical features: mountainous (Mount Olympus); a large number of islands, notably Crete, Corfu, and Rhodes, and Cyclades and Ionian Islands
Currency: drachma
GNP per capita (PPP): (US$) 14,595 (1999)
Resources: bauxite, nickel, iron pyrites, magnetite, asbestos, marble, salt, chromite, lignite
Population: 10,645,000 (2000 est)
Population density: (per sq km) 81 (1999 est)
Language: Greek (official)
Religion: Greek Orthodox, over 96%; about 1% Muslim
Time difference: GMT +2

GRENADA

Map page 72

Area: (including the southern Grenadine Islands, notably Carriacou and Petit Martinique) 344 sq km/133 sq mi
Capital: St. George's
Major towns/cities: Grenville, Sauteurs, Victoria, Gouyave
Physical features: southernmost of the Windward Islands; mountainous; Grand-Anse beach; Annandale Falls; the Great Pool volcanic crater
Currency: East Caribbean dollar
GNP per capita (PPP): (US$) 5,847 (1999)
Population: 94,000 (2000 est)
Population density: (per sq km) 286 (1999 est)
Language: English (official), some French-African patois
Religion: Roman Catholic 53%, Anglican about 14%, Seventh Day Adventist, Pentecostal, Methodist
Time difference: GMT -4

GUATEMALA

Map page 72

National name: República de Guatemala/Republic of Guatemala
Area: 108,889 sq km/ 42,042 sq mi
Capital: Guatemala
Major towns/cities: Quezaltenango, Escuintla, Puerto Barrios (naval base), Chinautla
Physical features: mountainous; narrow coastal plains; limestone tropical plateau in north; frequent earthquakes
Currency: quetzal
GNP per capita (PPP): (US$) 3,517 (1999 est)
Resources: petroleum, antimony, gold, silver, nickel, lead, iron, tungsten
Population: 11,385,000 (2000 est)
Population density: (per sq km) 102 (1999 est)
Language: Spanish (official), 22 Mayan languages (45%)
Religion: Roman Catholic 70%, Protestant 10%, traditional Mayan
Time difference: GMT -6

GUINEA

Map page 54

National name: République de Guinée/Republic of Guinea
Area: 245,857 sq km/ 94,925 sq mi
Capital: Conakry
Major towns/cities: Labé, Nzérékoré, Kankan, Kindia, Mamou, Siguiri
Physical features: flat coastal plain with mountainous interior; sources of rivers Niger, Gambia, and Senegal; forest in southeast; Fouta Djallon, area of sandstone plateaus, cut by deep valleys
Currency: Guinean franc
GNP per capita (PPP): (US$) 1,761 (1999)
Resources: bauxite (world's top exporter of bauxite and second-largest producer of bauxite ore), alumina, diamonds, gold, granite, iron ore, uranium, nickel, cobalt, platinum
Population: 7,430,000 (2000 est)
Population density: (per sq km) 30 (1999 est)

Language: French (official), Susu, Pular (Fulfude), Malinke, and other African languages
Religion: Muslim 85%, Christian 6%, animist
Time difference: GMT +/-0

GUINEA-BISSAU

Map page 54

National name: República da Guiné-Bissau/Republic of Guinea-Bissau
Area: 36,125 sq km/13,947 sq mi
Capital: Bissau (and chief port)
Major towns/cities: Bafatá, Bissorã, Bolama, Gabú, Bubaque, Cacheu, Catió, Farim
Physical features: flat coastal plain rising to savannah in east
Currency: Guinean peso
GNP per capita (PPP): (US$) 595 (1999)
Resources: bauxite, phosphate, petroleum (largely unexploited)
Population: 1,213,000 (2000 est)
Population density: (per sq km) 33 (1999 est)
Language: Portuguese (official), Crioulo (a Cape Verdean dialect of Portuguese), African languages
Religion: animist 58%, Muslim 40%, Christian 5% (mainly Roman Catholic)
Time difference: GMT +/-0

GUYANA

Map page 76

National name: Cooperative Republic of Guyana
Area: 214,969 sq km/ 82,999 sq mi
Capital: Georgetown (and chief port)
Major towns/cities: Linden, New Amsterdam, Bartica, Corriverton
Major ports: New Amsterdam
Physical features: coastal plain rises into rolling highlands with savannah in south; mostly tropical rain forest; Mount Roraima; Kaietur National Park, including Kaietur Falls on the Potaro (tributary of Essequibo) 250 m/821 ft
Currency: Guyanese dollar
GNP per capita (PPP): (US$) 3,242 (1999 est)
Resources: gold, diamonds, bauxite, copper, tungsten, iron, nickel, quartz, molybdenum
Population: 861,000 (2000 est)
Population density: (per sq km) 4 (1999 est)
Language: English (official), Hindi, American Indian languages
Religion: Christian 57%, Hindu 34%, Sunni Muslim 9%
Time difference: GMT -3

HAITI

Map page 72

National name: République d'Haïti/Republic of Haiti
Area: 27,750 sq km/ 10,714 sq mi
Capital: Port-au-Prince
Major towns/cities: Cap-Haïtien, Gonaïves, Les Cayes, St. Marc, Carrefour, Delmas
Physical features: mainly mountainous and tropical; occupies western third of Hispaniola Island in Caribbean Sea
Currency: gourde
GNP per capita (PPP): (US$) 1,407 (1999 est)
Resources: marble, limestone, calcareous clay, unexploited copper and gold deposits
Population: 8,222,000 (2000 est)
Population density: (per sq km) 291 (1999 est)
Language: French (20%), Creole (both official)
Religion: Christian 95% (of which 70% are Roman Catholic), voodoo 4%
Time difference: GMT -5

HONDURAS

Map page 72

National name: República de Honduras/Republic of Honduras
Area: 112,100 sq km/43,281 sq mi
Capital: Tegucigalpa
Major towns/cities: San Pedro Sula, La Ceiba, El Progreso, Choluteca, Juticalpa, Danlí
Major ports: La Ceiba
Physical features: narrow tropical coastal plain with mountainous interior, Bay Islands, Caribbean reefs
Currency: lempira
GNP per capita (PPP): (US$) 2,254 (1999 est)
Resources: lead, zinc, silver, gold, tin, iron, copper, antimony
Population: 6,485,000 (2000 est)
Population density: (per sq km) 56 (1999 est)
Language: Spanish (official), English, American Indian languages
Religion: Roman Catholic 97%
Time difference: GMT -6

HUNGARY

Map page 10

National name: Magyar Köztársaság/Republic of Hungary
Area: 93,032 sq km/35,919 sq mi
Capital: Budapest
Major towns/cities: Miskolc, Debrecen, Szeged, Pécs, Győr, Nyíregyháza, Székesfehérvár, Kecskemét
Physical features: Great Hungarian Plain covers eastern half of country; Bakony Forest, Lake Balaton, and Transdanubian Highlands in the west; rivers Danube, Tisza, and Raba; more than 500 thermal springs
Currency: forint
GNP per capita (PPP): (US$) 10,479 (1999)
Resources: lignite, brown coal, natural gas, petroleum, bauxite, hard coal
Population: 10,036,000 (2000 est)
Population density: (per sq km) 108 (1999 est)
Language: Hungarian (official)
Religion: Roman Catholic 65%, Calvinist 20%, other Christian denominations, Jewish, atheist
Time difference: GMT +1

ICELAND

Map page 8

National name: Lýðveldið Ísland/Republic of Iceland
Area: 103,000 sq km/39,768 sq mi
Capital: Reykjavík
Major towns/cities: Akureyri, Kópavogur, Hafnarfjördur, Keflavík, Vestmannaeyjar
Physical features: warmed by the Gulf Stream; glaciers and lava fields cover 75% of the country; active volcanoes (Hekla was once thought the gateway to Hell), geysers, hot springs, and new islands created offshore (Surtsey in 1963); subterranean hot water heats 85% of Iceland's homes; Sidujokull glacier moving at 100 meters a day
Currency: krona
GNP per capita (PPP): (US$) 26,283 (1999)
Resources: aluminum, diatomite, hydroelectric and thermal power, fish
Population: 281,000 (2000 est)
Population density: (per sq km) 3 (1999 est)
Language: Icelandic (official)
Religion: Evangelical Lutheran about 90%, other Protestant and Roman Catholic about 4%
Time difference: GMT +/-0

INDIA

Map page 44

National name: Bharat (Hindi)/India; Bharatiya Janarajya (unofficial)/Republic of India

Area: 3,166,829 sq km/1,222,713 sq mi
Capital: New Delhi
Major towns/cities: Mumbai (formerly Bombay), Kolkata (formerly Calcutta), Chennai (formerly Madras), Bangalore, Hyderabad, Ahmadabad, Kanpur, Pune, Nagpur, Bhopal, Jaipur, Lucknow, Surat
Major ports: Kolkata, Mumbai, Chennai
Physical features: Himalayas on northern border; plains around rivers Ganges, Indus, Brahmaputra; Deccan peninsula south of the Narmada River forms plateau between Western and Eastern Ghats mountain ranges; desert in west; Andaman and Nicobar Islands, Lakshadweep (Laccadive Islands)
Currency: rupee
GNP per capita (PPP): (US$) 2,149 (1999 est)
Resources: coal, iron ore, copper ore, bauxite, chromite, gold, manganese ore, zinc, lead, limestone, crude oil, natural gas, diamonds
Population: 1,013,662,000 (2000 est)
Population density: (per sq km) 315 (1999 est)
Language: Hindi, English, Assamese, Bengali, Gujarati, Kannada, Kashmiri, Konkani, Malayalam, Manipuri, Marathi, Nepali, Oriya, Punjabi, Sanskrit, Sindhi, Tamil, Telugu, Urdu (all official), more than 1,650 dialects
Religion: Hindu 80%, Sunni Muslim 10%, Christian 2.5%, Sikh 2%, Buddhist, Jewish
Time difference: GMT +5.5

INDONESIA

Map page 42

National name: Republik Indonesia/Republic of Indonesia
Area: 1,904,569 sq km/735,354 sq mi
Capital: Jakarta
Major towns/cities: Surabaya, Bandung, Medan, Semarang, Palembang, Tangerang, Tanjungkarang-Telukbetung, Ujung Pandang, Malang
Major ports: Surabaya, Semarang (Java), Ujung Pandang (Sulawesi)
Physical features: comprises 13,677 tropical islands (over 6,000 of them are inhabited): the Greater Sundas (including Java, Madura, Sumatra, Sulawesi, and Kalimantan (part of Borneo)), the Lesser Sunda Islands/Nusa Tenggara (including Bali, Lombok, Sumbawa, Flores, Sumba, Alor, Lomblen, Timor, Roti, and Savu), Maluku/Moluccas (over 1,000 islands including Ambon, Ternate, Tidore, Tanimbar, and Halmahera), and Irian Jaya (part of New Guinea); over half the country is tropical rain forest; it has the largest expanse of peatlands in the tropics
Currency: rupiah
GNP per capita (PPP): (US$) 2,439 (1999)
Resources: petroleum (principal producer of petroleum in the Far East), natural gas, bauxite, nickel (world's third-largest producer), copper, tin (world's second-largest producer), gold, coal, forests
Population: 212,107,000 (2000 est)
Population density: (per sq km) 110 (1999 est)
Language: Bahasa Indonesia (closely related to Malay; official), Javanese, Dutch, over 550 regional languages and dialects
Religion: Muslim 87%, Protestant 6%, Roman Catholic 3%, Hindu 2% and Buddhist 1% (the continued spread of Christianity, together with an Islamic revival, have led to greater religious tensions)
Time difference: GMT +7/9

IRAN

Map page 46

National name: Jomhûrî-ye Eslâmi-ye Îrân/Islamic Republic of Iran
Area: 1,648,000 sq km/636,292 sq mi
Capital: Teheran
Major towns/cities: Eşfahān, Mashhad, Tabrīz, Shīrāz, Ahvāz, Kermānshāh, Qom, Karaj
Major ports: Abādān
Physical features: plateau surrounded by mountains, including Elburz and Zagros; Lake Rezayeh; Dasht-e-Kavir desert; occupies islands of Abu Musa, Greater Tunb and Lesser Tunb in the Gulf
Currency: rial
GNP per capita (PPP): (US$) 5,163 (1999)
Resources: petroleum, natural gas, coal, magnetite, gypsum, iron ore, copper, chromite, salt, bauxite, decorative stone
Population: 67,702,000 (2000 est)
Population density: (per sq km) 41 (1999 est)
Language: Farsi (official), Kurdish, Turkish, Arabic, English, French
Religion: Shiite Muslim (official) 91%, Sunni Muslim 8%; Zoroastrian, Christian, Jewish, and Baha'i comprise about 1%
Time difference: GMT +3.5

IRAQ

Map page 46

National name: al-Jumhuriyya al'Iraqiyya/Republic of Iraq
Area: 434,924 sq km/167,924 sq mi
Capital: Baghdād
Major towns/cities: Al Mawşil, Al Başrah, Kirkūk, Al Ḩillah, An Najaf, An Nāşirīyah, Arbīl
Major ports: Al Başrah
Physical features: mountains in north, desert in west; wide valley of rivers Tigris and Euphrates running northwest-southeast; canal linking Baghdād and Persian Gulf opened in 1992
Currency: Iraqi dinar
GNP per capita (PPP): (US$) N/A
Resources: petroleum, natural gas, sulfur, phosphates
Population: 23,115,000 (2000 est)
Population density: (per sq km) 52 (1999 est)
Language: Arabic (80%) (official), Kurdish (15%), Assyrian, Armenian
Religion: Shiite Muslim 60%, Sunni Muslim 37%, Christian 3%
Time difference: GMT +3

IRELAND, REPUBLIC OF

Map page 16

National name: Poblacht Na hÉireann/Republic of Ireland
Area: 70,282 sq km/27,135 sq mi
Capital: Dublin
Major towns/cities: Cork, Limerick, Galway, Waterford, Dundalk, Bray
Major ports: Cork, Dun Laoghaire, Limerick, Waterford, Galway
Physical features: central plateau surrounded by hills; rivers Shannon, Liffey, Boyne; Bog of Allen; Macgillicuddy's Reeks, Wicklow Mountains; Lough Corrib, lakes of Killarney; Galway Bay and Aran Islands
Currency: Irish pound, or punt Eireannach
GNP per capita (PPP): (US$) 19,180 (1999)
Resources: lead, zinc, peat, limestone, gypsum, petroleum, natural gas, copper, silver
Population: 3,730,000 (2000 est)
Population density: (per sq km) 53 (1999 est)
Language: Irish Gaelic, English (both official)
Religion: Roman Catholic 92%, Church of Ireland, other Protestant denominations 3%
Time difference: GMT +/-0

ISRAEL

Map page 46

National name: Medinat Israel/State of Israel
Area: 20,800 sq km/8,030 sq mi (as at 1949 armistice)
Capital: Jerusalem (not recognized by the United Nations)
Major towns/cities: Tel Aviv-Yafo, Haifa, Bat-Yam, Ḩolon, Ramat Gan, Petah Tiqwa, Rishon le Ziyyon, Be'ér Sheva'
Major ports: Tel Aviv-Yafo, Haifa, 'Akko (formerly Acre), Elat
Physical features: coastal plain of Sharon between Haifa and Tel

Aviv noted since ancient times for its fertility; central mountains of Galilee, Samaria, and Judea; Dead Sea, Lake Tiberias, and River Jordan Rift Valley along the east are below sea level; Negev Desert in the south; Israel occupies Golan Heights, West Bank, East Jerusalem, and Gaza Strip (the last was awarded limited autonomy, with West Bank town of Jericho, in 1993)
Currency: shekel
GNP per capita (PPP): (US$) 16,867 (1999)
Resources: potash, bromides, magnesium, sulfur, copper ore, gold, salt, petroleum, natural gas
Population: 6,217,000 (2000 est)
Population density: (per sq km) 293 (1999 est)
Language: Hebrew, Arabic (both official), English, Yiddish, other European and west Asian languages
Religion: Israel is a secular state, but the predominant faith is Judaism 80%; also Sunni Muslim (about 15%), Christian, and Druze
Time difference: GMT +2

ITALY

Map page 24

National name: Repubblica Italiana/ Italian Republic
Area: 301,300 sq km/ 116,331 sq mi
Capital: Rome
Major towns/cities: Milan, Naples, Turin, Palermo, Genoa, Bologna, Florence
Major ports: Naples, Genoa, Palermo, Bari, Catania, Trieste
Physical features: mountainous (Maritime Alps, Dolomites, Apennines) with narrow coastal lowlands; continental Europe's only active volcanoes: Vesuvius, Etna, Stromboli; rivers Po, Adige, Arno, Tiber, Rubicon; islands of Sicily, Sardinia, Elba, Capri, Ischia, Lipari, Pantelleria; lakes Como, Maggiore, Garda
Currency: lira
GNP per capita (PPP): (US$) 20,751 (1999)
Resources: lignite, lead, zinc, mercury, potash, sulfur, fluorspar, bauxite, marble, petroleum, natural gas, fish
Population: 57,298,000 (2000 est)
Population density: (per sq km) 190 (1999 est)
Language: Italian (official), German and Ladin (in the north), French (in the Valle d'Aosta region), Greek and Albanian (in the south)
Religion: Roman Catholic 98% (state religion)
Time difference: GMT +1

JAMAICA

Map page 72

Area: 10,957 sq km/4,230 sq mi
Capital: Kingston
Major towns/cities: Montego Bay, Spanish Town, Portmore, May Pen
Physical features: mountainous tropical island; Blue Mountains (so called because of the haze over them)
Currency: Jamaican dollar
GNP per capita (PPP): (US$) 3,276 (1999)
Resources: bauxite (one of world's major producers), marble, gypsum, silica, clay
Population: 2,583,000 (2000 est)
Population density: (per sq km) 234 (1999 est)
Language: English (official), Jamaican Creole
Religion: Protestant 70%, Rastafarian
Time difference: GMT -5

JAPAN

Map page 38

National name: Nihon-koku/State of Japan
Area: 377,535 sq km/ 145,766 sq mi
Capital: Tōkyō
Major towns/cities: Yokohama, Ōsaka, Nagoya, Fukuoka, Kita-Kyūshū, Kyōto,

Sapporo, Kobe, Kawasaki, Hiroshima
Major ports: Ōsaka, Nagoya, Yokohama, Kobe
Physical features: mountainous, volcanic (Mount Fuji, volcanic Mount Aso, Japan Alps); comprises over 1,000 islands, the largest of which are Hokkaido, Honshu, Kyushu, and Shikoku
Currency: yen
GNP per capita (PPP): (US$) 24,041 (1999)
Resources: coal, iron, zinc, copper, natural gas, fish
Population: 126,714,000 (2000 est)
Population density: (per sq km) 335 (1999 est)
Language: Japanese (official), Ainu
Religion: Shinto, Buddhist (often combined), Christian (less than 1%)
Time difference: GMT +9

JORDAN

Map page 46

National name: Al-Mamlaka al-Urduniyya al-Hashemiyyah/ Hashemite Kingdom of Jordan
Area: 89,206 sq km/ 34,442 sq mi (excluding the West Bank 5,879 sq km/ 2,269 sq mi)
Capital: Ammān
Major towns/cities: Zarqā', Irbid, Ma'ān
Major ports: Aqaba
Physical features: desert plateau in east; Rift Valley separates east and west banks of River Jordan
Currency: Jordanian dinar
GNP per capita (PPP): (US$) 3,542 (1999)
Resources: phosphates, potash, shale
Population: 6,669,000 (2000 est)
Population density: (per sq km) 73 (1999 est)
Language: Arabic (official), English
Religion: over 90% Sunni Muslim (official religion), small communities of Christians and Shiite Muslims
Time difference: GMT +2

KAZAKHSTAN

Map page 34

National name: Kazak Respublikasy/Republic of Kazakhstan
Area: 2,717,300 sq km/ 1,049,150 sq mi
Capital: Astana (formerly Akmola)
Major towns/cities: Qaraghandy, Pavlodar, Semey, Petropavl, Shymkent
Physical features: Caspian and Aral seas, Lake Balkhash; Steppe region; natural gas and oil deposits in the Caspian Sea
Currency: tenge
GNP per capita (PPP): (US$) 4,408 (1999)
Resources: petroleum, natural gas, coal, bauxite, chromium, copper, iron ore, lead, titanium, magnesium, tungsten, molybdenum, gold, silver, manganese
Population: 16,223,000 (2000 est)
Population density: (per sq km) 6 (1999 est)
Language: Kazakh (related to Turkish; official), Russian
Religion: Sunni Muslim 50-60%, Russian Orthodox 30-35%
Time difference: GMT +6

KENYA

Map page 56

National name: Jamhuri ya Kenya/Republic of Kenya
Area: 582,600 sq km/ 224,941 sq mi
Capital: Nairobi
Major towns/cities: Mombasa, Kisumu, Nakuru, Eldoret, Nyeri
Major ports: Mombasa
Physical features: mountains and highlands in west and center; coastal plain in south; arid interior and tropical coast; semidesert in north; Great Rift Valley, Mount Kenya, Lake Nakuru (salt lake with world's largest colony of flamingos), Lake Turkana (Rudolf)

Currency: Kenyan shilling
GNP per capita (PPP): (US$) 975 (1999)
Resources: soda ash, fluorspar, salt, limestone, rubies, gold, vermiculite, diatonite, garnets
Population: 30,080,000 (2000 est)
Population density: (per sq km) 51 (1999 est)
Language: English, Kiswahili (both official), many local dialects
Religion: Roman Catholic 28%, Protestant 8%, Muslim 6%, traditional tribal religions
Time difference: GMT +3

KIRIBATI

Map page 60

National name: Ribaberikan Kiribati/Republic of Kiribati
Area: 717 sq km/277 sq mi
Capital: Bairiki (on Tarawa atoll)
Major towns/cities: principal islands are the Gilbert Islands, the Phoenix Islands, the Line Islands, Banaba
Major ports: Bairiki, Betio (on Tarawa)
Physical features: comprises 33 Pacific coral islands: the Kiribati (Gilbert), Rawaki (Phoenix), Banaba (Ocean Island), and three of the Line Islands including Kiritimati (Christmas Island); island groups crossed by Equator and International Date Line
Currency: Australian dollar
GNP per capita (PPP): (US$) 3,186 (1999)
Resources: phosphate, salt
Population: 83,000 (2000 est)
Population density: (per sq km) 107 (1999 est)
Language: English (official), Gilbertese
Religion: Roman Catholic, Protestant (Congregationalist)
Time difference: GMT -10/-11

KUWAIT

Map page 46

National name: Dowlat al-Kuwayt/State of Kuwait
Area: 17,819 sq km/6,879 sq mi
Capital: Kuwait (and chief port)
Major towns/cities: as-Salimiya, Al Farwānīyah, Ḥawallī, Abraq Kheetan, Al Jahrah, Al Aḥmadī, Al Fuḥayḥil
Physical features: hot desert; islands of Faylakah, Bubiyan, and Warbah at northeast corner of Arabian Peninsula
Currency: Kuwaiti dinar
GNP per capita (PPP): (US$) 24,270 (1997)
Resources: petroleum, natural gas, mineral water
Population: 1,972,000 (2000 est)
Population density: (per sq km) 106 (1999 est)
Language: Arabic (78%) (official), English, Kurdish (10%), Farsi (4%)
Religion: Sunni Muslim 45%, Shiite Muslim 40%; Christian, Hindu, and Parsi about 5%
Time difference: GMT +3

KYRGYZSTAN

Map page 34

National name: Kyrgyz Respublikasy/Kyrgyz Republic
Area: 198,500 sq km/ 76,640 sq mi
Capital: Bishkek (formerly Frunze)
Major towns/cities: Osh, Karakol, Kyzyl-Kiya, Tokmak, Djalal-Abad
Physical features: mountainous, an extension of the Tien Shan range
Currency: som
GNP per capita (PPP): (US$) 2,223 (1999)
Resources: petroleum, natural gas, coal, gold, tin, mercury, antimony, zinc, tungsten, uranium
Population: 4,699,000 (2000 est)
Population density: (per sq km) 24 (1999 est)

Language: Kyrgyz (a Turkic language; official), Russian
Religion: Sunni Muslim 70%, Russian Orthodox 20%
Time difference: GMT +5

LAOS
Map page 40

National name: Sathalanalat Praxathipatai Paxaxôn Lao/ Democratic People's Republic of Laos
Area: 236,790 sq km/ 91,424 sq mi
Capital: Vientiane
Major towns/cities: Louangphrabang (the former royal capital), Pakxé, Savannakhet
Physical features: landlocked state with high mountains in east; Mekong River in west; rain forest covers nearly 60% of land
Currency: new kip
GNP per capita (PPP): (US$) 1,726 (1999)
Resources: coal, tin, gypsum, baryte, lead, zinc, nickel, potash, iron ore; small quantities of gold, silver, precious stones
Population: 5,433,000 (2000 est)
Population density: (per sq km) 22 (1999 est)
Language: Lao (official), French, English, ethnic languages
Religion: Theravada Buddhist 85%, animist beliefs among mountain dwellers
Time difference: GMT +7

LATVIA
Map page 8

National name: Latvijas Republika/ Republic of Latvia
Area: 63,700 sq km/24,594 sq mi
Capital: Rīga
Major towns/cities: Daugavpils, Liepāja, Jūrmala, Jelgava, Ventspils
Major ports: Ventspils, Liepāja
Physical features: wooded lowland (highest point 312 m/1,024 ft), marshes, lakes; 472 km/293 mi of coastline; mild climate
Currency: lat
GNP per capita (PPP): (US$) 5,938 (1999)
Resources: peat, gypsum, dolomite, limestone, amber, gravel, sand
Population: 2,357,000 (2000 est)
Population density: (per sq km) 38 (1999 est)
Language: Latvian (official)
Religion: Lutheran, Roman Catholic, Russian Orthodox
Time difference: GMT +2

LEBANON
Map page 46

National name: Jumhouria al-Lubnaniya/Republic of Lebanon
Area: 10,452 sq km/4,035 sq mi
Capital: Beirut (and chief port)
Major towns/cities: Tripoli, Zahlé, Baabda, Ba'albek, Jezzine
Major ports: Tripoli, Soûr, Saida, Joûnié
Physical features: narrow coastal plain; fertile Bekka valley running north-south between Lebanon and Anti-Lebanon mountain ranges
Currency: Lebanese pound
GNP per capita (PPP): (US$) 4,129 (1999)
Resources: there are no commercially viable mineral deposits; small reserves of lignite and iron ore
Population: 3,282,000 (2000 est)
Population density: (per sq km) 310 (1999 est)
Language: Arabic (official), French, Armenian, English
Religion: Muslim 70% (Shiite 35%, Sunni 23%, Druze 7%, other 5%); Christian 30% (mainly Maronite 19%), Druze 3%; other Christian denominations including Greek Orthodox, Armenian, and Roman Catholic
Time difference: GMT +2

LESOTHO
Map page 58

National name: Mmuso oa Lesotho/Kingdom of Lesotho
Area: 30,355 sq km/11,720 sq mi
Capital: Maseru
Major towns/cities: Qacha's Nek, Teyateyaneng, Mafeteng, Hlotse, Roma, Quthing
Physical features: mountainous with plateaus, forming part of South Africa's chief watershed
Currency: loti
GNP per capita (PPP): (US$) 2,058 (1999)
Resources: diamonds, uranium, lead, iron ore; believed to have petroleum deposits
Population: 2,153,000 (2000 est)
Population density: (per sq km) 69 (1999 est)
Language: English (official), Sesotho, Zulu, Xhosa
Religion: Protestant 42%, Roman Catholic 38%, indigenous beliefs
Time difference: GMT +2

LIBERIA
Map page 54

National name: Republic of Liberia
Area: 111,370 sq km/ 42,999 sq mi
Capital: Monrovia (and chief port)
Major towns/cities: Bensonville, Gbarnga, Voinjama, Buchanan
Major ports: Buchanan, Greenville
Physical features: forested highlands; swampy tropical coast where six rivers enter the sea
Currency: Liberian dollar
GNP per capita (PPP): (US$) N/A
Resources: iron ore, diamonds, gold, barytes, kyanite
Population: 3,154,000 (2000 est)
Population density: (per sq km) 26 (1999 est)
Language: English (official), over 20 Niger-Congo languages
Religion: animist 70%, Sunni Muslim 20%, Christian 10%
Time difference: GMT +/-0

LIBYA
Map page 50

National name: Al-Jamahiriyya al-'Arabiyya al-Libiyya ash-Sha'biyya al-Ishtirakiyya al-'Uzma/Great Libyan Arab Socialist People's State of the Masses
Area: 1,759,540 sq km/ 679,358 sq mi
Capital: Tripoli
Major towns/cities: Banghāzī, Mişrātah, Az Zāwīyah, Tubruq, Ajdābiyā, Darnah
Major ports: Banghāzī, Mişrātah, Az Zāwīyah, Tubruq, Ajdābiyā, Darnah
Physical features: flat to undulating plains with plateaus and depressions stretch southward from the Mediterranean coast to an extremely dry desert interior
Currency: Libyan dinar
GNP per capita (PPP): (US$) N/A
Resources: petroleum, natural gas, iron ore, potassium, magnesium, sulfur, gypsum
Population: 5,605,000 (2000 est)
Population density: (per sq km) 3 (1999 est)
Language: Arabic (official), Italian, English
Religion: Sunni Muslim 97%
Time difference: GMT +1

LIECHTENSTEIN
Map page 22

National name: Fürstentum Liechtenstein/Principality of Liechtenstein

Area: 160 sq km/62 sq mi
Capital: Vaduz
Major towns/cities: Balzers, Schaan, Eschen
Physical features: landlocked Alpine; includes part of Rhine Valley in west
Currency: Swiss franc
GNP per capita (PPP): (US$) 24,000 (1998 est)
Resources: hydro power
Population: 33,000 (2000 est)
Population density: (per sq km) 199 (1999 est)
Language: German (official), an Alemannic dialect
Religion: Roman Catholic 80%, Protestant 7%
Time difference: GMT +1

LITHUANIA
Map page 8

National name: Lietuvos Respublika/ Republic of Lithuania
Area: 65,200 sq km/25,173 sq mi
Capital: Vilnius
Major towns/cities: Kaunas, Klaipéda, Šiauliai, Panevėžys
Physical features: central lowlands with gentle hills in west and higher terrain in southeast; 25% forested; some 3,000 small lakes, marshes, and complex sandy coastline; River Nenumas
Currency: litas
GNP per capita (PPP): (US$) 6,093 (1999)
Resources: small deposits of petroleum, natural gas, peat, limestone, gravel, clay, sand
Population: 3,670,000 (2000 est)
Population density: (per sq km) 56 (1999 est)
Language: Lithuanian (official)
Religion: predominantly Roman Catholic; Evangelical Lutheran, also Russian Orthodox, Evangelical Reformist, and Baptist
Time difference: GMT +2

LUXEMBOURG
Map page 14

National name: Grand-Duché de Luxembourg/Grand Duchy of Luxembourg
Area: 2,586 sq km/998 sq mi
Capital: Luxembourg
Major towns/cities: Esch, Differdange, Dudelange, Pétange
Physical features: on the River Moselle; part of the Ardennes (Oesling) forest in north
Currency: Luxembourg franc
GNP per capita (PPP): (US$) 38,247 (1999)
Resources: iron ore
Population: 431,000 (2000 est)
Population density: (per sq km) 165 (1999 est)
Language: Letzeburgisch (a German-Moselle-Frankish dialect; official), English
Religion: Roman Catholic about 95%, Protestant and Jewish 4%
Time difference: GMT +1

MACEDONIA
Map page 28

National name: Republika Makedonija/Republic of Macedonia (official internal name); Poranesna Jugoslovenska Republika Makedonija/Former Yugoslav Republic of Macedonia (official international name)
Area: 25,700 sq km/ 9,922 sq mi
Capital: Skopje
Major towns/cities: Bitola, Prilep, Kumanovo, Tetovo
Physical features: mountainous; rivers: Struma, Vardar; lakes: Ohrid, Prespa, Scutari; partly Mediterranean climate with hot summers

Currency: Macedonian denar
GNP per capita (PPP): (US$) 4,339 (1999)
Resources: coal, iron, zinc, chromium, manganese, lead, copper, nickel, silver, gold
Population: 2,024,000 (2000 est)
Population density: (per sq km) 78 (1999 est)
Language: Macedonian (related to Bulgarian; official), Albanian
Religion: Christian, mainly Orthodox 67%; Muslim 30%
Time difference: GMT +1

MADAGASCAR
Map page 58

National name: Repoblikan'i Madagasikara/République de Madagascar/Republic of Madagascar
Area: 587,041 sq km/ 226,656 sq mi
Capital: Antananarivo
Major towns/cities: Antsirabe, Mahajanga, Fianarantsoa, Toamasina, Ambatondrazaka
Major ports: Toamasina, Antsiranana, Mahajanga
Physical features: temperate central highlands; humid valleys and tropical coastal plains; arid in south
Currency: Malagasy franc
GNP per capita (PPP): (US$) 766 (1999)
Resources: graphite, chromite, mica, titanium ore, small quantities of precious stones, bauxite and coal deposits, petroleum reserves
Population: 15,942,000 (2000 est)
Population density: (per sq km) 26 (1999 est)
Language: Malagasy, French (both official), local dialects
Religion: over 50% traditional beliefs, Roman Catholic, Protestant about 40%, Muslim 7%
Time difference: GMT +3

MALAWI
Map page 58

National name: Republic of Malawi
Area: 118,484 sq km/ 45,735 sq mi
Capital: Lilongwe
Major towns/cities: Blantyre, Mzuzu, Zomba
Physical features: landlocked narrow plateau with rolling plains; mountainous west of Lake Nyasa
Currency: Malawi kwacha
GNP per capita (PPP): (US$) 581 (1999)
Resources: marble, coal, gemstones, bauxite and graphite deposits, reserves of phosphates, uranium, glass sands, asbestos, vermiculite
Population: 10,925,000 (2000 est)
Population density: (per sq km) 90 (1999 est)
Language: English, Chichewa (both official), other Bantu languages
Religion: Protestant 50%, Roman Catholic 20%, Muslim 2%, animist
Time difference: GMT +2

MALAYSIA
Map page 42

National name: Persekutuan Tanah Malaysia/Federation of Malaysia
Area: 329,759 sq km/ 127,319 sq mi
Capital: Kuala Lumpur
Major towns/cities: Johor Bahru, Ipoh, George Town (on Penang island), Kuala Terengganu, Kuala Bahru, Petaling Jaya, Kelang, Kuching (on Sarawak), Kota Kinabalu (on Sabah)
Major ports: Kelang
Physical features: comprises peninsular Malaysia (the nine Malay states - Johore, Kedah, Kelantan, Negri Sembilan, Pahang, Perak, Perlis, Selangor, Terengganu - plus Malacca and Penang);

states of Sabah and Sarawak on the island of Borneo; and the federal territory of Kuala Lumpur; 75% tropical rain forest; central mountain range; Mount Kinabalu, the highest peak in southeast Asia, is in Sabah; swamps in east; Niah caves (Sarawak)
Currency: ringgit
GNP per capita (PPP): (US$) 7,963 (1999)
Resources: tin, bauxite, copper, iron ore, petroleum, natural gas, forests
Population: 22,244,000 (2000 est)
Population density: (per sq km) 66 (1999 est)
Language: Bahasa Malaysia (Malay; official), English, Chinese, Tamil, Iban, many local dialects
Religion: Muslim (official) about 53%, Buddhist 19%, Hindu, Christian, local beliefs
Time difference: GMT +8

MALDIVES
Map page 44

National name: Divehi Raajjeyge Jumhuriyya/Republic of the Maldives
Area: 298 sq km/115 sq mi
Capital: Malé
Physical features: comprises 1,196 coral islands, grouped into 12 clusters of atolls, largely flat, none bigger than 13 sq km/5 sq mi, average elevation 1.8 m/6 ft; 203 are inhabited
Currency: rufiya
GNP per capita (PPP): (US$) 3,545 (1999)
Resources: coral (mining was banned as a measure against the encroachment of the sea)
Population: 286,000 (2000 est)
Population density: (per sq km) 933 (1999 est)
Language: Divehi (a Sinhalese dialect; official), English, Arabic
Religion: Sunni Muslim
Time difference: GMT +5

MALI
Map page 52

National name: République du Mali/Republic of Mali
Area: 1,240,142 sq km/ 478,818 sq mi
Capital: Bamako
Major towns/cities: Mopti, Kayes, Ségou, Tombouctou, Sikasso
Physical features: landlocked state with River Niger and savannah in south; part of the Sahara in north; hills in northeast; Senegal River and its branches irrigate the southwest
Currency: franc CFA
GNP per capita (PPP): (US$) 693 (1999)
Resources: iron ore, uranium, diamonds, bauxite, manganese, copper, lithium, gold
Population: 11,234,000 (2000 est)
Population density: (per sq km) 9 (1999 est)
Language: French (official), Bambara, other African languages
Religion: Sunni Muslim 80%, animist, Christian
Time difference: GMT +/-0

MALTA
Map page 24

National name: Repubblika ta'Malta/ Republic of Malta
Area: 320 sq km/124 sq mi
Capital: Valletta (and chief port)
Major towns/cities: Rabat, Birkirkara, Qormi, Sliema
Major ports: Marsaxlokk, Valletta
Physical features: includes islands of Gozo 67 sq km/26 sq mi and Comino 3 sq km/1 sq mi
Currency: Maltese lira
GNP per capita (PPP): (US$) 15,066 (1999 est)
Resources: stone, sand; offshore petroleum reserves were under exploration 1988-95

Population: 389,000 (2000 est)
Population density: (per sq km) 1,206 (1999 est)
Language: Maltese, English (both official)
Religion: Roman Catholic 98%
Time difference: GMT +1

MARSHALL ISLANDS
Map page 60

National name: Majol/ Republic of the Marshall Islands
Area: 181 sq km/70 sq mi
Capital: Dalap-Uliga-Darrit (on Majuro atoll)
Major towns/cities: Ebeye (the only other town)
Physical features: comprises the Ratak and Ralik island chains in the West Pacific, which together form an archipelago of 31 coral atolls, 5 islands, and 1,152 islets
Currency: US dollar
GNP per capita (PPP): (US$) 1,860 (1999 est)
Resources: phosphates
Population: 64,000 (2000 est)
Population density: (per sq km) 343 (1999 est)
Language: Marshallese, English (both official)
Religion: Christian (mainly Protestant) and Baha'i
Time difference: GMT +12

MAURITANIA
Map page 52

National name: Al-Jumhuriyya al-Islamiyya al-Mawritaniyya/ République Islamique Arabe et Africaine de Mauritanie/Islamic Republic of Mauritania
Area: 1,030,700 sq km/ 397,953 sq mi
Capital: Nouakchott (and chief port)
Major towns/cities: Nouâdhibou, Kaédi, Zouérat, Kiffa, Rosso, Atâr
Major ports: Nouâdhibou
Physical features: valley of River Senegal in south; remainder arid and flat
Currency: ouguiya
GNP per capita (PPP): (US$) 1,522 (1999 est)
Resources: copper, gold, iron ore, gypsum, phosphates, sulfur, peat
Population: 2,670,000 (2000 est)
Population density: (per sq km) 3 (1999 est)
Language: Hasaniya Arabic (official), Pulaar, Soninke, Wolof (all national languages), French (particularly in the south)
Religion: Sunni Muslim (state religion)
Time difference: GMT +/-0

MAURITIUS
Map page 58

National name: Republic of Mauritius
Area: 1,865 sq km/720 sq mi
Capital: Port Louis (and chief port)
Major towns/cities: Beau Bassin, Rose Hill, Curepipe, Quatre Bornes, Vacoas-Phoenix
Physical features: mountainous, volcanic island surrounded by coral reefs; the island of Rodrigues is part of Mauritius; there are several small island dependencies
Currency: Mauritian rupee
GNP per capita (PPP): (US$) 8,652 (1999)
Population: 1,158,000 (2000 est)
Population density: (per sq km) 616 (1999 est)
Language: English (official), French, Creole (36%), Bhojpuri (32%), other Indian languages
Religion: Hindu over 50%, Christian (mainly Roman Catholic) about 30%, Muslim 17%
Time difference: GMT +4

MEXICO

Map page 72

National name: Estados Unidos Mexicanos/United States of Mexico
Area: 1,958,201 sq km/ 756,061 sq mi
Capital: Mexico City
Major towns/cities: Guadalajara, Monterrey, Puebla, Ciudad Juárez, Tijuana
Major ports: 49 ocean ports
Physical features: partly arid central highlands; Sierra Madre mountain ranges east and west; tropical coastal plains; volcanoes, including Popocatepetl; Rio Grande
Currency: Mexican peso
GNP per capita (PPP): (US$) 7,719 (1999)
Resources: petroleum, natural gas, zinc, salt, silver, copper, coal, mercury, manganese, phosphates, uranium, strontium sulfide
Population: 98,881,000 (2000 est)
Population density: (per sq km) 50 (1999 est)
Language: Spanish (official), Nahuatl, Maya, Zapoteco, Mixteco, Otomi
Religion: Roman Catholic about 90%
Time difference: GMT -6/8

MICRONESIA, FEDERATED STATES OF

Map page 60

National name: Federated States of Micronesia (FSM)
Area: 700 sq km/270 sq mi
Capital: Palikir (in Pohnpei island state)
Major towns/cities: Kolonia (in Pohnpei), Weno (in Truk), Lelu (in Kosrae)
Physical features: an archipelago of 607 equatorial, volcanic islands in the West Pacific
Currency: US dollar
GNP per capita (PPP): (US$) 3,860 (1999 est)
Population: 119,000 (2000 est)
Population density: (per sq km) 165 (1999 est)
Language: English (official), eight officially recognized local languages (including Trukese, Pohnpeian, Yapese, and Kosrean), a number of other dialects
Religion: Christianity (mainly Roman Catholic in Yap state, Protestant elsewhere)
Time difference: GMT +10 (Chuuk and Yap); +11 (Kosrae and Pohnpei)

MOLDOVA

Map page 26

National name: Republica Moldova/ Republic of Moldova
Area: 33,700 sq km/13,011 sq mi
Capital: Chişinău (Russian Kishinev)
Major towns/cities: Tiraspol, Bălţi, Tighina
Physical features: hilly land lying largely between the rivers Prut and Dniester; northern Moldova comprises the level plain of the Bălţi Steppe and uplands; the climate is warm and moderately continental
Currency: leu
GNP per capita (PPP): (US$) 2,358 (1999)
Resources: lignite, phosphorites, gypsum, building materials; petroleum and natural gas deposits discovered in the early 1990s were not yet exploited in 1996
Population: 4,380,000 (2000 est)
Population density: (per sq km) 130 (1999 est)
Language: Moldovan (official), Russian, Gaganz (a Turkish dialect)
Religion: Eastern Orthodox 98.5%; remainder Jewish
Time difference: GMT +2

MONACO

Map page 18

National name: Principauté de Monaco/Principality of Monaco
Area: 1.95 sq km/0.75 sq mi
Physical features: steep and rugged; surrounded landwards by French territory; being expanded by filling in the sea
Currency: French franc
GNP per capita (PPP): (US$) 27,000 (1999 est)
Population: 34,000 (2000 est)
Population density: (per sq km) 16,074 (1999 est)
Language: French (official), Monégasgne (a mixture of the French Provençal and Italian Ligurian dialects), Italian
Religion: Roman Catholic about 90%
Time difference: GMT +1

MONGOLIA

Map page 36

National name: Mongol Uls/ State of Mongolia
Area: 1,565,000 sq km/ 604,246 sq mi
Capital: Ulaanbaatar
Major towns/cities: Darhan, Choybalsan, Erdenet
Physical features: high plateau with desert and steppe (grasslands); Altai Mountains in southwest; salt lakes; part of Gobi desert in southeast; contains both the world's southernmost permafrost and northernmost desert
Currency: tugrik
GNP per capita (PPP): (US$) 1,496 (1999)
Resources: copper, nickel, zinc, molybdenum, phosphorites, tungsten, tin, fluorospar, gold, lead; reserves of petroleum discovered in 1994
Population: 2,662,000 (2000 est)
Population density: (per sq km) 2 (1999 est)
Language: Khalkha Mongolian (official), Kazakh (in the province of Bagan-Ölgiy), Chinese, Russian, Turkic languages
Religion: there is no state religion, but traditional lamaism (Mahayana Buddhism) is gaining new strength; the Sunni Muslim Kazakhs of Western Mongolia have also begun the renewal of their religious life, and Christian missionary activity has increased
Time difference: GMT +8

MOROCCO

Map page 52

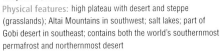

National name: Al-Mamlaka al-Maghribyya/Kingdom of Morocco
Area: 458,730 sq km/ 177,115 sq mi (excluding Western Sahara)
Capital: Rabat
Major towns/cities: Casablanca, Marrakech, Fès, Oujda, Kénitra, Tétouan, Meknès
Major ports: Casablanca, Tanger, Agadir
Physical features: mountain ranges, including the Atlas Mountains northeast-southwest; fertile coastal plains in west
Currency: dirham
GNP per capita (PPP): (US$) 3,190 (1999)
Resources: phosphate rock and phosphoric acid, coal, iron ore, barytes, lead, copper, manganese, zinc, petroleum, natural gas, fish
Population: 28,351,000 (2000 est)
Population density: (per sq km) 61 (1999 est)
Language: Arabic (75%) (official), Berber dialects (25%), French, Spanish
Religion: Sunni Muslim; Christian and Jewish minorities
Time difference: GMT +/-0

MOZAMBIQUE

Map page 58

National name: República de Moçambique/Republic of Mozambique

Area: 799,380 sq km/ 308,640 sq mi
Capital: Maputo (and chief port)
Major towns/cities: Beira, Nampula, Nacala, Chimoio
Major ports: Beira, Nacala, Quelimane
Physical features: mostly flat tropical lowland; mountains in west; rivers Zambezi and Limpopo
Currency: metical
GNP per capita (PPP): (US$) 797 (1999 est)
Resources: coal, salt, bauxite, graphite; reserves of iron ore, gold, precious and semiprecious stones, marble, natural gas (all largely unexploited in 1996)
Population: 19,680,000 (2000 est)
Population density: (per sq km) 24 (1999 est)
Language: Portuguese (official), 16 African languages
Religion: animist 48%, Muslim 20%, Roman Catholic 16%, Protestant 16%
Time difference: GMT +2

MYANMAR (BURMA)

Map page 40

National name: Pyedawngsu Myanma Naingngan/Union of Myanmar
Area: 676,577 sq km/ 261,226 sq mi
Capital: Yangon (formerly Rangoon) (and chief port)
Major towns/cities: Mandalay, Moulmein, Bago, Bassein, Taung-gyi, Sittwe,
Physical features: over half is rain forest; rivers Irrawaddy and Chindwin in central lowlands ringed by mountains in north, west, and east
Currency: kyat
GNP per capita (PPP): (US$) 1,200 (1999 est)
Resources: natural gas, petroleum, zinc, tin, copper, tungsten, coal, lead, gems, silver, gold
Population: 45,611,000 (2000 est)
Population density: (per sq km) 70 (1999 est)
Language: Burmese (official), English, tribal dialects
Religion: Hinayana Buddhist 89%, Christian 5%, Muslim 4%, animist 1.5%
Time difference: GMT +6.5

NAMIBIA

Map page 58

National name: Republic of Namibia
Area: 824,300 sq km/ 318,262 sq mi
Capital: Windhoek
Major towns/cities: Swakopmund, Rehoboth, Rundu
Major ports: Walvis Bay
Physical features: mainly desert (Namib and Kalahari); Orange River; Caprivi Strip links Namibia to Zambezi River; includes the enclave of Walvis Bay (area 1,120 sq km/432 sq mi)
Currency: Namibian dollar
GNP per capita (PPP): (US$) 5,369 (1999 est)
Resources: uranium, copper, lead, zinc, silver, tin, gold, salt, semiprecious stones, diamonds (one of the world's leading producers of gem diamonds), hydrocarbons, lithium, manganese, tungsten, cadmium, vanadium
Population: 1,726,000 (2000 est)
Population density: (per sq km) 2 (1999 est)
Language: English (official), Afrikaans, German, Ovambo (51%), Nama (12%), Kavango (10%), other indigenous languages
Religion: about 90% Christian (Lutheran, Roman Catholic, Dutch Reformed Church, Anglican)
Time difference: GMT +1

NAURU
Map page 60

National name: Republic of Nauru
Area: 21 sq km/8.1 sq mi

Capital: Yaren District (seat of government)
Physical features: tropical coral island in southwest Pacific; plateau encircled by coral cliffs and sandy beaches
Currency: Australian dollar
GNP per capita (PPP): (US$) 11,800 (1994 est)
Resources: phosphates
Population: 12,000 (2000 est)
Population density: (per sq km) 524 (1999 est)
Language: Nauruan, English (both official)
Religion: majority Protestant, Roman Catholic
Time difference: GMT +12

NEPAL
Map page 44

National name: Nepál Adhirajya/ Kingdom of Nepal
Area: 147,181 sq km/ 56,826 sq mi
Capital: Kathmandu
Major towns/cities: Biratnagar, Lalitpur, Bhadgaon, Pokhara, Birganj, Dahran Bazar
Physical features: descends from the Himalayas in the north through foothills to the River Ganges plain in the south; Mount Everest, Mount Kanchenjunga
Currency: Nepalese rupee
GNP per capita (PPP): (US$) 1,219 (1999)
Resources: lignite, talcum, magnesite, limestone, copper, cobalt
Population: 23,930,000 (2000 est)
Population density: (per sq km) 159 (1999 est)
Language: Nepali (official), Tibetan, numerous local languages
Religion: Hindu 90%, Buddhist 5%, Muslim 3%, Christian
Time difference: GMT +5.5

NETHERLANDS
Map page 14

National name: Koninkrijk der Nederlanden/Kingdom of the Netherlands
Area: 41,863 sq km/ 16,163 sq mi
Capital: Amsterdam (official), the Hague (legislative and judicial)
Major towns/cities: Rotterdam, the Hague (seat of government), Utrecht, Eindhoven, Groningen, Tilburg, Maastricht, Apeldoorn, Nijmegen, Breda
Major ports: Rotterdam
Physical features: flat coastal lowland; rivers Rhine, Schelde, Maas; Frisian Islands
Territories: Aruba, Netherlands Antilles (Caribbean)
Currency: guilder
GNP per capita (PPP): (US$) 23,052 (1999)
Resources: petroleum, natural gas
Population: 15,786,000 (1999 est)
Population density: (per sq km) 376 (1999 est)
Language: Dutch (official)
Religion: atheist 39%, Roman Catholic 31%, Dutch Reformed Church 14%, Calvinist 8%
Time difference: GMT +1

NEW ZEALAND
Map page 64

National name: Aotearoa/ New Zealand
Area: 268,680 sq km/ 103,737 sq mi
Capital: Wellington
Major towns/cities: Auckland, Hamilton, Christchurch, Manukau
Major ports: Auckland, Wellington
Physical features: comprises North Island, South Island, Stewart Island, Chatham Islands, and minor islands; mainly

---

mountainous; Ruapehu in North Island, 2,797 m/9,180 ft, highest of three active volcanoes; geysers and hot springs of Rotorua district; Lake Taupo (616 sq km/238 sq mi), source of Waikato River; Kaingaroa state forest. In South Island are the Southern Alps and Canterbury Plains
Territories: Tokelau (three atolls transferred in 1926 from former Gilbert and Ellice Islands colony); Niue Island (one of the Cook Islands, separately administered from 1903: chief town Alafi); Cook Islands are internally self-governing but share common citizenship with New Zealand; Ross Dependency in Antarctica
Currency: New Zealand dollar
GNP per capita (PPP): (US$) 16,566 (1999)
Resources: coal, clay, limestone, dolomite, natural gas, hydroelectric power, pumice, iron ore, gold, forests
Population: 3,862,000 (2000 est)
Population density: (per sq km) 14 (1999 est)
Language: English (official), Maori
Religion: Christian (Anglican 18%, Roman Catholic 14%, Presbyterian 13%)
Time difference: GMT +12

NICARAGUA
Map page 72

National name: República de Nicaragua/Republic of Nicaragua
Area: 127,849 sq km/ 49,362 sq mi
Capital: Managua
Major towns/cities: León, Chinandega, Masaya, Granada, Estelí
Major ports: Corinto, Puerto Cabezas, El Bluff
Physical features: narrow Pacific coastal plain separated from broad Atlantic coastal plain by volcanic mountains and lakes Managua and Nicaragua; one of the world's most active earthquake regions
Currency: cordoba
GNP per capita (PPP): (US$) 2,154 (1999)
Resources: gold, silver, copper, lead, antimony, zinc, iron, limestone, gypsum, marble, bentonite
Population: 5,074,000 (2000 est)
Population density: (per sq km) 39 (1999 est)
Language: Spanish (official), English, American Indian languages
Religion: Roman Catholic 95%
Time difference: GMT -6

NIGER
Map page 52

National name: République du Niger/Republic of Niger
Area: 1,186,408 sq km/ 458,072 sq mi
Capital: Niamey
Major towns/cities: Zinder, Maradi, Tahoua, Agadez, Birnin Konni, Arlit
Physical features: desert plains between hills in north and savannah in south; River Niger in southwest, Lake Chad in southeast
Currency: franc CFA
GNP per capita (PPP): (US$) 727 (1999)
Resources: uranium (one of world's leading producers), phosphates, gypsum, coal, cassiterite, tin, salt, gold; deposits of other minerals (including petroleum, iron ore, copper, lead, diamonds, and tungsten) have been confirmed
Population: 10,730,000 (2000 est)
Population density: (per sq km) 9 (1999 est)
Language: French (official), Hausa (70%), Djerma, other ethnic languages
Religion: Sunni Muslim 95%; also Christian, and traditional animist beliefs
Time difference: GMT +1

NIGERIA
Map page 54

National name: Federal Republic of Nigeria
Area: 923,773 sq km/356,668 sq mi

Capital: Abuja
Major towns/cities: Ibadan, Lagos, Ogbomosho, Kano, Oshogbo, Ilorin, Abeokuta, Zaria, Port Harcourt
Major ports: Lagos, Port Harcourt, Warri, Calabar
Physical features: arid savannah in north; tropical rain forest in south, with mangrove swamps along coast; River Niger forms wide delta; mountains in southeast
Currency: naira
GNP per capita (PPP): (US$) 744 (1999)
Resources: petroleum, natural gas, coal, tin, iron ore, uranium, limestone, marble, forest
Population: 111,506,000 (2000 est)
Population density: (per sq km) 118 (1999 est)
Language: English, French (both official), Hausa, Ibo, Yoruba
Religion: Sunni Muslim 50% (in north), Christian 35% (in south), local religions 15%
Time difference: GMT +1

NORTH KOREA
Map page 38

National name: Chosun Minchu-chui Inmin Konghwa-guk/ Democratic People's Republic of Korea
Area: 120,538 sq km/ 46,539 sq mi
Capital: P'yöngyang
Major towns/cities: Hamhüng, Ch'öngjin, Namp'o, Wönsan, Sinüiji
Physical features: wide coastal plain in west rising to mountains cut by deep valleys in interior
Currency: won
GNP per capita (PPP): (US$) 950 (1999 est)
Resources: coal, iron, lead, copper, zinc, tin, silver, gold, magnesite (has 40-50% of world's deposits of magnesite)
Population: 24,039,000 (2000 est)
Population density: (per sq km) 197 (1999 est)
Language: Korean (official)
Religion: Buddhist (predominant religion), Chondoist, Christian, traditional beliefs
Time difference: GMT +9

NORWAY
Map page 8

National name: Kongeriket Norge/ Kingdom of Norway
Area: 387,000 sq km/ 149,420 sq mi (including Svalbard and Jan Mayen)
Capital: Oslo
Major towns/cities: Bergen, Trondheim, Stavanger, Kristiansand, Drammen
Physical features: mountainous with fertile valleys and deeply indented coast; forests cover 25%; extends north of Arctic Circle
Territories: dependencies in the Arctic (Svalbard and Jan Mayen) and in Antarctica (Bouvet and Peter I Island, and Queen Maud Land)
Currency: Norwegian krone
GNP per capita (PPP): (US$) 26,522 (1999)
Resources: petroleum, natural gas, iron ore, iron pyrites, copper, lead, zinc, forests
Population: 4,465,000 (2000 est)
Population density: (per sq km) 14 (1999 est)
Language: Norwegian (official), Saami (Lapp), Finnish
Religion: Evangelical Lutheran (endowed by state) 88%; other Protestant and Roman Catholic 4%
Time difference: GMT +1

OMAN
Map page 46

National name: Saltanat `Uman/Sultanate of Oman
Area: 272,000 sq km/105,019 sq mi
Capital: Muscat

Major towns/cities: Sallālah, Ibrī, Suḥār, Al Buraymī, Nazwá, Sūr, Maṭraḥ
Physical features: mountains to the north and south of a high arid plateau; fertile coastal strip; Jebel Akhdar highlands; Kuria Muria Islands
Currency: Omani rial
GNP per capita (PPP): (US$) 8,690 (1997)
Resources: petroleum, natural gas, copper, chromite, gold, salt, marble, gypsum, limestone
Population: 2,542,000 (2000 est)
Population density: (per sq km) 9 (1999 est)
Language: Arabic (official), English, Urdu, other Indian languages
Religion: Muslim 75% (predominantly Ibadhi Muslim), about 25% Hindu
Time difference: GMT +4

PAKISTAN

Map page 46

National name: Islami Jamhuriyya e Pakistan/Islamic Republic of Pakistan
Area: 803,940 sq km/ 310,321 sq mi
Capital: Islamabad
Major towns/cities: Lahore, Rawalpindi, Faisalabad, Karachi, Hyderabad, Multan, Peshawar, Gujranwala, Quetta
Major ports: Karachi
Physical features: fertile Indus plain in east, Baluchistan plateau in west, mountains in north and northwest; the 'five rivers' (Indus, Jhelum, Chenab, Ravi, and Sutlej) feed the world's largest irrigation system; K2 mountain; Khyber Pass
Currency: Pakistan rupee
GNP per capita (PPP): (US$) 1,757 (1999)
Resources: iron ore, natural gas, limestone, rock salt, gypsum, silica, coal, petroleum, graphite, copper, manganese, chromite
Population: 156,483,000 (2000 est)
Population density: (per sq km) 189 (1999 est)
Language: Urdu (official), English, Punjabi, Sindhi, Pashto, Baluchi, other local dialects
Religion: Sunni Muslim 90%, Shiite Muslim 5%; also Hindu, Christian, Parsee, Buddhist
Time difference: GMT +5

PALAU

Map page 60

National name: Belu'u era Belau/Republic of Palau
Area: 508 sq km/196 sq mi
Capital: Koror (on Koror island)
Physical features: more than 350 (mostly uninhabited) islands, islets, and atolls in the west Pacific; warm, humid climate, susceptible to typhoons
Currency: US dollar
GNP per capita (PPP): (US$) N/A
Population: 19,000 (2000 est)
Population density: (per sq km) 39 (1999 est)
Language: Palauan, English (both official in most states)
Religion: Christian, principally Roman Catholic; Modekngei (indigenous religion)
Time difference: GMT +9

PANAMA

Map page 72

National name: República de Panamá/Republic of Panama
Area: 77,100 sq km/ 29,768 sq mi
Capital: Panamá
Major towns/cities: San Miguelito, Colón, David, La Chorrera, Santiago, Chitré,

Changuinola
Major ports: Colón, Cristóbal, Balboa
Physical features: coastal plains and mountainous interior; tropical rain forest in east and northwest; Archipelago de las Perlas in Gulf of Panama; Panama Canal
Currency: balboa
GNP per capita (PPP): (US$) 5,016 (1999)
Resources: limestone, clay, salt; deposits of coal, copper, and molybdenum have been discovered
Population: 2,856,000 (2000 est)
Population density: (per sq km) 36 (1999 est)
Language: Spanish (official), English
Religion: Roman Catholic 93%
Time difference: GMT -5

PAPUA NEW GUINEA

Map page 60

National name: Gau Hedinarai ai Papua-Matamata Guinea/Independent State of Papua New Guinea
Area: 462,840 sq km/ 178,702 sq mi
Capital: Port Moresby (on East New Guinea)
Major towns/cities: Lae, Madang, Arawa, Wewak, Goroka, Rabaul
Major ports: Port Moresby, Rabaul
Physical features: mountainous; swamps and plains; monsoon climate; tropical islands of New Ireland, New Britain, and Bougainville; Admiralty Islands, D'Entrecasteaux Islands, and Louisiade Archipelago; active volcanoes Vulcan and Tavurvur
Currency: kina
GNP per capita (PPP): (US$) 2,263 (1999 est)
Resources: copper, gold, silver; deposits of chromite, cobalt, nickel, quartz; substantial reserves of petroleum and natural gas (petroleum production began in 1992)
Population: 4,807,000 (2000 est)
Population density: (per sq km) 10 (1999 est)
Language: English (official), pidgin English, over 700 local languages
Religion: Christian 97%, of which 3% Roman Catholic; local pantheistic beliefs
Time difference: GMT +10

PARAGUAY

Map page 78

National name: República del Paraguay/Republic of Paraguay
Area: 406,752 sq km/ 157,046 sq mi
Capital: Asunción (and chief port)
Major towns/cities: Ciudad del Este, Pedro Juan Caballero, San Lorenzo, Fernando de la Mora, Lambare, Luque, Capiatá
Major ports: Concepción
Physical features: low marshy plain and marshlands; divided by Paraguay River; Paraná River forms southeast boundary
Currency: guaraní
GNP per capita (PPP): (US$) 4,193 (1999 est)
Resources: gypsum, kaolin, limestone, salt; deposits (not commercially exploited) of bauxite, iron ore, copper, manganese, uranium; deposits of natural gas discovered in 1994; exploration for petroleum deposits ongoing mid-1990s
Population: 5,496,000 (2000 est)
Population density: (per sq km) 13 (1999 est)
Language: Spanish (official), Guaraní (an indigenous Indian language)
Religion: Roman Catholic (official religion) 85%; Mennonite, Anglican
Time difference: GMT -3/4

PERU

Map page 76

National name: República del Perú/Republic of Peru
Area: 1,285,200 sq km/496,216 sq mi

Capital: Lima
Major towns/cities: Arequipa, Iquitos, Chiclayo, Trujillo, Huancayo, Piura, Chimbote
Major ports: Callao, Chimbote, Salaverry
Physical features: Andes mountains running northwest-southeast cover 27% of Peru, separating Amazon river-basin jungle in northeast from coastal plain in west; desert along coast north-south (Atacama Desert); Lake Titicaca
Currency: nuevo sol
GNP per capita (PPP): (US$) 4,387 (1999)
Resources: lead, copper, iron, silver, zinc (world's fourth-largest producer), petroleum
Population: 25,662,000 (2000 est)
Population density: (per sq km) 20 (1999 est)
Language: Spanish, Quechua (both official), Aymara, many indigenous dialects
Religion: Roman Catholic (state religion) 95%
Time difference: GMT -5

PHILIPPINES

Map page 40

National name: Republika Ñg Pilipinas/Republic of the Philippines
Area: 300,000 sq km/ 115,830 sq mi
Capital: Manila (on Luzon island) (and chief port)
Major towns/cities: Quezon City, Davao, Caloocan, Cebu, Bacolod, Cagayan de Oro, Iloilo
Major ports: Cebu, Davao (on Mindanao), Iloilo, Zamboanga (on Mindanao)
Physical features: comprises over 7,000 islands; volcanic mountain ranges traverse main chain north-south; 50% still forested. The largest islands are Luzon 108,172 sq km/41,754 sq mi and Mindanao 94,227 sq km/36,372 sq mi; others include Samar, Negros, Palawan, Panay, Mindoro, Leyte, Cebu, and the Sulu group; Pinatubo volcano (1,759 m/5,770 ft); Mindanao has active volcano Apo (2,954 m/9,690 ft) and mountainous rain forest
Currency: peso
GNP per capita (PPP): (US$) 3,815 (1999)
Resources: copper ore, gold, silver, chromium, nickel, coal, crude petroleum, natural gas, forests
Population: 75,967,000 (2000 est)
Population density: (per sq km) 248 (1999 est)
Language: Filipino, English (both official), Spanish, Cebuano, Ilocano, more than 70 other indigenous languages
Religion: Christian 94%, mainly Roman Catholic (84%), Protestant; Muslim 4%, local religions
Time difference: GMT +8

POLAND
Map page 10

National name: Rzeczpospolita Polska/Republic of Poland
Area: 312,683 sq km/ 120,726 sq mi
Capital: Warsaw
Major towns/cities: Łódź, Kraków, Wroclaw, Poznan, Gdansk, Szczecin, Katòwice, Bydgoszcz, Lublin
Major ports: Gdansk (Danzig), Szczecin (Stettin), Gdynia (Gdingen)
Physical features: part of the great plain of Europe; Vistula, Oder, and Neisse rivers; Sudeten, Tatra, and Carpathian mountains on southern frontier
Currency: zloty
GNP per capita (PPP): (US$) 7,894 (1999)
Resources: coal (world's fifth-largest producer), copper, sulfur, silver, petroleum and natural gas reserves
Population: 38,765,000 (2000 est)
Population density: (per sq km) 124 (1999 est)
Language: Polish (official)
Religion: Roman Catholic 95%
Time difference: GMT +1

PORTUGAL

Map page 20

National name: República Portuguesa/Republic of Portugal
Area: 92,000 sq km/35,521 sq mi (including the Azores and Madeira)
Capital: Lisbon
Major towns/cities: Porto, Coimbra, Amadora, Setúbal, Funchal, Braga, Vila Nova de Gaia
Major ports: Porto, Setúbal
Physical features: mountainous in the north (Serra da Estrêla mountains); plains in the south; rivers Minho, Douro, Tagus (Tejo), Guadiana
Currency: escudo
GNP per capita (PPP): (US$) 15,147 (1999)
Resources: limestone, granite, marble, iron, tungsten, copper, pyrites, gold, uranium, coal, forests
Population: 9,875,000 (2000 est)
Population density: (per sq km) 107 (1999 est)
Language: Portuguese (official)
Religion: Roman Catholic 97%
Time difference: GMT +/-0

QATAR

Map page 46

National name: Dawlat Qatar/ State of Qatar

Area: 11,400 sq km/4,401 sq mi
Capital: Doha (and chief port)
Major towns/cities: Dukhān, ad Dawhah, ar-Rayyan, Umm Salal, Musay'īd, aš-Šahniyah
Physical features: mostly flat desert with salt flats in south
Currency: Qatari riyal
GNP per capita (PPP): (US$) N/A
Resources: petroleum, natural gas, water resources
Population: 599,000 (2000 est)
Population density: (per sq km) 52 (1999 est)
Language: Arabic (official), English
Religion: Sunni Muslim 95%
Time difference: GMT +3

ROMANIA

Map page 26

National name: România/Romania
Area: 237,500 sq km/91,698 sq mi
Capital: Bucharest
Major towns/cities: Brasov, Timisoara, Cluj-Napoca, Iaşi, Constanta, Galati, Craiova
Major ports: Galati, Constanta, Brăila
Physical features: mountains surrounding a plateau, with river plains in south and east. Carpathian Mountains, Transylvanian Alps; River Danube; Black Sea coast; mineral springs
Currency: leu
GNP per capita (PPP): (US$) 5,647 (1999)
Resources: brown coal, hard coal, iron ore, salt, bauxite, copper, lead, zinc, methane gas, petroleum (reserves expected to be exhausted by mid- to late 1990s)
Population: 22,327,000 (2000 est)
Population density: (per sq km) 94 (1999 est)
Language: Romanian (official), Hungarian, German
Religion: Romanian Orthodox 87%; Roman Catholic and Uniate 5%; Reformed/Lutheran 3%, Unitarian 1%
Time difference: GMT +2

RUSSIA

Map page 32

National name: Rossiiskaya Federatsiya/Russian Federation
Area: 17,075,400 sq km/6,592,811 sq mi
Capital: Moscow
Major towns/cities: St. Petersburg, Nizhniy Novgorod, Samara, Yekaterinburg, Novosibirsk, Chelyabinsk, Kazan, Omsk, Perm',

Ufa

Physical features: fertile Black Earth district; extensive forests; the Ural Mountains with large mineral resources; Lake Baikal, world's deepest lake
Currency: rouble
GNP per capita (PPP): (US$) 6,339 (1999)
Resources: petroleum, natural gas, coal, peat, copper (world's fourth-largest producer), iron ore, lead, aluminum, phosphate rock, nickel, manganese, gold, diamonds, platinum, zinc, tin
Population: 146,934,000 (2000 est)
Population density: (per sq km) 9 (1999 est)
Language: Russian (official) and many East Slavic, Altaic, Uralic, Caucasian languages
Religion: traditionally Russian Orthodox; significant Muslim and Buddhist communities
Time difference: GMT +2-12

RWANDA

Map page 56

National name: Republika y'u Rwanda/Republic of Rwanda
Area: 26,338 sq km/10,169 sq mi
Capital: Kigali
Major towns/cities: Butare, Ruhengeri, Gisenyi, Kibungo, Cyangugu
Physical features: high savannah and hills, with volcanic mountains in northwest; part of lake Kivu; highest peak Mount Karisimbi 4,507 m/14,792 ft; Kagera River (whose headwaters are the source of the Nile)
Currency: Rwandan franc
GNP per capita (PPP): (US$) 690 (1998)
Resources: cassiterite (a tin-bearing ore), wolframite (a tungsten-bearing ore), natural gas, gold, columbo-tantalite, beryl
Population: 7,733,000 (2000 est)
Population density: (per sq km) 275 (1999 est)
Language: Kinyarwanda, French (both official), Kiswahili
Religion: about 50% animist; about 40% Christian, mainly Roman Catholic; 9% Muslim
Time difference: GMT +2

ST. KITTS AND NEVIS

Map page 72

National name: Federation of St. Christopher and St. Nevis
Area: 262 sq km/101 sq mi (St. Kitts 168 sq km/65 sq mi, Nevis 93 sq km/36 sq mi)
Capital: Basseterre (on St. Kitts) (and chief port)
Major towns/cities: Charlestown (Nevis), Newcastle, Sandy Point Town, Dieppe Bay Town
Physical features: both islands are volcanic; fertile plains on coast; black beaches
Currency: East Caribbean dollar
GNP per capita (PPP): (US$) 9,801 (1999)
Population: 38,000 (2000 est)
Population density: (per sq km) 160 (1999 est)
Language: English (official)
Religion: Anglican 36%, Methodist 32%, other Protestant 8%, Roman Catholic 10%
Time difference: GMT -4

ST. LUCIA

Map page 72

Area: 617 sq km/238 sq mi
Capital: Castries
Major towns/cities: Soufrière, Vieux Fort, Choiseul, Gros Islet
Major ports: Vieux-Fort
Physical features: mountainous island with fertile valleys; mainly tropical forest; volcanic peaks; Gros and Petit Pitons
Currency: East Caribbean dollar

GNP per capita (PPP): (US$) 5,022 (1999)
Resources: geothermal energy
Population: 154,000 (2000 est)
Population density: (per sq km) 252 (1999 est)
Language: English (official), French patois
Religion: Roman Catholic 85%; Anglican, Protestant
Time difference: GMT -4

ST. VINCENT AND THE GRENADINES

Map page 72

Area: 388 sq km/150 sq mi (including islets of the Northern Grenadines 43 sq km/17 sq mi)
Capital: Kingstown
Major towns/cities: Georgetown, Châteaubelair, Dovers
Physical features: volcanic mountains, thickly forested; La Soufrière volcano
Currency: East Caribbean dollar
GNP per capita (PPP): (US$) 4,667 (1999)
Population: 114,000 (2000 est)
Population density: (per sq km) 355 (1999 est)
Language: English (official), French patois
Religion: Anglican, Methodist, Roman Catholic
Time difference: GMT -4

SAMOA

Map page 60

National name: 'O la Malo Tu To'atasi o Samoa/Independent State of Samoa
Area: 2,830 sq km/1,092 sq mi
Capital: Apia (on Upolu island) (and chief port)
Major towns/cities: Lalomanu, Tuasivi, Falealupo, Falelatai, Taga
Physical features: comprises South Pacific islands of Savai'i and Upolu, with two smaller tropical islands and uninhabited islets; mountain ranges on main islands; coral reefs; over half forested
Currency: tala, or Samoan dollar
GNP per capita (PPP): (US$) 3,915 (1999)
Population: 180,000 (2000 est)
Population density: (per sq km) 63 (1999 est)
Language: English, Samoan (both official)
Religion: Congregationalist; also Roman Catholic, Methodist
Time difference: GMT -11

SAN MARINO

Map page 24

National name: Serenissima Repubblica di San Marino/Most Serene Republic of San Marino
Area: 61 sq km/24 sq mi
Capital: San Marino
Major towns/cities: Serravalle, Faetano, Fiorentino, Borgo Maggiore, Domagnano
Physical features: the slope of Mount Titano
Currency: Italian lira
GNP per capita (PPP): (US$) 20,000 (1997 est)
Resources: limestone and other building stone
Population: 27,000 (2000 est)
Population density: (per sq km) 417 (1999 est)
Language: Italian (official)
Religion: Roman Catholic 95%
Time difference: GMT +1

SÃO TOMÉ AND PRÍNCIPE
Map page 54

National name: República Democrática de São Tomé e Príncipe/Democratic Republic of São Tomé and Príncipe

Area: 1,000 sq km/386 sq mi
Capital: São Tomé
Major towns/cities: Santo Antônio, Sant Ana, Porto Alegre, Neves, Santo Amaro
Physical features: comprises two main islands and several smaller ones, all volcanic; thickly forested and fertile
Currency: dobra
GNP per capita (PPP): (US$) 1,335 (1999)
Population: 147,000 (2000 est)
Population density: (per sq km) 161 (1999 est)
Language: Portuguese (official), Fang (a Bantu language), Lungwa São Tomé (a Portuguese Creole)
Religion: Roman Catholic 80%, animist
Time difference: GMT +/-0

SAUDI ARABIA
Map page 46

National name: Al-Mamlaka al-'Arabiyya as-Sa'udiyya/ Kingdom of Saudi Arabia
Area: 2,200,518 sq km/ 849,620 sq mi
Capital: Riyadh
Major towns/cities: Jedda, Mecca, Medina, Ad Dammām, Tabūk, Buraydah
Major ports: Jedda, Ad Dammām, Jīzān, Yanbu
Physical features: desert, sloping to the Persian Gulf from a height of 2,750 m/9,000 ft in the west
Currency: riyal
GNP per capita (PPP): (US$) 10,472 (1999 est)
Resources: petroleum, natural gas, iron ore, limestone, gypsum, marble, clay, salt, gold, uranium, copper, fish
Population: 21,607,000 (2000 est)
Population density: (per sq km) 9 (1999 est)
Language: Arabic (official), English
Religion: Sunni Muslim 85%; there is a Shiite minority
Time difference: GMT +3

SENEGAL
Map page 54

National name: République du Sénégal/Republic of Senegal
Area: 196,200 sq km/ 75,752 sq mi
Capital: Dakar (and chief port)
Major towns/cities: Thiès, Kaolack, Saint-Louis, Ziguinchor, Diourbel, Mbour
Physical features: plains rising to hills in southeast; swamp and tropical forest in southwest; River Senegal; The Gambia forms an enclave within Senegal
Currency: franc CFA
GNP per capita (PPP): (US$) 1,341 (1999)
Resources: calcium phosphates, aluminum phosphates, salt, natural gas; offshore deposits of petroleum to be developed
Population: 9,481,000 (2000 est)
Population density: (per sq km) 47 (1999 est)
Language: French (official), Wolof, other ethnic languages
Religion: mainly Sunni Muslim; Christian 4%, animist 1%
Time difference: GMT +/-0

SEYCHELLES
Map page 58

National name: Republic of Seychelles
Area: 453 sq km/174 sq mi
Capital: Victoria (on Mahé island) (and chief port)
Major towns/cities: Cascade, Anse Boileau, Takamaka
Physical features: comprises two distinct island groups: one, the Granitic group, concentrated, the other, the Outer or Coralline group, widely scattered; totals over 100 islands and islets

Currency: Seychelles rupee
GNP per capita (PPP): (US$) 10,381 (1999)
Resources: guano; natural gas and metal deposits were being explored mid-1990s
Population: 77,000 (2000 est)
Population density: (per sq km) 174 (1999 est)
Language: Creole (an Asian, African, European mixture) (95%), English, French (all official)
Religion: Roman Catholic 90%
Time difference: GMT +4

SIERRA LEONE
Map page 54

National name: Republic of Sierra Leone
Area: 71,740 sq km/27,698 sq mi
Capital: Freetown
Major towns/cities: Koidu, Bo, Kenema, Makeni
Major ports: Bonthe
Physical features: mountains in east; hills and forest; coastal mangrove swamps
Currency: leone
GNP per capita (PPP): (US$) 414 (1999)
Resources: gold, diamonds, bauxite, rutile (titanium dioxide)
Population: 4,854,000 (2000 est)
Population density: (per sq km) 66 (1999 est)
Language: English (official), Krio (a Creole language), Mende, Limba, Temne
Religion: animist 45%, Muslim 44%, Protestant 8%, Roman Catholic 3%
Time difference: GMT +/-0

SINGAPORE
Map page 42

National name: Repablik Singapura/Republic of Singapore
Area: 622 sq km/240 sq mi
Capital: Singapore
Physical features: comprises Singapore Island, low and flat, and 57 small islands; Singapore Island is joined to the mainland by causeway across Strait of Johore
Currency: Singapore dollar
GNP per capita (PPP): (US$) 27,024 (1999)
Resources: granite
Population: 3,567,000 (2000 est)
Population density: (per sq km) 5,662 (1999 est)
Language: Malay, Mandarin Chinese, Tamil, English (all official), other Indian languages, Chinese dialects
Religion: Buddhist, Taoist, Muslim, Hindu, Christian
Time difference: GMT +8

SLOVAK REPUBLIC
Map page 10

National name: Slovenská Republika/Slovak Republic
Area: 49,035 sq km/18,932 sq mi
Capital: Bratislava
Major towns/cities: Košice, Nitra, Prešov, Banská Bystrica, Zilina, Trnava, Martin
Physical features: Western range of Carpathian Mountains, including Tatra and Beskids in north; Danube plain in south; numerous lakes and mineral springs
Currency: Slovak koruna (based on Czechoslovak koruna)
GNP per capita (PPP): (US$) 9,811 (1999)
Resources: brown coal, lignite, copper, zinc, lead, iron ore, magnesite
Population: 5,387,000 (2000 est)
Population density: (per sq km) 110 (1999 est)
Language: Slovak (official), Hungarian, Czech, other ethnic languages
Religion: Roman Catholic (over 50%), Lutheran, Reformist, Orthodox, atheist 10%
Time difference: GMT +1

SLOVENIA
Map page 22

National name: Republika Slovenija/ Republic of Slovenia
Area: 20,251 sq km/7,818 sq mi
Capital: Ljubljana
Major towns/cities: Maribor, Kranj, Celje, Velenje, Koper, Novo Mesto
Major ports: Koper
Physical features: mountainous; Sava and Drava rivers
Currency: tolar
GNP per capita (PPP): (US$) 15,062 (1999)
Resources: coal, lead, zinc; small reserves/deposits of natural gas, petroleum, salt, uranium
Population: 1,986,000 (2000 est)
Population density: (per sq km) 98 (1999 est)
Language: Slovene (related to Serbo-Croat; official), Hungarian, Italian
Religion: Roman Catholic 70%; Eastern Orthodox, Lutheran, Muslim
Time difference: GMT +1

SOLOMON ISLANDS
Map page 60

Area: 27,600 sq km/ 10,656 sq mi
Capital: Honiara (on Guadalcanal island) (and chief port)
Major towns/cities: Gizo, Auki, Kirakira, Buala
Major ports: Yandina
Physical features: comprises all but the northernmost islands (which belong to Papua New Guinea) of a Melanesian archipelago stretching nearly 1,500 km/900 mi. The largest is Guadalcanal (area 6,500 sq km/2,510 sq mi); others are Malaita, San Cristobal, New Georgia, Santa Isabel, Choiseul; mainly mountainous and forested
Currency: Solomon Island dollar
GNP per capita (PPP): (US$) 1,793 (1999)
Resources: bauxite, phosphates, gold, silver, copper, lead, zinc, cobalt, asbestos, nickel
Population: 444,000 (2000 est)
Population density: (per sq km) 16 (1999 est)
Language: English (official), pidgin English, more than 80 Melanesian dialects (85%), Papuan and Polynesian languages
Religion: more than 80% Christian; Anglican 34%, Roman Catholic 19%, South Sea Evangelical, other Protestant, animist 5%
Time difference: GMT +11

SOMALIA
Map page 56

National name: Jamhuuriyadda Soomaaliya/Republic of Somalia
Area: 637,700 sq km/ 246,215 sq mi
Capital: Mogadishu (and chief port)
Major towns/cities: Hargeysa, Berbera, Kismaayo, Marka
Major ports: Berbera, Marka, Kismaayo
Physical features: mainly flat, with hills in north
Currency: Somali shilling
GNP per capita (PPP): (US$) 600 (1999 est)
Resources: chromium, coal, salt, tin, zinc, copper, gypsum, manganese, iron ore, uranium, gold, silver; deposits of petroleum and natural gas have been discovered but remain unexploited
Population: 10,097,000 (2000 est)
Population density: (per sq km) 15 (1999 est)
Language: Somali, Arabic (both official), Italian, English
Religion: Sunni Muslim; small Christian community, mainly Roman Catholic
Time difference: GMT +3

SOUTH AFRICA

Map page 58

National name: Republiek van
Suid-Afrika/Republic of South
Africa
Area: 1,222,081 sq km/
471,845 sq mi
Capital: Cape Town (legislative),
Pretoria (administrative),
Bloemfontein (judicial)
Major towns/cities: Johannesburg, Durban, Port Elizabeth,
Vereeniging, Pietermaritzburg, Kimberley, Soweto, Tembisa
Major ports: Cape Town, Durban, Port Elizabeth, East London
Physical features: southern end of large plateau, fringed by
mountains and lowland coastal margin; Drakensberg Mountains,
Table Mountain; Limpopo and Orange rivers
Territories: Marion Island and Prince Edward Island in the
Antarctic
Currency: rand
GNP per capita (PPP): (US$) 8,318 (1999)
Resources: gold (world's largest producer), coal, platinum, iron
ore, diamonds, chromium, manganese, limestone, asbestos,
fluorspar, uranium, copper, lead, zinc, petroleum, natural gas
Population: 40,377,000 (2000 est)
Population density: (per sq km) 33 (1999 est)
Language: English, Afrikaans, Xhosa, Zulu, Sesotho (all official),
other African languages
Religion: Dutch Reformed Church and other Christian
denominations 77%, Hindu 2%, Muslim 1%
Time difference: GMT +2

SOUTH KOREA

Map page 38

National name: Daehan Minguk/
Republic of Korea
Area: 98,799 sq km/38,146 sq mi
Capital: Seoul
Major towns/cities: Pusan,
Taegu, Inch'ŏn, Kwangju,
Taejŏn, Songnam
Major ports: Pusan, Inch'ŏn
Physical features: southern end of a mountainous peninsula
separating the Sea of Japan from the Yellow Sea
Currency: won
GNP per capita (PPP): (US$) 14,637 (1999)
Resources: coal, iron ore, tungsten, gold, molybdenum,
graphite, fluorite, natural gas, hydroelectric power, fish
Population: 46,844,000 (2000 est)
Population density: (per sq km) 473 (1999 est)
Language: Korean (official)
Religion: Buddhist 48%, Confucian 3%, Christian 47%, mainly
Protestant; Chund Kyo (peculiar to Korea, combining elements of
Shaman, Buddhist, and Christian doctrines)
Time difference: GMT +9

SPAIN

Map page 20

National name: España/Spain
Area: 504,750 sq km/194,883 sq mi
(including the Balearic and Canary
islands)
Capital: Madrid
Major towns/cities:
Barcelona, Valencia, Zaragoza,
Sevilla, Málaga, Bilbao, Las
Palmas (on Gran Canarias island), Murcia, Palma (on Mallorca)
Major ports: Barcelona, Valencia, Cartagena, Málaga, Cádiz,
Vigo, Santander, Bilbao
Physical features: central plateau with mountain ranges,
lowlands in south; rivers Ebro, Douro, Tagus, Guadiana,
Guadalquivir; Iberian Plateau (Meseta); Pyrenees, Cantabrian
Mountains, Andalusian Mountains, Sierra Nevada
Territories: Balearic and Canary Islands; in North Africa: Ceuta,
Melilla, Alhucemas, Chafarinas Islands, Peñón de Vélez
Currency: peseta
GNP per capita (PPP): (US$) 16,730 (1999)
Resources: coal, lignite, anthracite, copper, iron, zinc, uranium,
potassium salts
Population: 39,630,000 (2000 est)

Population density: (per sq km) 79 (1999 est)
Language: Spanish (Castilian; official), Basque, Catalan, Galician
Religion: Roman Catholic 98%
Time difference: GMT +1

SRI LANKA

Map page 44

National name: Sri Lanka
Prajatantrika Samajavadi
Janarajaya/Democratic Socialist
Republic of Sri Lanka
Area: 65,610 sq km/25,332 sq mi
Capital: Sri Jayewardenepura
Kotte
Major towns/cities: Colombo,
Kandy, Dehiwala-Mount Lavinia, Moratuwa, Jaffna, Galle
Major ports: Jaffna, Galle, Negombo, Trincomalee
Physical features: flat in north and around coast; hills and
mountains in south and central interior
Currency: Sri Lankan rupee
GNP per capita (PPP): (US$) 3,056 (1999)
Resources: gemstones, graphite, iron ore, monazite, rutile,
uranium, iemenite sands, limestone, salt, clay
Population: 18,827,000 (2000 est)
Population density: (per sq km) 284 (1999 est)
Language: Sinhala, Tamil (both official), English
Religion: Buddhist 69%, Hindu 15%, Muslim 8%, Christian 8%
Time difference: GMT +5.5

SUDAN

Map page 50

National name: Al-Jumhuryyat
es-Sudan/Republic of Sudan
Area: 2,505,800 sq km/
967,489 sq mi
Capital: Khartoum
Major towns/cities: Omdurman,
Port Sudan, Juba, Wad Medani, El
Obeid, Kassala, Gedaref, Nyala
Major ports: Port Sudan
Physical features: fertile Nile valley separates Libyan Desert in
west from high rocky Nubian Desert in east
Currency: Sudanese dinar
GNP per capita (PPP): (US$) 1,298 (1999)
Resources: petroleum, marble, mica, chromite, gypsum, gold,
graphite, sulfur, iron, manganese, zinc, fluorspar, talc, limestone,
dolomite, pumice
Population: 29,490,000 (2000 est)
Population density: (per sq km) 12 (1999 est)
Language: Arabic (51%) (official), 100 local languages
Religion: Sunni Muslim 70%; also animist 25%, and Christian
5%
Time difference: GMT +2

SURINAME

Map page 76

National name: Republiek
Suriname/Republic of
Suriname
Area: 163,820 sq km/
63,250 sq mi
Capital: Paramaribo
Major towns/cities: Nieuw
Nickerie, Moengo, Brokopondo,
Nieuw Amsterdam, Albina,
Groningen
Physical features: hilly and forested, with flat and narrow
coastal plain; Suriname River
Currency: Suriname guilder
GNP per capita (PPP): (US$) 3,820 (1998 est)
Resources: petroleum, bauxite (one of the world's leading
producers), iron ore, copper, manganese, nickel, platinum, gold,
kaolin
Population: 417,000 (2000 est)
Population density: (per sq km) 3 (1999 est)
Language: Dutch (official), Spanish, Sranan (Creole), English,
Hindi, Javanese, Chinese, various tribal languages

Religion: Christian 47%, Hindu 28%, Muslim 20%
Time difference: GMT -3.5

SWAZILAND

Map page 58

National name: Umbuso waka
Ngwane/Kingdom of Swaziland
Area: 17,400 sq km/6,718 sq mi
Capital: Mbabane
(administrative), Lobamba
(legislative)
Major towns/cities: Manzini, Big
Bend, Mhlume, Nhlangano
Physical features: central valley; mountains in west (Highveld);
plateau in east (Lowveld and Lubombo plateau)
Currency: lilangeni
GNP per capita (PPP): (US$) 4,200 (1999)
Resources: coal, asbestos, diamonds, gold, tin, kaolin, iron ore,
talc, pyrophyllite, silica
Population: 1,008,000 (2000 est)
Population density: (per sq km) 56 (1999 est)
Language: Swazi, English (both official)
Religion: about 60% Christian, animist
Time difference: GMT +2

SWEDEN

Map page 8

National name: Konungariket
Sverige/Kingdom of Sweden
Area: 450,000 sq km/
173,745 sq mi
Capital: Stockholm
Major towns/cities:
Göteborg, Malmö, Uppsala,
Norrköping, Västerås, Linköping,
Örebro, Helsingborg
Major ports: Helsingborg, Malmö, Göteborg, Stockholm
Physical features: mountains in west; plains in south; thickly
forested; more than 20,000 islands off the Stockholm coast;
lakes, including Vänern, Vättern, Mälaren, and Hjälmaren
Currency: Swedish krona
GNP per capita (PPP): (US$) 20,824 (1999)
Resources: iron ore, uranium, copper, lead, zinc, silver,
hydroelectric power, forests
Population: 8,910,000 (2000 est)
Population density: (per sq km) 20 (1999 est)
Language: Swedish (official), Finnish, Saami (Lapp)
Religion: Evangelical Lutheran, Church of Sweden (established
national church) 90%; Muslim, Jewish
Time difference: GMT +1

SWITZERLAND

Map page 22

National name: Schweizerische
Eidgenossenschaft (German)/
Confédération Suisse (French)/
Confederazione Svizzera (Italian)/
Confederaziun Svizra
(Romansch)/ Swiss
Confederation
Area: 41,300 sq km/15,945 sq mi
Capital: Bern
Major towns/cities: Zürich, Geneva, Basel, Lausanne, Luzern,
St. Gallen, Winterthur
Major ports: river port Basel (on the Rhine)
Physical features: most mountainous country in Europe (Alps
and Jura mountains); highest peak Dufourspitze 4,634 m/15,203
ft in Apennines
Currency: Swiss franc
GNP per capita (PPP): (US$) 27,486 (1999)
Resources: salt, hydroelectric power, forest
Population: 7,386,000 (2000 est)
Population density: (per sq km) 178 (1999 est)
Language: German (65%), French (18%), Italian (10%),
Romansch (1%) (all official)
Religion: Roman Catholic 46%, Protestant 40%
Time difference: GMT +1

SYRIA
Map page 46

National name: al-Jumhuriyya al-Arabiyya as-Suriyya/Syrian Arab Republic
Area: 185,200 sq km/71,505 sq mi
Capital: Damascus
Major towns/cities: Aleppo, Homs, Al Lādhiqīyah, Hamāh, Ar Raqqah, Dayr az Zawr
Major ports: Al Lādhiqīyah
Physical features: mountains alternate with fertile plains and desert areas; Euphrates River
Currency: Syrian pound
GNP per capita (PPP): (US$) 2,761 (1999)
Resources: petroleum, natural gas, iron ore, phosphates, salt, gypsum, sodium chloride, bitumen
Population: 16,125,000 (2000 est)
Population density: (per sq km) 85 (1999 est)
Language: Arabic (89%) (official), Kurdish (6%), Armenian (3%), French, English, Aramaic, Circassian
Religion: Sunni Muslim 74%; other Islamic sects 16%, Christian 10%
Time difference: GMT +2

TAIWAN
Map page 38

National name: Chung-hua Min-kuo/Republic of China
Area: 36,179 sq km/13,968 sq mi
Capital: T'aipei
Major towns/cities: Kaohsiung, T'aichung, T'ainan, Panch'iao, Chungho, Sanch'ung
Major ports: Kaohsiung, Chilung
Physical features: island (formerly Formosa) off People's Republic of China; mountainous, with lowlands in west; Penghu (Pescadores), Jinmen (Quemoy), Mazu (Matsu) islands
Currency: New Taiwan dollar
GNP per capita (PPP): (US$) 18,950 (1998 est)
Resources: coal, copper, marble, dolomite; small reserves of petroleum and natural gas
Population: 22,113,000 (1999 est)
Population density: (per sq km) 685 (1999 est)
Language: Chinese (dialects include Mandarin (official), Min, and Hakka)
Religion: officially atheist; Buddhist 23%, Taoist 18%, I-Kuan Tao 4%, Christian 3%, Confucian and other 3%
Time difference: GMT +8

TAJIKISTAN
Map page 34

National name: Jumhurii Tojikston/Republic of Tajikistan
Area: 143,100 sq km/55,250 sq mi
Capital: Dushanbe
Major towns/cities: Khūjand, Qūrghonteppa, Külob, Ūroteppa, Kofarnihon
Physical features: mountainous, more than half of its territory lying above 3,000 m/10,000 ft; huge mountain glaciers, which are the source of many rapid rivers
Currency: Tajik ruble
GNP per capita (PPP): (US$) 981 (1999)
Resources: coal, aluminum, lead, zinc, iron, tin, uranium, radium, arsenic, bismuth, gold, mica, asbestos, lapis lazuli; small reserves of petroleum and natural gas
Population: 6,188,000 (2000 est)
Population density: (per sq km) 43 (1999 est)
Language: Tajik (related to Farsi; official), Russian
Religion: Sunni Muslim; small Russian Orthodox and Jewish communities
Time difference: GMT +5

TANZANIA
Map page 56

National name: Jamhuri ya Muungano wa Tanzania/United Republic of Tanzania
Area: 945,000 sq km/364,864 sq mi
Capital: Dodoma (official), Dar es Salaam (administrative)
Major towns/cities: Zanzibar, Mwanza, Mbeya, Tanga, Morogoro
Major ports: (former capital) Dar es Salaam
Physical features: central plateau; lakes in north and west; coastal plains; lakes Victoria, Tanganyika, and Nyasa; half the country is forested; comprises islands of Zanzibar and Pemba; Mount Kilimanjaro, 5,895 m/19,340 ft, the highest peak in Africa; Olduvai Gorge; Ngorongoro Crater, 14.5 km/9 mi across, 762 m/2,500 ft deep
Currency: Tanzanian shilling
GNP per capita (PPP): (US$) 478 (1999)
Resources: diamonds, other gemstones, gold, salt, phosphates, coal, gypsum, tin, kaolin (exploration for petroleum in progress)
Population: 33,517,000 (2000 est)
Population density: (per sq km) 35 (1999 est)
Language: Kiswahili, English (both official), Arabic (in Zanzibar), many local languages
Religion: Muslim, Christian, traditional religions
Time difference: GMT +3

THAILAND
Map page 40

National name: Ratcha Anachak Thai/Kingdom of Thailand
Area: 513,115 sq km/198,113 sq mi
Capital: Bangkok (and chief port)
Major towns/cities: Chiang Mai, Hat Yai, Khon Kaen, Songkhla, Nakhon Ratchasima, Nonthaburi, Udon Thani
Major ports: Nakhon Sawan
Physical features: mountainous, semiarid plateau in northeast, fertile central region, tropical isthmus in south; rivers Chao Phraya, Mekong, and Salween
Currency: baht
GNP per capita (PPP): (US$) 5,599 (1999)
Resources: tin ore, lignite, gypsum, antimony, manganese, copper, tungsten, lead, gold, zinc, silver, rubies, sapphires, natural gas, petroleum, fish
Population: 61,399,000 (2000 est)
Population density: (per sq km) 119 (1999 est)
Language: Thai, Chinese (both official), English, Lao, Malay, Khmer
Religion: Buddhist 95%; Muslim 5%
Time difference: GMT +7

TOGO
Map page 54

National name: République Togolaise/Togolese Republic
Area: 56,800 sq km/21,930 sq mi
Capital: Lomé
Major towns/cities: Sokodé, Kpalimé, Kara, Atakpamé, Bassar, Tsévié
Physical features: two savannah plains, divided by range of hills northeast-southwest; coastal lagoons and marsh; Mono Tableland, Oti Plateau, Oti River
Currency: franc CFA
GNP per capita (PPP): (US$) 1,346 (1999 est)
Resources: phosphates, limestone, marble, deposits of iron ore, manganese, chromite, peat; exploration for petroleum and uranium was under way in the early 1990s
Population: 4,629,000 (2000 est)
Population density: (per sq km) 79 (1999 est)
Language: French (official), Ewe, Kabre, Gurma, other local languages
Religion: animist about 50%, Catholic and Protestant 35%, Muslim 15%
Time difference: GMT +/-0

TONGA
Map page 60

National name: Pule'anga Fakatu'i 'o Tonga/Kingdom of Tonga
Area: 750 sq km/290 sq mi
Capital: Nuku'alofa (on Tongatapu island)
Major towns/cities: Neiafu, Vaini
Physical features: three groups of islands in southwest Pacific, mostly coral formations, but actively volcanic in west; of the 170 islands in the Tonga group, 36 are inhabited
Currency: pa'anga, or Tongan dollar
GNP per capita (PPP): (US$) 4,281 (1999)
Population: 99,000 (2000 est)
Population density: (per sq km) 131 (1999 est)
Language: Tongan (official), English
Religion: mainly Free Wesleyan Church; Roman Catholic, Anglican
Time difference: GMT +13

TRINIDAD AND TOBAGO
Map page 72

National name: Republic of Trinidad and Tobago
Area: 5,130 sq km/1,980 sq mi (Trinidad 4,828 sq km/1,864 sq mi and Tobago 300 sq km/115 sq mi)
Capital: Port of Spain (and chief port)
Major towns/cities: San Fernando, Arima, Point Fortin
Major ports: Scarborough
Physical features: comprises two main islands and some smaller ones in Caribbean Sea; coastal swamps and hills east-west
Currency: Trinidad and Tobago dollar
GNP per capita (PPP): (US$) 7,262 (1999)
Resources: petroleum, natural gas, asphalt (world's largest deposits of natural asphalt)
Population: 1,295,000 (2000 est)
Population density: (per sq km) 251 (1999 est)
Language: English (official), Hindi, French, Spanish
Religion: Roman Catholic 33%, Hindu 25%, Anglican 15%, Muslim 6%, Presbyterian 4%
Time difference: GMT -4

TUNISIA
Map page 52

National name: Al-Jumhuriyya at-Tunisiyya/Tunisian Republic
Area: 164,150 sq km/63,378 sq mi
Capital: Tunis (and chief port)
Major towns/cities: Sfax, L'Ariana, Bizerte, Gabès, Sousse, Kairouan
Major ports: Sfax, Sousse, Bizerte
Physical features: arable and forested land in north graduates toward desert in south; fertile island of Jerba, linked to mainland by causeway (identified with island of lotus-eaters); Shott el Jerid salt lakes
Currency: Tunisian dinar
GNP per capita (PPP): (US$) 5,478 (1999)
Resources: petroleum, natural gas, phosphates, iron, zinc, lead, aluminum fluoride, fluorspar, sea salt
Population: 9,586,000 (2000 est)
Population density: (per sq km) 58 (1999 est est)
Language: Arabic (official), French
Religion: Sunni Muslim (state religion); Jewish and Christian minorities
Time difference: GMT +1

TURKEY
Map page 46

National name: Türkiye Cumhuriyeti/Republic of Turkey
Area: 779,500 sq km/300,964 sq mi

Capital: Ankara
Major towns/cities: İstanbul, İzmir, Adana, Bursa, Gaziantep, Konya, Mersin, Antalya, Diyarbakduringr
Major ports: İstanbul and İzmir
Physical features: central plateau surrounded by mountains, partly in Europe (Thrace) and partly in Asia (Anatolia); Bosporus and Dardanelles; Mount Ararat (highest peak Great Ararat, 5,137 m/16,854 ft); Taurus Mountains in southwest (highest peak Kaldi Dag, 3,734 m/12,255 ft); sources of rivers Euphrates and Tigris in east
Currency: Turkish lira
GNP per capita (PPP): (US$) 6,126 (1999)
Resources: chromium, copper, mercury, antimony, borax, coal, petroleum, natural gas, iron ore, salt
Population: 66,591,000 (2000 est)
Population density: (per sq km) 84 (1999 est)
Language: Turkish (official), Kurdish, Arabic
Religion: Sunni Muslim 99%; Orthodox, Armenian churches
Time difference: GMT +3

TURKMENISTAN
Map page 34

National name: Türkmenistan/ Turkmenistan
Area: 488,100 sq km/ 188,455 sq mi
Capital: Ashkhabad
Major towns/cities: Chardzhev, Mary, Nebitdag, Dashkhovuz, Turkmenbashi
Major ports: Turkmenbashi
Physical features: about 90% of land is desert including the Kara Kum 'Black Sands' desert (area 310,800 sq km/120,000 sq mi)
Currency: manat
GNP per capita (PPP): (US$) 3,099 (1999)
Resources: petroleum, natural gas, coal, sulfur, magnesium, iodine-bromine, sodium sulfate and different types of salt
Population: 4,459,000 (2000 est)
Population density: (per sq km) 9 (1999 est)
Language: Turkmen (a Turkic language; official), Russian, Uzbek, other regional languages
Religion: Sunni Muslim
Time difference: GMT +5

TUVALU
Map page 60

National name: Fakavae Aliki-Malo i Tuvalu/ Constitutional Monarchy of Tuvalu
Area: 25 sq km/9.6 sq mi
Capital: Fongafale (on Funafuti atoll)
Physical features: nine low coral atolls forming a chain of 579 km/650 mi in the Southwest Pacific
Currency: Australian dollar
GNP per capita (PPP): (US$) 970 (1998 est)
Population: 12,000 (2000 est)
Population density: (per sq km) 423 (1999 est)
Language: Tuvaluan, English (both official), a Gilbertese dialect (on Nui)
Religion: Protestant 96% (Church of Tuvalu)
Time difference: GMT +12

UGANDA
Map page 56

National name: Republic of Uganda
Area: 236,600 sq km/91,351 sq mi
Capital: Kampala
Major towns/cities: Jinja, Mbale, Entebbe, Masaka, Mbarara, Soroti
Physical features: plateau with mountains in west (Ruwenzori Range, with Mount Margherita, 5,110 m/16,765 ft); forest and

grassland; 18% is lakes, rivers, and wetlands (Owen Falls on White Nile where it leaves Lake Victoria; Lake Albert in west); arid in northwest
Currency: Ugandan new shilling
GNP per capita (PPP): (US$) 1,136 (1999 est)
Resources: copper, apatite, limestone; believed to possess the world's second-largest deposit of gold (hitherto unexploited); also reserves of magnetite, tin, tungsten, beryllium, bismuth, asbestos, graphite
Population: 21,778,000 (2000 est)
Population density: (per sq km) 89
Language: English (official), Kiswahili, other Bantu and Nilotic languages
Religion: Christian 65%, animist 20%, Muslim 15%
Time difference: GMT +3

UKRAINE
Map page 30

National name: Ukrayina/ Ukraine
Area: 603,700 sq km/ 233,088 sq mi
Capital: Kiev
Major towns/cities: Kharkiv, Donets'k, Dnipropetrovs'k, L'viv, Kryvyy Rih, Zaporizhzhya, Odessa
Physical features: Russian plain; Carpathian and Crimean Mountains; rivers: Dnieper (with the Dnieper dam 1932), Donetz, Bug
Currency: hryvna
GNP per capita (PPP): (US$) 3,142 (1999)
Resources: coal, iron ore (world's fifth-largest producer), crude oil, natural gas, salt, chemicals, brown coal, alabaster, gypsum
Population: 50,456,000 (2000 est)
Population density: (per sq km) 84 (1999 est)
Language: Ukrainian (a Slavonic language; official), Russian (also official in Crimea), other regional languages
Religion: traditionally Ukrainian Orthodox; also Ukrainian Catholic; small Protestant, Jewish, and Muslim communities
Time difference: GMT +2

UNITED ARAB EMIRATES
Map page 46

National name: Dawlat Imarat al-'Arabiyya al Muttahida/State of the Arab Emirates (UAE)
Area: 83,657 sq km/ 32,299 sq mi
Capital: Abu Dhabi
Major towns/cities: Dubai, Sharjah, Ra's al Khaymah, Ajmān, Al 'Ayn
Major ports: Dubai
Physical features: desert and flat coastal plain; mountains in east
Currency: UAE dirham
GNP per capita (PPP): (US$) 18,825 (1999 est)
Resources: petroleum and natural gas
Population: 2,441,000 (2000 est)
Population density: (per sq km) 29 (1999 est)
Language: Arabic (official), Farsi, Hindi, Urdu, English
Religion: Muslim 96% (of which 80% Sunni); Christian, Hindu
Time difference: GMT +4

UNITED KINGDOM
Map page 16

National name: United Kingdom of Great Britain and Northern Ireland (U.K.)
Area: 244,100 sq km/ 94,247 sq mi
Capital: London
Major towns/cities: Birmingham, Glasgow, Leeds, Sheffield, Liverpool, Manchester, Edinburgh, Bradford, Bristol, Coventry, Belfast, Cardiff

Major ports: London, Grimsby, Southampton, Liverpool
Physical features: became separated from European continent in about 6000 BC; rolling landscape, increasingly mountainous toward the north, with Grampian Mountains in Scotland, Pennines in northern England, Cambrian Mountains in Wales; rivers include Thames, Severn, and Spey
Territories: Anguilla, Bermuda, British Antarctic Territory, British Indian Ocean Territory, British Virgin Islands, Cayman Islands, Falkland Islands, Gibraltar, Montserrat, Pitcairn Islands, St. Helena and Dependencies (Ascension, Tristan da Cunha), South Georgia, South Sandwich Islands, Turks and Caicos Islands; the Channel Islands and the Isle of Man are not part of the U.K. but are direct dependencies of the crown
Currency: pound sterling
GNP per capita (PPP): (US$) 20,883 (1999)
Resources: coal, limestone, crude petroleum, natural gas, tin, iron, salt, sand and gravel
Population: 58,830,000 (2000 est)
Population density: (per sq km) 240 (1999 est)
Language: English (official), Welsh (also official in Wales), Gaelic
Religion: about 46% Church of England (established church); other Protestant denominations, Roman Catholic, Muslim, Jewish, Hindu, Sikh
Time difference: GMT +/-0

UNITED STATES OF AMERICA
Map page 70

National name: United States of America (U.S.A.)
Area: 9,372,615 sq km/ 3,618,766 sq mi
Capital: Washington, D.C.
Major towns/cities: New York, Los Angeles, Chicago, Philadelphia, Detroit, San Francisco, Dallas, San Diego, San Antonio, Houston, Boston, Phoenix, Indianapolis, Honolulu, San José
Physical features: topography and vegetation from tropical (Hawaii) to arctic (Alaska); mountain ranges parallel with east and west coasts; the Rocky Mountains separate rivers emptying into the Pacific from those flowing into the Gulf of Mexico; Great Lakes in north; rivers include Hudson, Mississippi, Missouri, Colorado, Columbia, Snake, Rio Grande, Ohio
Territories: the commonwealths of Puerto Rico and Northern Marianas; Guam, the U.S. Virgin Islands, American Samoa, Wake Island, Midway Islands, Johnston Atoll, Baker Island, Howland Island, Jarvis Island, Kingman Reef, Navassa Island, Palmyra Island
Currency: US dollar
GNP per capita (PPP): (US$) 30,600 (1999)
Resources: coal, copper (world's second-largest producer), iron, bauxite, mercury, silver, gold, nickel, zinc (world's fifth-largest producer), tungsten, uranium, phosphate, petroleum, natural gas, timber
Population: 278,357,000 (2000 est)
Population density: (per sq km) 29 (1999 est)
Language: English, Spanish
Religion: Protestant 58%; Roman Catholic 28%; atheist 10%; Jewish 2%; other 4% (1998)
Time difference: GMT -5-11

URUGUAY
Map page 78

National name: República Oriental del Uruguay/Eastern Republic of Uruguay
Area: 176,200 sq km/ 68,030 sq mi
Capital: Montevideo
Major towns/cities: Salto, Paysandú, Las Piedras, Rivera, Tacuarembó
Physical features: grassy plains (pampas) and low hills; rivers Negro, Uruguay, Río de la Plata
Currency: Uruguayan peso
GNP per capita (PPP): (US$) 8,280 (1999)
Resources: small-scale extraction of building materials, industrial minerals, semiprecious stones; gold deposits are being

developed
Population: 3,337,000 (2000 est)
Population density: (per sq km) 19 (1999 est)
Language: Spanish (official), Brazilero (a mixture of Spanish and Portuguese)
Religion: mainly Roman Catholic
Time difference: GMT -3

UZBEKISTAN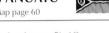
Map page 34

National name: Özbekiston Respublikasi/Republic of Uzbekistan
Area: 447,400 sq km/ 172,741 sq mi
Capital: Tashkent
Major towns/cities: Samarkand, Bukhara, Namangan, Andijon, Nukus, Karshi
Physical features: oases in deserts; rivers: Amu Darya, Syr Darya; Fergana Valley; rich in mineral deposits
Currency: som
GNP per capita (PPP): (US$) 2,092 (1999)
Resources: petroleum, natural gas, coal, gold (world's seventh-largest producer), silver, uranium (world's fourth-largest producer), copper, lead, zinc, tungsten
Population: 24,318,000 (2000 est)
Population density: (per sq km) 54 (1999 est)
Language: Uzbek (a Turkic language; official), Russian, Tajik
Religion: predominantly Sunni Muslim; small Wahhabi, Sufi, and Orthodox Christian communities
Time difference: GMT +5

VANUATU
Map page 60

National name: Ripablik blong Vanuatu/République de Vanuatu/Republic of Vanuatu
Area: 14,800 sq km/ 5,714 sq mi
Capital: Port-Vila (on Efate island) (and chief port)
Major towns/cities: Luganville (on Espíritu Santo)
Physical features: comprises around 70 inhabited islands, including Espíritu Santo, Malekula, and Efate; densely forested, mountainous; three active volcanoes; cyclones on average twice a year
Currency: vatu
GNP per capita (PPP): (US$) 2,771 (1999 est)
Resources: manganese; gold, copper, and large deposits of petroleum have been discovered but have hitherto remained unexploited
Population: 190,000 (2000 est)
Population density: (per sq km) 13 (1999 est)
Language: Bislama (82%), English, French (all official)
Religion: Christian 80%, animist about 8%
Time difference: GMT +11

VATICAN CITY STATE
Map page 24

National name: Stato della Città del Vaticano/Vatican City State
Area: 0.4 sq km/0.2 sq mi
Physical features: forms an enclave in the heart of Rome, Italy
Currency: Vatican City lira and Italian lira
GNP per capita (PPP): see Italy
Population: 1,000 (2000 est)
Population density: (per sq km) 2,500 (2000 est)
Language: Latin (official), Italian
Religion: Roman Catholic
Time difference: GMT +1

VENEZUELA
Map page 76

National name: República de Venezuela/Republic of Venezuela
Area: 912,100 sq km/ 352,161 sq mi
Capital: Caracas
Major towns/cities: Maracaibo, Maracay, Barquisimeto, Valencia, Ciudad Guayana, Petare
Major ports: Maracaibo
Physical features: Andes Mountains and Lake Maracaibo in northwest; central plains (llanos); delta of River Orinoco in east; Guiana Highlands in southeast
Currency: bolívar
GNP per capita (PPP): (US$) 5,268 (1999)
Resources: petroleum, natural gas, aluminum, iron ore, coal, diamonds, gold, zinc, copper, silver, lead, phosphates, manganese, titanium
Population: 24,170,000 (2000 est)
Population density: (per sq km) 26 (1999 est)
Language: Spanish (official), Indian languages (2%)
Religion: Roman Catholic 92%
Time difference: GMT -4

VIETNAM
Map page 40

National name: Công-hòa xã-hôi chu-nghia Viêt Nam/Socialist Republic of Vietnam
Area: 329,600 sq km/ 127,258 sq mi
Capital: Hanoi
Major towns/cities: Ho Chi Minh (formerly Saigon), Hai Phong, Da Nãng, Cân Tho, Nha Trang, Biên Hoa, Huê
Major ports: Ho Chi Minh (formerly Saigon), Da Nãng, Hai Phong
Physical features: Red River and Mekong deltas, center of cultivation and population; tropical rain forest; mountainous in north and northwest
Currency: dong
GNP per capita (PPP): (US$) 1,755 (1999)
Resources: petroleum, coal, tin, zinc, iron, antimony, chromium, phosphate, apatite, bauxite
Population: 79,832,000 (2000 est)
Population density: (per sq km) 237 (1999 est)
Language: Vietnamese (official), French, English, Khmer, Chinese, local languages
Religion: mainly Buddhist; Christian, mainly Roman Catholic (8-10%); Taoist, Confucian, Hos Hoa, and Cao Dai sects
Time difference: GMT +7

YEMEN
Map page 46

National name: Al-Jumhuriyya al Yamaniyya/Republic of Yemen
Area: 531,900 sq km/ 205,366 sq mi
Capital: Şan'ã
Major towns/cities: Aden, Ta'izz, Al Mukallã, Al Ḥudaydah, Ibb, Dhamãr
Major ports: Aden
Physical features: hot, moist coastal plain, rising to plateau and desert
Currency: riyal
GNP per capita (PPP): (US$) 688 (1999)
Resources: petroleum, natural gas, gypsum, salt; deposits of copper, gold, lead, zinc, molybdenum
Population: 18,112,000 (2000 est)
Population density: (per sq km) 33 (1999 est)
Language: Arabic (official)
Religion: Sunni Muslim 63%, Shiite Muslim 37%
Time difference: GMT +3

YUGOSLAVIA
Map page 26

National name: Savezna Republika Jugoslavija/Federal Republic of Yugoslavia
Area: 58,300 sq km/ 22,509 sq mi
Capital: Belgrade
Major towns/cities: Priština, Novi Sad, Niš, Kragujevac, Podgorica (formerly Titograd), Subotica
Physical features: federation of republics of Serbia and Montenegro and two former autonomous provinces, Kosovo and Vojvodina
Currency: new Yugoslav dinar
GNP per capita (PPP): (US$) 5,880 (1997 est)
Resources: petroleum, natural gas, coal, copper ore, bauxite, iron ore, lead, zinc
Population: 10,640,000 (2000 est)
Population density: (per sq km) 182 (1999 est)
Language: Serbo-Croat (official), Albanian (in Kosovo)
Religion: Serbian and Montenegrin Orthodox; Muslim in southern Serbia
Time difference: GMT +1

ZAMBIA
Map page 58

National name: Republic of Zambia
Area: 752,600 sq km/ 290,578 sq mi
Capital: Lusaka
Major towns/cities: Kitwe, Ndola, Kabwe, Mufulira, Chingola, Luanshya, Livingstone
Physical features: forested plateau cut through by rivers; Zambezi River, Victoria Falls, Kariba Dam
Currency: Zambian kwacha
GNP per capita (PPP): (US$) 686 (1999)
Resources: copper (world's fourth-largest producer), cobalt, zinc, lead, coal, gold, emeralds, amethysts and other gemstones, limestone, selenium
Population: 9,169,000 (2000 est)
Population density: (per sq km) 12 (1999 est)
Language: English (official), Bantu languages
Religion: about 64% Christian, animist, Hindu, Muslim
Time difference: GMT +2

ZIMBABWE
Map page 58

National name: Republic of Zimbabwe
Area: 390,300 sq km/ 150,694 sq mi
Capital: Harare
Major towns/cities: Bulawayo, Gweru, Kwekwe, Mutare, Kadoma, Chitungwiza
Physical features: high plateau with central high veld and mountains in east; rivers Zambezi, Limpopo; Victoria Falls
Currency: Zimbabwe dollar
GNP per capita (PPP): (US$) 2,470 (1999)
Resources: gold, nickel, asbestos, coal, chromium, copper, silver, emeralds, lithium, tin, iron ore, cobalt
Population: 11,669,000 (2000 est)
Population density: (per sq km) 30 (1999 est)
Language: English, Shona, Ndebele (all official)
Religion: 50% follow a syncretic (part Christian, part indigenous beliefs) type of religion, Christian 25%, animist 24%, small Muslim minority
Time difference: GMT +2

Index

HOW TO USE THE INDEX

This is an alphabetically arranged index of the places and features that can be found on the maps in this atlas. Each name is generally indexed to the largest scale map on which it appears. If that map covers a double page, the name will always be indexed by the left-hand page number.

Names composed of two or more words are alphabetized as if they were one word.

All names appear in full in the index, except for 'St.' and 'Ste.', which, although abbreviated, are indexed as though spelled in full.

Where two or more places have the same name, they can be distinguished from each other by the country or province name that immediately follows the entry. These names are indexed in the alphabetical order of the country or province.

Alternative names, such as English translations, can also be found in the index and are cross-referenced to the map form by the '=' sign. In these cases the names also appear in brackets on the maps.

Settlements are indexed to the position of the symbol; all other features are indexed to the position of the name on the map.

Abbreviations used in this index are explained in the list opposite.

FINDING A NAME ON THE MAP

Each index entry contains the name, followed by a symbol indicating the feature type (for example, settlement, river), a page reference, and a grid reference:

The grid reference locates a place or feature within a rectangle formed by the network of lines of longitude and latitude. A name can be found by referring to the letters and numbers placed around the maps. First find the letter, which appears along the top and bottom of the map, and then the number, down the sides. The name will be found within the rectangle uniquely defined by that letter and number. A number in brackets preceding the grid reference indicates that the name is to be found within an inset map.

SYMBOLS

✕	Continent name	↗	River, canal
Ⓐ	Country name	⬗	Lake, salt lake
a	State or province name	▻	Gulf, strait, bay
◼	Country capital	◣	Sea, ocean
▣	State or province capital	▭	Cape, point
●	Settlement	◦◦	Island or island group, rocky or coral reef
▲	Mountain, volcano, peak		
▲▲	Mountain range	✳	Place of interest
⬭	Physical region or feature	ℋ	Historical or cultural region

A

Aachen 14 J4
Aalen 12 F8
Aalst 14 G4
Aarau 22 D3
Aare 22 C3
Aarschot 14 G4
Aba 54 F3
Abādān 46 E3
Abadla 52 E2
Abaji 54 F3
Abakaliki 54 F3
Abakan 34 S7
Abancay 76 C6
Abano Terme 22 G5
Abashiri 38 L2
Abava 8 M8
Ābaya Hāyk' 56 F2
Abay Wenz 50 G5
Abbeville 14 D4
Abd al Kūrī 46 F7
Abéché 50 D5
Abengourou 54 D3
Abenójar 20 F6
Åbenrå 12 E1
Abensberg 12 G8
Abeokuta 54 E3
Aberaeron 16 H9
Aberdeen, *S.A.* 58 C6
Aberdeen, *U.K.* 16 K4
Aberdeen, *S.D., U.S.* 70 G2
Aberdeen, *Wash.,U.S.* 70 B2
Aberdeen Lake 68 M4
Aberystwyth 16 H9
Abez' 30 M1
Abhā 50 H4
Abidjan 54 D3
Abilene 70 G5
Abingdon 14 A3
Abnūb 50 F2
Aboisso 54 D3
Abomey 54 E3
Abong Mbang 54 G4
Abou Déia 50 C5
Abrantes 20 B5
Abrud 26 L3
Absaroka Range 70 D2
Abu Ballâs 50 E3
Abu Dhabi = Abū Ẓabī 46 G5
Abu Hamed 50 F4
Abuja 54 F3
Abumombazi 56 C3
Ābune Yosēf 50 G5
Abū Nujaym 50 C1
Abū Qarin 50 C1
Aburo 56 E3
Abu Simbel 50 F3
Abut Head 64 B6
Abuye Meda 56 F1
Abū Ẓabī 46 G5
Acaponeta 70 E7
Acapulco 72 E5
Acará 76 H4
Acarigua 76 D2
Accra 54 D3
Achaguas 72 L7
Achayvayam 36 W4
Acheng 38 H1
Achenkirch 22 G3
Achen See 22 G3
Achill Island 16 B8
Achim 12 E3
Achinsk 34 S6
Achit 30 L3
Aci Göl 28 M7
A Cihanbeyli 28 Q6
Acireale 24 K11
Acklins Island 72 K4
Aconcagua 74 D7
Açores 52 (1)B2
A Coruña 20 B1
Acquarossa 22 D4
Acqui Terme 22 D6
Acre 76 C5
Acri 24 L9
Ada 10 K12
Adam 46 G5
Adamas 28 G8
Adams Island 64 (2)B1
'Adan 46 E7
Adana 46 C2
Adda 22 E5
Ad Dahnā 46 E4
Ad Dakhla 52 B4
Ad Dammām 46 F4
Ad Dawādimī 46 D5
Ad Dawḩah 46 F4
Addis Ababa =
Ādīs Ābeba 56 F2
Ad Dīwānīyah 46 D3
Adelaide 62 G6
Adelaide Peninsula 68 M3
Adelaide River 62 F2
Aden = Adan 46 E7
Aderbissinat 54 F1
Adi 43 D3
Adige 22 G5
Ādīgrat 50 G5
Adilabad 44 C5
Adīrī 50 B2
Ādīs Ābeba 56 F2
Adi Ugri 50 G5
Adıyaman 46 C2
Adjud 26 Q3
Admiralty Island 68 E5
Admiralty Islands 60 E6
Adoni 44 C5
Adour 18 F10
Adra 20 H8
Adrano 24 J11
Adrar 52 E3
Adrar des Ifôghas 52 F5
Adrar Tamgak 52 G5
Adria 22 H5
Adriatic Sea 24 H4
Adycha 36 P3
Adygeya 30 H6
Adzopé 54 D3
Adz'vavom 30 L1
Aegean Sea 28 H5
A Estrada 20 B2
Afghanistan 46 H3
Afgooye 56 H3
'Afif 50 H3
Afikpo 54 F3
Afmadow 56 G3
A Fonsagrada 20 C1
Afragola 24 J8
Africa 48 F5
Afuá 76 G4
Afyon 28 N6
Agadez 52 G5
Agadir 52 D2
Agadyr' 34 N8
Agalega Islands 48 J7
Agan 36 B4
Āgaro 56 F2
Agartala 44 F4
Agathonisi 28 J7
Agattu Island 36 W6
Agde 18 J10
Agen 18 F9
Agia Triada 28 D7
Aginskoye 34 S6
Agiokampos 28 E5
Agios Efstratios 28 H5
Agios Georgios 28 F7
Agios Nikolaos 28 H9
Agnibilekrou 54 D3
Agnita 26 M4
Agra 44 C3
Ağri 46 D2
Agri 24 L8
Agrigento 24 H11
Agrinio 28 D6
Agropoli 24 K8
Agryz 30 K3
Agua Prieta 70 E5
Aguascalientes 72 D4
A Gudiña 20 C2
Aguelhok 52 F5
Águilas 20 J7
Agulhas Negras 76 H8
Ağva 28 M3
Ahar 46 E2
Ahaura 64 C6
Ahaus 14 K2
Ahititi 64 E4
Ahlen 14 K3
Ahmadabad 44 B4
Ahmadnagar 44 B5
Ahmadpur East 44 B3
Ahr 12 B6
Ahrensburg 12 F3
Ahvāz 46 E3
Aichach 12 G8
Aigialousa 28 S9
Aigina 28 F7
Aigina 28 F7
Aigio 28 E6
Aigosthena 28 F6
Aiguillon 18 F9
Aihui 36 M6
Aim 36 N5
Ain 18 L7
Aïn Beïda 52 G1
'Aïn Ben Tili 52 D3
Aïn Bessem 20 P8
Aïn el Hadjel 20 P9
Ain Oussera 52 F1
Ainsa 20 L2
Aïn Sefra 52 E2
Ain Taya 20 P8
Aïn-Tédélès 20 L8
Aïn Témouchent 20 J9
Airão 76 E4
Aire 16 L8
Air Force Island 68 S3
Airolo 22 D4
Airpanas 43 C4
Aisne 14 F5
Aitape 43 F3
Aitutaki 60 K7
Aiud 26 L3
Aix-en-Provence 18 L10
Aix-les-Bains 18 L8
Aizawl 44 F4
Aizkraukle 8 N8
Aizpute 8 L8
Ajaccio 24 C7
Aj Bogd Uul 38 B2
Ajdābiyā 50 D1
Ajka 10 G10
Ajmer 44 B3
Ajtos 26 Q7
Akaroa 64 D6
Akasha 50 F3
Akbalyk 34 P8
Akbasty 34 L8
Akçakoca 28 P3
Aken 12 H5
Aketi 56 C3
Akhisar 28 K6
Akhmîm 50 F2
Akimiski Island 68 Q6
Akita 38 L3
Akjoujt 52 C5
Akka 52 D3
Akkajaure 8 J3
Akmeqit 46 L2
Akobo 56 E2
Akola 44 C4
Akonolinga 54 G4
Akordat 50 G4
Akpatok Island 68 T4
Akqi 34 P9
Akra Drepano 28 G5
Akranes 8 (1)B2
Akra Sounio 28 F7
Akra Spatha 28 F9
Akra Trypiti 28 G9
Åkrehamn 8 C7
Akron 70 K3
Aksaray 28 R6
Aksarka 34 M4
Akşehir 28 P6
Akseki 28 P7
Aksha 36 J6
Akshiy 34 P9
Aksu 34 Q9
Aksuat 34 Q8
Āksum 50 G5
Aktau, *Kazakhstan* 6 K3
Aktau, *Kazakhstan* 34 N7
Aktogay, *Kazakhstan* 34 N8
Aktogay, *Kazakhstan* 34 P8
Aktuma 34 M8
Aktyubinsk 30 L4
Akula 56 C3
Akulivik 68 R4
Akune 38 J4
Akure 54 F3
Akureyri 8 (1)E2
Akwanga 54 F3
Alabama 70 J5
Alaejos 20 E3
Alagoas 76 K5
Alagoinhas 76 K6
Alagón 20 J3
Al 'Amārah 46 E3
Alaminos 40 F3
Åland 8 K6
Alanya 28 Q8
Alappuzha 44 C7
Al Argoub 52 B4
Al Arṭāwīyah 46 E4
Alaşehir 28 L6
Al 'Ashurīyah 50 H1
Alaska 66 S3
Alaska Range 66 R3
Alassio 22 D6
Alatri 24 H7
Alatyr' 30 J4
Alavus 8 M5
Al 'Ayn 46 G5
Alazeya 36 S2
Alba, *It.* 22 D6
Alba, *Spain* 20 E4
Albacete 20 J5
Alba Iulia 26 L3
Albania 28 B3
Albany 68 Q6
Albany, *Aus.* 62 C6
Albany, *Ga., U.S.* 70 K5
Albany, *N.Y., U.S.* 70 M3
Albany, *Oreg., U.S.* 70 B3
Albardão do João
Maria 78 L4
Al Bardī 50 D1
Al Başrah 46 E3
Albatross Bay 62 H2
Albatross Point 64 E4
Al Bayḑā' 50 D1
Albenga 22 D6
Albert 14 E4
Alberta 68 H6
Albertirsa 10 J10
Albert Kanaal 14 G3
Albert Lea 70 H3
Albert Nile 56 E3
Albertville 18 M8
Albi 18 H10
Albina 76 G2
Albino 22 E5
Ålborg 8 E8
Ålborg Bugt 8 F8
Albox 20 H7
Albstadt 12 E8
Albufeira 20 B7
Al Bū Kamāl 46 D3
Albuquerque 70 E4
Al Buraymī 46 G5
Alburquerque 20 D5
Albury 62 J7
Al Buşayyah 50 G1
Alcácer do Sal 20 B6
Alcala de Guadaira 20 E7
Alcala de Henares 20 G4
Alcalá la Real 20 G7
Alcamo 24 G11
Alcañiz 20 K3
Alcantarilla 20 J7
Alcaraz 20 H6
Alcaudete 20 F7
Alcazar de San Juan 20 G5
Alcobendas 20 G4
Alcoi 20 K6
Alcolea del Pinar 20 H3
Alcorcón 20 G4
Alcoutim 20 C7
Aldabra Islands 58 (2)A2
Aldan 36 M5
Aldan 36 N5
Aldeburgh 14 D2
Alderney 18 C4
Aldershot 14 B3
Aleg 52 C5
Aleksandrov-
Sakhalinskiy 36 Q6
Aleksandrovskiy
Zavod 36 K6
Aleksandrovskoye 30 Q2
Alekseyevka 34 N7
Aleksinac 26 J6
Alençon 18 F5
Aleppo = Ḩalab 46 C2
Aléria 24 D6
Alès 18 K9
Aleşd 10 M10
Alessandria 22 D6
Ålesund 8 D5
Aleutian Islands 66 T4
Aleutian Trench 32 W5
Alexander Archipelago 68 D5
Alexander Bay 58 B5
Alexandra 64 B7
Alexandreia 28 E4
Alexandria =
El Iskandarîya,
Egypt 50 E1
Alexandria, *Romania* 26 N6
Alexandria, *La., U.S.* 70 H5
Alexandria, *Va., U.S.* 70 L4
Alexandroupoli 28 H4
Alexis Creek 68 G6
Aley 34 Q7
Aleysk 34 Q7
Alfeld 12 E5
Alföld 26 H2
Alfonsine 22 H6
Alfreton 14 A1
Al Fuḩayḩil 46 E4
Al-Fujayrah 46 G4
Algeciras 20 E8
Algemes 20 K5
Algena 50 G4
Alger 52 F1
Algeria 52 E3
Al Ghayḑah 46 F6
Alghero 24 C8
Algiers = Alger 52 F1
Al Hadīthah 46 C3
Alhama de Murcia 20 J7
Al Ḩammādah al
Ḩamrā' 52 G3
Al Harūj al Aswad 50 C2
Al Ḩasakah 46 D2
Alhaurmín el Grande 20 F8
Al Ḩijāz 50 G2
Al Ḩillah 46 D3
Al Hoceima 52 E1
Al Ḩudaydah 50 H5
Al Hufūf 46 E4
Al Ḩumayḑah 46 C4
Aliağa 28 J6
Aliakmonas 28 E4
Äli Bayramlı 46 E2
Alicante 20 K6
Alice 70 G6
Alice Springs 62 F4
Alicudi 24 J10
Aligarh 44 C3
Alindao 56 C2
Alingås 8 G8
Aliwal North 58 D6
Al Jabal al Akhḑar 50 D1
Al Jaghbūb 50 D2
Al Jālamīd 50 G1
Al Jarah 46 E4
Al Jawf, *Libya* 50 D3
Al Jawf, *Saudi Arabia* 50 G2
Aljezur 20 B7
Al Jubayl 46 E4
Aljustrel 20 B7
Al Kāmil 46 G5
Al Kharj 46 E5
Al Khaşab 46 G4
Al Khawr 46 F4
Al Khufrah 50 D3
Al Khums 52 H2
Alkmaar 14 G2
Al Kūt 46 E3
Al Kuwayt 46 E4
Al Lādhiqīyah 46 C2
Allahabad 44 D3
Allakh-Yun' 36 P4
Alldays 58 D4
Allen 40 G4
Allentown 70 L3
Aller 12 E4
Aller = Cabañaquinta 20 E1
Alliance 70 F3
Allier 18 J8
Allinge 10 D2
Al Lith 50 H3
Almada 20 A6
Almadén 20 F6
Al Madīnah 50 G3
Al Mahbas 52 D3
Al Majma'ah 46 E4
Almalyk 34 M9
Al Manāmah 46 F4
Almansa 20 J6
Al Marj 50 D1
Almaty 34 P9
Al Mawşil 46 D2
Al Mazāḩimīyah 50 J3
Almazán 20 H3
Almeirim 76 G4
Almelo 14 J2
Almendralejo 20 D6
Almería 20 H8
Al'met'yevsk 34 J7
Almiros 28 E5
Almonte 20 D7
Almora 44 C3
Al Mubarraz 46 E4
Al Mukallā 46 E7
Al Mukhā 50 H5
Almuñécar 20 G8
Alnwick 16 L6
Alonnisos 28 F5
Alor 43 B4
Alor Setar 40 C5
Alotau 62 K2
Alpena 70 K3
Alphen 14 G2
Alpi Lepontine 22 D4
Alpi Orobie 22 E4
Alps 22 B5
Al Qalībah 50 G2
Al Qāmishlī 46 D2
Al Qaryāt 50 B1
Al Qaṭrūn 50 B3
Al Qunfudhah 50 H4
Al Qurayyāt 50 G1
Als 12 E1
Alsask 68 K6
Alsasua 20 H2
Alsfeld 12 E6
Alta 8 M2
Altaelva 8 M2
Altai Mountains 38 A1
Al Tamīnī 50 D1
Altamira 76 G4
Altamura 24 L8
Altanbulag 36 H6
Altay 34 R7
Altay, *China* 34 R8
Altay, *Mongolia* 38 B1
Altdorf 22 D4
Alte Mellum 12 D3
Altenberg 12 J6
Altenburg 12 H6
Altenkirchen 12 J2
Altkirch 22 C3
Alto Garças 76 G7
Alto Molócuè 58 F3
Altoona 70 L3
Alto Parnaíba 76 H5
Altötting 22 H2
Altun Shan 34 S10
Altus 70 G5
Al 'Ubaylah 46 F5
Alūksne 8 P8
Al 'Uqaylah 50 C1
Al 'Uwaynāt, *Libya* 50 B2
Al 'Uwaynāt, *Libya* 50 D3
Al 'Uwayqīlah 50 H1
Alvarães 76 E4
Älvdalen 8 H6
Älvsbyn 8 L4
Al Wajh 50 G2
Alwar 44 C3
Al Wari'ah 46 E4
Alxa Zouqi 38 D3
Alytus 10 P3
Alzey 12 D7
Alzira 20 K5
Amadi 56 E2
Amadjuak Lake 68 S4
Amadora 20 A6
Amahai 43 C3
Amaliada 28 D7
Amalner 44 C4
Amamapare 43 E3
Amambaí 78 K3
Amami-Ōshima 32 S7
Amanab 43 F3
Amandola 24 H6
Amantea 24 L9
Amapá 76 G3
Amapá 76 G3
Amarante 76 J5
Amarapura 40 B2
Amareleja 20 C6
Amarillo 70 F4
Amasya 46 C1
Amay 14 H4
Amazar 36 L6
Amazon = Amazonas 74 F4
Amazonas 76 D4
Amazonas 76 E4
Ambala 44 C2
Ambanjā 58 H2
Ambarchik 36 U3
Ambato 76 B4
Ambato Boeny 58 H3
Ambatondrazaka 58 H3
Amberg 12 G7
Ambikapur 44 D4
Ambilobe 58 H2
Ambohimahasoa 58 H4
Amboise 18 G6
Ambon 43 C3
Ambositra 58 H4
Ambovombe 58 H5
Amderma 34 L4
Amdo 44 F2
Ameland 14 H1
Amengel'dy 34 M7
American Samoa 60 J7
Amersfoort 14 H2
Amery 68 N5
Amery Ice Shelf 80 (2)M2
Ames 70 H3
Amfilochia 28 D6
Amfissa 28 E6
Amga 36 L5
Amga 36 N4
Amguid 52 G3
Amgun' 36 P6
Amherst 68 U7
Amiens 14 E5
Amirante Islands 58 (2)B2
Amlekhganj 44 D3
Åmli 8 E7
'Amm Adam 50 G4
'Ammān 46 C3
Ammassalik 68 Z3
Ammerland 14 K1
Ammersee 22 F2
Ammochostos 28 R9
Amo 40 C2
Amol 46 F2
Amorgos 28 H8
Amos 70 L2
Amourj 52 D5
Ampana 43 B3
Ampanihy 58 G4
Amparai 44 D7
Ampezzo 22 H4
Amposta 20 L4
Amrān 46 D6
Amravati 44 C4
Amritsar 44 B2
Amroha 44 C3
Amrum 12 D2
Amsterdam 14 G2
Amstetten 22 K2
Am Timan 50 D5
Amudar'ya 34 L9
Amundsen Gulf 68 G2
Amundsen Sea 80 (2)GG3
Amungen 8 H6
Amuntai 42 F3
Amur 36 P6
Amursk 36 P6
Amvrakikos Kolpos 28 C6
Anabanua 43 B3
Anabar 36 J2
Anaconda 70 D2
Anadolu Dağları 46 C1
Anadyr' 36 X4
Anadyrskaya
Nizmennost' 36 X3
Anadyrskiy Zaliv 36 Y3
Anafi 28 H8
'Ānah 46 D3
Analalava 58 H2
Anamur 28 Q8
Anantapur 44 C6
Anan'yiv 26 T2
Anapa 30 G6
Anápolis 76 H7
Anār 46 G3
Anārak 46 F3
Anardara 46 H3
Anatolia 28 M6
Añatuya 78 J4
Anchorage 66 R3
Ancona 24 H5
Ancud 78 G7
Anda 38 H1
Andalgalá 78 H4
Åndalsnes 8 D5
Andaman Islands 40 A4
Andaman Sea 40 A4
Andapa 58 H2
Andarāb 46 J2
Andenne 14 H4
Andéramboukane 54 E1
Andermatt 22 D4
Andernach 14 K4
Anderson 68 F3
Andes 74 D5
Andfjorden 8 J2
Andilamena 58 H3
Andipsara 28 H6
Andizhan 34 N9
Andkhvoy 46 J2
Andoas 76 B4
Andong 38 H3
Andorra 20 L2
Andorra la Vella 20 M2
Andover 14 A3
Andøya 8 H2
Andradina 78 L3
Andria 24 L7
Andriamena 58 H3
Andros 28 G7
Andros, *Greece* 28 G7
Andros,
The Bahamas 72 J4
Andrott 44 B6
Andrychów 10 J8
Andújar 20 F6
Andulo 58 B2
Aneto 20 L2
Angara 36 G5
Angarsk 36 G6
Ånge 8 H5
Angel de la Guarda 70 D6
Angeles 40 G3
Ängelholm 8 G8
Angeln 12 E2
Angermünde 12 K4
Angern 22 M2
Angers 18 E6
Anglesey 16 H8
Angmagssalik =
Ammassalik 68 Z3
Ango 56 D3
Angoche 58 F3
Angol 78 G6
Angola 48 E7
Angoulême 18 F8
Angren 34 M9
Anguilla 72 M5
Anina 26 J4
Ankang 38 D4
Ankara 28 Q5
Ankazoabo 58 G4
Anklam 12 J3
Ankpa 54 F3
Ånn 8 G5
Anna 30 H4
Annaba 52 G1
Annaberg Buchholz 12 H6
An Nafud 50 G2
An Nāirīyah 46 E3
An Najaf 46 D3
Annapolis 70 L4
Annapurna 44 D3
Ann Arbor 70 K3
An Nāşirīyah 50 J1
Annecy 22 B5
Annemasse 22 B4
Anniston 70 J5
Annobón 54 F5
Annonay 18 K8
An Nukhayb 46 D3
Anqing 38 F4
Ansbach 12 F7
Anshan 38 G2
Anshun 38 D5
Ansongo 52 F5
Antakya 46 C2
Antalaha 58 J2
Antalya 28 N8
Antalya Körfezi 28 N8
Antananarivo 58 H3
Antarctic Peninsula 80 (2)LL3
Antequera 20 F7
Anti-Atlas 52 D3
Antibes 22 C7
Antigua 72 M5
Antigua and Barbuda 72 M5
Antikythira 28 F9
Antiparos 28 G7
Antipaxoi 28 C5
Antipayuta 34 P4
Antipodes Islands 64 (3)A1
Antofagasta 78 G3
Antrim 16 F7
Antropovo 30 H3
Antsalova 58 G3
Antsirabe 58 H3

Name	Page	Grid
Bansko	28	F3
Bantry	16	C10
Banyo	54	G3
Banyoles	20	N2
Banyuwangi	42	E4
Baode	38	E3
Baoding	38	F3
Baoji	38	D4
Bao Lôc	40	D4
Baoro	56	B2
Baoshan	40	B1
Baotou	38	E2
Baoying	38	F4
Bap	44	B3
Bapaume	14	E4
Ba'qūbah	46	D3
Baquedano	78	H3
Bar	26	G7
Barabai	42	F3
Barakaldo	20	H1
Baramati	44	B5
Baramula	44	B2
Baran	44	C3
Baranavichy	30	E4
Baraolt	26	N3
Barbados	76	F1
Barbastro	20	L2
Barbate	20	E8
Barbuda	72	M5
Barcaldine	62	J4
Barcellona Pozzo di Gotto	24	K10
Barcelona, Spain	20	N3
Barcelona, Venezuela	72	M6
Barcelos, Brazil	76	E4
Barcelos, Spain	20	B3
Barclayville	54	C4
Barco de Valdeorras = O Barco	20	D2
Barcs	26	E4
Bardai	50	C3
Barddhamān	44	E4
Bardejov	10	L8
Bardonecchia	22	B5
Bareilly	44	C3
Barentin	14	C5
Barents Sea	34	E3
Barentu	50	G4
Bareo	42	F2
Barga	44	D2
Bargaal	56	J1
Bargteheide	12	F3
Barguzin	36	H6
Bari	24	L7
Barikot	44	B1
Barinas	76	C2
Bârîs	50	F3
Barisal	44	F4
Barito	43	A3
Barkam	38	C4
Barkava	8	P3
Barkly Tableland	62	F3
Barkol	34	S9
Bârlad	26	Q3
Bârlad	26	Q3
Bar-le-Duc	14	H6
Barletta	24	L7
Barmer	44	B3
Barmouth Bay	16	H9
Barnaul	34	Q7
Barnsley	16	L8
Barnstaple	16	H10
Barnstaple Bay	16	H10
Barpeta	44	F3
Barquisimeto	76	D1
Barr	22	C2
Barra, Brazil	76	J6
Barra, U.K.	16	E4
Barracão do Barreto	76	G5
Barracas	20	K5
Barra do Bugres	76	F7
Barra do Corda	76	H5
Barra do Cuanza	56	A5
Barra do Garças	76	G7
Barra do São Manuel	76	G5
Barragem de Santa Clara	20	B7
Barragem de Sobradinho	76	J5
Barragem do Castelo de Bode	20	B5
Barragem do Maranhão	20	C6
Barranca, Peru	76	B4
Barranca, Peru	76	B6
Barranquilla	72	K6
Barreiras	76	H6
Barreiro	20	A6
Barretos	76	H8
Barrie	70	L3
Barrow Creek	62	F4
Barrow-in-Furness	16	J7
Barrow Island	62	B4
Barrow Strait	68	N2
Barshatas	34	P8
Barsi	44	C5
Bar-sur-Aube	18	K5
Bar-sur-Seine	18	K5
Barth	12	H2
Bartın	28	Q3
Bartle Frere	60	E7
Bartlesville	70	G4
Bartoszyce	10	K3
Barus	42	C2
Baruun Urt	38	E1
Barwani	44	B4
Barysaw	30	E4
Basankusu	56	B3
Basarabeasca	26	R3
Basarabi	26	R5
Basco	24	G2
Basel	22	C3
Bashkiria	30	K4
Basilan	43	B1
Basildon	14	C3
Basiluzzo	24	K10
Basingstoke	16	L10
Başkale	46	D2
Basoko	56	C3
Bassano	70	D1
Bassano del Grappa	22	G5
Bassar	54	E3
Bassas da India	58	F4
Bassein	40	A3
Basse Santa Su	52	C6
Basse-Terre	72	M5
Bassikounou	52	D5
Bass Strait	62	H7
Bassum	12	D4
Bastak	46	F4
Basti	44	D3
Bastia	24	D6
Bastogne	14	H4
Batagai	36	N3
Batagay-Alyta	36	N3
Batak	28	G3
Batamay	36	M4
Batang	38	B5
Batangas	40	G4
Batan Islands	40	G2
Batanta	43	C3
Batchelor	62	F2
Batemans Bay	62	K7
Bath	16	K10
Bathinda	44	B2
Bathurst, Aus.	62	J6
Bathurst, Can.	68	T7
Bathurst Inlet	68	K3
Bathurst Island, Aus.	62	E2
Bathurst Island, Can.	68	M2
Batman	46	D2
Batna	52	G1
Baton Rouge	70	H5
Bátonyterenye	26	G2
Batouri	54	G4
Batticaloa	44	D7
Battipaglia	24	J8
Battle	68	J6
Battle Harbour	68	V6
Batu	56	F2
Batui	43	B3
Bat'umi	46	D1
Batu Pahat	42	C2
Baturino	34	R6
Baubau	43	B4
Bauchi	54	F2
Baukau	43	C4
Baume-les-Dames	18	M6
Bauru	78	M3
Bauska	8	N8
Bautzen	12	H3
Bawean	42	E4
Bawiti	50	E2
Bawku	54	D2
Bayamo	72	J4
Bayanaul	34	P7
Bayandelger	36	H7
Bayan Har Shan	38	B4
Bayanhongor	38	C1
Bayan Mod	38	C2
Bayan Obo	38	D2
Bayansumküre	34	Q9
Bay City	70	K3
Baydhabo	56	G3
Bayerische Alpen	22	G3
Bayeux	14	B5
Bayindir	28	K6
Baykit	34	T5
Baykonur	34	M8
Bay of Bengal	44	E5
Bay of Biscay	18	C9
Bay of Fundy	68	T3
Bay of Islands	64	E2
Bay of Plenty	64	F3
Bayonne	18	D10
Bayramaly	46	H2
Bayramiç	28	J5
Bayreuth	12	G7
Baysun	46	J2
Bayt al Faqīh	50	H5
Bay View	64	F4
Baza	20	H7
Bazas	18	E9
Beachy Head	14	C4
Beagle Gulf	62	E2
Bealanana	58	H2
Bear Island = Bjørnøya, Norway	34	B3
Bear Island, Rep. of I.	16	B10
Beas de Segura	20	H6
Beaufort	42	F1
Beaufort Sea	66	Q2
Beaufort West	58	C6
Beaumont, N.Z.	64	B7
Beaumont, U.S.	70	H5
Beaune	18	K6
Beauvais	14	E5
Beaver Creek	68	C4
Beawar	44	B3
Beazley	78	H5
Bebra	12	E6
Bečej	26	H4
Béchar	52	E2
Beckley	70	K4
Becks	64	B7
Beckum	12	L3
Beclean	26	M2
Bedelē	56	F2
Bedford	16	M9
Bedworth	14	A2
Beenleigh	62	K5
Be'ér Sheva'	46	B3
Beeville	70	G6
Bei'an	36	M7
Beihai	40	D2
Beijing	38	F3
Beipan	38	D5
Beipiao	38	G2
Beira	58	E3
Beirut = Beyrouth	46	C3
Beiuş	26	K3
Béja	52	G1
Bejaïa	52	G1
Béjar	20	E4
Bekdash	46	F1
Békés	10	L11
Békéscsaba	26	J3
Bekily	58	H4
Bela	46	J4
Bela Crkva	26	J5
Belaga	42	E2
Belarus	6	G2
Bela Vista	58	E5
Belaya	30	K3
Belaya Gora	36	R3
Bełchatów	10	J6
Belcher Islands	68	Q5
Beledweyne	56	H3
Belek	30	J10
Belém	76	C2
Belen	70	C1
Belfast	16	G7
Belfort	22	B3
Belgaum	34	T7
Belgium	14	G4
Belgorod	30	M4
Belgrade = Beograd	26	H5
Beli	30	G2
Belice	26	F4
Belinyu	42	D3
Belitung	42	D3
Belize	72	G5
Belize	72	G5
Bellac	18	G7
Bella Coola	68	F6
Bellary	44	C5
Belle Fourche	70	F3
Belle Île	18	B6
Belle Isle	68	V6
Bellême	18	F5
Belleville	70	L3
Bellingham	70	B2
Bellingshausen Sea	80	(2)JJ4
Bellinzona	22	E4
Bello	76	B2
Belluno	22	H4
Bellyk	36	E6
Belmonte, Brazil	76	K7
Belmonte, Spain	20	L5
Belmopan	72	G5
Belmullet	16	B7
Belogorsk	36	M6
Belogradčik	26	K6
Beloha	58	H5
Belo Horizonte	76	J7
Belo Monte	76	F2
Belomorsk	30	F2
Beloretsk	30	L4
Belo Tsiribihina	58	G3
Belovo	34	R7
Beloyarskiy	34	M5
Beloye More	30	G1
Belozersk	30	G2
Belozerskoye	30	N3
Belye Vody	34	M9
Belyy Yar	34	Q6
Belzig	12	H4
Bembibre	20	D2
Bena Dibele	56	C4
Benavente	20	E3
Benbecula	16	E3
Bend	70	B3
Bendorf	14	K4
Bene	58	E3
Benešov	10	D8
Benevento	24	J7
Bengbu	38	F4
Bengkalis	42	C2
Bengkulu	42	C3
Benguela	58	A2
Benguerir	52	D2
Benha	50	F1
Beni	56	E2
Beni	76	D6
Beni Abbès	52	E2
Benicarló	20	L4
Benidorm	20	K6
Benī Mazâr	50	F2
Beni Mellal	52	D2
Benin	54	F3
Benin City	54	F3
Beni Saf	20	J9
Beni Slimane	20	P8
Benito Juaréz	78	K6
Benjamin Constant	76	D4
Benkovac	22	L6
Ben More Assynt	16	H3
Ben Nevis	16	H4
Benoud	52	F2
Bensheim	12	D7
Benson, Ariz., U.S.	70	D5
Benson, Minn., U.S.	70	G2
Benteng	43	B4
Bentinck Island	62	G3
Bentung	43	A3
Benue	54	G3
Benxi	38	G2
Beo	40	H6
Beograd	26	H5
Berat	26	G4
Beravina	58	H3
Berber	50	F4
Berbera	50	H5
Berbérati	56	B3
Berck	14	D4
Berdigestyakh	36	M4
Berdsk	34	Q7
Berdyans'k	30	G5
Berdychiv	30	D5
Bereeda	56	J1
Berehove	26	K1
Berezina	30	C2
Berezniki	30	K3
Berettyó	26	J2
Berettyóújfalu	26	J2
Berettys	10	L10
Bereznik	30	H2
Berezniki	30	L3
Berezovo	30	N2
Berezovyy	36	P6
Berga	20	M2
Bergama	28	K5
Bergamo	22	E5
Bergara	20	H1
Bergby	8	J6
Bergedorf	12	F3
Bergen, Germany	12	J2
Bergen, Germany	12	E4
Bergen, Netherlands	14	G2
Bergen, Norway	8	C6
Bergen op Zoom	14	G3
Bergerac	18	F9
Bergheim	14	J4
Bergisch Gladbach	12	C6
Bergsfjordhalvøya	8	L1
Beringen	14	H3
Beringovskiy	36	X4
Bering Sea	66	V4
Bering Strait	66	T3
Berkner Island	80	(2)A2
Berkovica	26	L6
Berlin	12	J4
Bermejo	78	K4
Bermeo	20	H1
Bermuda	66	H6
Bern	22	C4
Bernalda	24	L8
Bernau	12	J4
Bernay	14	C5
Bernburg	12	G5
Berner Alpen	22	C4
Beroun	10	D8
Berounka	12	J7
Berovo	28	E3
Beroroa	20	N8
Bertoua	54	G4
Beruni	34	L9
Berwick-upon-Tweed	16	L6
Besalampy	58	G3
Besançon	18	M6
Besbay	34	K8
Bessemer	70	J5
Bestamak	34	P8
Bestuzhevo	30	H2
Bestyakh, Russia	36	L3
Bestyakh, Russia	36	M4
Betanzos	20	B1
Bētdâmbâng	40	C4
Bethlehem	58	D5
Béthune	14	E4
Betioky	58	G4
Betoota	62	H5
Betpak-Dala	34	M8
Betroka	58	H4
Bettiah	44	D3
Betul	44	C4
Betzdorf	12	C6
Beverley	16	M8
Beverungen	12	E5
Bey Dağlari	28	M8
Beykoz	28	M3
Beyla	54	C3
Beyneu	34	J8
Beypazari	28	P4
Beyra	56	H2
Beyrouth	46	C3
Beyşehir	28	P7
Beyşehir Gölü	28	P7
Bezhetsk	30	G3
Béziers	18	J10
Bhadgaon	44	E3
Bhadrakh	44	E4
Bhadravati	44	C6
Bhagalpur	44	E3
Bhairab Bazar	44	F4
Bhakkar	44	B2
Bhamo	40	B2
Bharuch	44	B4
Bhatpara	44	F4
Bhavnagar	44	B4
Bhawanipatna	44	D5
Bhilai	44	D4
Bhilwara	44	B3
Bhīmavaram	44	D5
Bhind	44	C3
Bhiwandi	44	B5
Bhiwani	44	C3
Bhopal	44	C4
Bhubaneshwar	44	E4
Bhuj	44	A4
Bhusawal	44	C4
Bhutan	44	E3
Biak	43	E3
Biała Podlaska	10	N5
Białogard	10	F3
Białystok	10	N4
Biarritz	18	D10
Biasca	22	G7
Bibbiena	22	G7
Biberach	22	E2
Bicaz	26	P3
Bicester	16	A3
Bickerton Island	62	G2
Bicske	26	F2
Bida	54	F3
Bidar	44	C5
Biddeford	70	H10
Biedenkopf	12	D6
Biel	22	C3
Bielefeld	12	D4
Biella	22	D5
Bielsko-Biała	10	J8
Bielsk Podlaski	10	N5
Bień Hoa	40	D4
Bietigheim-Bissingen	22	E2
Big	68	G2
Biga	28	K4
Bigadiç	28	L5
Big Desert	62	H7
Bighorn	70	E3
Bighorn Mountains	70	E3
Bight of Bangkok	40	C4
Bight of Benin	54	E3
Bight of Biafra	54	F4
Bignona	52	B6
Big River	68	K6
Big Spring	70	F5
Big Trout Lake	68	P6
Bihać	22	L6
Bijapur	44	C5
Bījār	46	E2
Bijeljina	26	G5
Bijelo Polje	26	G6
Bijie	38	D5
Bikaner	44	B3
Bikin	36	N7
Bikini	60	G4
Bilaspur	44	D4
Bila Tserkva	30	F5
Bilbao	20	H1
Bileća	26	F7
Bilecik	28	M4
Bilečko Jezero	26	F7
Biled	26	H4
Biłgoraj	10	M7
Bilhorod-Dnistrovs'kyy	30	F5
Bilibino	36	V3
Bilina	12	J6
Billings	70	E2
Bill of Portland	16	K11
Bilma	50	B4
Biloela	62	K4
Biloxi	70	J5
Bimini Islands	72	F2
Bina-Etawa	44	C4
Binche	14	G4
Bindi Bindi	62	C6
Bindura	58	E3
Bingen	12	C7
Binghamton	70	L3
Bingöl	46	D2
Binongko	43	B4
Bintuan	42	C5
Bintulu	42	E2
Bintuni	43	D3
Binyang	40	D2
Binzhou	38	F3
Biograd	22	L7
Birāk	52	H3
Birao	50	D5
Biratnagar	44	E3
Birdsville	62	G5
Bireun	42	B1
Bir Gandouz	52	B4
Birhan	50	G5
Birkenfeld	14	K5
Birmingham, U.K.	16	L9
Birmingham, U.S.	70	J5
Bîr Mogreïn	52	C3
Birnie	60	J6
Birnin-Gwari	54	F2
Birnin Kebbi	54	E2
Birnin Konni	54	F2
Birnin Kudu	54	F2
Birobidzhan	36	N7
Birsk	30	L3
Biržai	10	P1
Bi'r Zalțan	50	C2
Bisceglie	24	L7
Bischofshofen	22	J3
Bischofswerda	10	D6
Biševo	24	L7
Bishkek	34	N9
Bishop Auckland	16	L7
Bishop's Stortford	14	C3
Biskra	52	G2
Bislig	40	H5
Bismarck	70	F2
Bismarck Sea	60	E6
Bissau	52	B6
Bistcho Lake	68	H5
Bistrița	26	M2
Bistrița	26	P3
Bitburg	14	J5
Bitche	12	C7
Bitkine	50	C5
Bitola	28	D3
Bitonto	24	L7
Bitterfeld	12	H5
Bitterroot Range	70	C2
Bitti	24	D8
Bitung	43	C2
Biu	54	G2
Biyâvra	44	C4
Biysk	34	R7
Bjala, Bulgaria	26	N6
Bjala, Bulgaria	26	L6
Bjelovar	26	D4
Bjerkvik	8	J2
Bjørnøya	34	B3
B-Köpenick	12	J4
Bla	54	C2
Blackall	62	J4
Blackburn	16	K8
Blackpool	16	K8
Black Range	70	E5
Black Sea	6	J4
Black Sugarloaf	62	K6
Black Volta	54	D3
Blackwater	16	D9
Blackwater	62	J4
Blagoevgrad	28	F3
Blagoveshchenka	34	P7
Blagoveshchensk	36	M6
Blain	18	D6
Blaj	26	L3
Blanco	76	E6
Blangy-sur-Bresle	14	D5
Blankenberge	14	F3
Blankenburg	12	F5
Blankenheim	14	J4
Blantyre	58	F3
Blasket Islands	16	B9
Blaubeuren	22	E2
Blaye-et-Sainte-Luce	18	E8
Bled	22	K4
Blenheim	64	D5
Blevands Huk	12	D1
Blida	52	F1
Blind River	70	K2
Bloemfontein	58	D5
Bloemhof	58	D5
Blois	18	G6
Blönduós	8	(1)C2
Błonie	10	K5
Bloomington, Ill., U.S.	70	J3
Bloomington, Ind., U.S.	70	J4
Bludenz	22	E3
Bluefield	70	K4
Bluefields	72	H6
Blue Mountains	46	C3
Blue Nile = Bahr el Azraq	50	F5
Bluenose Lake	68	H3
Bluff	64	B8
Blumenau	78	M4
Blythe	70	D5
Bo	54	B3
Boac	40	G4
Boa Vista, Brazil	72	M7
Boa Vista, Cape Verde	54	(1)B1
Bobbili	44	D5
Bobbio	22	E6
Bobigny	14	E6
Bobingen	22	F2
Böblingen	22	E2
Bobo-Dioulasso	54	D2
Bobolice	10	F4
Bobr	10	E6
Bobrov	30	H4
Bôca do Acre	76	D5
Boca Grande	72	M7
Boca Grande	74	E3
Bocaiúva	76	J7
Bocaranga	56	B2
Bochnia	10	K8
Bocholt	12	B5
Bochum	12	C5
Bockenem	12	F4
Bodaybo	36	J5
Bode	12	G4
Bodélé	50	C4
Boden	8	L4
Bodham	8	A5
Bodmin	16	H11
Bodø	8	H3
Bodrog	10	L9
Bodrum	28	K7
Boende	56	C4
Boffa	54	B2
Bogale	40	B3
Boggabilla	62	K5
Boghni	20	P8
Bognor Regis	14	B4
Bogo	40	G4
Bogor	42	D4
Bogorodskoye	36	Q6
Bogotá	76	C3
Bogotol	34	R6
Bogra	44	E3
Boguchany	36	F5
Bogué	52	C5
Bo Hai	38	F3
Böhmerwald	12	H7
Bohol	40	G5
Bohumin	10	H8
Boiaçu	76	E4
Boise	70	C3
Bojnürd	46	G2
Bokatola	56	B4
Boké	54	B2
Bokoro	54	H2
Bokspits	58	C5
Bokungu	56	C4
Bolbec	14	C5
Boldu	26	Q4
Bole, China	34	Q9
Bole, Ghana	54	D3
Bolechiv	10	N8
Bolesławiec	10	E6
Bolgatanga	54	D2
Bolhrad	26	R4
Bolintin-Vale	26	N5
Bolivia	76	D7
Bollène	18	K9
Bollnäs	8	J6
Bolmen	8	G8
Bolobo	56	B4
Bologna	22	G6
Bolognesi	76	C6
Bolomba	56	B3
Bolotnoye	34	Q6
Bol'shaya Pyssa	30	J2
Bol'sherech'ye	30	P3
Bol'shezemel'skaya Tundra	34	J4
Bol Shirta	36	J4
Bolshoy Atlym	30	N2
Bol'shoy Osinovaya	36	W3
Bol'shoy Vlas'evo	36	Q6
Bol'shoy Yugan	30	P2
Bolsover	14	A1
Bolton	16	K8
Bolu	28	P4
Bolvadin	28	P6
Bolzano	22	G4
Boma	54	G6
Bombala	62	J7
Bombay = Mumbai	44	B5
Bomili	56	D3
Bom Jesus da Lapa	76	J6
Bomlo	8	C7
Bomnak	36	M6
Bomossa	54	H4
Bonaparte Archipelago	62	B2
Bonavista Bay	68	W7
Bondeno	22	G6

Bondo 56 C3
Bondokodi 62 C1
Bondoukou 54 D3
Bondowoso 42 E4
Bonerate 43 B4
Bongaigaon 44 F3
Bongandanga 56 C3
Bongao 43 A1
Bongor 54 H2
Bonifacio 24 D7
Bonn 12 C6
Bonneville 22 B4
Bonnie Rock 62 C6
Bonorva 24 C8
Bonthe 54 B3
Bontoc 40 G3
Bontosunggu 43 A4
Bonyhád 26 F3
Boorama 56 G2
Boosaaso 56 H1
Boothia Peninsula 68 M2
Booué 54 G5
Boppard 12 C6
Bor, Russia 36 D4
Bor, Sudan 56 E2
Bor, Turkey 28 S7
Bor, Yugoslavia 26 K5
Borah Peak 70 D3
Borås 8 G8
Borāzjān 46 F4
Bordeaux 18 E9
Bordeira 22 B3
Borden Peninsula 68 Q2
Border Town 62 H7
Bordj Bou Arréridj 52 F1
Bordj Bounaam 20 M9
Bordj Flye Sante Marie 52 E3
Bordj Messaouda 52 G2
Bordj Mokhtar 52 F4
Bordj Omar Driss 52 G3
Borgarnes 8 (1)C2
Borgholm 8 J8
Borgomanero 22 D5
Borgo San Dalmazzo 22 C6
Borgo San Lorenzo 22 G7
Borgosesia 22 D5
Borgo Val di Taro 22 E6
Bori Jenein 52 H2
Borislav 10 N8
Borisoglebsk 30 H4
Borken 14 J3
Borkou 50 C4
Borkum 14 J1
Borkum 14 J1
Borlänge 8 H6
Bormida 22 D6
Bormio 22 F4
Borna 12 H5
Borne 14 J2
Borneo 42 E3
Bornholm 8 H9
Borodino 34 R5
Borodinskoye 8 Q6
Boromo 54 D2
Borongan 40 H4
Borovichi 30 F3
Borovskoy 30 M4
Borriana 20 L5
Borroloola 62 G3
Borşa 26 M2
Borshchiv 26 P1
Borshchovochnyy Khrebet 36 J7
Borðeyri 8 (1)C2
Borüjerd 46 E3
Borzya 36 K6
Bosa 24 C8
Bosanska Dubica 26 D4
Bosanska Gradiška 26 E4
Bosanska Kostajnica 22 M5
Bosanska Krupa 26 D5
Bosanski Brod 26 F4
Bosanski Novi 26 D4
Bosanski Petrovac 26 D5
Bosansko Grahovo 22 M6
Bosca 26 J4
Bose 40 D2
Bosilegrad 26 K7
Boskovice 10 F8
Bosna 26 F5
Bosnia-Herzegovina 26 E5
Bosobolo 56 B3
Bosporus 46 A1
Bosporus = İstanbul Boğazı 28 M3
Bossámbélé 56 B2
Bossangoa 56 B2
Bosten Hu 34 R9
Boston, U.K. 16 M9
Boston, U.S. 70 M3
Botevgrad 26 L7
Botlikh 46 E1
Botna 26 R3
Botoşani 26 P2
Botou 38 F3
Botrange 14 J4
Botswana 58 C4
Bottrop 14 J3
Bou Ahmed 20 F9
Bouaké 54 D3
Bouar 56 B2
Bouârfa 20 N8
Boufarik 20 N8
Bougainville Island 60 F6
Bougainville Reef 62 J3
Bougouni 54 C2
Bougzoul 20 N9
Bouira 52 F1
Bou Ismaïl 20 M8
Bou Izakarn 52 D3
Boujdour 52 C3
Bou Kadir 20 M8
Boukra 52 C3
Boulder 70 D4
Boulder City 70 D4
Boulia 62 G4

Boulogne-sur-Mer 14 D4
Bouna 54 D3
Boundiali 54 C3
Bounty Islands 60 H10
Bourem 52 E5
Bourg 18 E8
Bourg-de-Piage 18 L9
Bourg-en-Bresse 18 L7
Bourges 18 H6
Bourgoin-Jallieu 18 L8
Bourke 62 J6
Bournemouth 16 L11
Bou Saâda 52 F1
Boussu 50 C5
Boussu 14 F4
Boutilimit 52 C5
Bouzghaïa 20 M8
Bowen 62 J4
Bowling Green 70 J4
Bowman Bay 68 E2
Bo Xian 38 F4
Boxwood Hill 62 C6
Boyang 38 F5
Boyarka 36 F2
Boyle 16 D8
Boyuibe 78 J3
Bozcaada 28 K3
Boz Dağ 28 M7
Bozkır 28 Q7
Bozoum 56 B2
Bozüyük 28 N5
Bra 22 C6
Brač 26 D6
Bracciano 24 G6
Bräcke 8 H5
Bracknell 14 B3
Brad 26 K3
Bradano 24 L8
Bradford 16 L8
Brady 70 G5
Braga 20 B3
Bragança, Brazil 76 H4
Bragança, Portugal 20 D3
Brahmapur 44 D5
Brahmaputra 44 F3
Bráila 26 Q4
Braintree 14 C3
Brake 12 D1
Bramming 12 D1
Bramsche 12 D4
Branco 76 E3
Brandberg 58 A4
Brandenburg 12 H4
Brandon 68 M7
Brandvlei 58 C6
Brandýs 10 D7
Braniewo 10 J3
Brasileia 76 D6
Brasília 76 H7
Braslaw 8 P9
Braşov 26 N4
Bratislava 10 G9
Bratsk 36 G5
Bratskoye Vodokhranilishche 36 G5
Braţul 26 R4
Bratunac 26 G5
Braunau 22 J2
Braunschweig 12 F4
Bray 16 F8
Brazil 76 F4
Brazzaville 56 B4
Brčko 26 F5
Bream Bay 64 E2
Břeclav 10 F9
Breda 14 G3
Bredasdorp 58 C6
Bredstedt 12 D1
Bredy 30 M4
Bree 14 H3
Bree 18 L2
Bregenz 22 E3
Breiðafjörður 8 (1)A2
Bremangerlandet 8 B6
Bremen 12 D3
Bremerhaven 12 D3
Bremervörde 12 E3
Brenham 70 G5
Brennero 22 G4
Breno 22 F5
Brentwood 14 C3
Brescia 22 F5
Bressanone 22 G4
Bressay 16 M1
Bressuire 18 E7
Brest, Belarus 30 D4
Brest, France 18 A5
Breteuil 14 E5
Bretten 12 D7
Breves 76 G4
Brewarrina 62 J5
Brežice 26 C4
Brézina 52 F2
Brezno 10 J9
Bria 56 C2
Briançon 22 B6
Briceni 26 Q1
Bridgend 16 J10
Bridgeport 70 M3
Bridgetown 76 F1
Bridgewater 68 U8
Bridgwater 16 J10
Bridlington 16 M7
Brienzer See 22 D4
Brig 22 C4
Brighton 14 B4
Brignoles 22 B7
Brikama 54 A2
Brilon 12 D5
Brindisi 24 M8
Brisbane 62 K5
Bristol 16 K10
Bristol Bay 66 S4
Bristol Channel 16 H10
British Columbia 68 F5

Britstown 58 C6
Brive-la-Gaillarde 18 G8
Briviesca 20 G2
Brixham 16 J11
Brlik 34 N9
Brno 10 F8
Broad Sound 62 J4
Broadus 70 E2
Brod 26 J9
Brodeur Peninsula 68 P2
Brodick 16 G6
Brodnica 10 J4
Broken Arrow 72 K1
Broken Hill 62 H6
Brokopondo 76 F2
Bromölla 10 D1
Bromsgrove 16 K9
Bröndersley 8 E8
Broni 22 E5
Brooke's Point 40 F5
Brookhaven 70 H5
Brooks 68 J6
Brooks Range 66 S3
Broome 62 D3
Brora 16 J3
Brösarp 8 H9
Broughton Island 68 U3
Brovary 30 F4
Brownsville 70 G6
Brownwood 70 G5
Bruchsal 12 D7
Bruck, Austria 22 L3
Bruck, Austria 22 M2
Bruck an der Mur 26 C2
Brugge 14 F3
Brühl 14 J4
Bruint 44 G3
Brumado 76 J6
Brumath 12 C8
Brunei 42 E2
Brunflo 8 H5
Brunico 24 F2
Brunsbüttel 12 E3
Brunswick 70 K5
Bruntál 10 G8
Brussels = Bruxelles 14 G4
Bruxelles 14 G4
Bryan 70 G5
Bryanka 34 S6
Bryansk 30 F4
Brzeg 10 G7
Brzeg Dolny 10 F6
Brzeziny 10 J6
B-Spandau 10 C5
Bubi 58 E4
Bucak 28 N7
Bucaramanga 76 C2
Buchanan 54 B3
Buchan Gulf 68 S2
Bucharest = Bucureşti 26 P5
Buchholz 12 E3
Buchy 18 M5
Bückeburg 12 E4
Bučovice 10 F8
Bucureşti 26 P5
Budapest 26 G2
Bude 16 H11
Budennovsk 30 H6
Büdingen 12 E6
Budoni 24 D8
Budrio 22 G6
Budva 26 G7
Buenaventura, Col. 76 B3
Buenaventura, Mexico 70 E6
Buenos Aires 78 K5
Buffalo, N.Y., U.S. 70 L3
Buffalo, S.D., U.S. 70 F2
Buffalo Lake 68 J4
Buffalo Narrows 68 K5
Buftea 26 N5
Bug 10 L5
Bugojno 26 E5
Bugrino 34 H4
Bugsuk 40 F5
Bugul'ma 30 K4
Buguruslan 30 K4
Buhuşi 26 P3
Builth Wells 16 J9
Buinsk 30 J4
Buir Nuur 38 F1
Bujanovac 26 J7
Buje 22 J5
Bujumbura 56 D4
Bukachacha 36 K6
Bukavu 56 D4
Bukhara 46 H2
Bukittinggi 42 C3
Bukoba 56 E4
Bula, Indonesia 43 D3
Bula, P.N.G. 43 F4
Bülach 22 D3
Bulan 40 G4
Bulawayo 58 D4
Buldan 28 L7
Buldir Island 36 X6
Bulgaria 26 M7
Buli 43 C2
Bulle 22 C4
Bulls 64 E5
Bulukumba 43 B4
Bulun 36 M2
Bumba 56 C3
Bumbeşti Jiu 26 L4
Buna 56 F3
Bunbury 62 C6
Buncrana 16 E6
Bunda 56 E4
Bundaberg 62 K4
Bünde 12 D4
Bungunya 62 J5
Buñol 20 L5
Buôn Mê Thuôt 40 D4
Buotama 36 M4

Bura 56 F4
Buran 34 R8
Buranj 44 D2
Buraydah 46 D4
Burco 56 H2
Burdur 28 N7
Burdur Gölü 28 N7
Burë 50 G5
Büren 14 L3
Burg 12 G4
Burgas 26 Q7
Burgdorf 22 C3
Burghausen 22 H2
Burglengenfeld 12 H7
Burgos 20 G2
Burgsvik 8 K8
Burhaniye 28 K5
Burhanpur 44 C4
Burjassot 20 K5
Burketown 62 G3
Bur-Khaybyt 36 P3
Burkina Faso 54 D2
Burlin 30 K4
Burlington, Colo., U.S. 70 F4
Burlington, Ia., U.S. 70 H3
Burlington, Vt., U.S. 70 M3
Burma = Myanmar 40 B2
Burnet 70 G5
Burnie 62 J8
Burns 46 C3
Burns Lake 68 F6
Burqin 34 R8
Burra 62 G6
Burrel 28 C3
Bururi 56 D4
Burton-upon-Trent 16 L9
Buru 43 C3
Burundi 56 D4
Bury St. Edmunds 14 C2
Büshehr = Büshehr 46 F4
Büshehr 46 F4
Bushire = Büshehr 46 F4
Businga 56 C3
Busira 56 C4
Bussum 14 H2
Busto Arsizio 22 D5
Buta 56 C3
Butare 56 D4
Butaritari 60 H5
Bute 16 G5
Butembo 56 D3
Buton 43 B3
Butte 70 D2
Butuan 40 H5
Butwal 44 D3
Butzbach 12 D6
Bützow 12 G3
Buy 30 H3
Büyükada 28 L4
Büyükçekmece 28 L4
Buzai Gumbad 46 K2
Buzançais 18 G7
Buzău 26 P4
Buzău 26 Q4
Buzuluk 30 K4
Byam Martin Island 68 L2
Byaroza 8 N10
Bydgoszcz 10 H4
Bygdin 8 D6
Bygland 8 D7
Bykovskiy 36 M2
Bylot Island 68 R2
Byskeälven 8 L4
Bystřice 10 G8
Bystrzyca Kłodzka 10 F7
Bytča 10 H8
Bytom 10 H7
Bytów 10 G3
Bzura 10 J5

C

Caaguazú 78 K4
Caballococha 76 C5
Cabañaquinta 20 E1
Cabanatuan 40 G3
Cabdul Qaadir 50 H5
Cabeza del Buey 20 E6
Cabezas 76 E7
Cabimas 76 C1
Cabinda 54 G6
Cabinda 54 G6
Cabo Bascuñán 78 G4
Cabo Beata 72 K5
Cabo Camarón 72 G5
Cabo Carvoeiro 20 A5
Cabo Catoche 72 G4
Cabo Corrientes, Col. 76 B2
Cabo Corrientes, Mexico 72 C4
Cabo Corrubedo 20 A2
Cabo Cruz 72 J5
Cabo de Espichel 20 A6
Cabo de Gata 20 H8
Cabo de Hornos 78 H10
Cabo de la Nao 20 L6
Cabo de Palos 20 K7
Cabo de São Roque 76 K5
Cabo de Sao Tomé 76 H8
Cabo de São Vicente 20 A7
Cabo de Trafalgar 20 D8

Cabo dos Bahías 78 H8
Cabo Fisterra 20 A2
Cabo Frio 78 N3
Cabo Gracias a Dios 72 H6
Cabo Mondego 20 A4
Cabo Norte 76 H3
Cabo Orange 76 G3
Cabo Ortegal 20 B1
Cabo Peñas 20 E1
Cabo Rojo 54 A2
Cabo Roxo 78 H9
Cabo San Francisco de Paula 78 H8
Cabo San Juan 54 F4
Cabo San Lucas 72 D7
Cabo Santa Elena 72 H6
Cabo Tortosa 20 L4
Cabo Tres Puntas 78 H8
Cabot Strait 68 U7
Cabrera 20 N5
Čačak 26 H6
Cáceres, Brazil 76 F7
Cáceres, Spain 20 D5
Cacheu 54 A2
Cachimbo 76 G5
Cachoeira do Sul 78 L4
Cachoeiro de Itapemirim 76 J8
Cacola 58 B2
Caconda 58 B2
Čadca 10 H8
Cadillac 70 E2
Cádiz 20 D8
Caen 14 B5
Caernarfon 16 H8
Cagayan de Oro 40 G5
Cagli 22 H7
Cagliari 24 C9
Cagnes-sur-Mer 22 C7
Caguas 72 L5
Cahama 58 A3
Cahersiveen 16 B10
Cahir 16 E9
Cahors 18 G9
Cahul 26 R4
Caia 58 F3
Caianda 58 C2
Caicos Islands 72 K4
Cairns 62 J3
Cairo = El Qâhira 50 F1
Cairo Montenotte 22 D6
Calabar 54 F3
Calabozo 76 D2
Calabro 24 L9
Calafat 26 K6
Calahorra 20 J2
Calais 14 D4
Calama, Brazil 76 E5
Calama, Peru 78 H3
Calamar 76 C3
Calamian Group 40 F4
Calamocha 20 J4
Călan 26 L4
Calanscio Sand Sea 50 D2
Calapan 40 G4
Călăraşi, Moldova 26 R2
Călăraşi, Romania 26 Q5
Calatafim 24 G11
Calatayud 20 J3
Calauag 40 G4
Calbayog 40 G4
Calçoene 76 G3
Calcutta = Kolkata 44 E4
Caldas da Rainha 20 A5
Caldera 78 G4
Calf of Man 16 H7
Calgary 68 J6
Cali 76 B3
Caliente 70 D4
California 70 B4
Callao 76 B6
Caloundra 62 K5
Caltagirone 24 J11
Caltanissetta 24 J11
Caluquembe 58 A2
Caluula 56 J1
Calvi 24 C6
Calvinia 58 B6
Calw 22 D2
Camaçari 76 K6
Camacupa 58 B2
Camagüey 72 J4
Camaiore 22 F7
Camana 76 C7
Camargue 18 K10
Camariñas 20 A1
Camarones 78 H7
Ca Mau 40 D5
Camberley 16 M10
Cambodia 40 C4
Cambrai 14 F4
Cambre 20 B1
Cambrian Mountains 16 H10
Cambridge, N.Z. 64 E3
Cambridge, U.K. 16 N9
Cambridge, U.S. 70 L4
Cambridge Bay 68 K3
Cambrils 20 M3
Cameroon 54 H4
Cametá 76 H4
Çamiçigölü 28 K7
Camiguin 43 B3
Camiranga 76 H4
Camocim 76 J4
Camooweal 62 G3
Camopi 76 G3
Campbell Island 64 (2)C8
Campbell River 68 F7
Campbeltown 16 G6

Campeche 72 F5
Câmpeni 26 L3
Câmpia Turzii 26 L3
Câmpina 26 N4
Campina Grande 76 L5
Campinas 78 M3
Campobasso 24 J7
Campo de Criptana 20 G5
Campo de Diauarum 76 G6
Campo Gallo 78 J4
Campo Grande 78 L3
Campo Maior 78 L3
Campo Mourão 78 L3
Campos 78 N3
Câmpulung 26 N4
Câmpulung Moldovenesc 26 N2
Cam Ranh 40 D4
Çan 28 K4
Canada 66 M4
Canadian 70 F4
Çanakkale 28 J4
Çanakkale Boğazı 28 J4
Canal de Panamá 72 J7
Canary Islands = Islas Canarias 52 B3
Cañaveras 20 H4
Canberra 62 J7
Cancún 72 G4
Çandarli Körfezi 28 J6
Candelaro 26 C8
Candlemas Island 74 J9
Cangamba 58 B2
Cangas 20 B2
Cangas de Narcea 20 D1
Cangyuan 40 B2
Cangzhou 38 F3
Canicattì 24 H11
Canindé 76 K4
Çankırı 28 R4
Canna 16 F4
Cannanore 44 B6
Cannanore 44 C6
Cannes 22 C7
Cannock 14 A2
Cantanduanes 40 G4
Canterbury 14 D3
Canterbury Bight 64 C7
Canterbury Plains 64 C6
Cân Tho 40 D5
Canto do Buriti 76 J5
Canton 70 K3
Canumã 76 F5
Canutama 76 E5
Canyon 70 F5
Cao Bāng 40 D2
Caorle 22 H5
Cap Blanc 24 D11
Cap Bon 52 H1
Cap Corse 24 D5
Cap d'Agde 18 J10
Cap d'Antifer 14 C5
Cap de Fer 52 G1
Cap de Formentor 20 P5
Cap de la Hague 18 D4
Cap de Nouvelle-France 68 S4
Cap de ses Salines 20 P5
Cap des Trois Fourches 20 H9
Cape Agulhas 58 C6
Cape Alexandra 78 P9
Cape Apostolos Andreas 46 B2
Cape Arid 62 D6
Cape Arnaoutis 28 Q9
Cape Arnhem 62 G2
Cape Barren Island 62 J8
Cape Bauld 68 V6
Cape Blanco 70 B3
Cape Borda 62 G7
Cape Breton Island 68 U7
Cape Brett 64 E2
Cape Byron 62 K5
Cape Campbell 64 E5
Cape Canaveral 70 K6
Cape Carnot 62 F6
Cape Chidley 68 U4
Cape Christian 68 T2
Cape Churchill 68 N5
Cape Clear 16 C10
Cape Coast 54 E3
Cape Cod 66 H5
Cape Columbine 58 B6
Cape Comorin 44 C7
Cape Crawford 62 G3
Cape Croker 62 F2
Cape Dalhousie 68 H2
Cape Direction 62 H2
Cape Disappointment 78 P9
Cape Dominion 68 R3
Cape Dorchester 68 R3
Cape Dorset 68 R4
Cape Dyer 68 U3
Cape Egmont 64 D5
Cape Farewell, Greenland 66 F4
Cape Farewell, N.Z. 64 D5
Cape Fear 70 L5
Cape Finisterre = Cabo Fisterra 20 A2
Cape Flattery, Aus. 62 J2
Cape Flattery, U.S. 70 B2
Cape Foulwind 64 C5
Cape Fria 58 A3
Cape Girardeau 70 H4
Cape Greko 28 S10
Cape Grenville 62 H2
Cape Grim 62 H8
Cape Harrison 68 V6
Cape Hatteras 70 L4
Cape Henrietta Maria 68 Q5
Cape Horn = Cabo de Hornos 78 H10

Fdérik 52 C4
Featherston 64 E5
Fécamp 14 C5
Federated States of Micronesia 60 E5
Fedorovka 30 M4
Fehmarn 12 G2
Feijó 76 C5
Feilding 64 E5
Feira de Santana 76 K6
Feistritz 22 L3
Fejø 12 G2
Feldbach 22 L4
Feldkirch 22 E3
Feldkirchen 22 K4
Felidu Atoll 44 B8
Felixstowe 14 D3
Feltre 22 G4
Femø 12 G2
Femund 8 F5
Fenghua 38 G5
Fengning 38 F2
Feng Xian 38 D4
Feni 44 F4
Fenyang 38 E3
Feodosiya 30 G5
Feres 28 J4
Fergana 46 K1
Fergus Falls 70 G2
Ferkessédougou 54 C3
Ferlach 22 K4
Fermo 24 H5
Fernandópolis 78 L3
Ferrara 22 G6
Ferreira do Alentejo 20 B7
Ferrol 20 B1
Fès 52 E2
Fetești 26 Q5
Fethiye 28 M8
Fetisovo 46 F1
Fetlar 16 M1
Feucht 12 G7
Feuchtwangen 12 F7
Feyzābād 46 K2
Fianarantsoa 58 H4
Fianga 56 B2
Fichē 56 F2
Fidenza 22 F6
Fieni 26 N4
Fier 28 B4
Figari 24 D7
Figeac 18 G9
Figline Valdarno 22 G7
Figueira da Foz 20 B4
Figueres 20 N2
Figuig 52 E2
Figuil 54 G3
Fiji 60 H8
Filadélfia 78 J3
Fil'akovo 10 J9
Filiași 26 L5
Filicudi 24 J10
Fīltu 56 G2
Finale Ligure 22 D6
Fingoè 58 E3
Finike 28 N8
Finland 8 P3
Finlay 68 F5
Finley 62 J7
Finnsnes 8 K2
Finsterwalde 12 J5
Fırat 46 E3
Firenze 22 G7
Firminy 18 K8
Firozabad 44 C3
Firozpur 44 B2
Firth of Clyde 16 G6
Firth of Forth 16 K5
Firth of Lorn 16 G5
Firth of Thames 64 E3
Fish 58 B5
Fisher Strait 68 Q4
Fishguard 16 H9
Fiskenæsset = Qeqertarsuatsiaat 68 W4
Fismes 14 F5
Fitzroy Crossing 62 E3
Fivizzano 22 F6
Fizi 56 D4
Flå 8 E6
Flannan Islands 16 E3
Flåsjön 8 H4
Flateyri 8 (1)B1
Flathead Lake 70 D2
Flat Point 64 E5
Flekkefjord 8 D7
Flensburg 12 E2
Flensburg Fjord 12 E2
Flers 14 B6
Flinders Island 62 J7
Flinders Ranges 62 G6
Flinders Reefs 62 J3
Flin Flon 68 L6
Flint 70 K3
Flint Island 60 L7
Flirey 22 A2
Flöha 12 J6
Florac 18 J9
Florence = Firenze, *It.* 22 G7
Florence, *U.S.* 70 L5
Florencia 76 B3
Florennes 14 G4
Florenville 14 H5
Flores, *Azores* 52 (1)A2
Flores, *Indonesia* 43 B4
Flores Sea 43 A4
Florești 26 R2
Floriano 76 J5
Florianópolis 78 M4
Florida 70 K6
Florida 78 K5
Florida Keys 66 K7
Florina 28 D4
Florø 8 C6
Flumendosa 24 D9
Fly 43 F4
Foça 28 J6
Foča 26 F6
Focșani 26 Q4
Foggia 24 K7
Fogo 54 (1)B1
Fogo Island 68 W7
Fohnsdorf 22 K3
Föhr 12 D2
Foix 18 G11
Folegandros 28 G8
Foleyet 70 K2
Foligno 24 G6
Folkestone 14 D3
Follonica 24 E6
Fomboni 58 G2
Fondi 24 H7
Fongafale 60 H6
Fontainebleau 18 H5
Fontana 24 M8
Fonte Boa 76 D4
Fontenay-le-Comte 18 E7
Fontur 8 (1)F1
Fonyód 24 M2
Forbach, *France* 14 J5
Forbach, *Germany* 14 L6
Forchheim 12 G7
Førde 8 C6
Forfar 16 K5
Forges-les-Eaux 14 D5
Forlì 22 H6
Formazza 22 D4
Formentera 20 M6
Formia 24 H7
Formiga 78 M3
Formosa, *Brazil* 76 H7
Formosa, *Paraguay* 78 K4
Fornovo di Taro 22 F6
Forsayth 62 H3
Forssa 8 M6
Forst 12 K5
Fort Abbas 44 B3
Fortaleza 76 K4
Fort Augustus 16 H4
Fort Beaufort 58 D6
Fort Chipewyan 68 J5
Fort-de-France 72 M6
Fort Dodge 70 H3
Forte dei Marmi 22 F7
Fortezza 22 G4
Fort Frances 70 H2
Fort George 68 R6
Fort Good Hope 68 F3
Forth 16 H5
Fort Hope 68 P6
Fortín Coronel Eugenio Garay 78 J3
Fort Lauderdale 70 K6
Fort Liard 68 G4
Fort Mackay 68 J5
Fort McMurray 68 J5
Fort McPherson 68 D3
Fort Munro 46 J4
Fort Myers 70 K6
Fort Nelson 68 G5
Fort Norman 68 F4
Fort Peck Reservoir 70 E2
Fort Pierce 70 K6
Fort Portal 56 E3
Fort Providence 68 H4
Fortrose 64 B8
Fort Rupert 68 R6
Fort St. John 68 G5
Fort Severn 68 P5
Fort Shevchenko 34 J9
Fort Simpson 68 G4
Fort Smith, *Can.* 68 J4
Fort Smith, *U.S.* 70 H4
Fort Stockton 70 F5
Fortune Bay 68 V7
Fort Vermilion 68 H5
Fort Wayne 70 G3
Fort William 16 G5
Fort Worth 70 G5
Foshan 40 E2
Fosna 8 F5
Fossano 22 C6
Fossombrone 22 H7
Fougamou 54 G5
Fougères 18 D5
Foula 16 K1
Foulness 14 C3
Foumban 54 G3
Fourmies 14 G4
Fournoi 28 J7
Fouta Djallon 54 B2
Foveaux Strait 64 A8
Foxe Basin 68 R3
Foxe Channel 68 R4
Foxe Peninsula 68 R4
Fox Glacier 64 B6
Fox Islands 66 T4
Foz 20 C1
Foz do Cunene 58 A3
Foz do Iguaçu 78 L4
Fraga 20 L3
Franca 78 M3
Francavilla al Mare 24 J6
France 18 G7
Franceville 54 G5
Francistown 58 D4
Franeker 14 H1
Frankenberg 12 D5
Frankenthal 12 D7
Frankfort 70 K4
Frankfurt, *Germany* 12 K4
Frankfurt, *Germany* 12 D6
Franklin Bay 68 F2
Franklin D. Roosevelt Lake 70 C2
Franklin Mountains 68 F3
Franklin Strait 68 M2
Franz Josef Glacier 64 C6
Franz Josef Land = Zemlya Frantsa-Iosifa 34 J2
Fraser 68 G6
Fraserburg 58 C6
Fraserburgh 16 L4
Fraser Island 62 K5
Frasertown 64 F4
Frauenfeld 22 D3
Fredensborg 10 B2
Fredericton 68 T7
Frederikshåb = Paamiut 68 X4
Frederikshavn 8 F8
Frederikssund 10 B2
Frederiksværk 8 G9
Fredrikstad 8 F7
Freeport 70 G6
Freeport City 72 J3
Free State 58 D5
Freetown 54 B3
Fregenal de la Sierre 20 D6
Freiberg 12 J6
Freiburg 22 C3
Freilassing 22 H3
Freising 22 G2
Freistadt 22 K2
Fréjus 18 M10
Fremantle 62 C6
Fremont 70 G3
French Guiana 76 G3
French Pass 64 D5
French Polynesia 60 L7
Frenda 52 F1
Fresnes-sur-Apances 22 A3
Fresnillo 72 D4
Fresno 70 C4
Freudenstadt 22 D2
Freyung 12 J8
Frias 78 H4
Fribourg 22 C4
Friedburg 22 G2
Friedrichshafen 22 E3
Friesach 22 K4
Friesoythe 12 C3
Frisian Islands 14 H1
Fritzlar 12 E5
Frobisher Bay 68 T4
Frolovo 30 H5
Frome 16 K10
Frontera 72 F5
Frontignan 18 J10
Frosinone 24 H7
Frøya 8 D5
Fruges 14 E4
Frýdek Místek 10 H8
Fuding 38 G5
Fuengirola 20 F8
Fuentesauco 20 E3
Fuerte Olimpo 78 K3
Fuerteventura 52 C3
Fugu 38 E3
Fuhai 34 R8
Fujin 36 N7
Fuji-san 38 K3
Fukue-jima 38 H4
Fukui 38 K3
Fukuoka 38 J4
Fukushima 38 L3
Fulda 12 E6
Fulda 12 E6
Fuling 38 D5
Funafuti 60 H6
Funchal 52 B2
Fundão 20 C4
Funing 40 D2
Funtua 54 F2
Furmanovka 34 N9
Furmanovo 30 J5
Furneaux Group 62 J8
Fürstenberg 12 J3
Fürstenfeldbruck 22 G2
Fürstenwalde 12 K4
Fürth 12 F7
Furukawa 38 L3
Fushun 38 G2
Fusong 36 M8
Füssen 22 F3
Futog 26 G4
Fuxhou 38 F5
Fu Xian 38 D3
Fuxin 38 G2
Fuyang 38 F4
Fuyu 38 G1
Fuyun 34 R8
Fuzhou 40 F1
Fyn 12 F1
Fynshav 12 F2

G

Gaalkacyo 56 H2
Gabès 52 H2
Gabon 54 G5
Gaborone 58 D4
Gabrovo 26 N7
Gacé 14 C6
Gacko 26 F6
Gäddede 8 H4
Gadsden 70 J5
Găești 26 N5
Gaeta 24 H7
Gafsa 52 G2
Gaggenau 22 D2
Gagnoa 54 C3
Gaildorf 22 E2
Gaillac 18 G10
Gainesville, *Fla., U.S.* 70 K6
Gainesville, *Ga., U.S.* 70 K5
Gala 44 E3
Gălăbovo 28 H2
Galana 56 F4
Galanta 22 N2
Galapagos Islands = Islas Galápagos 76 (1)B1
Galashiels 16 K6
Galatas 28 F7
Galați 26 R4
Galdhøpiggen 8 D6
Galich 30 H3
Gallabat 50 G5
Galle 44 D7
Gallipoli 24 N8
Gällivare 8 L3
Gallup 70 E4
Galtat Zemmour 52 C3
Galveston Bay 70 G6
Galway 16 C8
Galway Bay 16 C8
Gamalakhe 58 E6
Gambēla 56 E2
Gambell 36 Z4
Gambier Islands 60 N8
Gamboma 56 B4
Gamboula 56 B3
Gan 36 L7
Ganado 70 E4
Gäncä 46 E1
Gandajika 56 C5
Gander 68 W7
Ganderkesee 12 D3
Gandesa 20 L3
Gāndhīdhām 44 B4
Gandhinagar 44 B4
Gandia 20 K6
Gandu 76 K6
Ganganagar 44 B3
Gangara 54 F2
Gangdise Shan 44 D2
Ganges 18 J10
Ganges 44 E3
Gangi 24 J11
Gangtok 44 E3
Gannett Peak 70 E3
Ganta 54 C3
Ganye 54 G3
Ganzhou 38 E5
Gao 52 E5
Gaoual 52 C6
Gap 22 B6
Gapan 40 G3
Garanhuns 76 K5
Garba 54 J3
Garbsen 12 E4
Gardelegen 12 G4
Garden City 70 F4
Gardēz 46 J3
Gardone Val Trompia 22 F5
Gargždai 10 L2
Gariau 43 D3
Garies 58 B6
Garissa 56 F4
Garlasco 22 D5
Garliava 10 N3
Garmisch-Partenkirchen 22 G3
Garonne 18 E9
Garoowe 56 H2
Garoua 54 G3
Garoua Boulai 54 G3
Garry Lake 68 L3
Garsen 56 G4
Garut 42 D4
Garwa 44 D4
Garwolin 10 L6
Gary 70 J3
Garyarsa 44 D2
Garzê 38 B4
Gasan Kuli 46 F2
Gasht 46 H4
Gashua 54 G2
Gastre 78 H7
Gatchina 30 F3
Gateshead 16 L7
Gauja 8 N8
Gaula 8 F5
Gaurella 44 D4
Gauteng 58 D5
Gava 20 N3
Gavdos 28 G10
Gävle 8 J6
Gawler 62 G6
Gawler Ranges 62 G6
Gaxun Nur 38 C2
Gaya, *India* 44 E4
Gaya, *Niger* 54 E2
Gayndah 62 K5
Gayny 30 K2
Gaza 50 F1
Gaz-Achak 34 L9
Gazandzhyk 34 K10
Gaziantep 46 C2
Gazipaşa 28 Q8
Gazli 34 L9
Gbaaka 54 C3
Gbarnga 54 C3
Gdańsk 10 H3
Gdov 8 P7
Gdyel 20 K9
Gdynia 10 H3
Gebel Katherina 50 F2
Gebze 28 M4
Gedaref 50 G5
Gediz 28 K6
Gediz 28 M6
Gedser 12 G2
Geel 14 H3
Geelong 62 H7
Geesthacht 12 F3
Gê'gyai 44 D2
Geidam 54 G2
Geilenkirchen 14 J4
Geilo 8 E6
Geinhausen 12 E6
Geislingen 22 E2
Geita 56 E4
Gejiu 40 C2
Gela 24 J11
Geladī 56 H2
Geldern 14 J3
Geleen 14 H4
Gelibolu 28 J4
Gelibolu Yarimadasi 28 J4
Gelsenkirchen 14 K3
Gembloux 14 G4
Gembu 54 G3
Gemena 56 B3
Gemlik 28 M4
Gemlik Körfezi 28 L4
Gemona del Friuli 22 J4
Genalē Wenz 56 G2
General Acha 78 J6
General Alvear 78 H6
General Pico 78 J6
General Pinedo 78 J4
General Roca 78 H6
General Santos 40 H5
Genève 22 B4
Gengma 40 B2
Genil 20 F7
Genk 14 H4
Genoa = Genova 22 D6
Genova 22 D6
Gent 14 F3
Genteng 42 D4
Genthin 12 H4
George 62 B6
George 58 C6
George 68 T5
George Town, *Aus.* 62 J8
George Town, *Malaysia* 42 C1
Georgetown, *Aus.* 62 H3
Georgetown, *Gambia* 54 B2
Georgetown, *Guyana* 76 F2
Georgia 46 D1
Georgia 70 K5
Georgian Bay 70 K2
Gera 12 H6
Geraldine 64 C7
Geraldton, *Aus.* 62 B5
Geraldton, *Can.* 70 J2
Gérardmer 22 B2
Gerede 28 Q4
Gerefsried 22 G3
Gereshk 46 H3
Gérgal 20 H7
Gerik 40 C5
Germany 12 E6
Germencik 28 K7
Germering 22 G2
Germersheim 14 L5
Gernika 20 H1
Gerolzhofen 12 F7
Gêrzê 44 D2
Geser 43 D3
Getafe 20 G4
Getxo 20 H1
Geugnon 18 K7
Gevgelija 28 E3
Gewanē 50 H5
Geyik Dağ 28 Q8
Geyve 28 N4
Ghadāmis 52 G2
Ghana 54 D3
Ghanzi 58 C4
Ghardaïa 52 F2
Gharo 46 J5
Gharyān 52 H2
Ghāt 50 B2
Ghazaouet 52 E1
Ghaziabad 44 C3
Ghazipur 44 D3
Ghazn 46 J3
Gheorgheni 26 N3
Gherla 26 L2
Ghizar 44 B1
Ghotāru 44 B3
Giannitsa 28 E4
Giannutri 24 F6
Giarre 24 K11
Gibraleón 20 D7
Gibraltar 20 E8
Gibson Desert 62 D4
Gideån 8 K5
Gien 18 H6
Gießen 12 D6
Gifhorn 12 F4
Gifu 38 K3
Gigha 16 G6
Giglio 24 E6
Giglio Castello 24 E6
Gijón 20 E1
Gila Bend 70 D5
Gilău 26 L3
Gilbert Islands 60 H5
Gilbués 76 H5
Gilching 22 G2
Gilf Kebir Plateau 50 E3
Gilgandra 62 J6
Gilgit 44 B1
Gilimanuk 42 E4
Gillam 68 N5
Gillette 70 E3
Gillingham 14 C3
Gīmbī 56 F2
Gimli 68 M6
Gimol'skoe Ozero 8 R5
Ginīr 56 G2
Gioia del Colle 24 L8
Gioia Tauro 24 K10
Gioura 28 F5
Girga 50 F2
Girona 20 N3
Gironde 18 E8
Girvan 16 H6
Gisborne 64 G4
Gisenyi 56 D4
Gitega 56 D4
Giurgiu 26 N6
Givet 14 G4
Givors 18 K8
Giyon 56 F2
Gizhiga 36 U4
Gizhiginskaya Guba 36 T4
Giżycko 10 L3
Gjiri i Vlorës 28 B4
Gjirokaster 28 C4
Gjoa Haven 68 M3
Gjøvik 8 F6
Glacier Peak 70 B2
Gladstone 62 K4
Glamoč 26 D5
Glan 12 C7
Glan 43 C1
Glarner Alpen 22 D4
Glasgow, *U.K.* 16 H6
Glasgow, *U.S.* 70 E2
Glauchau 12 H6
Glazov 34 J6
Gleisdorf 22 L3
Glendale 70 D5
Glendambo 62 G6
Glendive 70 F2
Glenmorgan 62 J5
Glennallen 68 B4
Glenn Innes 62 K5
Glenrothes 16 J5
Glina 22 M5
Gliwice 10 H7
Glodeni 26 Q2
Głogów 10 F6
Glomfjord 8 H3
Glomma 8 F5
Glorieuses 48 H7
Gloucester 16 K10
Głowno 10 J6
Głuchołazy 10 G7
Glückstadt 12 E3
Gmünd, *Austria* 22 J4
Gmünd, *Austria* 22 L2
Gmunden 22 J3
Gniezno 10 G5
Gnjilane 28 D2
Gnoien 12 H3
Goalpara 44 F3
Goba 56 F2
Gobabis 58 B4
Gobernador Gregores 78 G8
Gobi Desert 38 C2
Gobustan 46 E1
Goce Delčev 28 F3
Goch 14 J3
Gochas 58 B4
Godé 56 G2
Godhra 44 B4
Gödöllő 26 G2
Gods Lake 68 N6
Godthåb = Nuuk 68 W4
Goeree 14 F3
Goes 14 F3
Goiânia 76 H7
Goiás 76 G6
Goiás 76 G7
Gökçeada 28 H4
Gökova Körfezi 28 K8
Göksun 46 C2
Golaghat 44 F3
Golbāf 46 G4
Gölbasi 46 C2
Gol'chikha 34 Q3
Gölcük 28 K5
Gołdap 10 M3
Gold Coast 62 K5
Golden Bay 64 D5
Goldsboro 70 L4
Goldsworthy 62 C4
Goleniów 10 D4
Golfe d'Ajaccio 24 C7
Golfe de Gabès 52 H2
Golfe de Hammamet 52 H1
Golfe de Porto 24 C6
Golfe de Sagone 24 C6
Golfe de Saint-Malo 18 C5
Golfe de Tunis 24 E11
Golfe de Valinco 24 C7
Golfe du Lion 18 J10
Golfo de Almería 20 H8
Golfo de Batabanó 72 H4
Golfo de Cádiz 20 C7
Golfo de California 72 B3
Golfo de Chiriquí 72 H7
Golfo de Corcovado 78 F7
Golfo de Cupica 76 B2
Golfo de Fonseca 72 G6
Golfo de Guayaquil 76 A4
Golfo de Honduras 72 G5
Golfo del Darién 76 B2
Golfo dell' Asinara 24 C7
Golfo de los Mosquitos 76 A2
Golfo de Mazarrón 20 J7
Golfo de Morrosquillo 76 B1
Golfo de Panamá 72 J7
Golfo de Penas 78 F8
Golfo de San Jorge 78 H8
Golfo de Tehuantepec 72 E5
Golfo de València 20 L5
Golfo de Venezuela 76 C1
Golfo di Augusta 24 K11
Golfo di Catania 24 K11
Golfo di Gaeta 24 H7
Golfo di Gela 24 J11
Golfo di Genova 24 C4
Golfo di Manfredonia 24 L7
Golfo di Olbia 24 D8
Golfo di Oristano 24 C9
Golfo di Orosei 24 D8
Golfo di Palmas 24 C10
Golfo di Policastro 24 K9
Golfo di Salerno 24 J8
Golfo di Sant'Eufemia 24 K10
Golfo di Squillace 24 L10
Golfo di Taranto 24 L8
Golfo di Trieste 22 J5
Golfo di Venezia 22 H5
Golfo San Matías 78 J6
Gölhisar 28 M8
Gölmarmara 28 K6
Golyshmanovo 34 M6
Goma 56 D4
Gombe 54 G2
Gombi 54 G2
Gomera 52 B3
Gómez Palacio 70 F6
Gonam 36 M5
Gonbad-e Kavus 46 G2
Gonda 44 D3

Japan 38 K4
Japan Trench 60 E2
Japurá 76 D4
Jaramillo 78 H8
Jardim 78 K3
Jarosław 10 M7
Järpen 8 G5
Jarud Qi 38 G2
Järvenpää 8 N6
Jarvis 60 K6
Jasel'da 8 N10
Jäsk 46 H3
Jason Islands 78 J9
Jastrebarsko 22 L5
Jászberény 26 G2
Jataí 76 G7
Jatapu 76 F4
Jaunpur 44 D3
Java = Jawa 42 E4
Javarthushuu 36 J7
Java Sea 42 E4
Javoriv 10 N8
Jawa 42 E4
Jawhar 56 H3
Jayapura 43 F3
Jaza'ir Farasān 50 H4
Jazīrat Būbīyān 46 E4
Jbel Ayachi 52 E2
Jbel Bou Naceur 52 E2
Jbel Toubkal 52 D2
Jebba 54 E3
Jebel Gimbala 50 D5
Jebel Uweinat 50 E3
Jedburgh 16 K6
Jedda = Jiddah 46 C5
Jedeida 24 D12
Jędrzejów 10 K7
Jefferson City 70 H4
Jega 54 E2
Jēkabpils 8 N8
Jelgava 8 M8
Jemaja 42 D2
Jena 12 G6
Jendouba 52 G1
Jequié 76 J6
Jequitinhonha 76 J7
Jerada 52 E2
Jeremoabo 76 K6
Jerez de la Frontera 20 D8
Jerez de los Caballeros 20 D6
Jericho 62 J4
Jerramungup 62 C6
Jersey 18 C4
Jerusalem = Yerushalayim 46 C3
Jesenice 26 B3
Jesenik 10 G7
Jesi 22 J7
Jessore 44 E4
Jesup 70 K5
Jeumont 14 G4
Jever 12 C3
Jeypore 44 D5
Jezioro 10 J4
Jezioro Gardno 8 J9
Jezioro Jeziorsko 10 H6
Jezioro Łebsko 10 F3
Jezioro Śniardwy 10 L4
Jezioro Wigry 10 N2
Jhang Maghiana 44 B2
Jhansi 44 C3
Jharsuguda 44 D4
Jhelum 44 B2
Jialing Jiang 38 D4
Jiamusi 38 J1
Ji'an 38 E5
Jiangle 38 F5
Jiangling 38 E4
Jiangmen 38 E6
Jiangyou 38 C4
Jianyang 38 F5
Jiaonan 38 F3
Jiaozou 38 E3
Jiaxing 38 G4
Jiayuguan 38 B3
Jibou 26 L2
Jičín 10 E7
Jiddah 46 C5
Jiesjavrre 8 N2
Jiexiu 38 E3
Jihlava 10 E8
Jijia 26 Q2
Jijiga 56 G2
Jilib 56 G3
Jilin 38 H2
Jima 56 F2
Jimbolia 26 H4
Jiménez 70 F6
Jimsar 34 R9
Jinan 38 F3
Jinchang 38 C3
Jincheng 38 E3
Jindřichův Hradec 10 E8
Jingdezhen 38 F5
Jinggu 38 C6
Jinghe 34 Q9
Jinghong 38 C6
Jingmen 38 E4
Jingning 38 D3
Jingxi 38 D6
Jingyuan 38 C3
Jinhua 38 F5
Jining, *China* 38 E2
Jining, *China* 38 F3
Jinja 56 E3
Jinka 56 F2
Jinsha 38 C5
Jinshi 38 E5
Jinta 38 B2
Jinxi 38 G2
Jinzhou 38 G2
Jirgatol 46 K2
Jirin Gol 38 F2
Jirkov 12 J6
Jiroft 46 G4
Jirriiban 56 H2
Jishou 38 D5
Jiu 26 L4
Jiujiang 38 F5
Jiwani 46 H4
Jixi 38 J1
Jīzān 50 H4
Jizera 10 D7
J. J. Castelli 76 D4
Joal-Fadiout 52 B6
João Pessoa 76 L5
Jódar 20 G7
Jodhpur 44 B3
Joensuu 30 E2
Jōetsu 38 K3
Jõgeva 8 P7
Johannesburg 58 D5
John o' Groats 16 J3
Johnson's Crossing 68 E4
Johnston Island 60 J4
Johor Bahru 42 C2
Joigny 18 J5
Joinville, *Brazil* 78 M4
Joinville, *France* 18 L5
Jokkmokk 8 K3
Jökulsá-á Fjöllum 8 (1)E1
Jolfa 46 E2
Joliet 70 J3
Jolo 43 B1
Jolo 43 B1
Jonava 10 P2
Jonesboro 70 H4
Jones Sound 68 P1
Jonglei Canal 56 E2
Jongunjärvi 8 P4
Joniškis 10 N1
Jönköping 8 H8
Jonquière 70 M2
Joplin 70 H4
Jordan 46 C3
Jorhat 44 F3
Jörn 8 L4
Jos 54 F3
José de San Martin 78 G7
Joseph Bonaparte Gulf 62 E2
Joure 14 H2
Juan de Nova 58 G3
Juàzeiro 76 J5
Juàzeiro do Norte 76 K5
Juba 56 E3
Jubba 56 G3
Júcar 20 J5
Juchitán 72 F5
Judenburg 22 K3
Juhre 36 L8
Juist 12 B3
Juiz de Fora 78 N3
Juli 76 C7
Juliaca 76 C7
Juliana Top 76 F3
Jülich 14 J4
Jullouville 14 A6
Jumilla 20 J6
Jumla 44 D3
Junagadh 44 B4
Junction City 70 G4
Jundah 62 H4
Juneau 68 E5
Jungfrau 22 C4
Junggar Pendi 34 R8
Junsele 8 J5
Jun Xian 38 E4
Jūra 10 M2
Jura 16 G5
Jura 22 B4
Jurbarkas 10 M2
Jurhe 38 G2
Jurilovca 26 R5
Jūrmala 8 M8
Jūrmala 30 D3
Juruá 76 D4
Juruena 76 F5
Juruena 76 F6
Justo Daract 78 H5
Jutaí 76 D5
Jüterbog 12 J5
Juwain 46 H3
Ju Xian 38 F3
Jüymand 46 G3
Juzur al Halaniyat 46 G6
Jylland 8 E8
Jyvädskylä 30 E2
Jyväskylä 8 N5

K

K2 44 C1
Kaakhka 46 G2
Kaamanen 8 P2
Kaarta 52 C6
Kabaena 43 B4
Kabakly 46 H2
Kabala 54 B3
Kabale 56 E4
Kabalo 56 D5
Kåbdalis 8 L3
Kabompo 58 C2
Kabongo 56 D5
Kabugao 40 G3
Kābul 46 J3
Kabwe 58 D2
Kachikattsy 36 M4
Kachug 36 H6
Kadama 44 B6
Kadaň 10 C7
Kadınhanı 28 Q6
Kadoka 70 F3
Kadoma 58 D3
Kadugli 50 E5
Kaduna 54 F2
Kadzherom 30 L2
Kaédi 52 C5
Kaeo 64 D2
Kaesŏng 38 H3
Kafanchan 54 F3
Kaffrine 54 A2
Kafiau 43 C3
Kåfjord 8 N1
Kafr el Sheikh 50 F1
Kafue 58 D3
Kaga Bandoro 56 B2
Kagoshima 38 J4
Kahemba 56 B5
Kahnūj 46 G4
Kahraman Maraş 46 C2
Kahurangi Point 64 C5
Kaiama 54 E3
Kai Besar 43 D4
Kaifeng 38 E4
Kaihu 64 D2
Kaihua 38 F5
Kai Kecil 43 D4
Kaikohe 64 D2
Kaikoura 64 D6
Kaili 38 D5
Kaimana 43 D3
Käina 8 M7
Kainji Reservoir 54 E2
Kaipara Harbour 64 D3
Kairouan 52 H1
Kaiserslautern 12 C7
Kaišiadorys 10 P3
Kaitaia 64 D2
Kaiwatu 43 C4
Kaiyuan 40 C2
Kajaani 8 P4
Kakamega 56 E3
Kakata 54 B3
Kakhovs'ke Vodoskhovyshche 30 F5
Käkināda 44 D5
Kalabagh 44 B2
Kalabahi 43 B4
Kalabakan 42 F2
Kalach 30 H4
Kalachinsk 30 P3
Kalach-na-Donu 30 H5
Kalahari Desert 58 C4
Kalajoki 8 M4
Kalakan 36 K5
Kalam 44 B1
Kalamata 28 E7
Kalamazoo 70 J3
Kalampaka 28 D5
Kalana 54 C2
Kalaotoa 43 B4
Kalavryta 28 E6
Kalbarri 62 B5
Kale 28 L7
Kaledupa 43 B4
Kalemie 56 D5
Kalemyo 44 F4
Kalevala 8 R4
Kalewa 44 F4
Kalgoorlie 62 D6
Kalianda 42 D4
Kalibo 40 G4
Kalima 56 D4
Kalimantan 42 E2
Kaliningrad 10 K3
Kaliningradskiy Zaliv 10 J3
Kalispell 70 D2
Kalisz 10 H6
Kalixälven 8 M3
Kalkan 28 M8
Kalkaring 62 F3
Kallavesi 8 P5
Kallsjön 8 G5
Kalmar 8 J8
Kalmykiya 30 J5
Kalmykovo 30 K5
Kalocsa 26 F3
Kalol 44 B4
Kalpakio 28 C5
Kalpeni 44 B6
Kaltenkirchen 12 E3
Kaluga 30 G4
Kalyan 44 B5
Kalymnos 28 J7
Kalymnos 28 J8
Kama 6 K1
Kama 56 D4
Kamaishi 38 L3
Kaman 28 R5
Kamande 56 D4
Kamango 34 U6
Kamares 28 G8
Kambarka 30 K3
Kamchatka 36 U6
Kamchatskiy Zaliv 36 U5
Kamenica 28 E2
Kamenka, *Russia* 30 H1
Kamenka, *Russia* 30 H4
Kamen'-na-Obi 34 Q7
Kamensk-Shakhtinskiy 30 H5
Kamensk-Ural'skiy 30 M3
Kamenz 10 D6
Kamet 44 C2
Kamina 56 C5
Kamituga 56 D4
Kamloops 68 G6
Kampala 56 E3
Kampen 14 H2
Kâmpóng Cham 40 D4
Kâmpóng Chhnăng 40 C4
Kâmpot 40 C4
Kamsuuma 56 G3
Kam"yanets'-Podil's'kyy 30 E5
Kamyanyets 8 M10
Kamyshin 30 J4
Kamyzyak 30 J5
Kan 50 F6
Kananga 56 C5
Kanazawa 38 K3
Kanbalu 44 G4
Kanchipuram 44 C6
Kandahār 46 J3
Kandalaksha 8 S3
Kandalakshskiy Zaliv 30 F1
Kandi 54 E2
Kandira 28 N3
Kandy 44 D7
Kang 58 C4
Kangaatsiaq 68 W3
Kangān 46 F4
Kangar 42 C1
Kangaroo Island 62 G7
Kangchenjunga 44 E3
Kangding 38 C4
Kangeq 68 Y4
Kangerluarsoruseq 68 W4
Kangerlussuatsiaq 68 Y4
Kangersuatsiaq 68 W2
Kangetet 56 F3
Kangiqsualujjuaq 68 T5
Kangiqsujuaq 68 S4
Kangirsuk 68 S4
Kangmar 44 E3
Kangnŭng 38 H3
Kango 54 G4
Kangping 38 G2
Kaniama 56 C5
Kanin Nos 34 G4
Kanji Reservoir 48 D4
Kanjiža 26 H3
Kankaanpää 8 M6
Kankan 54 C2
Kankossa 52 C5
Kano 54 F2
Kanoya 38 J4
Kanpur 44 D3
Kansas 70 G4
Kansas City 70 H4
Kansk 34 T6
Kanta 56 F2
Kantchari 54 E2
Kantemirovka 30 G5
Kanye 58 C4
Kaohsiung 38 G6
Kaolack 52 B6
Kaoma 58 C2
Kapanga 56 C5
Kap Arkona 10 C3
Kapchagay 34 P9
Kap Cort Adelaer = Kangeq 68 Y4
Kap Farvel = Nunap Isua 68 Y5
Kapfenberg 22 L3
Kapıdağı Yarimadası 28 K4
Kapiri Mposhi 58 D2
Kapit 42 E2
Kapiti Island 64 E5
Kaplice 22 K2
Kapoeta 56 E3
Kaposvár 26 E3
Kappel 12 C6
Kappeln 12 E2
Kappl 22 F3
Kapsan 38 H2
Kapuskasing 70 K2
Kapuvár 26 E2
Kara 34 M4
Kara, *Russia* 34 M4
Kara, *Togo* 54 E3
Kara Ada 28 K8
Kara-Balta 34 N9
Karabekaul 46 H2
Kara-Bogaz-Gol 46 F1
Karabutak 30 M5
Karacabey 28 L4
Karacaköy 28 L3
Karacal Tepe 28 Q8
Karachayevo-Cherkesiya 30 H6
Karachi 46 J5
Karaganda 34 N8
Karaginskiy Zaliv 36 V5
Karaj 46 F2
Kara-Kala 46 G2
Karakalpakiya 34 K9
Karakol 34 P9
Karakoram 32 L6
Karaksar 36 K6
Kara-Kul' 34 N9
Karam 36 H5
Karaman 28 R7
Karamay 34 R8
Karamea 64 D5
Karamea Bight 64 C5
Karamürsel 28 M4
Karaoy 34 N8
Karapınar 28 R7
Kara-Say 34 P9
Karasburg 58 B5
Kara Sea = Karskoye More 34 L3
Karasu 28 N3
Karasuk 34 P7
Karasuk 34 P7
Karatal 34 P8
Karatobe 30 K5
Karaton 30 K5
Karazhal 30 P5
Karbalā' 46 D3
Karcag 26 H2
Karditsa 28 D5
Kärdla 8 M7
Kărdžali 28 H3
Kareliya 8 R4
Karepino 30 L2
Karesuando 8 M2
Kargasok 34 Q6
Kargat 34 P6
Kargil 44 C2
Kargopol' 30 G2
Kariba 58 D3
Kariba Dam 58 D3
Karibib 58 B4
Karimata 42 D3
Karimnagar 44 C5
Karkaralinsk 34 P8
Karkinits'ka Zatoka 30 F5
Karlik Shan 38 A2
Karlovac 26 C4
Karlovasi 28 J7
Karlovo 28 G2
Karlovy Vary 12 H6
Karlshamn 10 D1
Karlskoga 8 H7
Karlskrona 8 H8
Karlsruhe 12 D8
Karlstad 8 G7
Karlstadt 12 E7
Karmala 44 C5
Karmøy 8 C7
Karnafuli Reservoir 44 F4
Karnal 44 C3
Karnische Alpen 22 H4
Karnobat 28 J2
Karodi 46 J4
Karonga 56 E5
Karpathos 28 K9
Karpathos 28 K9
Karpenisi 28 D6
Karpogory 30 H2
Karrabük 28 Q3
Karratha 62 C4
Kars 46 D1
Karsakpay 30 N5
Kärsava 8 P8
Karshi 46 J2
Karskoye More 34 L3
Karslyaka 28 K6
Karstula 8 N5
Kartal 28 M4
Kartaly 30 M4
Kartayel' 30 K2
Kartuzy 10 H3
Karufa 43 D3
Karumba 62 H3
Karur 44 C6
Karvina 10 H8
Karwar 44 B6
Karystos 28 G6
Kasai 56 B4
Kasaji 58 C2
Kasama 58 E2
Kasansay 34 N9
Kasba Lake 68 L4
Kasempa 58 D2
Kasenga 58 D2
Kāshān 46 F3
Kashi 46 L2
Kashima 38 L3
Kāshmar 46 G2
Kashmor 46 J4
Kasimov 30 H4
Kasli 30 M3
Kasongo 56 D4
Kasos 28 K9
Kaspiysk 46 E1
Kassala 50 G4
Kassandreia 28 F4
Kassel 12 E5
Kasserine 52 G1
Kastamonu 28 R3
Kastelli 28 F9
Kastoria 28 D4
Kasulu 56 E4
Kasur 44 B2
Kata 36 G5
Katchall 44 F7
Katerini 28 E4
Katete 58 E2
Katha 44 G4
Katherine 62 F2
Kathiawar 46 K5
Kathmandu 44 E3
Kati 54 C2
Katihar 44 E3
Katiola 54 C3
Kato Nevrokopi 28 F3
Katonga 56 E3
Katoomba 62 K6
Katowice 10 J7
Katrineholm 8 J7
Katsina 54 F2
Katsina-Ala 54 F3
Kattakurgan 46 J2
Kattavia 28 K9
Kattegat 8 F8
Katun' 34 R7
Katwijkaan Zee 14 G2
Kauai 60 L3
Kaufbeuren 22 F3
Kauhajoki 8 M5
Kaunas 10 N3
Kauno 10 P3
Kaunus 6 G2
Kaura Namoda 54 F2
Kavadarci 28 D3
Kavajë 28 B3
Kavala 28 G4
Kavali 44 C5
Kavaratti 44 B6
Kavarna 26 R6
Kawakawa 64 E2
Kawambwa 56 D5
Kawau Island 64 E3
Kaweka 64 F4
Kawhia 64 E4
Kawkareik 40 B3
Kawthaung 40 B4
Kaya 54 D2
Kayak 34 U3
Kayes 54 B2
Kaymaz 28 P5
Kaynar 34 P8
Kayseri 46 C2
Kayyerkan 34 R4
Kazachinskoye 36 E5
Kazach'ye 36 P2
Kazakdar'ya 34 K9
Kazakhstan 34 L8
Kazan 68 M4
Kazan' 30 J3
Kazanlăk 28 H2
Kazan-rettō 60 E3
Kāzerūn 46 F4
Kazincbarcika 26 H1
Kazungula 58 D3
Kazymskiy Mys 34 M5
Kea 28 G7
Kea 28 G7
Kearney 70 G3
Kébémèr 52 B5
Kebkabiya 50 D5
Kebnekaise 8 K3
K'ebrī Dehar 56 G2
K'ech'a Terara 56 F2
Keçiborlu 28 N7
Kecskemet 26 G3
Kėdainiai 10 N2
Kediri 42 E4
Kédougou 54 B2
Kędzierzyn-Koźle 10 H7
Keele 68 F4
Keetmanshoop 58 B5
Kefallonia 28 C6
Kefamenanu 43 B4
Keflavík 8 (1)B2
Kegen' 34 P9
Keg River 68 H5
Keheili 50 F4
Kehl 22 C2
Keila 8 N7
Keitele 8 N5
Kekerengu 64 D5
Kékes 26 H2
Kelai Thiladhunmathee Atoll 44 B7
Kelheim 22 G2
Kelibia 24 F12
Kells 16 F8
Kelmë 10 M2
Kélo 54 H3
Kelowna 68 H7
Keluang 42 C2
Kem' 30 F2
Kemalpaşa 28 K6
Kemasik 42 C2
Kemer, *Turkey* 28 M8
Kemer, *Turkey* 28 N8
Kemerovo 34 R6
Kemi 8 N4
Kemijärvi 8 P3
Kemijärvi 8 P3
Kemijoki 8 P3
Kemmuna 24 J12
Kemnath 12 G7
Kempten 22 F3
Kendal 16 K7
Kendari 43 B3
Kendawangan 42 E3
Kendégué 54 H2
Kendujhargarh 44 E4
Kenema 54 B3
Keneurgench 46 G1
Kenge 56 B4
Kengtung 40 B2
Kenhardt 58 C5
Kénitra 52 D2
Kenmare 16 C10
Kennewick 70 C2
Keno Hill 68 D4
Kenora 70 H2
Kentau 34 M9
Kentucky 70 J4
Kenya 48 G5
Keokuk 70 H3
Kępno 10 H6
Kepulauan Anambas 42 D2
Kepulauan Aru 43 E4
Kepulauan Ayu 43 D2
Kepulauan Balabalangan 42 F3
Kepulauan Banggai 43 B3
Kepulauan Barat Daya 43 C4
Kepulauan Batu 42 B3
Kepulauan Bonerate 43 A4
Kepulauan Kai 43 D4
Kepulauan Kangean 42 F4
Kepulauan Karimunjawa 42 D4
Kepulauan Karkaralong 43 B2
Kepulauan Laut Kecil 42 F3
Kepulauan Leti 43 C4
Kepulauan Lingga 42 C2
Kepulauan Lucipara 43 C4
Kepulauan Mentawai 42 B3
Kepulauan Nanusa 43 C2
Kepulauan Natuna 42 D2
Kepulauan Riau 42 C2
Kepulauan Sabalana 42 F4
Kepulauan Sangir 43 C2
Kepulauan Solor 43 B4
Kepulauan Sula 43 B3
Kepulauan Talaud 43 C2
Kepulauan Tanimbar 43 D4
Kepulauan Tengah 42 F4
Kepulauan Togian 43 B3
Kepulauan Tukangbesi 43 B4
Kepulauan Watubela 43 D3
Kerch 30 G5
Kerchevskiy 30 L3
Kerempe Burnu 28 R2
Keren 50 G4
Kericho 56 F4
Keri Keri 64 D2
Kerio 56 F3
Kerki 46 J2
Kerkrade 14 J4
Kerkyra 28 B5
Kerkyra 28 B5
Kerma 50 F4
Kermadec Islands 60 H8
Kermadec Trench 60 J9
Kermān 46 G3
Kermānshāh 46 E3
Keros 28 H8
Kerpen 14 J4
Kerrville 70 G6
Kerulen 36 J7
Keryneia 28 R9
Keşan 28 J4
Keşiş Dağları 46 C2
Keszthely 26 E3

116

117

Morcenx 18 E9
Mordaga 36 L6
Mordoviya 30 H4
Morecambe 16 K7
Moree 62 J5
Morehead 43 F4
More Laptevykh 36 L1
Morelia 72 D5
Morella 20 K4
Moreton Island 62 K5
Morez 18 M7
Morfou 28 Q9
Morgan 62 G6
Morges 22 B4
Mori 38 L2
Morioka 38 L3
Morkoka 36 J4
Morlaix 18 B5
Mornington Island 62 G3
Morocco 48 C2
Morogoro 56 F5
Moro Gulf 40 G5
Morombe 58 G4
Mörön 36 G7
Morondava 58 G4
Morón de la Frontera 20 E7
Moroni 58 G2
Moron Us He 44 F2
Morotai 43 C2
Moroto 56 E3
Morpeth 16 L6
Morris 70 G2
Morristown 70 K4
Mors 8 E8
Morshansk 30 H4
Mortain 14 B6
Morteros 78 J5
Morvern 16 G5
Morwell 62 J7
Mosbach 12 E7
Moscow = Moskva 30 G3
Mosel 14 K4
Moselle 14 G6
Moses Lake 70 C2
Mosgiel 64 C7
Moshi 56 F4
Mosjøen 8 G4
Moskenesøy 8 F3
Moskva 30 G3
Mosonmagyaróvár 22 N3
Moss 8 F7
Mossburn 64 B7
Mosselbaai 58 C6
Mossoró 76 K5
Most 12 J6
Mostaganem 20 L9
Mostar 26 E6
Mostoles 20 G4
Møsvatn 8 E7
Mot'a 50 G5
Motala 8 H7
Motherwell 16 J6
Motihari 44 D3
Motilla del Palancar 20 J5
Motiti Island 64 F3
Motril 20 G8
Motru 26 K5
Motu One 60 L7
Motygino 34 S6
Mouchard 22 A4
Moudjéria 52 C5
Moudros 28 H5
Mouila 54 G5
Moulins 18 J7
Moulmein 40 B3
Moundou 50 C6
Mount Adam 78 J9
Mount Adams 70 B2
Mountain Nile =
Bahr el Jebel 56 E2
Mount Alba 64 B7
Mount Aloysius 62 E5
Mount Anglem 64 A8
Mount Apo 40 H5
Mount Ararat 46 D2
Mount Arrowsmith 64 C6
Mount Aspiring 64 B7
Mount Assiniboine 68 H6
Mount Augustus 62 C4
Mount Baco 40 G3
Mount Baker 70 B2
Mount Bartle Frere 62 J3
Mount Bogong 62 J7
Mount Brewster 64 B7
Mount Bruce 62 C4
Mount Cameroun 48 D5
Mount Columbia 68 H6
Mount Cook 64 C6
Mount Cook 64 C6
Mount Donald 64 A7
Mount Egmont 64 E4
Mount Elbert 70 E4
Mount Elgon 56 E3
Mount Essendon 62 D4
Mount Evelyn 62 F2
Mount Everest 44 E3
Mount Fairweather 68 D5
Mount Gambier 62 H7
Mount Garnet 62 J3
Mount Hood 70 B2
Mount Hutt 64 C6
Mount Huxley 64 B7
Mount Isa 62 G4
Mount Jackson 80 (2)MM2
Mount Karisimbi 56 D4
Mount Kendall 64 D5
Mount Kenya =
Kirinyaga 56 F4
Mount Kilimanjaro 56 F4
Mount Kirkpatrick 80 (2)AA1
Mount Kosciuszko 62 J7
Mount Liebig 62 F4
Mount Lloyd George 68 G5
Mount Logan 68 C4
Mount Magnet 62 C5
Mount Maunganui 64 F3
Mount McKinley 66 S3
Mount Meharry 62 C4
Mount Menzies 80 (2)L2
Mount Minto 80 (2)Y2
Mount Mulanje 58 F3
Mount Murchison 64 C6
Mount Nyiru 56 F3
Mount Olympus 70 B2
Mount Ord 62 E3
Mount Ossa 62 J8
Mount Owen 64 D5
Mount Paget 78 P9
Mount Pleasant 70 K3
Mount Pulog 40 G3
Mount Rainier 70 B2
Mount Ratz 68 E5
Mount Richmond 64 D5
Mount Roberts 62 K5
Mount Robson 68 H6
Mount Roosevelt 68 F5
Mount Roraima 76 E2
Mount Ross 64 E5
Mount Shasta 70 B3
Mount Somers 64 C6
Mount Stanley 56 D3
Mount Tahat 48 D3
Mount Travers 64 D6
Mount Usborne 78 K9
Mount Vernon 70 J4
Mount Victoria,
Myanmar 40 A2
Mount Victoria, *P.N.G.* 60 E6
Mount Waddington 68 F6
Mount Washington 68 S8
Mount Whitney 70 C4
Mount Woodroffe 62 F5
Mount Ziel 62 F4
Moura 20 C6
Mousa 16 L2
Moussoro 50 C5
Moutamba 54 G5
Mouth of the
Shannon 16 B9
Mouths of the
Amazon 74 G3
Mouths of the
Danube 26 S4
Mouths of the
Ganges 44 E4
Mouths of the Indus 46 J5
Mouths of the
Irrawaddy 40 A3
Mouths of the
Krishna 44 D5
Mouths of the
Mekong 40 D5
Mouths of the Niger 54 F4
Moûtiers 22 B5
Moutong 43 B2
Mouzarak 54 H2
Moyale 56 F3
Moyen Atlas 52 D2
Moyenvic 14 J6
Moyero 34 U4
Moyynty 34 N8
Mozambique 58 E3
Mozambique
Channel 58 F4
Mozhga 30 K3
Mozirje 22 K4
Mpanda 56 E5
Mpika 58 E2
Mporokoso 56 E5
Mpumalanga 58 D5
Mrągowo 10 L4
Mrkonjić-Grad 22 N6
M'Sila 52 F1
Mtsensk 30 G4
Mtwara 56 G6
Muang Khammouan 40 C3
Muang Không 40 D4
Muang Khôngxédôn 40 D3
Muang Khoua 40 C2
Muang Pakxan 40 C3
Muang Phin 40 D3
Muang Sing 40 C2
Muang Xai 40 C2
Muar 42 C2
Muarabungo 42 C3
Muaradua 42 C3
Muarasiberut 42 B3
Muaratewen 42 E3
Muarawahau 42 F2
Mubarek 34 M10
Mubende 56 E3
Mubrani 43 D3
Muck 16 F5
Muckadilla 62 J5
Muconda 56 C6
Mucur 28 S5
Mudanjiang 38 H2
Mudanya 28 L4
Mudurnu 28 P4
Mufulira 58 D2
Mughshin 46 F6
Muğla 28 L7
Mugodzhary 30 L5
Muhammad Qol 50 G3
Mühldorf 22 H2
Mühlhausen 12 F5
Muhos 8 N4
Muhu 8 M7
Muhulu 56 D4
Mukacheve 10 M9
Mukdahan 40 C3
Mukomuko 42 C3
Mukry 46 J2
Mukuku 58 D2
Mulaku Atoll 44 B8
Mulde 12 H5
Mulgrave Island 62 H2
Mulhacén 20 G7
Mülheim 14 J3
Mulhouse 22 C3
Muling 38 J1
Mull 16 G5
Mullaittivu 44 D7
Mullewa 62 C5
Müllheim 22 C3
Mullingar 16 E8
Mulobezi 58 D3
Multan 46 K3
Mumbai 44 B5
Mumbwa 58 D2
Muna 43 B4
Munaðarnes 8 (1)C1
Münchberg 12 G6
München 22 G2
Münden 12 E5
Mundo Novo 76 J6
Mundrabilla 62 E6
Munera 20 H5
Mungbere 56 D3
Munger 44 E3
Munich = München 22 G2
Munster, *France* 22 C2
Munster, *Germany* 12 F4
Münster, *Germany* 14 K3
Munte 43 A2
Muojärvi 8 Q4
Muonio 8 M3
Muqdisho 56 H3
Mur 22 L4
Murang'a 56 F4
Murashi 30 J3
Murat 46 D2
Muratlı 28 K3
Murchison 64 D5
Murcia 20 J7
Murdo 70 F3
Mureș 26 J3
Muret 18 G10
Murghob 46 K2
Muriaé 76 J8
Müritz 12 H3
Muriwai 64 F4
Murmansk 8 S2
Murnau 22 G3
Murom 30 H3
Muroran 38 L2
Muros 20 A2
Murray 62 H6
Murray Bridge 62 G7
Murray River Basin 62 H6
Murska Sobota 22 M4
Murter 22 L7
Murtosa 20 B4
Murud 44 B5
Murupara 64 F4
Mururoa 60 M8
Murwara 44 D4
Murzūq 52 H3
Mürzzuschlag 22 L3
Muş 46 D2
Mūša 10 N1
Musala 28 F2
Muscat = Masqaţ 46 G5
Musgrave Ranges 62 E5
Mushin 54 E3
Muskegon 70 J3
Musmar 50 G4
Musoma 56 E4
Mussende 56 B6
Mustafakemalpaşa 28 L4
Mut, *Egypt* 50 E2
Mut, *Turkey* 28 R8
Mutare 58 E3
Mutarnee 62 J3
Mutnyy Materik 30 L1
Mutoray 34 U5
Mutsamudu 58 G2
Mutsu 38 L2
Muttaburra 62 H4
Mutur 44 D7
Muyezerskiy 8 R5
Muyinga 56 E4
Muynak 34 K9
Muzaffarnagar 44 C3
Muzaffarpur 44 E3
Muzillac 18 C6
Muztagata 34 N10
Mwali 58 G2
Mwanza 56 E4
Mweka 56 C4
Mwenda 56 D6
Mwene-Ditu 56 C5
Mwenezi 58 E4
Mwenezi 58 E4
Mwinilunga 58 C2
Myanmar 40 B2
Myaungmya 40 A3
Myingyan 40 B2
Myitkyina 40 B1
Myjava 22 N2
Myjava 22 N2
Mykolayiv 10 N8
Mykonos 28 H7
Mymensingh 44 F4
Mynbulak 34 L9
Myndagayy 36 N4
Myōjin 38 K4
Myonggan 38 H2
Mýrdalsjökull 8 (1)D3
Myrina 28 H5
Myrtle Beach 70 L5
Mys Alevina 36 S5
Mys Aniva 38 L1
Mys Buorkhaya 36 N2
Mys Dezhneva 36 Z3
Mys Elizavety 36 Q6
Mys Enkan 36 P5
Mys Govena 36 V5
Mys Kanin Nos 30 H1
Mys Kril'on 38 L1
Myślenice 10 J8
Myślibórz 10 D5
Mys Lopatka, *Russia* 36 T6
Mys Lopatka, *Russia* 36 S2
Mys Navarin 36 X4
Mys Nemetskiy 8 S2
Mys Olyutorskiy 36 W5
Mysore 44 C6
Mys Peschanyy 34 J9
Mys Povorotnyy 38 J2
Mys Prubiynyy 30 F5
Mys Shelagskiy 36 V2
Mys Sivuchiy 36 U5
Mys Terpeniya 36 Q7
Mys Tolstoy 36 T5
Mys Yuzhnyy 36 T5
Mys Zhelaniya 34 M2
Myszksw 10 J7
My Tho 40 D4
Mytilini 28 J5
Mývatn 8 (1)E2
Mže 12 H7
Mzimba 58 E2
Mzuzu 58 E2

N

Naas 16 F8
Nabas 40 G4
Naberezhnyye Chelny 30 K3
Nabeul 24 E12
Nabire 43 E3
Nacala 58 G2
Nacaroa 58 F2
Náchod 10 F7
Nadiad 44 B4
Nador 52 E2
Nadvirna 26 M1
Nadym 30 P1
Nadym 30 P2
Næstved 12 G1
Nafpaktos 28 D6
Nafplio 28 E7
Naga 40 G4
Nagano 38 K3
Nagaon 44 F3
Nagarzê 44 F3
Nagasaki 38 J4
Nagaur 44 B3
Nagercoil 44 C7
Nago 38 H5
Nagold 12 D8
Nagorsk 30 K3
Nagoya 38 K4
Nagpur 44 C4
Nagqu 44 F2
Nagyatád 22 N4
Nagykállś 26 J2
Nagykanizsa 22 N4
Nagykáta 10 J10
Nagykőrös 26 G2
Naha 38 H5
Nahanni 68 G4
Nahanni Butte 68 G4
Nahr en Nile = Nile 50 F2
Naiman Qi 38 G2
Nain 68 U5
Nairn 16 J4
Nairobi 56 F4
Naivasha 56 F4
Naizishan 38 H2
Najafābād 46 F3
Nájera 20 H2
Najibabad 44 C3
Najin 38 J2
Najrān 50 H4
Nakamura 38 J4
Nakhodka, *Russia* 34 P4
Nakhodka, *Russia* 38 J2
Nakhon Ratchasima 40 C3
Nakhon Sawan 40 B3
Nakhon Si
Thammarat 40 B5
Nakina 68 P6
Nakło nad Notecią 10 G4
Nakonde 56 E5
Nakskov 12 G2
Nakten 8 H5
Nakuru 56 F4
Nal'chik 46 D1
Nallihan 28 P4
Nālūt 52 H2
Namanga 56 F4
Namangan 34 N9
Namapa 58 F2
Namasagali 56 E3
Nam Can 40 C5
Nam Co 44 F2
Namdalen 8 G4
Nam Dinh 40 D2
Namib Desert 58 A4
Namibe 58 A3
Namibia 58 B4
Namidobe 58 F3
Namlea 43 C3
Namo 43 A3
Nampa 46 C3
Nampala 54 C1
Nam Ping 40 B3
Namp'o 38 H3
Nampula 58 F3
Namsos 8 F4
Namtsy 36 M4
Namur 14 G4
Namwala 58 D3
Nan 40 C3
Nanaimo 70 B2
Nanao 38 K3
Nanchang 38 F5
Nanchong 38 D4
Nancy 22 B2
Nanda Devi 44 C2
Nänded 44 C5
Nandurbar 44 B4
Nandyal 44 C5
Nanfeng 38 F5
Nangalala 62 G2
Nangapinoh 42 E3
Nangatayap 42 E3
Nangis 18 J5
Nangong 38 F3
Nang Xian 44 F3
Nanjing 38 F4
Nannine 62 C5
Nanning 40 D2
Nanortalik 68 X4
Nanpan 40 D2
Nanping 38 F5
Nansei-shotō 38 H5
Nantes 18 D6
Nanton 70 D1
Nantong 38 G4
Nanumea 60 H6
Nanuque 76 J7
Nanutarra
Roadhouse 62 C4
Nanyang 38 E4
Napalkovo 34 N3
Napas 36 C4
Napasoq 68 W3
Napier 64 F4
Naples = Napoli, *It.* 24 J8
Naples, *U.S.* 70 K6
Napo 76 C4
Napoli 24 J8
Nara 52 D5
Narathiwat 40 C5
Narbonne 18 H10
Nardò 24 N8
Nares Strait 66 J2
Narew 10 N5
Narew 10 L5
Narib 58 B4
Narmada 44 C4
Narnaul 44 C3
Narni 24 G6
Narok 56 F4
Närpes 8 L5
Narrabi 62 J6
Narrandera 62 J6
Narsimhapur 44 C4
Nart 38 F2
Narva 8 P7
Narva 8 Q7
Narva Bay 8 P7
Narvik 8 J2
Nar'yan Mar 30 K1
Naryn 36 F6
Năsăud 26 M2
Nashua 70 M3
Nashville 70 J4
Našice 26 F4
Nasik 44 B4
Nasir 56 E2
Nassarawa 54 F3
Nassau 72 J3
Nässjö 8 H8
Nastapoka Islands 68 R5
Nasugbu 40 G4
Naswá 46 G5
Nata 58 D4
Natal 76 K5
Natara 36 L3
Natashquan 68 U6
Natchez 70 H5
Natchitoches 70 H5
National Park 64 E4
Natitingou 54 E2
Natuna Besar 42 D2
Naucelle 18 H9
Nauchas 58 B4
Nauders 22 F4
Naujoji Akmenė 10 M1
Naumburg 12 G5
Nauru 60 G6
Nauta 76 C4
Nautonwa 44 D3
Navahermosa 20 F5
Navahrudak 8 N10
Navalero 20 H3
Navalmoral de la
Mata 20 E5
Navalvillar de Pela 20 E5
Navapolatsk 30 E3
Navlya 30 F4
Navoi 34 M9
Navojoa 70 E6
Navrongo 54 D2
Navsari 44 B4
Nawabshah 46 J4
Nāwah 46 J3
Naxçıvan 46 E2
Naxos 28 H7
Naxos 28 H7
Nayakhan 36 T4
Näy Band 46 G3
Nayoro 38 L2
Nazaré 20 A5
Nazarovo 34 S6
Nazca 76 C6
Nazca Ridge 78 E3
Naze 38 H5
Nazilli 28 L7
Nazino 34 P6
Nazrēt 56 F2
Nazwá 46 G5
Nazyvayevsk 30 P3
Ncojane 58 C4
Ndélé 56 C2
Ndjamena 50 B5
Ndjolé 54 G5
Ndola 58 D2
Nea Ionia 28 E5
Neapoli 28 F8
Nea Roda 28 F4
Nea Zichni 28 F3
Nebbi 56 E3
Nebitdag 46 F2
Nebo 62 J4
Nebraska 70 F3
Neckar 12 D7
Neckar 12 D8
Neckarsulm 12 E7
Necker Island 60 K3
Necochea 78 K6
Nédély 50 C4
Nedre Soppero 8 L3
Needles 70 D5
Nefedovo 30 P3
Nefta 52 G2
Neftçala 46 E2
Neftekamsk 30 K3
Neftekumsk 30 H6
Nefteyugansk 30 P2
Nefza 24 D12
Negage 56 B5
Negēlē 56 F2
Negele 56 F2
Negev 50 F1
Negomane 58 F2
Negombo 44 C7
Negotin 26 K5
Negotino 28 E3
Négrine 52 G2
Negro, *Arg.* 78 J7
Negro, *Brazil* 76 E4
Negros 40 G5
Negru Vodă 26 R6
Nehbandān 46 G3
Nehe 36 M7
Nehoiu 26 P4
Neijiang 38 C5
Nei Monggol 38 E2
Neiva 76 B3
Neixiang 38 E4
Nejanilini Lake 68 M5
Nek'emtē 56 F2
Nelidovo 30 F3
Nellore 44 C6
Nel'ma 36 P7
Nelson 68 N5
Nelson, *Can.* 70 C2
Nelson, *N.Z.* 64 D5
Nelspruit 58 E5
Nēma 52 D5
Neman 10 M2
Nēman 8 N10
Nemours 18 H5
Nemperola 43 B5
Nemunas 10 P3
Nemuro 38 M2
Nen 36 L7
Nenagh 16 D9
Nene 14 B2
Nenjiang 36 M7
Nepa 36 H5
Nepal 44 D3
Nepalganj 44 D3
Nepomuk 12 J7
Ner 10 H5
Nera 24 G6
Neratovice 12 K6
Neris 10 P2
Nerja 20 G8
Neryungri 36 L5
Nesebăr 26 Q7
Netherlands 14 H2
Netherlands Antilles 72 L6
Nettilling Lake 68 S3
Neubrandenburg 12 J3
Neuburg 12 G8
Neuchâtel 22 B3
Neuenhagen 12 J4
Neufchâteau,
Belgium 14 H5
Neufchâteau, *France* 18 L5
Neufchâtel-en-Bray 14 D5
Neuhof 12 E6
Neukirchen 12 D2
Neumarkt 12 G7
Neumünster 12 F2
Neunkirchen, *Austria* 22 M3
Neunkirchen,
Germany 12 C7
Neuquén 78 H6
Neuruppin 12 H4
Neusiedler 10 F10
Neusiedler See 22 M3
Neuss 14 J3
Neustadt, *Germany* 12 F2
Neustadt, *Germany* 12 F7
Neustadt, *Germany* 12 G6
Neustadt, *Germany* 12 G8
Neustadt, *Germany* 12 H7
Neustadt, *Germany* 14 L5
Neustrelitz 12 J3
Neu-Ulm 12 F8
Neuwerk 12 D3
Neuwied 14 K4
Nevada 70 C4
Nevada 70 H4
Nevado Auzangate 76 C6
Nevado de Colima 72 D5
Nevado de Cumbal 76 B3
Nevado de
Huascaran 76 B5
Nevado de Illampu 76 D7
Nevado Sajama 76 D7
Nevados de Cachi 78 H4
Never 36 L6
Nevers 18 J7
Nevesinje 26 F6
Nevėžis 8 M9
Nevinnomyssk 30 H6
Nevşehir 28 S6
Newala 56 F6
New Amsterdam 76 F2
Newark 70 M3
Newark-on-Trent 14 B1
New Bedford 70 M3
New Britain 60 F6
New Brunswick 68 T7
Newbury 14 A3
New Bussa 54 E3
Newcastle 62 K6
Newcastle-under-
Lyme 16 K8
Newcastle upon Tyne 16 L6
Newcastle Waters 62 F3
New Delhi 44 C3
Newfoundland 68 V7
Newfoundland 68 V7
New Georgia Islands 60 F6
New Glasgow 68 U7
New Guinea 32 S10
New Hampshire 70 M3
New Hanover 60 F6
New Haven 70 M3
Newhaven 14 C4
New Iberia 72 F2

New Ireland 60 F6
New Jersey 70 M3
Newman 62 C4
Newmarket 14 C2
New Mexico 70 E5
New Orleans 70 H6
New Plymouth 64 E4
Newport, *Eng., U.K.* 14 A4
Newport, *Wales, U.K.* 16 K10
Newport, *U.S.* 70 B3
New Providence 72 J3
Newquay 16 G11
Newry 16 F7
New Siberia Islands = Novosibirskiye Ostrova 36 P1
New South Wales 62 H6
Newton 70 G4
Newtownards 16 G7
New Ulm 70 G3
New York 70 L3
New York 70 M3
New Zealand 64 B5
Neya 30 H3
Neyrīz 46 F4
Neyshābūr 46 G2
Ngabang 42 D2
Ngalu 43 B5
Ngamring 44 E3
Ngaoundéré 54 G3
Ngara 56 E4
Ngawihi 64 E5
Ngo 54 H5
Ngoura 50 C5
Ngozi 56 D4
Nguigmi 54 G2
Nguru 54 G2
Nhachengue 58 F4
Nha Trang 40 D4
Nhulunbuy 62 G2
Niafounké 52 E5
Niakaramandougou 54 C3
Niamey 54 E2
Niangara 56 D3
Nia-Nia 56 D3
Nias 42 B2
Nicaragua 72 G6
Nicastro 24 L10
Nice 22 C7
Nicobar Islands 40 A5
Nicosia = Lefkosia 28 R9
Nida 10 K7
Nidym 36 F4
Nidzica 10 K4
Niebüll 12 D2
Niedere Tauern 22 J3
Niefang 54 G4
Niemegk 12 H4
Nienburg 12 E4
Niesky 12 K5
Nieuw Amsterdam 76 F2
Nieuw Nickerie 76 F2
Nieuwpoort 14 E3
Niğde 28 S7
Niger 52 G5
Niger 54 E2
Nigeria 54 F2
Nigoring Hu 38 B3
Niigata 38 K3
Nijar 20 H8
Nijmegen 14 H3
Nikel' 8 R2
Nikolayevsk-na-Amure 36 Q6
Nikol'sk 30 J3
Nikol'skoye 36 V5
Nikopol' 30 F5
Nikšić 26 F7
Nilande Atoll 44 B8
Nile 50 F3
Nimach 44 B4
Nîmes 18 K10
Nimule 56 E3
Nin 22 L6
Nine Degree Channel 44 B7
9 de Julio 78 J6
Ning'an 38 H2
Ningbo 38 G5
Ningde 38 F5
Ninghai 38 G5
Ninh Binh 40 D2
Ninh Hoa 40 D4
Niobrara 70 G3
Nioro 52 D5
Nioro du Sahel 54 C1
Niort 18 E7
Nipigon 70 J2
Niquelândia 76 H6
Nirmal 44 C5
Niš 26 J6
Nisa 20 C5
Niscemi 24 J11
Nisporeni 26 R2
Nisyros 28 K8
Niterói 78 N3
Nitra 10 H9
Nitra 10 H9
Nitsa 30 M3
Niue 60 K7
Nivelles 14 G4
Nizamabad 44 C5
Nizhnekamsk 30 K3
Nizhnekamskoye Vodokhranilishche 30 K3
Nizhneudinsk 36 F5
Nizhnevartovsk 30 Q2
Nizhneyansk 36 P2
Nizhniy Lomov 30 H4
Nizhniy Novgorod 30 H3
Nizhniy Tagil 30 M3
Nizhnyaya Tunguska 36 H4
Nizhyn 30 F4
Nizip 46 C2
Nizza Monferrato 22 D6
Njazidja 58 G2
Njombe 56 E5
Njombe 56 E5
Nkambe 54 G3
Nkhotakota 58 E2
Nkongsamba 54 F4
Nkurenkuru 58 B3
Nobeoka 38 J4
Noci 24 M8
Nogales 70 D5
Nogat 10 J3
Nogent-le-Rotrou 18 F5
Noginsk 30 G3
Noginskiy 34 S5
Nogliki 36 Q6
Noia 20 B2
Noire 40 C2
Noirmoutier-en-l'Île 18 C6
Nok Kundi 46 H4
Nokou 52 H6
Nola, *C.A.R.* 56 B3
Nola, *It.* 24 J8
Nolinsk 30 J3
Nomoi Islands 60 F5
Nong Khai 40 C3
Noord-beveland 14 F3
Noord-Oost-Polder 14 H2
Noordwijk aan Zee 14 G2
Norak 46 J2
Nordaustlandet 80 (1)L1
Nordborg 12 E1
Norden 12 C3
Nordenham 12 D3
Norderney 12 C3
Norderney 12 C3
Norderstedt 12 F3
Nordfjordeid 8 D6
Nordfriesische Inseln 12 D2
Nordhausen 12 F5
Nordhorn 14 K2
Nordkapp 8 N1
Nordkinn 8 P1
Nordkinnhalvøya 8 P1
Nordkvaløya 8 J1
Nordli 8 G4
Nördlingen 12 F8
Nord-Ostsee-Kanal 12 E2
Nordstrand 12 D2
Nordvik 34 W3
Nore 16 E9
Norfolk 70 L4
Norfolk Island 60 G8
Noril'sk 34 R4
Norman 70 G4
Normandia 76 F3
Normanton 62 H3
Norman Wells 68 F3
Nørre Åby 12 E1
Nørre Alslev 12 G2
Norrköping 8 J7
Norrtälje 8 K7
Norseman 62 D6
Norsk 36 N6
Northallerton 16 L7
Northam 62 C6
North America 66 L5
Northampton, *Aus.* 62 B5
Northampton, *U.K.* 14 B2
North Andaman 40 A4
North Battleford 68 K6
North Bay 70 L2
North Cape 64 D2
North Carolina 70 K4
North Channel 16 G6
North Dakota 70 F2
Northeim 12 F5
Northern Cape 58 C5
Northern Ireland 16 E7
Northern Mariana Islands 60 E4
Northern Province 58 D4
Northern Territory 62 F4
North Foreland 14 D3
North Horr 56 F3
North Island 64 D3
North Korea 38 H3
North Platte 70 F3
North Platte 70 F3
North Ronaldsay 16 K2
North Sea 16 N4
North Stradbroko Island 62 K5
North Taranaki Bight 64 D4
North Uist 16 E4
Northumberland Strait 68 U7
North West 58 C5
North West Basin 62 C4
North West Cape 62 B4
North West Christmas Island Ridge 60 K4
North West Highlands 16 G4
Northwest Territories 68 G4
Norton Sound 66 T3
Nortorf 12 E2
Norway 8 F5
Norwegian Sea 8 B4
Norwich 14 D2
Nos 30 H1
Nos Emine 26 Q7
Nosevaya 30 K1
Noshiro 38 K2
Nos Kaliakra 26 R6
Noşratābād 46 G4
Nos Šabla 26 R6
Nossen 12 J5
Nosy Barren 58 G3
Nosy Bé 58 H2
Nosy Boraha 58 J3
Nosy Mitsio 58 H2
Nosy Radama 58 H2
Nosy-Varika 58 H4
Notec 10 G4
Notios Evvoikos Kolpos 28 F6
Notre Dame Bay 68 V7
Notsé 54 E3
Nottingham 14 A2
Nottingham Island 68 R4
Nouâdhibou 52 B4
Nouakchott 52 B5
Nouâmghar 52 B5
Nouméa 60 G8
Nouvelle Calédonie 60 G8
Nova Gorica 22 J5
Nova Gradiška 26 E4
Nova Iguaçu 78 N3
Nova Mambone 58 F4
Nova Pazova 26 H5
Novara 22 D5
Nova Scotia 68 T8
Nova Xavantina 76 G6
Novaya Igirma 36 G5
Novaya Karymkary 30 N2
Novaya Kasanka 30 J5
Novaya Lyalya 30 M3
Novaya Zemlya 34 J3
Nova Zagora 26 P7
Novelda 20 K6
Nové Město 10 F8
Nové Mesto 10 G9
Nové Zámky 10 H10
Novgorod 30 F3
Novi Bečej 26 H4
Novigrad 24 H3
Novi Iskăr 26 L7
Novi Ligure 22 D6
Novi Marof 22 M4
Novi Pazar, *Bulgaria* 26 Q6
Novi Pazar, *Yugoslavia* 26 H6
Novi Sad 26 G4
Novi Vinodolski 22 K5
Novoaleksandrovsk 30 H5
Novoalekseyevka 30 L4
Novoanninsky 30 H4
Novocheboksarsk 30 J3
Novocherkassk 30 H5
Novodvinsk 30 H2
Novo Hamburgo 78 L4
Novohrad-Volyns'kyy 30 E4
Novokazalinsk 30 M5
Novokuybyshevsk 30 J4
Novokuznetsk 34 R7
Novoletov'ye 34 U3
Novo Mesto 22 L5
Novomoskovsk 30 G4
Novonazimovo 36 E5
Novorossiysk 30 G6
Novorybnoye 36 H2
Novoselivka 26 S2
Novosergiyevka 30 K4
Novosibirsk 34 Q6
Novosibirskiye Ostrova 36 P1
Novosil' 30 G4
Novotroitsk 30 L4
Novouzensk 30 J4
Novozybkov 30 F4
Novvy 34 V3
Nový Bor 12 K6
Nový Jičín 10 H8
Novyy Port 34 N4
Novyy Uoyan 36 J5
Novyy Urengoy 34 P4
Novyy Urgal 36 N6
Novyy Uzen' 34 J9
Nowa Dęba 10 L7
Nowa Ruda 10 F7
Nowogard 10 E4
Nowo Warpno 12 K3
Nowra 62 K6
Now Shahr 46 F2
Nowy Dwór Mazowiecki 10 K5
Nowy Sącz 10 K8
Nowy Targ 10 K8
Nowy Tomyśl 10 F5
Noyabr'sk 34 P5
Noyon 14 E5
Nsombo 58 D2
Ntem 54 G4
Ntwetwe Pan 58 C4
Nu 44 G2
Nuasjärvi 8 Q4
Nubian Desert 50 F3
Nudo Coropuna 76 C7
Nueltin Lake 68 M4
Nueva Lubecka 78 G7
Nueva Rosita 70 F6
Nueva San Salvador 72 G6
Nuevo Casas Grandes 70 E5
Nuevo Laredo 70 G6
Nugget Point 64 B8
Nuhaka 64 F4
Nuku'alofa 60 J8
Nuku Hiva 60 M6
Nukumanu Islands 60 F6
Nukunonu 60 J6
Nukus 34 K9
Nullagine 62 D4
Nullarbor Plain 62 E6
Numan 54 G3
Numbulwar 62 G2
Numfor 43 E3
Numto 30 P2
Nunap Isua 68 Y5
Nunarsuit 68 X4
Nunavik 68 W2
Nunavut 68 M3
Nuneaton 14 A2
Nungnain Sum 38 F1
Nunivak Island 66 T4
Nunligram 36 Y3
Nuoro 24 D8
Nuquí 76 B2
Nura 30 P4
Nurābād 46 F3
Nurata 46 J1
Nurmes 8 Q5
Nürnberg 12 G7
Nürtingen 22 E2
Nurzec 10 M5
Nushki 46 J4
Nutak 68 U5
Nuuk 68 W4
Nuussuaq 68 W2
Nyagan' 30 N2
Nyahururu 56 F3
Nyala 50 D5
Nyalam 44 E3
Nyamlell 56 D2
Nyamtumbo 56 F6
Nyandoma 30 H2
Nyantakara 56 E4
Nyborg 12 F1
Nybro 8 H8
Nyda 34 N4
Nyima 44 E2
Nyingchi 44 F3
Nyírbátor 26 K2
Nyíregyháza 10 L10
Nykarleby 8 M5
Nykøbing 12 G2
Nyköping 8 J7
Nylstroom 58 D4
Nymburk 10 E7
Nynäshamn 8 J7
Nyngan 62 J6
Nyon 22 B4
Nysa 10 D6
Nysa 10 G7
Nysted 12 G2
Nyukhcha 30 J2
Nyunzu 56 D5
Nyurba 36 K4
Nyuya 36 K4
Nzega 56 E4
Nzérékoré 54 C3
N'zeto 56 A5
Nzwami 58 G2

O

Oahu 60 L3
Oakham 14 B2
Oakland 70 B4
Oakley 70 F4
Oak Ridge 70 K4
Oamaru 64 C7
Oaxaca 72 E5
Ob' 30 N2
Oban 16 G5
O Barco 20 D2
Oberdrauburg 22 H4
Oberhausen 14 J3
Oberkirch 12 D8
Oberndorf 22 H3
Oberstdorf 22 F3
Oberursel 12 D6
Obervellach 10 C11
Oberwart 22 M3
Obi 43 C3
Obidos 76 F4
Obigarm 46 K2
Obihiro 38 L2
Obluch'ye 36 N7
Obninsk 30 G3
Obo, *C.A.R.* 56 D2
Obo, *China* 38 C3
Oborniki 10 F5
Obouya 54 H5
Oboyan' 30 G4
Obskaya Guba 34 N4
Obuasi 54 D3
Ob'yachevo 30 J2
Ocala 70 K6
Ocaña, *Col.* 76 C2
Ocaña, *Spain* 20 G5
Ocean Falls 68 F6
Oceania 60 G7
Oceanside 70 C5
Och'amch'ire 46 D1
Ochsenfurt 12 E7
Oda 54 D3
Ōdate 38 L2
Odda 8 D6
Odemira 20 B7
Ödemiş 28 L6
Odense 12 F1
Oder = Odra 10 F6
Oderzo 22 H5
Odesa 30 F5
Odessa = Odesa, *Ukraine* 30 F5
Odessa, *U.S.* 70 F5
Odienné 54 C3
Odorheiu Secuiesc 26 N3
Odra 10 F6
Odžaci 26 G4
Oeh 38 C2
Oeiras 76 J5
Oelsnitz 12 H6
Oeno 60 N8
Oestev 78 H7
Offenbach 12 D6
Offenburg 22 C2
Ogasawara-shotō 32 T7
Ogbomosho 54 E3
Ogden 70 D3
Ogdensburg 68 R8
Ogilvie Mountains 68 C4
Oglio 22 E5
Ogosta 26 L6
Ogre 8 N8
Ogre 8 N8
O Grove 20 B2
Ogulin 22 L5
Ohai 64 A7
Ohanet 52 G3
Ohio 70 J4
Ohio 70 K3
Ohre 12 J6
Ohrid 28 C3
Ohura 64 E4
Oia 28 H8
Oiapoque 76 G3
Oise 14 E5
Ōita 38 J4
Ojinaga 70 F6
Ojos del Salado 78 H4
Oka 36 G6
Okaba 43 E4
Okahandja 58 B4
Okanagan Lake 70 C2
Okano 54 G4
Okara 44 B2
Okarem 46 F2
Okato 64 D4
Okavango Delta 58 C3
Okayama 38 J4
Okene 54 F3
Oker 12 F4
Okha, *India* 46 J5
Okha, *Russia* 36 Q6
Okhansk 30 L3
Okhotsk 36 Q5
Okhtyrka 30 F4
Okinawa 38 H5
Okinawa 38 H5
Oki-shotō 38 J3
Okitipupa 54 E3
Oklahoma 70 G5
Oklahoma City 70 G4
Okoyo 54 H5
Okranger 8 E5
Oksino 30 K1
Oktinden 8 H4
Oktyabr'sk 30 L5
Oktyabr'skiy 30 K4
Okurchan 36 S5
Okushiri-tō 38 K2
Ólafsvík 8 (1)B2
Öland 8 J8
Olanga 8 Q3
Olava 12 J7
Olavarría 78 J6
Oława 10 G7
Olbia 24 D8
Olching 22 G2
Old Crow 68 D3
Oldenburg, *Germany* 12 D3
Oldenburg, *Germany* 12 F2
Oldenzaal 14 J2
Oldham 16 L8
Old Head of Kinsale 16 D10
Olecko 10 M3
Olekma 36 L5
Olekminsk 36 L4
Oleksandriya 30 F5
Olenegorsk 8 S2
Olenek 36 J3
Olenëk 36 L2
Olenëkskiy Zaliv 36 L2
Oleśnica 10 G6
Olesno 10 H7
Olhão 20 C7
Olib 22 K6
Olinda 76 L5
Oliva 20 K6
Olivet 18 G6
Olmos 76 B5
Olochi 36 K6
Olonets 30 F2
Olongapo 40 G4
Oloron-Ste-Marie 18 E10
Olot 20 N2
Olovyannaya 36 K6
Olpe 14 K3
Olsztyn 10 K4
Olt 26 M4
Olten 22 C3
Olteniţa 26 P5
Oltu 46 D1
Oluanpi 40 G2
Olvera 20 E8
Olympia 70 B2
Olympos 28 E4
Olympus 28 Q10
Olyutorskiy 36 W4
Olyutorskiy Zaliv 36 V4
Om' 34 N6
Oma 44 D2
Omagh 16 E7
Omaha 70 G3
Omakau 64 B7
Oman 46 G5
Omapere 64 D2
Omarama 64 B7
Omaruru 58 B4
Omba, *China* 44 E2
Omba, *Russia* 34 E4
Omboué 54 F5
Ombrone 24 F6
Omdurman = Umm Durman 50 F4
Omegna 22 D5
Omeo 62 J7
Om Hajer 50 G5
Omis 22 M7
Ommen 14 J2
Omolon 36 T3
Omoloy 36 N3
Omo Wenz 56 F2
Omsk 34 N6
Omsukchan 36 S4
Omulew 10 L4
Ōmuta 38 H4
Onang 43 A3
Onda 20 K5
Ondangwa 58 B3
Ondjiva 58 B3
Ondo 54 E3
Öndörhaan 38 E1
One and a Half Degree Channel 44 B8
Onega 30 G2
O'Neill 70 G3
Oneşti 26 P3
Onezhskoye Ozero 30 F2
Ongole 44 D5
Onguday 34 R7
Onilahy 58 G4
Onitsha 54 F3
Onon 36 J7
Onon 36 J7
Onslow Bay 72 J2
Ontario 68 N6
Ontinyent 20 K6
Oodnadatta 62 G5
Oostburg 14 F3
Oostelijk-Flevoland 14 H2
Oostende 14 E3
Oosterhout 14 G3
Oosterschelde 14 F3
Oost-Vlieland 14 H1
Ootsa Lake 68 F6
Opala 56 C4
Oparino 30 J3
Opava 10 G8
Opochka 30 E3
Opoczno 10 K6
Opole 10 G7
Opornyy 34 J8
Opotiki 64 F4
Opunake 64 D4
Opuwo 58 A3
Oradea 26 J2
Orahovac 26 H7
Orai 44 C3
Oran 20 K9
Orán 78 J3
Orange 58 C5
Orange, *Aus.* 62 J6
Orange, *France* 18 K9
Orangemund 58 B5
Orango 54 A2
Oranienburg 12 J4
Orapa 58 D4
Orăştie 26 L4
Oraviţa 26 J4
Orbec 18 F4
Orbetello 24 F6
Orco 22 C5
Ordes 20 B1
Ordes Santa Comba 20 B1
Ordu 46 C1
Öreälven 8 K4
Örebro 8 H7
Oregon 70 B3
Orekhovo-Zuyevo 30 G3
Orel 30 G4
Ören 28 K7
Orenburg 30 L4
Orestiada 28 J3
Orewa 64 E3
Orford Ness 14 D2
Orhei 26 R2
Orihuela 20 K6
Orillia 70 L3
Orinoco 76 D2
Orinoco Delta = Delta del Orinoco 76 E2
Orissaare 8 M7
Oristano 24 C9
Orivesi 8 Q5
Orkla 8 F5
Orkney Islands 16 K3
Orlando 70 K6
Orléans 18 G6
Orlik 36 F6
Orly 14 E6
Ormara 46 H4
Ormoc 40 G4
Ormos Almyrou 28 G9
Ormos Mesara 28 G9
Ornans 18 M6
Ornö 8 K7
Örnsköldsvik 8 K5
Orocué 76 C3
Orona 60 J6
Oronoque 76 F3
Oroqen Zizhiqi 36 L6
Orosei 24 D8
Orosháza 26 H3
Oroszlany 10 H10
Orotukan 36 S4
Orroroo 62 G6
Orsa 8 H6
Orsay 18 H5
Orsha 30 F4
Orsk 30 L4
Orşova 26 K5
Ørsta 8 D5
Ortaklar 28 K7
Orthez 18 E10
Ortigueira 20 C1
Ortisei 22 G4
Ortles 22 F4
Ortona 24 J6
Orūmīyeh 46 E2
Oruro 76 D7
Orvieto 24 G6
Orville 18 L6
Ōsaka 38 K4
Osăm 26 M6
Oschatz 12 J5
Oschersleben 12 G4
O Seixo 20 B3
Osh 34 N9
Oshawa 70 L3
Oshkosh 70 J3
Oshogbo 54 E3
Osijek 26 F4
Osimo 22 J7
Oskarshamn 8 J8
Oslo 8 F7
Oslofjorden 8 F7
Osmancık 46 B1
Osmaniye 46 C2
Osnabrück 14 L2
Osor 22 K6
Osorno 78 G7
Osprey Reef 62 J2
Oss 14 H3
Ossa de Montiel 20 H6
Ossora 36 U5
Ostashkov 30 F3
Oste 12 E3
Osterburg 12 G4
Østerdalen 8 F6
Osterholz-Scharmbeck 12 D3
Osterode 12 F5
Östersund 8 H5

Salinas, *Brazil* 76 J7
Salinas, *Ecuador* 76 A4
Salinas, *U.S.* 70 B4
Salinas Grandes 78 J4
Salinópolis 76 H4
Salisbury, *U.K.* 14 A3
Salisbury, *U.S.* 70 L4
Salisbury Island 68 R4
Salla 8 Q3
Salluit 68 R4
Salmon 70 C2
Salmon Arm 68 H6
Salo 8 M6
Salò 22 F5
Salon-de-Provence 18 L10
Salonta 26 J3
Sal'sk 30 H5
Salsomaggiore Terme 22 E6
Salta 78 H3
Saltee Islands 16 F9
Saltillo 70 F6
Salt Lake City 70 D3
Salto 78 K5
Salto del Guairá 78 K3
Salûm 50 E1
Saluzzo 22 C6
Salvador 76 K6
Salvadore 74 H5
Salween 40 B2
Salyan 46 E2
Salym 30 P3
Salzach 22 H2
Salzburg 22 J3
Salzgitter 12 F4
Salzwedel 12 G4
Samaipata 76 E7
Samar 40 H4
Samara 30 K4
Samarinda 42 F3
Samarkand 46 J2
Sambalpur 44 D4
Sambas 42 D2
Sambava 58 J2
Sambhal 44 C3
Sambir 10 N8
Sambo 43 A3
Samboja 42 F3
Sambre 14 F4
Same 56 F4
Sami 28 C6
Samoa 60 J7
Samobor 22 L5
Samoded 30 H2
Šamokov 26 L7
Šamorín 10 G9
Samos 28 J7
Samos 28 J7
Samothraki 28 H4
Samothraki 28 H4
Sampit 42 E3
Samsang 40 D3
Samsø 8 F9
Samsun 46 C1
Samtredia 46 D1
Samut Songkhram 40 B4
San 10 L7
San 54 D2
Şan'ā 50 H4
Sanaga 54 G4
San Ambrosio 78 F4
Sanana 43 C3
Sanana 43 C3
Sanandaj 46 E2
San Antonia Abad 20 M6
San Antonio, *Chile* 78 G5
San Antonio, *U.S.* 72 E3
San Antonio de los Cobres 78 H3
San Antonio-Oeste 78 H7
Sanāw 46 F6
San Benedetto del Tronto 24 H6
San Bernardino 70 C5
San Bernardo 78 H5
San Borja 76 D6
San Carlos, *Chile* 78 G6
San Carlos, *Phil.* 40 G3
San Carlos, *Venezuela* 76 D3
San Carlos de Bariloche 78 G7
San Carlos de Bolívar 78 J6
San Carlos del Zulia 76 C2
San Cataldo 24 H11
Sanchahe 38 H1
Sanchakou 34 P10
Sanchor 44 B4
Sanchursk 30 J3
San Clemente Island 70 C5
San Cristobal 60 G7
San Cristóbal, *Arg.* 78 J5
San Cristóbal, *Venezuela* 76 C2
San Cristóbal de las Casas 72 F5
Sancti Spíritus 72 J4
Sandakan 42 F1
Sandane 8 D6
Sandanski 28 F3
Sanday 16 K2
Sandby 12 G2
Sandefjord 8 F7
Sanderson 70 F5
Sandfire Flat Roadhouse 62 D3
San Diego 70 C5
Sandıklı 28 N6
Sandnes 8 C7
Sandnessjøen 8 G4
Sandoa 56 C5
Sandomierz 10 L7
San Donà di Piave 22 H5
Sandoway 44 F5
Sandpoint 70 C2
Sandray 16 E5
Sandviken 8 J6
Sandy Cape 62 K4
Sandy Island 62 D2
Sandy Lake 68 N6
Sandy Lake 68 N6
San Felipe 70 D5
San Félix 78 E4
San Fernando, *Chile* 78 G5
San Fernando, *Phil.* 40 G3
San Fernando, *Spain* 20 D8
San Fernando de Apure 76 D2
San Fernando de Atabapo 76 D3
San Francisco, *Arg.* 78 J5
San Francisco, *U.S.* 70 B4
Sangamner 44 B5
Sangān 46 H3
Sangar 36 M4
Sangāreddi 44 C5
Sangasanga 42 F3
Sângeorz-Băi 26 M2
Sangerhausen 12 G5
Sanggau 42 E2
Sangha 54 H4
Sanghar 46 J4
San Gimignano 22 G7
San Giovanni in Fiore 24 L9
San Giovanni Valdarno 22 G7
Sangir 43 C2
Sangkhla Buri 40 B3
Sangkulirang 42 F2
Sangli 44 B5
Sangmélima 54 G4
Sangsang 44 E3
Sangue 76 F6
Sangüesa 20 J2
San Jose 70 B4
San José 72 H7
San Jose de Buenavista 40 G4
San José de Chiquitos 76 E7
San Jose de Jáchal 78 H5
San José del Cabo 72 C4
San José de Ocuné 76 C3
San Juan 72 H4
San Juan, *Arg.* 78 H5
San Juan, *Costa Rica* 72 H6
San Juan, *Puerto Rico* 72 L5
San Juan, *Venezuela* 76 D2
San Juan Bautista, *Paraguay* 78 K4
San Juan Bautista, *Spain* 20 M5
San Juan de los Cayos 76 D1
San Juan de los Morros 76 D2
San Juan Mountains 70 E4
San Julián 78 H8
Sankt-Peterburg 30 F3
Sankuru 56 C4
Sanlıurfa 46 C2
Sanlúcar de Barrameda 20 D8
San Lucas 72 C4
San Luis 78 H5
San Luis Obispo 70 B4
San Luis Potosí 72 D4
San Marino 22 H7
San Marino 22 H7
San Martín 76 E6
Sanmenxia 38 E4
San Miguel 72 G6
San Miguel 76 E7
San Miguel de Tucumán 78 H4
San Miniato 22 F7
San Nicolas de los Arroyos 78 J5
Sânnicolau Mare 26 H3
Sanok 10 M8
San Pablo 40 G4
San-Pédro 54 C4
San Pedro, *Arg.* 78 J3
San Pedro, *Bolivia* 76 E7
San Pedro, *Paraguay* 78 K3
San Pedro, *Phil.* 40 G4
San Pedro Sula 72 G5
San Pellegrino Terme 22 E5
San Pietro 24 C9
San Rafael 78 H5
San Remo 22 C7
San Roque 20 E8
Sansalé 54 B2
San Salvador 72 G6
San Salvador 72 K4
San Salvador de Jujuy 78 H3
Sansar 44 C4
San Sebastián = Donostia 20 J1
San Sebastian de los Reyes 20 G4
Sansepolcro 22 H7
San Severo 24 K7
Sanski Most 22 M6
Santa Ana, *Bolivia* 76 D7
Santa Ana, *El Salvador* 72 G6
Santa Bárbara 70 E6
Santa Catalina 78 H4
Santa Catarina 78 L4
Santa Clara, *Columbia* 76 D4
Santa Clara, *Cuba* 70 K7
Santa Comba Dão 20 B4
Santa Cruz 78 G9
Santa Cruz, *Bolivia* 76 E7
Santa Cruz, *Phil.* 40 G3
Santa Cruz, *U.S.* 70 B4
Santa Cruz de Tenerife 52 B3
Santa Cruz Islands 60 G7
Santa Elena 76 E3
Santa Eugenia 20 A2
Santa Fe 70 E4
Santa Fé 78 J5
Sant'Agata di Militello 24 J10
Santa Isabel 60 F6
Santa Isabel 78 H6
Santa la Grande 70 K7
Santa Margarita 70 D7
Santa Margherita Ligure 22 E6
Santa Maria 52 (1)B2
Santa Maria, *Brazil* 78 L4
Santa Maria, *U.S.* 70 B5
Santa Maria das Barreiras 76 H5
Santa Marinella 24 F6
Santa Marta, *Col.* 72 K6
Santa Marta, *Spain* 20 D6
Santana do Livramento 78 K5
Santander 20 G1
Sant'Antioco 24 C9
Sant'Antioco 24 C9
Santanyí 20 P5
Santa Pola 20 K6
Santarém, *Brazil* 76 G4
Santarém, *Spain* 20 B5
Santa Rosa, *Arg.* 78 J6
Santa Rosa, *Acre, Brazil* 76 C5
Santa Rosa, *R.G.S., Brazil* 78 L4
Santa Rosa, *U.S.* 70 B4
Santa Vitória do Palmar 78 L5
Sant Boi 20 N3
Sant Carlos de la Ràpita 20 L4
Sant Celoni 20 N3
Sant Feliu de Guixols 20 P3
Santiago 78 G5
Santiago, *Brazil* 78 L4
Santiago, *Dominican Republic* 72 K5
Santiago, *Phil.* 40 G3
Santiago, *Spain* 20 B2
Santiago de Cuba 72 J5
Santiago del Estero 78 J4
Santo André 78 M3
Santo Antão 54 (1)A1
Santo Antônio de Jesus 76 K6
Santo Antônio do Içá 76 D4
Santo Domingo 72 L5
Santo Domingo de los Colorados 76 B4
Santoña 20 G1
Santos 78 M3
San Vicente 40 G3
San Vincenzo 24 E5
Sanya 40 D3
Sao Bernardo do Campo 76 E4
São Borja 78 K4
São Carlos 78 M3
São Félix, *M.G., Brazil* 76 G6
São Félix, *Pará, Brazil* 76 G5
São Filipe 54 (1)B2
São Francisco 76 J6
São João de Madeira 20 B4
São Jorge 52 (1)B2
São José do Rio Prêto 78 L3
São Luís 76 J4
São Miguel 52 (1)B2
Saône 18 K7
São Nicolau 54 (1)B1
São Paulo 78 L3
São Paulo 78 M3
São Paulo de Olivença 76 D4
São Raimundo Nonato 76 J5
São Tiago 54 (1)B1
São Tomé 54 F4
São Tomé 54 F4
São Tomé and Príncipe 54 F4
São Vicente 54 (1)A1
São Vicente 78 M3
Sapanca 28 M4
Saparua 43 C3
Sapele 54 F3
Sapes 28 H4
Sapientza 28 D8
Sa Pobla 20 P5
Sapporo 38 L2
Sapri 24 K8
Sapudi 42 E4
Saqqez 46 E2
Sara Buri 40 C4
Sarajevo 26 F6
Sarakhs 46 H2
Saraktash 30 L4
Saramati 44 G3
Saran 34 N8
Sarandë 28 C5
Sarangani Islands 43 C1
Saranpul 30 M2
Saransk 30 J4
Sarapul 30 K3
Sarapul'skoye 36 P7
Sarata 26 S3
Saratov 30 J4
Saravan 46 H4
Sarawak 42 E2
Saray 28 K3
Sarayköy 28 L7
Sarayönü 28 Q6
Sarbāz 46 H4
Sarbīsheh 46 G3
Sárbogárd 26 F3
Sardegna 24 E8
Sardinia = Sardegna 24 E8
Sar-e Pol 46 J2
Sargodha 46 K3
Sarh 54 H3
Sārī 46 F2
Saria 28 K9
Sarikei 42 E2
Sarina 62 J4
Sariñena 20 K3
Sarīr Tibesti 50 C3
Sariwŏn 38 H3
Sarıyer 28 M3
Sark 18 C4
Sarkad 26 J3
Sarkand 34 P8
Sarkikaraağaç 28 P6
Şarkişla 46 C2
Şarköy 28 K4
Sarmi 43 E3
Särna 8 G6
Sarnia 70 K3
Sarny 30 E4
Sarolangun 42 C3
Saronno 22 E5
Saros Körfezi 28 J4
Sárospatak 10 L9
Sarre 18 M5
Sarrebourg 18 N5
Sarreguemines 18 N4
Sarria 20 C2
Sartène 24 C7
Sartyn'ya 30 M2
Saruhanli 28 K6
Sárvár 22 M3
Sarviz 26 F2
Sarykamyshkoye Ozero 34 K9
Saryozek 34 P9
Saryshagan 34 N8
Sarysu 34 M8
Sary-Tash 46 K2
Sarzana 22 E6
Sasaram 44 D4
Sasebo 38 H4
Saskatchewan 68 K6
Saskatchewan 68 L6
Saskatoon 68 K6
Saskylakh 34 W3
Sassandra 54 C4
Sassari 24 C8
Sassnitz 12 J2
Sasso Marconi 22 G6
Sassuolo 22 F6
Satadougou 54 B2
Satara 44 B5
Satna 44 D4
Sátoraljaújhely 10 L9
Satti 44 C2
Sättna 8 J5
Satu Mare 26 K2
Satun 42 B1
Sauce 78 K5
Saudi Arabia 46 D4
Saulgau 22 E2
Saulieu 18 K6
Sault Ste. Marie, *Can.* 70 K2
Sault Ste. Marie, *U.S.* 70 K2
Saumlakki 43 D4
Saumur 18 E6
Saunders Island 74 J9
Saura 34 J9
Saurimo 56 C5
Sauðárkrókur 8 (1)D2
Sava 22 L5
Savaii 60 J7
Savalou 54 E3
Savannah 66 K6
Savannah 70 K5
Savannakhet 40 C3
Savaştepe 28 K5
Save 58 E4
Savè 54 E3
Sāveh 46 F2
Saverne 12 C8
Savigliano 22 C6
Savona 22 D6
Savonlinna 8 Q6
Savu 43 B5
Sawahlunto 42 C3
Sawai Madhopur 44 C3
Sawqirah 46 G6
Sawu Sea 43 B4
Sayanogorsk 34 S7
Sayansk 36 G6
Sayhūt 46 F6
Säylac 50 H5
Saynshand 38 E2
Sayram Hu 34 Q9
Say'ūn 46 E6
Say-Utes 34 J9
Sazan 28 B4
Sazin 46 K2
Sbaa 52 E3
Scafell Pike 16 J7
Scalea 24 K9
Scarborough 16 M7
Scargill 64 D6
Scarp 16 E3
Schaalsee 12 F3
Schaffhausen 22 D3
Schagen 14 G2
Scharbeutz 12 F2
Schärding 22 J2
Scharhörn 12 D3
Scheeßel 12 E3
Schefferville 68 T6
Scheibbs 22 L3
Schelde 14 F3
Scheveningen 14 G2
Schiedam 14 G3
Schiermonnikoog 14 H1
Schiermonnikoog 14 J1
Schio 22 G5
Schiza 28 D8
Schkeuditz 12 H5
Schlei 12 E2
Schleiden 14 J4
Schleswig 12 E2
Schlieben 12 J5
Schlüchtern 12 E6
Schneeberg 12 G6
Schneeberg 12 H6
Schönebeck 12 G4
Schongau 22 F3
Schöningen 12 F4
Schouwen 14 F3
Schramberg 22 D2
Schrems 22 L2
Schull 16 C10
Schwabach 12 G7
Schwäbische Alb 22 E2
Schwäbisch-Gmünd 22 E2
Schwäbisch-Hall 12 E7
Schwalmstadt 12 E6
Schwandorf 12 H7
Schwarzenbek 12 F3
Schwarzenberg 12 H6
Schwarzwald 22 D3
Schwaz 22 G3
Schwechat 10 F9
Schwedt 10 D4
Schweich 14 J5
Schweinfurt 12 F6
Schwenningen 22 D2
Schwerin 12 G3
Schweriner See 12 G3
Schwetzingen 12 D7
Schwyz 22 D3
Sciacca 24 H11
Scicli 24 J12
Scotia Ridge 78 K9
Scotia Sea 80 (2)A4
Scotland 16 H5
Scott Inlet 68 T2
Scott Island 80 (2)Z3
Scott Reef 62 D2
Scottsbluff 70 F3
Scranton 70 L3
Scunthorpe 16 M8
Seal 68 M5
Sea of Azov 30 G5
Sea of Japan 38 J2
Sea of Marmara = Marmara Denizi 28 L4
Sea of Okhotsk 36 Q5
Sea of the Hebrides 16 E4
Searcy 70 H4
Seattle 70 B2
Sebeş 26 L4
Sebkha Azzel Matti 52 F3
Sebkha de Timimoun 52 E3
Sebkha de Tindouf 52 D3
Sebkha Mekerrhane 52 F3
Sebkha Oum el Drouss Telli 52 C4
Sebkhet de Chemchâm 52 C4
Sebnitz 12 K6
Secchia 22 F6
Sechura 76 A5
Secretary Island 64 A7
Secunderabad 44 C5
Sécure 76 D7
Sedan 14 G5
Sedano 20 G2
Seddon 64 D5
Seddonville 64 C5
Sedeh 46 G3
Sedico 22 H4
Seeheim 58 B5
Seelow 12 K4
Sées 18 F5
Seesen 12 F5
Seevetal 12 E3
Séez 22 B5
Seferihisar 28 J6
Segamat 42 C2
Segezha 30 F2
Seghnān 46 K2
Ségou 54 C2
Segovia 20 F4
Segré 18 E6
Séguédine 52 H4
Segura 20 H6
Sehithwa 58 C4
Sehnde 12 E4
Seiland 8 M1
Seinäjoki 8 M5
Seine 18 F4
Sekayu 42 C3
Sekondi 54 D3
Selassi 43 D3
Selat Bangka 42 D3
Selat Berhala 42 C3
Selat Dampir 43 D3
Selat Karimata 42 D3
Selat Makassar 42 F3
Selat Mentawai 42 B3
Selat Sunda 42 D4
Selb 12 H6
Selby 70 F2
Selçuk 28 K7
Selebi-Phikwe 58 D4
Sélestat 22 C2
Selfoss 8 (1)C3
Sélibabi 52 C5
Seljord 8 E7
Selkirk 70 G1
Selkirk Mountains 68 H6
Selm 14 K3
Selpele 43 D3
Selvas 76 C5
Selwyn Lake 68 L5
Selwyn Mountains 68 E4
Semanit 28 B4
Semarang 42 E4
Sematan 42 D2
Sembé 54 G4
Semiozernoye 34 L7
Semipalatinsk 34 Q7
Semiyarka 34 P7
Semois 14 H5
Semporna 42 F2
Sena Madureira 76 D5
Senanga 58 C3
Sendai 38 L3
Senec 22 N2
Senegal 54 A2
Sénégal 54 B1
Senftenberg 12 J5
Sengerema 56 E4
Senhor do Bonfim 76 J6
Senica 10 G9
Senigallia 22 J7
Senj 22 K6
Senja 8 J2
Senlis 14 E5
Sennar 46 B7
Senneterre 70 L2
Sens 18 J5
Senta 26 H4
Seoni 44 C4
Seoul = Sŏul 38 H3
Separation Point 64 D5
Sepinang 42 F2
Sept-Îles 68 T6
Seraing 14 H4
Serakhs 46 H2
Seram 43 D3
Seram Sea 43 C3
Serang 42 D4
Serbia = Srbija 26 H5
Serdobsk 30 H4
Serebryansk 34 Q8
Sered' 26 E1
Şereflikoçhisar 28 R6
Seregno 22 E5
Serein 18 J6
Seremban 42 C2
Serenje 58 E2
Sergelen 38 E1
Sergeyevka 30 N4
Sergipe 76 K6
Sergiyev Posad 30 G3
Seria 42 E2
Serifos 28 G7
Serifos 28 G7
Serik 28 P8
Seringapatam Reef 62 D2
Sermata 43 C4
Seronga 58 C3
Serov 30 M3
Serowe 58 D4
Serpa 20 C7
Serpneve 26 S3
Serpukhov 30 G4
Serra Acari 76 F3
Serra Curupira 76 E3
Serra da Chela 58 A3
Serra da Espinhaço 76 J7
Serra da Ibiapaba 76 J4
Serra da Mantiqueira 78 M3
Serra de Maracaju 78 K3
Serra do Cachimbo 76 F5
Serra do Caiapó 76 G7
Serra do Dois Irmãos 76 J5
Serra do Roncador 76 G6
Serra dos Carajás 76 G5
Serra dos Parecis 76 E6
Serra do Tiracambu 76 H4
Serra Estrondo 76 H5
Serra Formosa 76 F6
Serra Geral de Goiás 76 H6
Serra Geral do Paranã 76 H7
Serra Lombarda 76 G3
Serra Pacaraima 76 E3
Serra Parima 76 E3
Serra Tumucumaque 76 F3
Serre da Estrela 20 C4
Serres, *France* 18 L9
Serres, *Greece* 28 F3
Serrinha 76 K6
Sertã 20 B5
Serui 43 E3
Servia 28 D4
Sêrxü 38 B4
Sese Islands 56 E4
Sesfontein 58 A3
Sesheke 58 C3
Sessa Aurunca 24 H7
Sestri Levante 22 E6
Sestroretsk 8 Q6
Sestrunj 22 K6
Sestu 24 D9
Sesvete 22 M5
Sète 18 J10
Sete Lagoas 76 J7
Setesdal 8 D7
Sétif 52 G1
Settat 52 D2
Setúbal 20 B6
Sŏul 60 C2
Seurre 18 L7
Sevastopol' 6 H3
Sevenoaks 14 C3
Sévérac-le-Château 18 J9
Severn, *Can.* 68 P5
Severn, *U.K.* 16 K10
Severnaya Dvina 30 H2
Severnaya Zemlya 34 U1
Severn Estuary 16 J10
Severnoye 30 K4
Severnyy 34 L4
Severobaykal'sk 36 H5
Severodvinsk 30 G2
Severo-Kuril'sk 36 T6
Severomorsk 8 S2
Severoural'sk 30 M2
Severo-Yeniseyskiy 34 S5
Sevier Lake 70 D4
Sevilla 20 E7
Sevlievo 26 N7
Seyakha 34 N3
Seychelles 58 (2)B2
Seychelles Islands 48 J6
Seydişehir 28 P7
Seymchan 36 S4
Seymour, *Aus.* 62 J7
Seymour, *U.S.* 70 G5
Seyðisfjörður 8 (1)G2
Sézanne 18 J5

Theniet el Had 20 N9
Theodore Roosevelt 76 E5
The Pas 68 L6
Thermaikos Kolpos 28 E4
Thermopolis 70 E3
The Sisters 64 (1)B1
The Solent 14 A4
Thessaloniki 28 E4
Thetford 16 N9
The Twins 64 D5
The Wash 16 N9
The Weald 14 B3
The Whitsundays 62 J4
Thiers 18 J8
Thiès 54 A2
Thika 56 F4
Thimphu 44 E3
Þingvallavatn 8 (1)C2
Thionville 14 J5
Thira 28 H8
Thira 28 H8
Thirasia 28 H8
Thirsk 16 L7
Thiruvananthapuram 44 C7
Thisted 8 E8
Þistilfjörður 8 (1)F1
Thiva 28 F6
Thiviers 18 F8
Þjórsá 8 (1)D2
Tholen 14 G3
Thompson 68 H6
Thompson 68 M5
Thonon-les-Bains 22 B4
Þórisvatn 8 (1)D2
Þorlákshöfn 8 (1)C3
Þorshöfn 8 (1)F1
Thouars 18 E7
Thrakiko Pelagos 28 H4
Three Kings Island 64 C2
Thuin 14 G4
Thun 22 C4
Thunder Bay 70 J2
Thuner See 22 C4
Thung Song 40 B5
Thüringer Wald 12 F6
Thurso 16 J3
Thusis 22 E4
Tianjin 38 F3
Tianmen 38 E4
Tianshui 38 D4
Tianshuihai 46 L2
Tianyang 38 D6
Tiaret 52 F1
Tibati 54 G3
Tibboburra 62 H5
Tibesti 50 C3
Tibet = Xizang 44 E2
Tiburón 72 B3
Tîchît 52 D5
Tichla 52 C4
Ticino 22 D4
Ticul 72 G4
Tidjikdja 52 C5
Tieling 38 G2
Tielongtan 44 C1
Tielt 14 F3
Tienen 14 G4
Tien Shan 34 Q9
Tien Yen 40 D2
Tiétar 20 E4
Tiflis = T'bilisi 48 H1
Tifton 70 K5
Tifu 43 C3
Tighina 26 S3
Tignère 54 G3
Tigre 76 B4
Tigris 46 D3
Tijuana 70 C5
Tikanlik 34 R9
Tikhoretsk 30 H5
Tikhvin 30 F3
Tikrīt 46 D3
Tiksi 36 M2
Tilburg 14 H3
Tilichiki 36 V4
Tillabéri 54 E2
Tilos 28 K8
Timanskiy Kryazh 30 K2
Timaru 64 C7
Timashevsk 30 G5
Timber Creek 62 F3
Timerloh 42 C2
Timimoun 52 F3
Timișoara 26 J4
Timmins 70 K2
Timon 76 J5
Timor 43 C4
Timor Sea 62 E2
Timor Timur 43 C4
Tinaca Point 60 C5
Tin Alkoum 52 H4
Tinchebray 14 B6
Tindivanam 44 C6
Tindouf 52 D3
Tineo 20 D1
Tinfouchy 52 D3
Tinglev 12 E2
Tingo Maria 76 B5
Tingri 44 E3
Tingsryd 10 E1
Tiniroto 64 F4
Tinnsjø 8 E7
Tinogasta 78 H4
Tinos 28 H7
Tinos 28 H7
Tinsukia 44 G3
Tîntâne 52 C5
T'i'o 50 H5
Tipperary 16 D9
Tirana = Tiranë 28 B3
Tiranë 28 B3
Tirari Desert 62 G5
Tiraspol 26 S3
Tire 28 K6
Tiree 16 F5
Tiroungoulou 56 C2
Tirschenreuth 12 H7
Tirso 24 C9
Tiruchchirāppalli 44 C6
Tirunelveli 44 C7
Tirupati 44 C6
Tiruppur 44 C6
Tiruvannamalai 44 C6
Tisa 26 H4
Tišnov 10 F8
Tisza 10 M9
Tiszafóldvár 26 H3
Tiszafüred 26 H2
Tiszaújváros 10 L10
Tit-Ary 34 Z3
Titel 26 H4
Titlagarh 44 D4
Titova Korenica 22 L6
Titovo Velenje 24 K2
Titu 26 N5
Tivaouane 52 B6
Tiverton 16 J11
Tivoli 24 G7
Tizi Ouzou 52 F1
Tiznit 52 D3
Tjeldøya 8 H2
Tjørkolm 8 D7
Tlemcen 52 E2
Tmassah 50 C2
Toad River 68 F5
Toamasina 58 H3
Tobago 72 M6
Tobelo 43 C2
Tobermorey 62 G4
Tobermory, *U.K.* 16 F5
Tobermory, *U.S.* 70 K2
Tobi 43 D2
Toboali 42 D3
Tobol 30 M4
Tobol 30 M4
Tobol'sk 30 N3
Tobseda 30 K1
Tocantins 76 H5
Tocantins 76 H5
Toce 22 D4
Tocopilla 78 G3
Todeli 43 B3
Todi 24 G6
Togo 54 E3
Toimin 24 H2
Tokar 50 G4
Tokat, *Sudan* 46 C6
Tokat, *Turkey* 46 C1
Tokelau 60 J6
Tokmak 34 P9
Tokoroa 64 E4
Tokounou 54 C3
Toksun 34 R9
Tok-tō 38 J3
Toktogul 34 N9
Tokushima 38 J4
Tōkyō 38 K3
Tolaga Bay 64 G4
Tôlañaro 58 H4
Tolbo 34 S8
Toledo, *Brazil* 78 L3
Toledo, *Spain* 20 F5
Toledo, *U.S.* 70 K3
Toliara 58 G4
Tolitoli 43 B2
Tol'ka 34 Q5
Tol'ka 34 Q5
Tollense 12 J3
Tolmezzo 22 J4
Tolmin 22 J4
Tolna 26 F3
Tolosa 20 H1
Tol'yatti 30 J4
Tolybay 34 L7
Tom' 34 R6
Tomakomai 38 L2
Tomar, *Brazil* 76 E4
Tomar, *Portugal* 20 B5
Tomari 36 Q7
Tomaszów Lubelski 10 N7
Tomaszów Mazowiecki 10 K6
Tombouctou 52 E5
Tombua 58 A3
Tomé 78 G6
Tomelloso 20 H5
Tomini 43 B2
Tommot 36 M5
Tomo 76 D2
Tompo 36 P4
Tom Price 62 C4
Tomra 44 E2
Tomsk 34 Q6
Tomtor 36 Q4
Tomu 43 D3
Tonalá 72 F5
Tondano 43 B2
Tønder 12 D2
Tonga 56 E2
Tonga 60 J7
Tonga Islands 60 J8
Tongareva 60 K6
Tonga Trench 60 J8
Tongbai 38 E4
Tongchuan 38 D4
Tongeren 14 H4
Tonghae 38 H3
Tongliao 38 G2
Tongling 38 F4
Tongshi 40 D3
Tongyu 38 G2
Tónichi 70 E6
Tonj 56 D2
Tonk 44 C3
Tonkābon 46 F2
Tônlé Sab 40 C4
Tonnay-Charente 18 E8
Tönning 12 D2
Toora-Khem 34 T7
Toowoomba 62 K5
Topeka 70 G4
Topki 34 R6
Toplița 26 N3
Topol'čany 10 H9
Topolobampo 70 E6
Torbali 28 K6
Torbat-e Heydarīyeh 46 G2
Torbat-e Jām 46 H2
Tordesillas 20 F3
Töre 8 M4
Torells 20 N2
Torgau 12 H5
Torgelow 10 C4
Torhout 14 F3
Torino 22 C5
Tori-shima 38 L4
Torneälven 8 L3
Torneträsk 8 K2
Tornio 8 N4
Toro 20 E3
Toronto 70 L3
Tororo 56 E3
Toros Dağları 28 Q8
Torquay 16 J11
Torreblanca 20 L4
Torre de Moncorvo 20 C3
Torrejón de Ardoz 20 G4
Torrelapaja 20 J3
Torrelavega 20 F1
Torremolinos 20 F8
Torrent 20 K5
Torreón 70 F6
Torre-Pacheco 20 K7
Torres Strait 62 H2
Torres Vedras 20 A5
Torrevieja 20 K6
Tortolì 24 D9
Tortona 22 D6
Tortosa 20 L4
Torūd 46 G2
Toruń 10 H4
Tory Island 16 D6
Torzhok 30 G3
Tostedt 12 E3
Tosya 28 S3
Totaranui 64 D5
Tôtes 14 D5
Tot'ma 30 H3
Totora 76 D7
Tottori 38 J3
Touba, *Côte d'Ivoire* 54 C3
Touba, *Senegal* 54 A2
Tougan 54 D2
Touggourt 52 G2
Tougouri 54 D2
Touil 52 C5
Toul 18 L5
Toulépleu 54 C3
Toulon 18 L10
Toulouse 18 G10
Toummo 52 H4
Toungoo 40 B3
Tourcoing 14 F4
Tournai 14 F4
Tournon-sur-Rhône 18 K8
Tours 18 F6
Touws River 58 C6
Towari 43 B3
Towcester 14 B2
Townshend Island 62 K4
Townsville 62 J3
Toxkan 34 P9
Toyama 38 K3
Tozeur 52 G2
Trâblous 46 C3
Trabzon 46 C1
Traiskirchen 22 M2
Trakai 8 N9
Tralee 16 C9
Tralee Bay 16 B9
Tramán Tepuí 76 E2
Tranås 8 H7
Trancoso 20 C4
Trang 40 B5
Trangan 43 D4
Transantarctic Mountains 80 (2)B1
Trapani 24 G11
Trappes 14 E6
Traun 22 K2
Traunreut 22 H3
Traunsee 22 J3
Traversay Islands 74 H9
Traverse City 70 J3
Travnik 26 E5
Trbovlje 22 L4
Trebbia 22 E6
Třebíč 10 E8
Trebinje 26 F7
Trebišov 26 J1
Trebnje 22 L5
Trebon 22 K1
Tregosse Islets 62 K3
Trélazé 18 E6
Trelew 78 H7
Trelleborg 8 G9
Tremp 20 L2
Trenčín 10 H9
Trent 16 M8
Trento 22 G4
Trenton 70 M3
Trepassey 68 W7
Tres Arroyos 78 J6
Três Corações 76 H8
Tres Esquinas 76 B3
Tres Lagos 78 G8
Trespaderne 20 G2
Treuchtlingen 22 F2
Treviglio 22 E5
Treviso 22 H5
Triangle 58 E4
Tricase 24 N9
Trichur 44 C6
Trier 14 J5
Trieste 22 J5
Triglav 22 J4
Trikala 28 D5
Trilj 22 M7
Trincomalee 44 D7
Trinidad 76 E1
Trinidad, *Bolivia* 76 E6
Trinidad, *U.S.* 70 F4
Trinidad, *Uruguay* 78 K5
Trinidad and Tobago 76 E1
Trino 22 D5
Tripoli, *Greece* 28 E7
Tripoli = Trâblous, *Lebanon* 46 C3
Tripoli = Tarābulus, *Libya* 52 H2
Trischen 12 D2
Tristan da Cunha 48 B9
Trivandrum = Thiruvananthapuram 44 C7
Trjavna 26 N7
Trjavna 28 H2
Trnava 26 E1
Trogir 26 D6
Troina 24 J11
Troisdorf 12 C6
Trois Rivières 70 M2
Troitsk 30 M4
Troitsko-Pechorsk 30 L2
Trojan 26 M7
Trollhättan 8 G7
Trombetas 76 F4
Tromsø 8 K2
Trondheim 8 F5
Trondheimsfjörden 8 E5
Troodos 28 Q10
Trotuș 26 P3
Trout Lake, *N.W.T., Can.* 68 G4
Trout Lake, *Ont., Can.* 68 N6
Troy 70 J5
Troyes 18 K5
Trstenik 26 J6
Trujillo, *Peru* 76 B5
Trujillo, *Spain* 20 E5
Truro, *Can.* 68 U7
Truro, *U.K.* 16 G11
Trusovo 34 J4
Trutnov 10 E7
Trzcianka 10 F4
Trzebnica 10 G6
Tržič 22 K4
Tsetserleg 36 G7
Tshabong 58 C5
Tshane 58 C4
Tshikapa 56 C5
Tshuapa 56 C4
Tsiafajavona 58 H3
Tsimlyanskoy Vodokhranilishche 30 H5
Tsiroanomandidy 58 H3
Tsugaru-kaikyō 38 K2
Tsumeb 58 B3
Tsumkwe 58 C3
Tsushima 38 H4
Tua 20 C3
Tual 43 D4
Tuân Giao 40 C2
Tuapse 30 G6
Tubarão 78 M4
Tübingen 22 E2
Tubize 14 G4
Tubruq 50 D1
Tubuai 60 M8
Tubuai Islands 60 L8
Tucano 76 K6
Tuchola 10 G4
Tucson 70 D5
Tucumcari 70 F4
Tucupita 76 E2
Tucuruí 76 H4
Tudela 20 J2
Tuguegarao 40 G3
Tugur 36 P6
Tui 20 B2
Tuktoyaktuk 68 E3
Tula 30 G4
Tulcea 26 R4
Tullamore 16 E8
Tulle 18 G8
Tulln 22 M2
Tuloma 8 S2
Tulsa 70 G4
Tulsequah 68 E5
Tulun 36 G6
Tulung La 44 F3
Tulu Weiel 56 E2
Tumaco 76 B3
Tumān 46 H2
Tumen 38 H2
Tumereng 76 E2
Tumkur 44 C6
Tumut 62 J7
Tunceli 46 C2
Tunduru 58 F2
Tundža 26 P8
Tungir 36 L5
Tungku 42 F1
Tungsten 68 F4
Tungusk 34 S5
Tunis 52 H1
Tunisia 52 E2
Tunja 76 C2
Tupelo 70 J5
Tupik 36 L6
Tupiza 78 H3
Tuquan 38 G1
Tura, *India* 44 F3
Tura, *Russia* 36 G4
Turan 34 S7
Turangi 64 E4
Turayf 50 G1
Turbat 46 H4
Turbo 76 B2
Turda 26 L3
Turek 10 H5
Turgay 34 L8
Turgay 34 L8
Turgayskaya Stolovaya Strana 34 L7
Turgutlu 28 K6
Turhal 46 C1
Turin = Torino 22 C5
Turinsk 30 M3
Turka 36 H6
Türkeli Adası 28 K4
Turkestan 34 M9
Turkey 46 B2
Turkmenbashi 46 F1
Turkmenistan 46 G2
Turks and Caicos Islands 72 K4
Turks Islands 72 K4
Turku 8 M6
Turma 36 N6
Turnhout 14 G3
Turnov 10 E7
Turnu Măgurele 26 M6
Turpan 34 R9
Turpan Pendi 34 S9
Turquino 74 D2
Turtas 30 N3
Turtkul' 46 H1
Turtle Island 62 K3
Turu 34 U5
Turugart Pass 34 P9
Turukhan 36 C3
Turukhansk 34 R4
Turukta 36 K4
Tuscaloosa 70 J5
Tuticorin 44 C7
Tutonchany 36 E4
Tutrakan 26 P5
Tuttlingen 22 D3
Tutuila 60 K7
Tuvalu 60 H6
Tuxpan, *Mexico* 70 E7
Tuxpan, *Mexico* 70 G7
Tuxtla Gutiérrez 72 F5
Tuyên Quang 40 D2
Tuy Hoa 40 D4
Tuymazy 30 K4
Tuz Gölü 28 R6
Tuzla 26 F5
Tver' 30 G3
Tweed 16 K6
Twilight Cove 62 E6
Twin Falls 70 D3
Twizel 64 C7
Tyachiv 26 L1
Tygda 36 M6
Tyler 70 G5
Tylkhoy 36 U4
Tym 34 Q6
Tynda 36 L5
Tyne 16 K6
Tynemouth 16 L6
Tynset 8 F5
Tyra 34 S7
Tyrifjorden 8 F6
Tyrnavos 28 E5
Tyrrhenian Sea 24 F8
Tyry 36 P4
Tysa 10 N9
Tyukyan 36 K4
Tyumen' 34 M6
Tyung 36 K3
Tyva 36 F6

U

Uarini 76 D4
Uaupés 76 D3
Ubá 76 J8
Ubaitaba 76 K6
Ubangi 56 B3
Úbeda 20 G6
Uberaba 76 H7
Uberlândia 76 H7
Überlingen 22 E3
Ubon Ratchathani 40 C3
Ubrique 20 E8
Ucayali 76 B5
Uchami 34 T5
Ucharal 34 Q8
Uchkuduk 34 L9
Uckermark 12 J3
Uda, *Russia* 36 F5
Uda, *Russia* 36 N6
Udachnyy 36 J3
Udagamandalam 44 C6
Udaipur 44 B4
Uddevalla 8 F7
Uddjaure 8 K4
Udine 22 J4
Udmurtiya 30 K3
Udon Thani 40 C3
Udupi 44 B6
Uecker 12 J3
Ueckermünde 12 J3
Uele 56 C3
Uelen 36 AA3
Uel'kal 36 Y3
Uelzen 12 F4
Ufa 30 L3
Ufa 30 L4
Uganda 56 E3
Ugep 54 F3
Ugine 22 B5
Uglegorsk 36 Q7
Uglich 30 G3
Ugljan 22 L6
Ugol'naya Zyryanka 36 R3
Ugol'nyye Kopi 36 X4
Ugulan 36 S4
Uh 26 K1
Uherské Hradiště 10 G8
Uherský Brod 10 G8
Uil 30 K5
Uil 30 K5
Uitenhage 58 D6
Újfehértó 26 J2
Ujiji 56 D4
Ujjain 44 C4
Ujung Pandang 43 A4
Ukerewe Island 56 E4
Ukhta 34 J5
Ukiah 70 B4
Ukmergė 10 P2
Ukraine 6 G3
Ulaanbaatar 36 H7
Ulaangom 34 S8
Ulan 38 B3
Ulan Bator = Ulaanbaatar 38 D1
Ulan-Ude 36 H6
Ulchin 38 H3
Ulcinj 26 G8
Uldz 36 J7
Ulety 36 J6
Ulhāsnagar 44 B5
Uliastay 34 T8
Ulindi 56 D4
Ullapool 16 G4
Ullŭng do 38 J3
Ulm 22 F2
Ulog 26 F6
Ulongue 58 E2
Ulu 36 M4
Ulubat Gölü 28 L4
Ulugqat 46 K2
Ulungur Hu 34 R8
Ulunkhan 36 J5
Uluru 62 F5
Ulu-Yul 36 D5
Ulva 16 F5
Ulverston 16 J7
Ulya 36 Q5
Ul'yanovsk 30 J4
Ulytau 34 M8
Umag 24 H3
Uman' 30 F5
Umanak = Uummannaq 68 W2
Umarkot 46 J4
Umba 30 F1
Umeå 8 L5
Umeälven 8 J4
Umfolozi 58 E5
Ummal Arānib 52 H3
Umm Durman 50 F4
Umm Keddada 50 E5
Umm Lajj 50 G3
Umm Ruwaba 50 F5
Umtata 58 D6
Umuarama 78 L3
Underberg 58 D5
Ungava Bay 68 T5
Ungheni 26 Q2
Ungwana Bay 56 G4
União da Vitória 78 L4
Unije 22 K6
Unini 76 E4
Union City 72 G1
United Arab Emirates 46 F5
United Kingdom 16 G6
United States 66 M5
Unna 14 K3
Unst 16 M1
Unstrut 12 G5
Unzha 30 H3
Upernavik 68 W2
Upington 58 C5
Upolu 60 J7
Upper Hutt 64 E5
Upper Klamath Lake 70 B3
Upper Lough Erne 16 E7
Uppsala 8 J7
Upsala 70 H2
Urad Houqi 38 D2
Ural 30 K5
Ural Mountains = Ural'skiy Khrebet 6 L1
Ural'sk 30 K4
Ural'skiy Khrebet 6 L1
Urambo 56 E5
Uranium City 68 K5
Uraricoera 76 E3
Uraricoera 76 E3
Uray 30 M2
Urbania 22 H7
Urbino 22 H7
Urdzhar 34 Q8
Uren' 30 J3
Urengoy 34 P4
Urgench 46 H1
Urho 34 R8
Uritskiy 30 N4
Urla 28 J6
Urlați 26 P5
Uroševac 26 J7
Uro-teppa 46 J2
Urt 38 C2
Uruaçu 76 H6
Uruapan 72 D5
Urucurituba 76 F4
Uruguaiana 78 K4
Uruguay 78 K5
Uruguay 78 K5
Ürümqi 34 R9
Uruti 64 E4
Uryupino 36 L6
Uryupinsk 30 H4
Urzhum 30 K3
Urziceni 26 P5
Usa 34 L4
Uşak 28 M6
Usedom 12 J3
Useless Loop 62 B5
Usfān 46 C5
Ushtobe 34 P8
Usingen 12 D6
Usk 16 J10
Usman' 30 G4
Usol'ye Sibirskoye 36 G6
Ussel 18 H8
Ussuri 38 J1
Ussuriysk 38 J2
Usta 30 J3
Ust'-Alekseyevo 30 J2
Ust'-Barguzin 36 H6
Ust' Chaun 36 W3
Ústí 10 F8
Ustica 24 H10
Ust'-Ilimsk 36 G5
Ústí nad Labem 10 D7

Ust'-Ishim 34 N6
Ustka 10 F3
Ust'-Kamchatsk 36 U5
Ust'-Kamenogorsk 34 Q8
Ust'-Kamo 34 T5
Ust'-Karenga 36 K6
Ust'-Khayryuzovo 36 T5
Ust'-Kulom 30 K2
Ust'-Kut 36 G5
Ust'-Kuyga 36 P3
Ust'-Maya 36 N4
Ust'-Mukduyka 34 R4
Ust'-Muya 36 K5
Ust' Nem 30 K2
Ust'-Nera 36 Q4
Ust'-Nyukzha 36 L5
Ust'-Olenek 36 K2
Ust'-Omchug 36 R4
Ust' Ozernoye 36 D5
Ust' Penzhino 36 V4
Ust'-Pit 36 E5
Ustrem 30 N2
Ust'-Sopochnoye 36 T5
Ust' Tapsuy 30 M2
Ust'-Tarka 34 P6
Ust'-Tatta 36 N4
Ust'-Tsil'ma 34 J4
Ust' Un'ya 30 L2
Ust'-Urkima 36 L5
Ust'-Usa 30 L1
Ust'-Uyskoye 34 L7
Usu 34 Q9
Utah 70 D4
Utata 36 G6
Utena 8 N9
Uthal 46 J4
Utica 70 M3
Utiel 20 J5
Utrecht 14 H2
Utrera 20 E7
Utsjoki 8 P2
Utsunomiya 38 K3
Uttaradit 40 C3
Utva 30 K4
Uummannaq 68 W2
Uusikaupunki 8 L6
Uvalde 72 E3
Uvargin 36 X3
Uvat 30 N3
Uvinza 56 E5
Uvira 56 D4
Uvs Nuur 34 S7
Uy 30 M4
Uyar 34 S6
Uyuk 34 N9
Uyuni 78 H3
Uzbekistan 34 L9
Uzgen 34 N9
Uzhhorod 26 K1
Užice 26 G6
Uzunköprü 26 P8

V

Vaal 58 D5
Vaasa 8 L5
Vác 26 G2
Vacaria 78 M4
Vachi 46 E1
Vadodara 44 B4
Vado Ligure 22 D6
Vadsø 8 Q1
Vaduz 22 E3
Værøy 8 G3
Vaganski Vhr 22 L6
Vagay 30 N3
Váh 10 H8
Vakh 30 Q2
Valbonnais 22 A6
Valcheta 78 H7
Valdagno 22 G5
Valday 30 F3
Val-de-Meuse 22 A2
Valdemoro 20 G4
Valdepeñas 20 G6
Valdez 68 B4
Valdivia 78 G6
Val-d'Or 70 L2
Valdosta 70 K5
Valdres 8 E6
Valea lui Mihai 26 K2
Valence 18 K9
Valencia, *Spain* 20 K5
Valencia, *Venezuela* 76 D1
Valencia de Alcántara 20 C5
Valenciennes 14 F4
Vălenii de Munte 26 P4
Valentia Island 16 B10
Valentine 70 F3
Valenza 22 D5
Valera 76 C2
Valga 30 E3
Val Horn 70 F5
Valjevo 26 G5
Valka 8 N8
Val'karay 36 X3
Valkeakoski 8 N6
Valkenswaard 14 H3
Valladolid, *Mexico* 72 G4
Valladolid, *Spain* 20 F3
Valle 8 D7
Valledupar 76 C1
Vallée de Azaouagh 52 F5
Vallée du Tîlemsi 52 F5
Vallentuna 8 K7
Valletta 24 J13
Valley of the Kings 50 F2
Valli di Comacchio 22 H6
Vallorbe 22 B4
Valls 20 M3
Valmiera 8 N8
Valognes 14 A5
Valparai 44 C6
Valparaíso 78 G5
Valsad 44 B4
Val'tevo 30 H2
Valuyki 30 G4
Valverde del Camino 20 D7
Vammala 8 M6
Van 46 D2
Vanadzor 46 E1
Vanavara 36 G4
Vancouver, *Can.* 66 P5
Vancouver, *U.S.* 70 B2
Vancouver Island 68 F7
Vanderbijlpark 58 D5
Vanderhoof 68 G6
Van Diemen Gulf 62 F2
Vänern 8 G7
Vangaindrano 58 H4
Van Horn 70 F5
Vanimo 43 F3
Vanino 36 Q7
Vankarem 36 Y3
Vanna 8 K1
Vännäs 8 K5
Vannes 18 C6
Vanrhynsdorp 58 B6
Vantaa 8 N6
Vanua Levu 60 H7
Vanuatu 60 G7
Vanzevat 30 N2
Vanzhil'kynak 36 C4
Varāmīn 46 F2
Varanasi 44 D3
Varangerfjorden 8 R2
Varaždin 26 D3
Varazze 22 D6
Varberg 8 G8
Varda 28 D6
Vardar 28 E3
Varde 8 E9
Vardø 8 R1
Varel 12 D3
Varėna 10 P3
Varese 22 D5
Vârful Moldoveanu 26 M4
Vârfurile 26 K3
Varginha 78 M3
Varkaus 8 P5
Varna 26 Q6
Värnamo 8 H8
Varnsdorf 12 K6
Várpalota 26 F2
Varzi 22 E6
Varzy 18 J6
Vásárosnamény 26 K1
Vaslui 26 Q3
Västerås 8 J7
Västervik 8 J8
Vasto 24 J6
Vasvár 22 M3
Vatan 18 G6
Vathia 28 E8
Vatican City 24 F7
Vatnajökull 8 (1)E2
Vatomandry 58 H3
Vatra Dornei 26 N2
Vättern 8 H7
Vawkavysk 10 P4
Växjö 8 H8
Vayuniya 44 D7
Vazhgort 30 J2
Vecht 14 J2
Vechta 14 L2
Vecsés 26 G2
Vedaranniyam 44 C6
Vedea 26 N6
Veendam 14 J1
Veenendaal 14 H2
Vega 8 F4
Vegreville 68 J6
Vejen 12 E1
Vejer de la Frontera 20 E8
Vejle 8 E9
Vel' 34 G5
Vela Luka 26 D7
Velenje 22 L4
Veles 28 D3
Vélez-Málaga 20 F8
Velika Gorica 22 M5
Velika Plana 26 J5
Velikaya 36 W4
Velikiye Luki 30 F3
Velikiy Ustyug 30 J2
Veliko Tărnovo 26 N6
Vélingara 54 B2
Velingrad 26 L7
Velita Kladuša 22 L5
Velké Meziříčí 10 F8
Velký Krtíš 10 J9
Velletri 24 G7
Vellinge 10 C2
Vellore 44 C6
Velopoula 28 F8
Vel'sk 30 H2
Velten 12 J4
Venaria 22 C5
Vence 22 C7
Venda Nova 20 C3
Vendôme 18 G6
Venev 30 G4
Venezia 22 H5
Venezuela 76 D2
Vengurla 44 B5
Venice = Venezia, *It.* 22 H5
Venice, *U.S.* 70 J6
Venlo 14 J3
Venray 14 H3
Venta 30 D3
Venta de Baños 20 F3
Ventimiglia 22 C7
Ventotene 24 H8
Ventspils 8 L8
Vera, *Arg.* 78 J4
Vera, *Spain* 20 J7
Veracruz 72 E5
Veraval 44 B4
Verbania 22 D5
Vercelli 22 D5
Verdalsøra 8 F5
Verde 76 G8
Verden 12 E4
Verdun 14 H5
Vereeniging 58 D5
Vereshchagino 36 D4
Verín 20 C3
Verkhneimbatsk 36 D4
Verkhne-Imbatskoye 34 R5
Verkhnetulomskoe Vodokhranilishche 8 R2
Verkhneural'sk 30 L4
Verkhniy Baskunchak 30 J5
Verkhnyaya Amga 36 M5
Verkhnyaya Toyma 30 J2
Verkhnyaya Tura 30 L3
Verkhovyna 26 M1
Verkhoyansk 36 N3
Verkhoyanskiy Khrebet 36 M3
Vermillion 70 G3
Vermont 70 M3
Verneuil 14 C6
Vernon, *France* 14 D5
Vernon, *U.S.* 70 G5
Veroia 28 E4
Verona 22 F5
Versailles 14 E6
Verviers 14 H4
Veselí 22 N2
Vesijarvi 8 N6
Vesoul 12 B9
Vesterålen 8 G2
Vestfjorden 8 G3
Vestmannaeyjar 8 (1)C3
Vestvagøy 8 G2
Vesuvio 24 J8
Veszprém 26 E2
Vet 58 D5
Vetluga 30 J3
Vetluga 30 J3
Veurne 14 E3
Vevey 22 B4
Viana do Castelo 20 B3
Vianden 14 J5
Viangchan 40 C3
Viareggio 22 F7
Viborg 8 E8
Vibo Valentia 24 L10
Vibraye 18 F5
Vic 20 N3
Vicenza 22 G5
Vichuga 30 H3
Vichy 18 J7
Victor Harbor 62 G7
Victoria 62 H7
Victoria, *Arg.* 78 J5
Victoria, *Can.* 68 G7
Victoria, *Chile* 78 G6
Victoria, *Malta* 24 J12
Victoria, *Romania* 26 M4
Victoria, *Seychelles* 58 (2)C1
Victoria, *U.S.* 70 G6
Victoria de las Tunas 72 J4
Victoria Falls 58 D3
Victoria Island 68 J2
Victoria Land 80 (2)W2
Victoria River 62 F3
Victoria Strait 68 M3
Victoria West 58 C6
Vidalia 70 K5
Vidamlja 10 N5
Videle 26 N5
Vidin 26 K6
Viedma 78 J7
Vienenburg 12 F5
Vienna = Wien 22 M2
Vienne 18 F7
Vienne 18 K8
Vientiane = Viangchan 40 C3
Vierzon 18 H6
Vieste 24 L7
Vietnam 40 D3
Viêt Tri 40 D2
Vigan 40 G3
Vigevano 22 D5
Vigia 76 H4
Vigo 20 B2
Vigo di Cadore 22 H4
Viho Valentia 24 L10
Vijaywada 44 D5
Vík 8 (1)D3
Vikna 8 E4
Vila de Conde 20 B3
Vilafranca del Penedäs 20 M3
Vila Franca de Xira 20 A6
Vila Nova de Gaia 20 B3
Vilanova y la Geltru 20 M3
Vila Real 20 C3
Vila-real 20 K5
Vilar Formoso 20 D4
Vila Velha 76 G3
Vilhelmina 8 J4
Vilhena 76 E6
Vilija 8 N9
Viljandi 8 N7
Vilkaviškis 10 N3
Villa Ahumada 72 C2
Villablino 20 D2
Villacarrillo 20 G6
Villach 22 J4
Villacidro 24 C9
Villa Constitución 70 D7
Villa de Cos 72 D4
Villafranca de los Barros 20 D6
Villafranca di Verona 22 F5
Villagarcia 20 B2
Villahermosa 72 F5
Villa Huidobro 78 J5
Villalba 20 C1
Villalpando 20 E3
Villamartín 20 E8
Villa Montes 78 J3
Villanueva de Cordoba 20 F6
Villaputzu 24 D9
Villarrobledo 20 H5
Villa San Giovanni 24 K10
Villavelayo 20 H2
Villavicencio 76 C3
Villaviciosa 20 E1
Villazon 78 H3
Villedieu-les-Poêles 14 A6
Villefranche-de-Rouergue 18 H9
Villefranche-sur-Saône 18 K8
Villena 20 K6
Villeneuve-sur-Lot 18 F9
Villers-Bocage 14 B5
Villers-Cotterêts 14 F5
Villerupt 14 H5
Villeurbanne 18 K8
Villingen 22 D2
Vilnius 8 N9
Vilsbiburg 22 H2
Vilshofen 22 J2
Vilvoorde 14 G4
Vilyuy 36 L4
Vilyuysk 36 L4
Vilyuyskoye Vodokhranilishche 36 J4
Vimoutiers 14 C6
Vimperk 22 J1
Viña del Mar 78 G5
Vinaròs 20 L4
Vincennes 70 J4
Vinh 40 D3
Vinkovci 26 F4
Vinnytsya 30 E5
Vinson Massif 80 (2)JJ2
Vinstri 8 E6
Vinzili 30 N3
Viöl 12 E2
Vioolsdrift 58 B5
Vipava 22 J5
Vipiteno 22 G4
Vir 22 L6
Virac 40 G4
Virawah 44 B4
Vire 14 B6
Virginia 70 H2
Virginia 70 L4
Virginia Beach 70 L4
Virgin Islands, *U.K.* 74 E2
Virgin Islands, *U.S.* 74 E2
Virihaure 8 J3
Virôchey 40 D4
Virovitica 26 E4
Virton 14 H5
Virtsu 8 M7
Virudunagar 44 C7
Vis 26 D6
Visby 8 K8
Viscount Melville Sound 68 J2
Viseu, *Brazil* 76 H4
Viseu, *Portugal* 20 C4
Vișeu de Sus 26 M2
Vishakhapatnam 44 D5
Vishera 34 K5
Vishnevka 34 N7
Visoko 26 F6
Visp 22 C4
Vissegrad 26 G6
Visselhövede 12 E4
Vistula = Wisła 6 F2
Viterbo 24 G6
Vitez 26 E5
Viti Levu 60 H7
Vitim 36 J5
Vitolište 28 D3
Vitória 78 N3
Vitória da Conquista 76 J6
Vitoria-Gasteiz 20 H2
Vitré 18 D5
Vitry-le-François 14 G6
Vitsyebsk 30 F3
Vitteaux 18 K6
Vittel 22 A2
Vittoria 24 J12
Vittorio Veneto 22 H5
Viveiro 20 C1
Vivi 34 T4
Vivonne 18 F7
Vize 28 K3
Vizhas 30 J1
Vizianagaram 44 D5
Vizinga 34 H5
Vizzini 24 J11
Vjosë 28 C4
Vladikavkaz 46 D1
Vladimir 30 H3
Vladivostok 38 J2
Vlasotince 26 K7
Vlasovo 36 N2
Vlieland 14 G1
Vlissingen 14 F3
Vlorë 28 B4
Vltava 10 D8
Vöcklabruck 22 J2
Vodice 22 L7
Vodnjan 22 J6
Vogelsberg 12 E6
Voghera 22 D6
Vohipeno 58 H4
Vöhringen 22 F2
Voi 56 F4
Voinjama 54 C3
Voiron 18 L8
Voitsberg 22 L3
Vojens 12 E1
Vojmsjön 8 J4
Vojvodina 26 G4
Volary 12 J8
Volcán Antofalla 78 H4
Volcán Barú 72 H7
Volcán Cayambe 76 B3
Volcán Citlaltépetl 66 L7
Volcán Corcovado 78 G7
Volcán Cotopaxi 76 B4
Volcán Domuyo 78 G6
Volcán Lanin 78 G6
Volcán Llullaillaco 78 H3
Volcán San Pedro 78 H3
Volcán Tajumulco 72 F5
Volga 30 J5
Volgodonsk 30 H5
Volgograd 30 H5
Völkermarkt 22 K4
Volkhov 30 F3
Völklingen 14 J5
Volksrust 58 D5
Volochanka 34 S3
Volodarskoye 30 N4
Vologda 30 H3
Volonga 30 J1
Volos 28 E5
Volosovo 8 Q7
Volta Redonda 76 J8
Volterra 22 F7
Voltri 22 D6
Volzhskiy 30 H5
Voorne 14 F3
Voranava 8 N9
Vorderrhein 22 E4
Vordingborg 12 G1
Voreios Evvoïkos Kolpos 28 E6
Voreria Pindos 28 C4
Vorkuta 30 M1
Vormsi 8 M7
Vorona 30 H4
Voronezh 30 G4
Vorstershoop 58 C5
Võru 8 P8
Vosges 22 C2
Voss 8 D6
Vostochno-Sibirskoye More 36 U2
Vostochnyy Sayan 34 T7
Vostok Island 60 L6
Votkinsk 34 J6
Vozhgora 30 J2
Vraca 26 L6
Vranje 26 J7
Vranov 10 L9
Vranov nad Toplau 26 J1
Vrbas 26 E5
Vrbas 26 G4
Vrbovsko 22 L5
Vrendenburg 58 B6
Vriddhachalam 44 C6
Vršac 26 J4
Vryburg 58 C5
Vryheid 58 E5
Vsetín 10 G8
Vstrechnyy 36 V3
Vućitrh 26 J7
Vukovar 26 G4
Vuktyl' 30 L2
Vulcănești 26 R4
Vulcano 24 J10
Vung Tau 40 D4
Vuollerim 8 L3
Vuotso 8 P2
Vyatka 30 K3
Vyazemskiy 36 N7
Vyaz'ma 30 F3
Vyborg 8 Q6
Vychegda 30 K2
Vyksa 30 H3
Vylkove 26 S4
Vynohradiv 10 N9
Vyshniy Volochek 30 F3
Vyškov 10 G8
Vytegra 30 G2

W

Wa 54 D3
Waal 14 H3
Waalwijk 14 H3
Wabē Shebelē Wenz 56 G2
Wabush 68 T6
Waco 70 G5
Wad Banda 50 E5
Waddān 50 C2
Waddeneilanden 14 G1
Waddenzee 14 H1
Wādī al Fārigh 50 C1
Wādī al Hamīm 50 D1
Wadi Halfa 50 F3
Wad Medani 50 F5
Wafangdian 38 G3
Wager Bay 68 P3
Wagga Wagga 62 J7
Wahai 43 C3
Waiau 64 D6
Waiblingen 22 E2
Waidhofen 22 K3
Waidhofen an der Ybbs 26 B2
Waigeo 43 D3
Waiheke Island 64 E3
Waihi 64 E3
Waikabubak 43 A4
Waikaia 64 B7
Waikaremoana 64 F4
Waikato 64 E4
Waikawa 64 B8
Waimana 64 F4
Waimate 64 C7
Waingapu 62 B1
Waiouru 64 E4
Waipara 64 D6
Waipawa 64 F4
Waipiro 64 G4
Waipu 64 E2
Waipukurau 64 F5
Wairoa 64 F4
Waitakaruru 64 E3
Waitaki 64 C7
Waitangi 64 (1)B1
Waitara 64 E4
Waitotara 64 E4
Waiuku 64 E3
Wajir 56 G3
Wakayama 38 K4
Wakefield 16 L8
Wake Island 60 G4
Wakkanai 38 L1
Waku-Kungo 58 B2
Wałbrzych 10 F7
Walcheren 14 F3
Wałcz 10 F4
Waldmünchen 12 H7
Waldshut-Tiengen 22 D3
Walen See 22 E3
Wales 16 J9
Wales Island 68 P3
Walgett 62 J6
Walkerville 62 J7
Wallis et Futuna 60 J7
Walpole 62 C6
Walsall 16 L9
Walsrode 12 E4
Waltershausen 12 F6
Walvis Bay 58 A4
Wamba 56 D3
Wana 46 J3
Wanaaring 62 H5
Wanaka 64 B7
Wandel Sea 66 A1
Wandingzhen 40 B2
Wanganui 64 E4
Wanganui 64 E4
Wangen 22 E3
Wangerooge 12 C3
Wangiwangi 43 B4
Wan Hsa-la 40 B2
Wanxian 38 D4
Wanyuan 38 D4
Warangal 44 C5
Warburg 12 D5
Ward 64 E5
Wardha 44 C4
Waregem 14 F4
Waremme 14 H4
Waren 12 H3
Warendorf 14 K3
Warka 10 L6
Warmandi 43 D3
Warminster 16 K10
Warrenton 58 C5
Warri 54 F3
Warrington 16 K8
Warrnambool 62 H7
Warsaw = Warszawa 10 K5
Warstein 12 D5
Warszawa 10 K5
Warta 10 F5
Warwick 16 L9
Washap 46 H4
Washburn Lake 68 K2
Washington 70 B2
Washington D.C. 66 J6
Wassenaar 14 G2
Wasserburg 22 H2
Watampone 43 B3
Watansoppeng 43 A3
Waterford 16 E9
Waterloo, *Belgium* 14 G4
Waterloo, *U.S.* 70 H3
Watertown 70 L3
Watford 14 B3
Watmuri 43 D4
Watrous 68 K6
Watsa 56 D3
Watson Lake 68 F4
Wau 56 D2
Waukegan 70 J3
Wausau 70 J3
Waverley 64 E4
Wavre 14 G4
Wawa 70 K2
Wāw al Kabīr 50 C2
Waxxari 34 R10
Waycross 70 K5
Weber 64 F5
Webi Shaabeelle 56 G3
Weddell Island 78 J9
Weddell Sea 80 (2)A2
Wedel 12 E3
Weert 14 H3
Węgorzewo 10 L3
Wei 38 D4
Weichang 38 F2
Weida 12 H6
Weiden 12 H7
Weifang 38 F3
Weihai 38 G3
Weilburg 12 D6
Weilheim 22 G3
Weimar 12 G6
Weinan 38 D4
Weinheim 12 D7
Weining 38 C5
Weipa 62 H2
Weiser 46 C3
Weißenburg 12 F7
Weißenfels 12 G5
Weißwasser 12 K5
Weixi 40 B1
Wejherowo 10 H3
Welkom 58 D5
Welland 14 B2
Wellawaya 44 D7
Wellesley Islands 62 G3
Wellingborough 18 E1
Wellington, *N.Z.* 64 E5
Wellington, *U.S.* 70 G4
Wells 46 D3
Wellsford 64 E3
Wels 22 K2
Welshpool 16 J9
Welwyn Garden City 14 B3
Wenatchee 70 B2
Wenchang 40 E3
Wenga 56 B3
Wenman 76 (1)A1
Wentworth 62 H6
Wen Xian 38 C4
Wenzhou 38 G5
Werdēr 56 H2

Name	Page	Ref
Werder	12	H4
Werl	14	K3
Werneck	12	F7
Wernigerode	12	F5
Werra	12	F6
Wertheim	12	E7
Wesel	14	J3
Wesel Dorsten	12	B5
Weser	12	E4
Wessel Islands	62	G2
West Antarctica	80	(2)GG2
West Cape	60	G10
Westerland	12	D2
Western Australia	62	D5
Western Cape	58	B6
Western Ghats	44	B5
Western Reef	64	(1)B1
Western Sahara	52	C4
Wester Ross	16	G4
Westerschelde	14	F5
Westerstede	14	K1
Westervoort	14	J3
Westerwald	14	K4
West Falkland	78	J9
West Lunga	58	C2
Weston-super-Mare	16	K10
West Palm Beach	70	K6
Westport, N.Z.	64	C5
Westport, Rep. of I.	16	C8
Westray	16	J2
West Siberian Plain = Zapadno-Sibirskaya Ravnina	34	P5
West-Terschelling	14	H1
West Virginia	70	K4
Wetar	43	C4
Wetaskiwin	68	J6
Wete	56	F5
Wetzlar	12	D6
Wewak	43	F3
Wexford	16	F9
Wexford Harbour	16	F9
Weyburn	70	F2
Weymouth	16	K11
Whakatane	64	F3
Whale Cove	68	N4
Whalsay	16	M1
Whangamata	64	E3
Whangamomona	64	E4
Whangarei	64	E2
Wharfe	16	L7
Whitby	16	M7
White	68	L8
White Bay	68	V6
White Cliffs	62	H6
Whitecourt	68	H6
Whitehaven	16	J7
Whitehorse	68	E4
White Island	64	F3
Whitemark	62	J8
White Mountains	68	S8
White Nile = Bahr el Abiad	50	F5
White Sea = Beloye More	30	G1
White Volta	54	D3
Whitstable	14	D3
Whyalla	62	G6
Wichita	70	G4
Wichita Falls	70	G5
Wick	16	J3
Wickenburg	70	D5
Wicklow	16	F9
Wicklow Mountains	16	F8
Widawka	10	J6
Wieluń	10	H6
Wien	22	M2
Wiener Neustadt	22	M3
Wieringermeer Polder	14	G2
Wiesbaden	12	D6
Wiesloch	12	D7
Wiesmoor	12	C3
Wigan	16	K8
Wil	22	E3
Wilcannia	62	H6
Wildeshausen	12	D4
Wilhelmshaven	12	D3
Wilkes Land	80	(2)U2
Willemstad	76	D1
Williams	62	C6
Williams Lake	68	G6
Willis Group	62	K3
Williston, S.A.	58	C6
Williston, U.S.	70	F2
Williston Lake	68	G5
Willow	68	B4
Willowmore	58	C6
Wilmington	70	L5
Wilson's Promontory	62	J7
Wiluna	62	D5
Winchester	16	L10
Windhoek	58	B4
Windischgarsten	22	K3
Windorah	62	H5
Windsor, Can.	70	K4
Windsor, U.K.	14	B3
Windward Islands	74	N6
Windward Passage	74	D2
Wingate Mountains	62	E2
Winisk	68	B4
Winisk	68	P5
Winisk	68	P6
Winisk Lake	68	P6
Winnemucca	46	C3
Winnfield	70	H5
Winnipeg	68	M7
Winschoten	14	K1
Winsen	12	F3
Winston-Salem	70	K4
Winterberg	12	D5
Winter Harbour	68	J2
Winterswijk	14	J3
Winterthur	22	D3
Winton, Aus.	62	H4
Winton, N.Z.	64	B8
Wisbech	14	C2
Wisconsin	70	H2
Wisil Dabarow	56	H2
Wisła	10	H4
Wisła	10	H8
Wisłoka	10	L8
Wismar	12	G3
Wissembourg	12	C7
Witney	14	A3
Witten	14	K3
Wittenberge	12	G3
Wittenoom	62	C4
Wittingen	12	F4
Wittlich	14	J5
Wittmund	12	C3
Wittstock	12	H3
Witzenhausen	12	E5
W. J. van Blommesteinmeer	76	G2
Wkra	10	K5
Władysławowo	10	H3
Włocławek	10	J5
Włodawa	10	N6
Wodzisław Śląski	10	H7
Wohlen	22	D3
Wokam	43	D4
Woking	16	M10
Wolfen	12	H5
Wolfenbüttel	12	F4
Wolfratshausen	22	G3
Wolfsberg	22	K4
Wolfsburg	12	F4
Wolgast	12	J2
Wollaston Lake	68	K5
Wollaston Peninsula	68	H3
Wollongong	62	K6
Wołomin	10	L5
Wolsztyn	10	F5
Wolvega	14	J2
Wolverhampton	16	K9
Wönsan	38	H3
Woodbridge	14	D2
Woodstock	14	A3
Woodville	64	E5
Woodward	70	G4
Woody Head	64	E3
Worcester, S.A.	58	B6
Worcester, U.K.	16	K9
Worcester, U.S.	70	M3
Wörgl	22	H3
Workington	16	J7
Worksop	14	A1
Worms	12	D7
Wörth	12	D7
Worthing	16	M11
Worthington	70	G3
Wosu	43	B3
Wotu	43	B3
Wowoni	43	B3
Wrangell	68	E5
Wrangell Mountains	68	C4
Wray	70	F3
Wrexham	16	K8
Wrigley	68	G4
Wrocław	10	G6
Września	10	G5
Wu	38	D5
Wubin	62	C6
Wubu	38	F3
Wuchang	38	H2
Wuchuan	38	E2
Wuday'ah	46	E6
Wudu	38	C4
Wuhai	38	D3
Wuhan	38	F3
Wuhu	38	F4
Wüjang	44	C2
Wukari	54	F3
Wuli	44	F2
Wunsiedel	12	G6
Wunstorf	12	E4
Wuppertal	12	C5
Würzburg	12	E7
Wurzen	12	H5
Wushi	34	P9
Wusuli	38	J1
Wutach	22	D3
Wuwei	38	C3
Wuxi	38	G4
Wuxu	40	D2
Wuyuan	38	D2
Wuzhong	38	D3
Wuzhou	40	E2
Wye	16	J9
Wyndham	62	E3
Wynniatt Bay	68	J2
Wyoming	70	E3
Wyszków	10	L5

X

Name	Page	Ref
Xaafuun	56	J1
Xàbia	20	L6
Xaçmaz	46	E1
Xaidulla	34	P10
Xainza	44	E2
Xai-Xai	58	E4
Xam Nua	40	C2
Xankändi	46	E2
Xanten	14	J3
Xanthi	28	F7
Xapuri	76	D6
Xar Moron	38	K8
Xàtiva	20	K6
Xi	40	E2
Xiahe	38	C3
Xiamen	40	F2
Xi'an	38	E3
Xiangcheng	38	E4
Xiangfan	38	E4
Xianggang	40	E2
Xianghoang	40	C3
Xianghuang Qi	38	E2
Xiangtan	38	E5
Xiangtan	38	E5
Xianyang	38	D4
Xiaogan	38	E4
Xiao Hinggan Ling	36	M7
Xiaonanchuan	44	F1
Xichang	40	C1
Xigazê	44	E3
Xilinhot	38	F2
Xincai	38	E4
Xinghe	38	E2
Xinghua	38	F4
Xingtai	38	F3
Xingu	76	G5
Xingyi	40	C1
Xining	38	C3
Xinjie	38	D3
Xinjin	38	G3
Xintai	38	E3
Xinxiang	38	E3
Xinyang	38	E4
Xinyuan	34	Q9
Xinzhou	38	E3
Xinzo de Limia	20	C2
Xique-Xique	76	J6
Xi Ujimqin Qi	38	F2
Xiushu	38	E5
Xiwu	44	G2
Xixia	38	E4
Xi Xiang	38	D4
Xizang	44	D2
Xizang Gaoyuan	44	D2
Xuanhua	38	E2
Xuchang	38	E4
Xuddur	56	G3
Xuwen	40	E2
Xuzhou	38	F4

Y

Name	Page	Ref
Ya'an	38	D3
Yabassi	54	F4
Yabēlo	56	F3
Yablonovyy Khrebet	36	J6
Yabuli	38	H2
Yacuma	76	D6
Yadgir	44	D5
Yagel'naya	34	P4
Yagodnyy	30	N3
Yahk	68	H7
Yako	54	D2
Yakoma	56	C3
Yaksha	30	L2
Yaku-shima	38	J4
Yakutsk	36	M4
Yala	40	C5
Yalova	28	M4
Yalta	30	F6
Yalu	38	H2
Yalutorovsk	30	N3
Yamagata	38	L3
Yamarovka	36	J6
Yambio	56	D3
Yamburg	34	P4
Yamdena	43	D4
Yamoussoukro	54	C3
Yampil'	26	R1
Yamsk	36	S5
Yana	36	N3
Yan'an	38	D3
Yanbu'al Bahr	46	C5
Yancheng	38	G4
Yandun	38	A2
Yangambi	56	C3
Yangbajain	44	F2
Yangjiang	40	E2
Yangon	40	B3
Yangquan	38	E3
Yangshuo	40	E2
Yangtze = Chang Jiang	38	D4
Yanhuqu	44	D2
Yani-Kurgan	34	M9
Yanji	38	H2
Yano-Indigirskaya Nizmennost'	36	N2
Yanqi	34	R9
Yanqing	38	F2
Yanshan	40	C2
Yanskiy Zaliv	36	N2
Yantai	38	G3
Yantarnyy	10	J3
Yaoundé	54	G4
Yap	60	D5
Yapen	43	E3
Yaqui	70	E6
Yaraka	62	H4
Yaransk	30	J3
Yardımcı Burnu	28	E8
Yare	14	D2
Yaren	60	G6
Yarensk	30	J2
Yari	76	C3
Yarkant	46	L2
Yarkovo	30	N3
Yarlung Zangbo	44	F3
Yarmouth	68	T8
Yaroslavl'	30	G3
Yar Sale	30	P1
Yartsevo	30	F3
Yashkul'	30	J5
Yasnyy	30	L4
Yatağan	28	L7
Yathkyed Lake	68	M4
Yatsushiro	38	J4
Yavari	76	C3
Yawatongguzlangar	34	Q10
Yaya	34	R6
Yazd	46	F3
Yazdān	46	H3
Ydra	28	F7
Ye	40	B3
Yea	62	J7
Yecheng	46	L2
Yecla	20	J6
Yefremov	30	G4
Yegendybulak	34	P8
Yei	56	E3
Yekaterinburg	30	M3
Yelets	30	G4
Yelizovo	36	T6
Yell	16	L1
Yellowknife	68	J4
Yellow River = Huang He	38	C3
Yellow Sea	38	G3
Yellowstone	70	E2
Yellowstone Lake	46	H2
Yeloten	34	J5
Yelva	54	E2
Yemen	46	D7
Yemetsk	30	H2
Yenakiyeve	30	G5
Yengisar	46	L2
Yenihisar	28	K7
Yenisey	34	S6
Yeniseysk	34	S6
Yeniseyskiy Kryazh	34	S5
Yeo Lake	62	D5
Yeovil	16	K11
Yeppoon	62	K4
Yeraliyev	34	J9
Yerbogachen	36	H4
Yerevan	46	D1
Yerkov	28	S5
Yerkoy	28	S5
Yermak	34	P7
Yermitsa	30	K1
Yerniva	34	J5
Yershov	30	J4
Yerupaja	76	B6
Yerushalayim	46	D3
Yesil'	30	N4
Yeşilköy	28	L4
Yessey	34	V4
Yevpatoriya	30	F5
Yeyik	34	Q10
Yeysk	30	G5
Yibin	38	C5
Yichang	38	E4
Yichun, China	38	E5
Yichun, China	38	H1
Yilan	38	H1
Yıldız Dağları	28	K2
Yinchuan	38	D3
Yingcheng	38	E4
Yingkou	38	G2
Yingtan	38	F5
Yining	34	Q9
Yirga Alem	56	F2
Yitomio	8	M3
Yitulihe	36	L6
Yiyang	38	E5
Yli-Kitka	8	Q3
Ylivieska	8	N4
Ylöjärvi	8	M6
Yoboki	50	H5
Yogyakarta	42	E4
Yohuma	56	C3
Yokadouma	54	G4
Yoko	54	G3
Yokohama	38	K3
Yola	54	G3
Yonago	38	J3
Yong'an	40	F1
Yongdeng	38	C3
Yongren	40	C1
Yongxiu	38	F5
York	16	L8
Yorkton	68	L6
Yoshkar Ola	30	J3
Youghal	16	E10
Youghal Bay	16	E10
Youngstown	70	K3
Youvarou	54	D1
Ystad	10	C2
Ytre Sula	8	B5
Ytyk-Kyuyel'	36	N4
Yuan	40	C2
Yuanjiang	40	C2
Yuanmou	40	C1
Yuanping	38	E3
Yucatán	72	F5
Yucatan Channel	72	G4
Yuci	38	E3
Yudoma	36	N4
Yuendumu	62	F4
Yueyang	38	E5
Yugorenok	36	P5
Yugo-Tala	36	S3
Yugoslavia	26	H6
Yukagirskoye Ploskogor'ye	36	S3
Yukon	66	S3
Yukon Territory	68	D4
Yukorskiy Poluostrov	34	L4
Yukta	36	H4
Yuli	34	R9
Yulin, China	38	D3
Yulin, China	40	E2
Yumen	38	B3
Yumin	34	Q8
Yunak	28	P6
Yuncheng	38	E3
Yun Xian	40	C2
Yuogi Feng	34	Q6
Yurga	34	Q6
Yurimaguas	76	B5
Yurla	30	K3
Yuroma	30	J1
Yur'yevets	30	H3
Yu Shan	40	G2
Yushkozero	8	S4
Yushu, China	38	B4
Yushu, China	38	H1
Yutian	34	Q10
Yuxi	38	C6
Yuyao	38	G4
Yuzhno-Sakhalinsk	36	Q7
Yuzhnoural'sk	30	M4
Yverdon-les-Bains	22	B4
Yvetot	14	C5

Z

Name	Page	Ref
Zaandam	14	G2
Ząbkowice Śląskie	10	F7
Zabok	22	L4
Zābol	46	H3
Zabrze	10	H7
Zacatecas	70	F7
Zadar	22	L6
Zadonsk	30	G4
Zafora	28	J8
Zafra	20	D6
Zagora	52	D2
Zagreb	22	L5
Zagyva	10	K10
Zāhedān	46	H4
Zahirabad	44	C5
Zahlé	46	D3
Zahrān	46	D6
Zaječar	26	K6
Zakamensk	36	G6
Zákho	46	D2
Zakopane	10	J8
Zakynthos	28	C7
Zakynthos	28	C7
Zala	22	M4
Zalaegerszeg	26	E3
Zalakomár	26	E3
Zalari	36	G6
Zalaszentgrót	22	N4
Zalāu	26	L2
Zalim	46	D5
Zalingei	50	D5
Zaliv Aniva	36	Q7
Zaliv Kara-Bogaz Gol	46	F1
Zaliv Kresta	36	Y3
Zaliv Paskevicha	30	L5
Zaliv Shelikhova	36	T5
Zaliv Terpeniya	36	Q7
Zamakh	46	E6
Zambezi	58	E2
Zambezi	58	E3
Zambia	58	D2
Zamboanga	40	G5
Zambrów	10	M5
Zamora	20	D3
Zamość	10	N7
Zanda	44	C2
Zandvoort	14	G2
Zangguy	46	L2
Zanjān	46	E2
Zannone	24	H8
Zanzibar	56	F5
Zanzibar Island	56	F5
Zaouatallaz	52	G4
Zaozernyy	34	S6
Zapadnaya Dvina	30	E3
Zapadno-Sibirskaya Ravnina	34	P5
Zapadnyy Sayan	34	S7
Zapolyarnyy	8	R2
Zaporizhzhya	30	G5
Zaprešić	22	L5
Zaqatala	46	E1
Zarafshan	34	L9
Zaragoza	20	K3
Zarand	46	G3
Zaranj	46	H3
Zarasai	8	P9
Zaraza	76	D2
Zarechensk	8	R3
Zaria	54	F3
Zărneşti	26	N4
Zarqā'	46	D3
Žary	10	E6
Zarzadilla de Totana	20	J7
Žatec	10	C7
Zavetnoye	30	H5
Zavidovići	26	F5
Zavitinsk	34	M6
Zayarsk	34	U6
Zaysan	34	Q8
Zayü	40	B1
Zazafotsy	58	H4
Zbraslav	10	D8
Zēbāk	46	K2
Zeebrugge	14	F3
Zehdenick	12	J4
Zeilona Góra	10	E6
Zeist	14	H2
Zeitz	12	H5
Zelenoborskiy	8	S3
Zelenograd	30	G3
Zelenogradsk	10	K3
Zelenokumsk	30	H6
Zelina	26	D4
Zella-Mehlis	12	F5
Zell am See	22	H3
Zémio	56	D2
Zemlya Alexsandry	34	G1
Zemlya Frantsa-Iosifa	34	J2
Zemlya Vil'cheka	34	L1
Zempoalteptl	72	E5
Zenica	26	E5
Zerbst	12	H5
Zermatt	22	C4
Zeta Lake	68	K2
Zeulenroda	12	H5
Zeven	12	E3
Zevenaar	14	J3
Zeya	36	M6
Zeya	36	M6
Zeyskoye Vodokhranilishche	36	M5
Zgierz	10	J6
Zgorzelec	10	E6
Zhailma	30	M4
Zhaksy	30	N4
Zhaksykon	30	N5
Zhaltyr	30	N4
Zhanatas	34	M9
Zhangbei	38	E2
Zhangguangcai Ling	38	H2
Zhangjiakou	38	E2
Zhangling	36	L6
Zhangwu	38	G2
Zhangye	38	B3
Zhangzhou	40	F2
Zhanjiang	40	E2
Zhaodong	36	M7
Zhaoqing	40	E2
Zhaosu	34	Q9
Zhaotong	38	C5
Zhaoyuan	38	H1
Zharkamys	34	K8
Zharkent	34	P9
Zharma	34	Q8
Zharyk	34	N8
Zhaxigang	44	C2
Zheleznogorsk	30	G4
Zhengzhou	38	E4
Zhenjiang	38	F4
Zherdevka	30	H4
Zhetybay	34	J9
Zhezkazgan	34	M8
Zhigalovo	36	H5
Zhigansk	36	L3
Zhilinda	36	J2
Zhob	46	J3
Zholymbet	34	N7
Zhongba	44	D3
Zhongdian	38	B5
Zhongning	38	D3
Zhongshan	40	E2
Zhongze	38	G5
Zhoukou	38	E4
Zhuanghe	38	G3
Zhucheng	38	F3
Zhumadian	38	E4
Zhuo Xian	38	F3
Zhytomyr	30	E4
Žiar	10	H9
Zibo	38	F3
Zichang	38	D3
Zierikzee	14	F3
Ziesar	12	H4
Zighan	50	D2
Zigon	40	B3
Zigong	38	C5
Ziguinchor	52	B6
Žilina	10	H8
Zillah	50	C2
Zima	36	G6
Zimbabwe	58	D3
Zimmi	54	B3
Zimnicea	26	N6
Zinder	54	F2
Zinjibār	50	J5
Zinnowitz	12	J2
Zirc	10	G10
Žirje	24	K5
Zistersdorf	22	M2
Zitava	10	H9
Zittau	12	K6
Ziway Häyk'	56	F2
Zixing	40	E1
Zlaté Moravce	10	H9
Zlatoust	30	L3
Zlín	10	G8
Zlītan	52	H2
Zlocieniec	10	F4
Złoczew	10	H6
Złotów	10	G4
Zmeinogorsk	34	Q7
Znamenskoye	34	N6
Žnin	10	G5
Znojmo	22	M2
Zoigê	38	C4
Zolotinka	36	M5
Zomba	58	F3
Zongo	56	B3
Zonguldak	28	P3
Zouar	50	C4
Zouérat	52	C4
Zovka	10	N7
Zrenjanin	26	H4
Zschopau	12	J6
Zug	22	D3
Zugdidi	46	D1
Zuger See	22	D3
Zugspitze	12	F9
Zuid-beveland	14	F3
Zunyi	38	D5
Županja	26	F4
Zürich	22	D3
Zuru	54	F3
Žut	24	K5
Zutphen	14	J2
Zuwārah	50	B4
Zuyevka	30	J3
Zvishavane	58	E4
Zvolen	10	J9
Zvornik	26	G5
Zwedru	54	C3
Zweibrücken	14	K5
Zwettl	22	L2
Zwickau	12	H6
Zwiesel	12	H7
Zwoleń	10	L6
Zwolle	14	J2
Zyryanka	36	S3
Zyryanovsk	34	Q8
Żywiec	10	J8